REVELATION
The Apocalypse Uncovered

The book of Revelation

unveils Jesus Christ

as the great Rescuer of the human race.

The slain and risen Lamb of God

fulfilled mankind's destiny

with death and judgment.

The significance of the implications of this

cannot be exaggerated.

It reaches into the entire past, present

and future of human history.

Behold how beautiful
how valuable
how loved and how innocent
you are!
You are the Bride!

The Apocalypse
UNCOVERED!

New Updated Release May 2023

THE MIRROR BIBLE is translated from the original text and paraphrased in contemporary speech with commentary.

Copyright © 2012 by Francois du Toit. All rights reserved.

THE MIRROR text may be quoted in any form (written, visual, electronic, or audio), up to and inclusive of fifty (50) verses, without express written permission of The Author providing the verses quoted do not account for 25 percent or more of the total text of the work in which they are quoted.

Notice of copyright must appear as follows on either the title page or the copyright page of the work in which THE MIRROR is quoted: "Scripture taken from THE MIRROR. Copyright © 2012. Used by permission of The Author."

When quotations from THE MIRROR text are used in 'nonsaleable' media, such as church bulletins, orders of service, posters, transparencies, or similar media, a complete copyright notice is not required but "The Mirror" must appear at the end of each quotation.

Permission requests for commercial and noncommercial use that exceed the above guidelines must be directed to and approved in writing by The Author email, info@mirrorword.net

Editing preparation for printing: Sean Osmond

Mirror Word Logo by: Wilna Furstenburg

Cover Design by: Sean Osmond

Published by Mirror Word Publishing

Should you wish to order printed copies in bulk, [2 or more] pls contact us at info@mirrorword.net

Contact us if you wish to help sponsor Mirror Bibles in Spanish, Shona or Xhosa.

Highly recommended books by the same author: Divine Embrace, God Believes in You, The Logic of His Love.

Children's books: The Eagle Story, by Lydia and Francois du Toit, illustrated by Carla Krige

Stella's Secret by Lydia du Toit and illustrated by Wendy Francisco.

The Little Bear and The Mirror

KAA Of The Great Kalahari

Lydia's books are also available on Kindle and in German and Spanish

The Mirror Bible, Divine Embrace God Believes in You and The Logic of His Love are also available on Kindle. The new updated Mirror Bible App is avaiable on our website

www.mirrorword.net

Subscribe to Francois facebook updates http://www.facebook.com/francois.toit

The Mirror Translation fb group http://www.facebook.com/groups/179109018883718/

ISBN 978-0-9922236-2-5

The Mirror Study Bible is a paraphrased translation from the Greek text. While strictly following the literal meaning of the original, sentences have been constructed so that the larger meaning is continually emphasized by means of an expanded text.

Some clarifying notes are included in italics. This is a paraphrased study rather than a literal translation. While the detailed shades of meaning of every Greek word and its components have been closely studied, this is done taking into account the consistent context of the entire chapter within the wider epistle, and bearing in mind that Jesus is what the Scriptures are all about and humankind is what Jesus is all about.

To assist the reader in their study, I have numerically superscripted the Greek word and corresponded it with the closest English word in the italicized commentary that follows. This is to create a direct comparison of words between the two languages.

I translated several Pauline epistles in the eighties
But these were never published.

In 2007 I started with the Mirror Translation.

This is an ongoing process and will eventually include the entire New Testament

as well as select portions of the Old Testament.

Completed books and chapters as of April 2021 are:

Luke, John, Romans, 1 Corinthians, 2 Corinthians,

Galatians, Ephesians, Philippians, Colossians,

1 Thessalonians, 2 Timothy, Titus, Hebrews, James, 1 Peter 1,2,3, 2 Peter 1

1 John 1-5,

Revelation

I dedicate this book to you.

As you ponder these pages,

I pray, that Holy Spirit quicken

your spirit with fresh insight

and resonance as you engage

in the
Romance of the Ages!

www.mirrorword.net

The recently updated and revised 444 page book, Divine Embrace is an excellent study companion to the Book of Revelation

The Mirror Study Bible is a work in progress.

Since its 1st Edition print in 2012, the MSB has become a very bulky book.

The single book size of **the 11th Edition** *exceeds 1200 pages, so, our Print on Demand Ingram publishers would in future print 3 Separate Volumes of approximately 500 pages each.*

The new, 3 Volume 11th Edition is <u>merged into a Single Volume book</u> which is printed in <u>South Africa</u>.

(Following the sequence of the books as in the 3 separate Volumes.)

The **Merged, single Volume MSB** is also available as an E-Book on all e-book platforms as well as on Kindle.

<u>Internationally</u> the MSB is printed in a set of 3 Volumes

*Volume 1 is dedicated to **Dr Luke***

    Luke's brilliant account of the Life of Jesus - The Gospel of Luke

    & his account of the Acts of the apostles

*Volume 2 features **Paul**'s writings as well as **James** and **Peter**.*

    ***Paul**'s Brilliant **Epistles** &*

    *The Amazing Book of **Hebrews***

    ***James** - The Younger Brother of Jesus*

    *Priceless **Peter***

*Volume 3 - features **John's** writings*

    *John's beautiful **Gospel***

    *The **Epistle** of John*

    ***Revelation** - John's Amazing unveiling of the triumph of the Lamb*

*A **4th Volume** will eventually feature **Matthew** and **Mark**.*

At the completion of the New Testament, the MSB will also be printed as a one volume book on thin "Bible-paper"

TABLE OF CONTENTS

My Philosophy	8
Endorsements	10
Understanding the Bible	11
Introduction to Revelation	16

    -Symbolism
    -Prophetic
    -The Lamb of God
    -The Throne of God
    -The Day of the Lord
    -Eschatology Redefined
    -The Son of Man is the Son of God
    -Jewish Audience
    -The Theme of the Book
    -The Text

Revelation Chapter 1	28
- Notes on the Number Seven	34
- Notes on the Day of the Lord	35
- Notes on the Ekklesia	37
Revelation Chapter 2	40
- Notes on The Son of Man is the Son of God	47
- Notes on Food offered to Idols	50
- Notes on the Rod of Iron	55
Revelation Chapter 3	57
- Notes on Thief in the Night	65
- Notes on Our God Identity	68
- Notes on the City Bride	73
Revelation Chapter 4	79
Revelation Chapter 5	82
Revelation Chapter 6	86
Revelation Chapter 7	90
Revelation Chapter 8	94
Revelation Chapter 9	98
- The Fallen Star is The Bright Morning Star	103
- Notes on The Abyss	105
- Notes on Idols and Demons	110
Revelation Chapter 10	114

- Notes on the Solemn Oath	116
Revelation Chapter 11	117
- Notes on the Measure of the temple	121
- Notes on the 2 Witnesses in Sackcloth	124
- Notes on the Inner Shrine	127
Revelation Chapter 12	132
- Notes on Ophis the Old Serpent	136
Revelation Chapter 13	139
- Notes on Counterfeit Christianity	145
- Notes on the Mark of the Beast	149
- Notes on an Open heaven	153
Revelation Chapter 14	158
- Notes from Mt Sinai to Mt Zion	162
- Notes on the 144,000 Virgins	165
Revelation Chapter 15	167
Revelation Chapter 16	170
- Notes on the Brazen Altar	174
- Notes on Armageddon	176
Revelation Chapter 17	189
- Notes on the Lamb's Book of Life	195
- Notes on End Times Redefined	207
- Notes on the Triumph of the Lamb	217
- Notes on Babylon's Fall	222
Revelation Chapter 18	223
Revelation Chapter 19	226
- Notes on the Hidden Name	232
- Notes on the Shepherd King	238
- Notes on the Wine-press of God's Passion	240
- Notes on the Lake of Fire and the 2nd Death	249
Revelation Chapter 20	269
- Notes on the Thousand Years	274
- Notes on the Testimony of Jesus	280
- Notes on Israel	286
Revelation Chapter 21	291

- Notes on the New heaven and New Earth	297
- The Splendor of the Gates - the redeemed beauty of the Bride	301
Revelation Chapter 22	303
Notes on Revelation 22	305
Biographical Note	313
References and Resources	314

My philosophy in doing the Mirror Bible is reflected in the following example:

I do not read music, but have often witnessed our son, Stefan, approach a new piece on the piano.

His eyes see so much more than mere marks scribbled on a page;

he hears the music.

His trained mind engages even the subtleties and the nuances of the original composition, and is able to repeat the authentic sound,

knowing that the destiny of the music would never be reduced to the page;

but is always in the next moment,

where the same intended beauty is heard

and repeated again!

The best translation would always be the incarnation!

I so value the enormity of the revelation of the incarnation.

Yet, before flesh, the Word was προς

face to face with God!

And fragile text

scribbled thru the ages in memoirs of stone, parchment and papyrus pages -

carrying eternity in thought

and continues to translate faith

to faith!

Now we have the same spirit of faith as he encountered when he wrote...

"I believe

and so I speak!"

Conversation ignites!

"Did not our hearts burn within our being when He spoke familiar text of ancient times, in the voices of Moses and the prophets and David and Abraham,

who saw his day

and announced its dawn in our hearts!

The mystery that was hidden for ages and generations

is now revealed!

In dealing daily with ancient text,

rediscovering thoughts buried in time, I am often overwhelmed and awed at the magnificence of eternity captured in little time capsules,

opening vistas of beauty beyond our imagination- face to face with the same face to faceness of the Logos

and God

and us - conceived in their dream!

And irresistibly intrigued by the invitation to come and drink -

to taste and see -

from the source -

and to hear a saint reminiscing and reminding himself of the utterance of another earth dweller-brother, David, who wrote a song 1000 BC,

"Return to your rest, oh my soul!

For the Lord has dealt bountifully with you!

I believe and so I speak!"

And with fresh wounds bleeding from the many angry blows he was dealt with, Paul echoes,

"We have the same spirit of faith as he had who wrote, 'I believe and so I speak!' We too believe and so we speak!"

Let's celebrate the "sameness" of Jesus

yesterday - yes, as far as history and beyond time can go -

and today! This very finite, fragile moment -

plus, the infinite future!

Inexhaustible, beyond boundaries and the confines of space and time!

ENDORSEMENTS

In a world where Bible translations and paraphrases are ubiquitous, *The Mirror Study Bible* is uniquely beautiful and helpful! Submitted to the original texts and the abiding guidance of the Holy Spirit, Francois du Toit carefully and meticulously opens and explores the treasures of Scripture. Not only does it satisfy the demands of the intellect, but it overwhelms the heart.

Wm Paul Young - *Author of The Shack*

I have plunged myself deep into the Apocalypse, reading articles, books, and commentaries. Francois, your translation rocks. I am so very proud of you and can only imagine what you have had to suffer to give birth to this translation. Union, union, union! Blindness, blindness, blindness! Union wins! Hallelujah! What a beautiful, stunning translation.

John must be in ecstatic joy!
Here is a translation of the book of Revelation that is true to the heart of the beloved John, true to the prophetic tradition, and true to our Lord Jesus—the King of kings, and Lord of lords. But be warned, Francois' paraphrase challenges everything you thought you knew about this book. Here is one among many examples: "The reach of the Lamb" instead of "The wrath of the Lamb." Odds are many will strongly react to Francois' interpretation, but du Toit steadfastly allows the worship of the encountered heart to see what John is showing us. Astonishingly beautiful, and wonderfully controversial.

C. Baxter Kruger *Ph.D., author of the international bestsellers The Shack Revisited and Patmos*

Francois' love for the text, his sheer exegetical courage and his astonishing ability to express essential biblical pre-suppositions in the intimate Love language of God, has opened for Judith and me a renewed and transformative biblical understanding.

Bob and Judith Mumford - *www.lifechangers.org*

UNDERSTANDING THE BIBLE - THE INCARNATION CODE

The Bible is a dangerous book. It has confused and divided more people than any other document. Yet its profound and simple message continues to appeal, overwhelm and transform the lives of multitudes of men and women of any age or culture. It is still the best seller on the planet.

Scriptures have been used to justify some of the greatest atrocities in human history. People were tortured, burned at the stake and multitudes murdered based on somebody's understanding of the Scriptures. Jesus, Paul and believers throughout the ages faced their greatest opposition from those who knew the Scriptures.

If it is such a dangerous document, how does one approach the book? What is the key that unlocks its mystery message?

The Romance of the ages is revealed here. The heart of the Lover, our Maker is hidden in Scripture and uncovered in the pages of this book. He says in Isaiah 65:1, "I was ready to be found by those who did not seek me. I said, 'Here am I, here am I.'" (RSV) This sounds like mirror-language. Here I am echoes within us: "Here I am."

What would it be that attracts God to engage with us?

Man began in God. You are the greatest idea that God has ever had.

It is not our brief history on planet Earth that introduces us to God. He has always known us. We are not the invention of our parents. Maybe your arrival was a big surprise to them, but according to Jeremiah 1:5, God knew you before he formed you in your mother's womb.

The Bible records how the invisible Engineer of the universe found image and likeness expression in visible form in human life.

When God imagined you, they imagined a being whose intimate friendship would intrigue Father, Son and Holy Spirit for eternity. Mankind would be partner in God's triune oneness. Their image and likeness would be unmasked in human life.

Jesus says in John 10:30, "I and the Father are one." None of the other disciples better captured the conclusion of the mission of Jesus than John in John 14:20, In that day you will know that we are in seamless union with one another. I am in my Father, you are in me and I am in you.

God has found us in Christ before we were lost in Adam. We are associated in Christ from before the foundation of the world (Ephesians 1:4). Elohim knew us, even before we were mystically formed in our mother's womb. Now in Christ, we are invited to know ourselves even as we have always been known (1 Corinthians 13:12).

Jesus Christ is the context and meaning of Scripture; his work of redeeming the image and likeness of God in human form is what the Bible is all about (Colossians 1:13-15).

He reveals that there is no place in the universe where God would rather be; the fullness of Deity physically resides in him. Jesus proves that human life is tailor-made for God. He mirrors our completeness. (While the expanse cannot measure or define God, their exact likeness is displayed in human form. The human body frames the most complete space for Deity to dwell in. See Colossians 1:19 & Colossians 2:9,10)

The entire Bible is about Jesus, and Jesus is all about you. This makes the Bible the most relevant book. Jesus is God's mind made up about "you-manity". The meaning of his name declares our salvation. In him, God rescued our authentic identity and innocence.

The prophetic shadow of the Old Testament introduces us to the Promise and the Promise points to the Person. He is the Messiah-Christ, the Incarnate Word. He represents the entire human race. In the economy of God, Jesus mirrors man. The heart dream of God realized in the redemption of humanity; in one man, through one act of righteousness, in a single sacrifice, he rescued the human race.

The conclusion is clear. It took just one offense to condemn mankind; one act of righteousness declares the same mankind innocent. The disobedience of the one exhibits mankind as sinners; the obedience of another exhibits mankind as righteous (Romans 5:18, 19 *The Mirror).*

We see then, that as one act of sin exposed the whole race of mankind to judgment and condemnation, so one act of perfect righteousness presents all mankind freely acquitted in the sight of God (Romans 5:19 *J.B. Phillips).* God has shown me that I should not call anyone common or unclean (Acts 10:28 RSV).

When Jesus joins the two confused disciples on their way back from Jerusalem, he introduces himself to them through the eyes of Scripture: "And beginning with Moses and all the Prophets, he interpreted to them in all the Scriptures the things concerning himself" (Luke 24:27 RSV). Then in Luke 24:44, he does the same when he appears to his disciples: "He said to them, 'These are my words which I spoke to you, while I was still with you, that everything written about me in the law of Moses and the Prophets and the Psalms must be fulfilled.'" (RSV) Luke 24:45 says, "Then he opened their minds to understand the Scriptures."(RSV)

Philip joins the chariot of the chief treasurer and asks him, "Sir, do you understand what you are reading?" (Phillip knew that it is possible to read the right book but get the wrong message.) The passage of the Scripture which he was reading was from Isaiah 53:7, "As a sheep led to the slaughter or a lamb before its shearer is dumb, so he opens not his mouth." And beginning with this Scripture Phillip told him the Good News of Jesus. (Acts 8:35) Jesus is the context of Scripture. (Isaiah 53:4, 5)

The destiny of the Logos was not to be caged in a book or a doctrine but to be documented and unveiled in human form. Human life is the most articulate voice of Scripture. Jesus is God's language; mankind is his audience (Hebrews 1:1-3).

Diligent research and study is not the key to understanding the Scriptures; Jesus says, "You study and search the Scriptures thinking that in them you will find eternal life, but if you miss me, you miss the point."

The Message translation reads, "You have your heads in your Bibles constantly because you think you'll find eternal life there. But you miss the forest for the trees. These Scriptures are all about me"(John 5:39).

The mission of Jesus was not to begin the Christian religion or to win protest votes against Moses, Mohammed, or Buddha. His mandate was twofold; first to reveal and then to redeem the blueprint image and likeness of the invisible God in human form. Instead of an instruction manual, the Bible is a mirror revealing our redeemed identity.

We are not window-shopping the promises; we gaze into the mirror of our true likeness and discover the integrity of our redeemed innocence.

Any form of striving to become more like Jesus through personal devotion and diligence, no matter how sincere, bears the same fruit of failure and guilt. Jesus did not come to condemn the world but to free the world. Religion has majored on guilt and willpower-driven sentiment, which engaged mankind in futile efforts to save or improve themselves.

The Bible was never meant to be a manual; its message is all about Immanuel. God with us. Every definition of distance is canceled in Christ (Isaiah 40:4, 5). When Scripture is interpreted as a mere instruction manual for moral behavior its message is veiled. 2 Corinthians 3:15 says, "Whenever Moses is read the veil remains."

In John 1:17, "Moses represents the law; Jesus reveals grace and truth." It is only in the mirror where the miracle transformation takes place and the blueprint image of our Maker is again realized in us (2 Corinthians 3:18).

Jesus did not come as an example for us, but of us. Beholding Jesus in any other way, sentimentally or religiously, will bring no lasting change. Now in Christ we may know ourselves, even as we have always been known (1 Corinthians 13:12).

This is the truth that frees us to live the life of our design (John 8:32).

John writes that "this is not a new message; it is the word that was from the beginning. Yet it is new, for that which is true in him, is equally true in you" (1 John 2:7, 8).

We know that the Son of God has come, and he has given us understanding to know him who is true; and this is the understanding, that we are in him who is true. (1 John 5:20).

Paul brands his gospel with the words grace and peace in order to distinguish the message of the revelation of the finished work of Christ from the law of Moses. It is a matter of grace vs. reward and peace vs. striving, guilt and condemnation. Grace and peace express the sum total of every beneficial purpose of God towards us realized in Christ.

To discover yourself in the mirror is the key that unlocks the door to divine encounter. Tangible beyond touch the genesis of our being is unveiled. Our most intimate and urgent quest is satisfied here.

The days of window-shopping the Bible are over. "And we all, with new understanding, see ourselves in him as in a mirror; thus we are changed from an inferior mindset to the revealed opinion of our true Origin" (2 Corinthians 3:18).

As much as the world of science depends upon the senses to perceive, measure and calculate the facts to then form reliable conclusion, faith perceives the reality of God and extends the evidence to reason. Faith is to the spirit what your senses are to your body, while the senses engage in the fragile and fading, faith celebrates perfection. Faith is not wishful thinking; Jesus Christ is the substance of faith. He is both the author and conclusion of our faith. He is the accurate measure of the blueprint of our design.

The gift of Christ measures the extravagant dimensions of grace; where everyone is equally advantaged. Ephesians 4:7. This is the mystery that was hidden for ages and generations; it is Christ in you (Colossians 1:27). He is not hiding in history or in outer space, or in the future. He is *I am* in you. Anticipate the revelation of Christ within you. There is no greater motivation for studying Scripture.

Jesus did not point to the sky when he gave the address of the kingdom of God; he said, "The kingdom of God is within you" (Luke 17:21).

In Matthew 13:44, he says, "The kingdom of heaven is like a treasure hidden in an agricultural field, which a man found and covered up. Then in his joy he goes and sells all that he has and buys that field." "He saw the joy of his image and likeness redeemed in mankind when he braved the cross and despised the shame of it." (Hebrews 12:2)

There is so much more to the field than what meets the eye. Jesus has come to unveil the real value of the field. Human life can never again be underestimated. The treasure exceeds any agricultural value that any harvest could possibly yield. The treasure defines the authentic value of the field.

Paul says, "We have this treasure in earthen vessels." (2 Corinthians 4:7 RSV). Yet our own unbelief veils our minds to keep us from recognizing the image of God, revealed in Christ, as the authentic reflection of our original identity (2 Corinthians 4:4).

We are not designed to live by bread alone. Bread represents the harvest of our own labor. Jesus invites us to look away from our own labor and to lift up our eyes and to see a harvest that is already ripe. A harvest is only ripe when the seed in the fruit matches the seed that was sown.

The single grain of wheat did not abide alone. (John 12: 24, John 4:35, John 2:19-21, Hosea 6:2, Ephesians 2:5).

The destiny of the word was not the book but the living epistle. Human life as revealed and redeemed in Christ is God's voice; mankind is his audience. "You yourselves are all the endorsement we need. Your very lives are a letter that anyone can read by just looking at you. Christ himself wrote it—not with ink, but with God's living Spirit; not chiseled into stone, but carved into human lives—and we publish it." 2 Corinthians 3:2-3 —*The Message*

2 Corinthians 3:3 reads, "The fact that you are a Christ-Epistle shines as bright as day. This is what our ministry is all about. The Spirit of God is the living ink. Every trace of the Spirit's influence on the heart is what gives permanence to this conversation. We are not talking law-language here; this is more dynamic and permanent than letters chiseled in stone; this conversation is embroidered in your inner consciousness." *(It is the life of your design that grace echoes within you.)*

Any sincere student of classical music would sensitively seek to so capture and interpret the piece, so as not to distract from the original sound of the composition. To form an accurate conclusion in the study of our origin would involve a peering over the Creator's shoulder as it were, in order to gaze through his eyes and marvel at his anticipation. His invisible image and likeness is about to be unveiled in human form.

Personal opinion or traditional belief holds no ground against the fountain freshness of his thoughts. The word of truth accurately preserves his original idea in the resonance of our hearts.

Jesus studied scripture with a different intent; he knew that he was reflected there. Familiar with the text, he brought context.

Imagine God finding a word, worthy to hold his ultimate thought; his final, eternal, most intimate message to mankind.

He frames this thought, not in an ancient language of men or celestial messengers, but in an "earthen jar", Jesus, the incarnate Word, the one who gives express image to the invisible God in human person.

In him dying humanity's death, he brings closure to every lie that we believed about ourselves, and in God co-quickening us in his resurrection, he powerfully introduces us to the redeemed life of our design.

Now, with every definition of veil removed, we may behold him as in a mirror, and discover and celebrate our own completeness endorsed in him.

INTRODUCTION TO REVELATION

INTRODUCTION TO THE BOOK OF REVELATION

The language of the Book of Revelation is purely symbolic. Its rich imagery celebrates the Champion of the Ages, the slain and risen Lamb of God bringing closure to every definition of judgment in his death and resurrection.

Jesus is not a literal Lamb, nor a literal Lion. As the Son of God he is the Incarnate Word that has always been face to face with God. He is the Word in whom all things exist.

The stars are not literal stars neither is the underworld a literal fathomless pit, or the Lake ablaze with Brimstone a literal place.

Throughout the unfolding conversation, pictures come to mind that have already been part of the narrative of God's prophetic dealings with Israel for generations, symbolically pointing to a Person and a Moment recorded historically in time, where the resolve of God concludes powerfully in the glorious triumph of the Lamb over every definition of Devil. In fact, every possible idea of Sin, Judgment, Death, Hades, Satan, Devil, Demon, Dragon, Beast and False Prophet-Prostitute is addressed and dissolved and thus rendered redundant. See Revelation 17:14 These join forces in that hour to wage war against the Lamb, but the Lamb defeats them since he is the Lord of lords and the King of kings. And, sharing with him in his victory, are his kindred, recognizing their origin in this conversation; they too are now of the same persuasion. The Lamb led them into freedom from their lost identity, and their doubts.

As far as God is concerned, it is indeed, Mission accomplished. The salvation of humankind is no longer a possible outcome of events, it is the grandest announcement of the redemption of the Romance of the Ages.

Revelation 20:15 And everything that was not written in the Book of Life was poured into the Lake of fire. *(The authentic ID of human life is defined in the Book of Life - or the Tree of Life, representing the redeemed life of our design, versus the alternative Tree of the knowledge of good and evil, representing humanity's identity under scrutiny and questioning. The "I am not-Tree" heads up a system of a works and performance-based philosophy, judging the masses of humanity as condemned to eternal torment.*

To have your name written in the Book of Life simply suggests that you discover your identity there in the Zoe-life redeemed by the Lamb. You may have only known yourself according to the flesh, as Simon, the son of Jonah, while you really are Petros; Mr Rock, a chip off the old Block. Every evidence of an inferior identity is cast into the lake of Sulphur burning away the dross to reveal the gold. Any idea of an identity outside of the Book of Life, is dissolved. The Lamb's Book of Life and not the law of personal achievement and performance, defines us.)

The book of Revelation is the unveiling of Jesus Christ as the great Rescuer of the human race. As the slain and risen Lamb of God, he fulfilled mankind's destiny with death and judgment. The significance of the implications of this cannot be exaggerated. It reaches into the entire past, present and future of human history.

It unveils the extent of the triumph of the Lamb of God in redeeming the innocence, the sense of belonging, the inherent value, identity and royalty of the entire human race and securing their Wedlock-union in the Romance of the ages. In his blood he brought closure to an incompetent sacrificial system which failed in its attempt to manage mankind's sinfulness and their sin-consciousness. Jesus Christ who is fully God and fully man, represents us individually; he gave himself as our "Scapegoat" in dying our death, then raised us together with him in his resurrection. As first-born from the dead, he re-birthed us and redeemed his image and likeness within us.

Colossians 1:26, Mankind's most sought after quest, the mystery which has remained elusive and concealed for ages and generations, is now fully realized in our redeemed innocence.

Colossians 1:27, Within us, God is delighted to exhibit the priceless treasure of this glorious unveiling of Christ's indwelling in order that every person on the planet, whoever they are, may now come to the greatest discovery of all time and recognize Christ in them as in a mirror. He is the desire of the nations and completes their every expectation. *[Haggai 2:6,7]*

Colossians 1:28, This is the essence and focus of our message; we awaken and re-align everyone's mind, instructing every individual by bringing them into full understanding *(flawless clarity)* in order that we may prove *(present)* everyone perfect in Christ. *(Translating **vous** + **tithemi**, to re-align every mind with God's mind.)*

While the slain and risen Lamb of God is the immediate focus of the graphic and prophetic symbolism of Revelation - the time of its writing – about 68 AD – is also soon followed by the tragic events of 70 AD. However, the central message of the book is of a far more dramatic and timelessly relevant significance.

The message in the Revelation of the Lamb is not static but dynamic; people across the planet would face challenges at any time of testing and experience temptation to conform to diabolical religious mindsets at the expense of their true identity and freedom. Sadly history will repeat itself, in "judgments" of horrific proportions until we fully realize the finished work of Jesus and what it was that the Lamb of God accomplished when, instead of demanding a sacrifice, he gave himself as sacrifice and took away the 'sin' of the world - thus bringing hostility and every excuse for separation to an end. Tragedy, crisis and wars are not acts of God. Judgment is not God's business. God's business is salvation.

DATE: The "Syriac version" of the New Testament, which dates back to the second century AD, states that Revelation was written during the reign of Nero bringing a date of 64-68 AD. This date is also confirmed in the "Muratorian Fragment" which dates back to 170-190 AD A quote, arguably attributed to Papius (130 AD), states that John the Apostle was martyred before the destruction of Jerusalem in AD 70.

INTRODUCTION TO REVELATION

SYMBOLISM: John uses the word *sēmainō* in Revelation 1:1 which is an important word to introduce the idea of a symbolic sign; to signify; to picture; to portray. Seeing symbolism and imagery in their context is the key that unlocks the mystery of the book. John would regularly employ pictures that his mostly Jewish audience was already familiar with in their own prophetic writings.

1 Corinthians 10:11 Now these prophetic pictures were written to alert us to the fact that they pointed to what we are now witnessing in the gospel; we are confronted with the completeness of everything that was promised.

PROPHETIC: Revelation 1:10, I was in a spiritual trance where I witnessed the day of the Lord - I heard a loud voice behind me, clear and distinct, like the sound of a trumpet.

The fact that John hears a word **behind him** is so significant. It means that what he hears already happened within its prophetic context. This reminds of the incident recorded in Genesis 22:7 & 8 where Abraham was asked by Isaac, "We have the fire and the wood; but where is the lamb for a burnt offering?" Abraham answered, "God will provide a lamb for the burnt offering, Son." Then, in Genesis 22:13, we read that Abraham lifted up his eyes and looked, and behold, **behind him** was a ram, caught in a thicket by its horns. Jesus refers to this in John 8:56-58 when he says, "Abraham saw my day." And, "Before Abraham was, I am."

Revelation 1:12, Having turned about to face the voice, I saw seven lampstands made out of gold. *(John's attention is drawn back to the prophetic context of the OT Scriptures. The inner sanctuary of the temple is the setting. Exodus 25:36, "The entire lampstand was fashioned from one piece of hammered, pure gold." Exodus 25:37, "Make seven of these lamps for the Table. Arrange the lamps so they throw their light out in front." [prophetic light.] Exodus 25:34, "The lampstand itself is to have four flower cups shaped like almond blossoms, with buds and petals." The almond tree is the prophetic tree; of all the trees, its blossoms awaken first after its winter sleep. It also pictures the resurrection, the first born from the dead. Jeremiah 1:11,12, "Jeremiah, what do you see?" I answered, "I see a branch of an almond tree." Then the LORD said to me, I am **awake** over my word to perform it. The Hebrew word שקד shaqad, means awake; it is also the word for an almond tree.*

The table in the temple is also a significant theme in the Revelation of Jesus Christ. Where every meal is a daily reminder of the incarnation and clearly points to the New Covenant, Bridal-banquet of the Marriage feast of the Lamb.)

Much of what John saw, reflected in the Jewish mind as familiar prophetic pointers and symbols. See the prophetic imagery in Ezekiel 1:1-28 mirrored in Revelation 4. The symbolic pictures John sees of judgment would immediately remind his typical Jewish audience of their prophets' imagery about judgment. This time however, the slaughtered and risen Lamb brings brand new context. Israel's unfaithfulness is met and eclipsed by God's faithfulness. The Lamb's death and resurrection confronts every idea of judgment that was mankind's due.

Revelation 1:19, Now therefore, without delay, give an accurate account in documenting everything that you have seen; both as they are and also what

INTRODUCTION TO REVELATION

their immediate, intentional context has brought about. It is important to see the relevance in mirror-matching all these things, both in their prophetic context as well as in their fulfillment.

Revelation 10:11, And he said to me, Necessity is laid upon you to now disclose with new insight the prophetic word again - this prophecy's time has come and is now relevant and you will declare it before many peoples and different nations and their kings in their specific mother tongue languages.

Revelation 12:10, Then I heard a very loud voice in the heavens announcing, "This is the moment which the entire prophetic word pointed to and culminates in; it is the realization of mankind's salvation. The power of the kingdom of our God and its authority is endorsed in the I-am-ness of his Christ. The business of accusation is bankrupt. The 24/7 industry of condemning the brotherhood of mankind before the face of God has been annihilated."

Revelation 22:10, He told me not to seal this conversation in futuristic, prophetic language since its time has come.

THE LAMB OF GOD: In the scandalous genius of God, the slain and risen Lamb is the central theme of the book. "Look. The Lion has conquered. He who is of the tribe of Judah, the root of David is qualified to open the scroll and its seven seals." So I looked to see the Lion and there, as if fused into one with the throne and in unison with the four Living Beings, taking center stage in the midst of the elders, I saw a little Lamb, alive and standing; even though it appeared to have been violently butchered in sacrifice. It had seven horns and seven eyes, which are the seven Spirits of God, sent out to accomplish his bidding in all the earth. (*Revelation 5:5,6. Also Zechariah 3:9 For behold, upon the stone which I have set before Joshua, upon a single stone with seven facets [eyes], I will engrave its inscription, says the LORD of hosts, I will remove the guilt of the earth in a single day.*)

1 Peter 1:18, It is clear to see that you were ransomed from the futile, fallen mindset that you inherited from your fathers, not by the currency of your own labor, represented by the fluctuating values of gold and silver, and the economy of your religious efforts;

1 Peter 1:19, but you were redeemed with the priceless blood of Christ; he is the ultimate sacrifice; spotless and without blemish. He completes the prophetic picture. (*In him God speaks the most radical scapegoat language of the law of judgment and brings final closure to a dead and redundant system. In Psalm 40:6,7, it is clearly stated that God does not require sacrifices or offerings. Jesus is the Lamb of God. He collides victoriously with the futile sacrificial system whereby offerings are constantly made to the pseudo, moody, monster gods of our imagination. This is the scandal of the cross. God does not demand a sacrifice that would change the way he thinks about mankind; he provides the sacrifice of himself in Christ in order to forever eradicate sin-consciousness from our minds and radically change the way we think about our Maker, one another and ourselves. [Sin-consciousness is in essence a works-based consciousness.] God did not clothe Adam with the skin of an animal because of a divine need to be appeased, but because of their unconditional*

love for Adam; they spoke the language of Adam's own judgment: Adam, not God, was embarrassed about his nakedness. The clothing was not to make God look at Adam differently, but to make Adam feel better about himself. And ultimately it was to prophetically prepare Adam for the unveiling of the mystery of mankind's redemption in the incarnation. Here Deity would clothe themselves in human skin, in a Son; and the Lion of Judah would become the Lamb of God in order to free our minds to re-discover his image and likeness in our skin. See 1 Peter 1:2.)

In 1 Corinthians 2:2 Paul makes a very bold and radical statement, confining his ministry focus to "know" the full scope and consequence of the revelation of mankind's redeemed innocence as communicated in the cross of Jesus Christ. This is the essence of the mystery of God. He writes, "My mind is fully made up about you. The only possible way in which I can truly know you, is in the light of God's mystery, which is Christ in you. Jesus died mankind's death on the cross and thus brought final closure to any other basis of judgment. *(The word, **krino**, to judge, to determine, to deem in a forensic sense, here, in the Aorist tense, **ekrina**, which suggests a once and for all completed act.)*

Also, in 2 Corinthians 5:14 Paul makes this emphatic statement in the immediate context of the constraining impact of the Agape of Christ within his spirit; "I am persuaded that One has died for all, therefore all have died." In the Mirror it reads, "The love of Christ resonates within us and leaves us with only one conclusion: Jesus died mankind's death; therefore, in God's logic every individual simultaneously died."

THE THRONE OF GOD: Revelation 4:1, Oh wow. What I see takes my breath away. A wide-open door in the heavenly realm. The first thing I heard was this voice addressing me. It was distinct and clear like the sound of a trumpet; it captured my attention, inviting me to enter. "Come up here and I will show you how everything coincides with what you have already seen."

Revelation 4:2 So here I am, immersed in this unrestricted space of spirit ecstasy. As the vision opens, I immediately notice the throne and One seated upon it.

Revelation 20:11, And I saw a huge white throne and it was as if heaven and earth fled away from the presence of the One seated upon the throne and its place was never found again. *(This means that there is no accusation in the heavens or upon the earth that could possibly stand in the presence of the Lamb, the One seated upon the throne of the judgment of righteousness – his throne gives testimony and is established upon the legitimacy and authority of mankind's redeemed innocence.*

"Having accomplished purification of sins, he sat down." Hebrews 1:3.

There was never a time where God's royal rule was in question. Giving himself as a scapegoat to be murdered by his own creatures, he assumes a weakness that does not compromise his authority at all. In the genius of his wisdom he defeats the entire system of judgment under the law of performance governing the tree

INTRODUCTION TO REVELATION

of the knowledge of good and evil. The seeming frailty of the slain Lamb never compromised the authority of the Lion of Judah.)

THE DAY OF THE LORD: Revelation 1:10, I was in a spiritual trance where I witnessed the day of the Lord - I heard a loud voice behind me, clear and distinct, like the sound of a trumpet. *(The day of the Lord is the very day to which the prophetic voice of the Spirit of Christ pointed - Jesus the Messiah, is the fulfillment of the day. See 1 Peter 1:10 and 11 where Peter specifically mentions the fact that throughout Scripture the Prophets mentioned the day of the Lord as pointing to the sufferings of the Christ and the consequent glory. Their urgent quest was to search out when this would happen and who the Messiah would be. In Acts 17:31 Paul addresses the Greek Philosophers and reminds them of their own ancient writings and he quotes two of their well-known philosophers: in 600BC Epimenedes wrote a song saying, "We live and move and have our being in God"; and Aratus wrote in 300BC that we are indeed God's offspring. Paul then announces to them that the God whom they worship in ignorance is not far from each one of us. He is not more Immanuel to the Jew than what he is to the Gentile. Now follows the punch line of the gospel: in the context of his Jewish background and personal encounter with Jesus Christ, Paul declares to them the Good News of mankind's redeemed innocence. "God has overlooked the times of ignorance, and now is urging all of mankind, whoever and wherever they are, to a radical mind-shift, since he has prophetically **fixed a day** on which he would judge the world in righteousness **by a man whom he has appointed**, and of this [righteous judgment] he has given proof to all by raising him from the dead." Acts 17:30,31. See also Romans 4:25 where, in Paul's understanding, the resurrection of Jesus from the dead includes mankind's co-resurrection and seals their acquittal and redeemed innocence. This is the predicted subsequent glory that was to follow the cross. Hosea 6:2, After two days he will revive us; on the third day, he will raise us up. Whatever glory was lost in Adam, would be redeemed again in Jesus Christ.)*

See extended commentary at the end of Revelation chapter 1 on this theme. Also Extended Notes on Eschatology at the end of Revelation 17.)

John 5:25, Oh how I desire for you to get this. The prophetic hour has come. This is the moment for the dead to hear the voice of the Son of God - C'mon. Hear and live.

ESCHATOLOGY REDEFINED: Revelation 1:17, Observing all this, I fell at his feet like a dead man; then, kneeling down, he ordained me with his right hand upon me and said, Do not be afraid. I am the origin and the conclusion *[eschatology]* of all things. *See Isaiah 44:6.*

Hebrews 1:1 Throughout [1]ancient times God spoke in many fragments and glimpses of prophetic thought to our fathers. Now, this entire conversation has [2]finally dawned in sonship. Suddenly, what seemed to be an ancient language falls fresh and new like the dew on the tender grass. He is the sum total of every utterance of God. He is whom the Prophets pointed to and we are his immediate audience. (*The word [1]palai, meaning, of old, ancient; from palin through the idea of oscillatory repetition or retrocession; anew, afresh. See Deuteronomy 32:1 "Give ear, Oh heavens, and I will speak; and let the earth hear the words of my mouth. Deuteronomy 32:2 May my teaching drop as the rain, my speech distil as the dew, as the gentle rain upon the tender grass, and as the showers upon the herb.... Deuteronomy 32:18 You were unmindful of the Rock that begot you, and you forgot the God who gave you birth. Like in James 1:24, we have forgotten what manner of people we are - we have forgotten the face of our birth. Jesus successfully rescued the real you, not the pseudo, make-belief you. God has never believed less of you than what he was able to communicate in the sonship that Jesus mirrored and redeemed.*

*The word ²**eschatos** means extreme; last in time or in space; the uttermost part, the final conclusion. What God said about 'you-manity' in Jesus defines eschatology.)*

John 6:39, My Sender's desire is for me to rescue every single individual - ¹this is his gift to me - that I will lose ²no detail of mankind's original identity mirrored in me. My rescuing mission will conclude in their joint-resurrection. This is the ³completeness of time. *(This is his gift to me, ¹ho dedoke moi. The phrase, ²hina pan apoleso Exodus auto, meaning, that I should lose nothing out of it. In the conclusion/fullness of time - ³te eschate hemera - This phrase occurs only in John - in chapters 6:39, 6:40, 6:44 and 6:54. See also John 4:23, The end of an era has arrived - the future is here. Whatever prophetic values were expressed in external devotional forms and rituals are now eclipsed in true spirit worship from within - face to face with the Father - acknowledging our genesis in him - this is his delight. The Father's desire is the worshipper more than the worship.)*

John 6:40, And this is the desire of my Father, that everyone who ¹sees the son, through his eyes, and finds the conclusion of (eis) their persuasion in him, will resonate (echo) the life of the ages. And I will ²raise him up on the ³final day. *(The word ¹theōreo means to gaze attentively. See Hosea 6:2, After two days he will revive us; ²on the third day he will raise us up, that we may live before him. The word ³eschatos means extreme; last in time or in space; the uttermost part, the final conclusion. What God said about 'you-manity' in their co-resurrection in Jesus, defines eschatology. Hebrews 1:1-3; Ephesians 2:5,6.)*

1 Peter 1:20, He was always destined in God's prophetic thought; God knew even before the ¹fall of the world order that his Son would be the Lamb, to be made manifest in these ²last days, because of you. *(You are the reason Jesus died and was raised. The word, ¹kataballo, meaning "to fall away, to put in a lower place," instead of themelios, meaning "foundation" [see Ephesians 2:20]; thus, translated "the fall of the world," instead of "the foundation of the world." The entire "Fall" was a falling away in our minds from our true identity as image and likeness bearers of Elohim. Just like Eve, were we all deceived to believe a lie about ourselves, which is the fruit of the "I-am-not-tree". We all, like sheep, have gone astray [Isaiah 53:6]. The word ²eschatos means extreme; last in time or in space; the uttermost part, the final conclusion.)*

Jurgen Moltmann *writes, The **eschaton** is not the temporal end of our historical days. Eschatology is the presence of eternity in every moment of this present history. Anyone who hears the thunderous word of the eternal God in the moment loses interest in the future.*

THE SON OF MAN IS THE SON OF GOD: Revelation 1:13, And encircled by the lampstands there was one who appeared to be of **human offspring, a son of man**. Clothed with a long robe and with a golden girdle round his chest. *(See Isaiah 6:1, I saw the Lord sitting on a high and lofty throne and the*

INTRODUCTION TO REVELATION

train of his robes filled the temple. The lavish splendor and grandeur of his royal majesty was the very atmosphere of the temple.)

Revelation 1:14, His head of hair was luminous white, like wool covered in fresh, shiny snow and his eyes were ablaze with fire. *(Resembling the Ancient of days. See Daniel 7:9 and Daniel 10:6. His body also was like beryl, and his face as the appearance of lightning, and his eyes as lamps of fire, and his arms and his feet alike in color to polished brass, and the voice of his words like the voice of a multitude.)*

Revelation 1:15, His feet looked like brilliant bronze fashioned in a furnace and his voice was like the sound of many cascading waterfalls. *(Triumphant in the fiery furnace of the altar/cross.)* Revelation 1:16, In his right hand he held seven stars and his words were like a sharp two-edged sword proceeding from his mouth. His face shone like the sun in its full strength.

Revelation 2:18, Write also to the leader of the ekklesia in Thyatira. **The Son of God** with eyes ablaze and feet shining like burnished bronze says...*(Here Jesus introduces himself as the son of God. The Rock foundation of the ekklesia that Jesus is both the Architect and Master-builder of, is the unveiling of the Father. The son of man [Revelation 1:13] is the son of God. Blessed are you, Simon, son of Jonah. Flesh and blood did not reveal this to you, but My Father. I say, you are Rock, a chip [**petros**] of the old Block [**petra**]. And upon this **petra**, I will build my ekklesia and the gates of Hades will not prevail against it. Matthew 16:13-19.*

See Deuteronomy 32:18, You were unmindful of the Rock that begot you, and you forgot the God who gave you birth. Also, Isaiah 51:1, Look to the Rock from which you were hewn, the quarry from which you were dug.

Here in Revelation 2:18, as in Revelation 1:15, his feet looked like brilliant, burnished bronze fashioned in a furnace. As the Lamb of God who presented his body in sacrifice on the "Bronze Altar", he descended into mankind's deepest darkness and triumphantly led mankind out into a place where the enemies of the human race [the Satanas-System] was made our footstool. See Hebrews 1:13, You are the extension of my right hand, my executive authority; take your position and witness how I make your enemies a place upon which you may rest your feet. Also 1 Corinthians 15:25, His dominion is destined to subdue all hostility and contradiction under his feet. (Psalm 110:1, The Lord said to my Lord, sit at my right hand until I make your enemies your footstool. Jesus is Lord of Lords; in his victory mankind is restored to lordship; "I say you are gods, all of you are sons of the Most High" [Psalm 82:6 RSV] Matthew 22:42-45.)

JEWISH AUDIENCE: Much of what John saw was reflected in the Jewish mind as familiar prophetic pictures, pointers and symbols. See the prophetic imagery in Ezekiel 1:1-28 repeated in Revelation 4. The symbolic pictures John sees about judgment would immediately remind his typical Jewish audience of their prophets' imagery of judgment. This time however, the slaughtered and risen Lamb brings brand new context. Israel's unfaithfulness is met and eclipsed by God's faithfulness. The Lamb's death and resurrection confronts every idea of judgment that was mankind's due.

As it was in Pharaoh's day, stubborn minds which were set in their perceptions had to be convinced - the 144,000 were sealed and therefore

INTRODUCTION TO REVELATION

protected from harm - yet they were witnesses of the prophetic/historic fate of Pharaoh. This is now repeated in dramatic fashion in front of their eyes to persuade them of the prophetic picture of deliverance from slavery which is now concluded in the Lamb's death, burial and resurrection and celebrated for ages upon ages by the entire universe.

Revelation 14:1, Oh wow. You've got to see this. The little Lamb, standing on mount Zion and with him a hundred and forty four thousands with the Lamb's Name and the Name of his Father written on their foreheads. *(Sonship redeemed. Hebrews 1:1-3. Note the 144,000's in plural, representing the symbolic value that includes the entire prophetic significance of the Jews as well as the prophetic context of their representing the entire human race. In you, all the nations of the earth will bless themselves. See Extended Notes at the end of Revelation 14 on* **From Mt Sinai to Mt Zion.***)*

Although John's immediate audience is primarily Jewish, seven times in the book of Revelation human society is addressed in the most all-inclusive fashion, with a similar grouping of words. Revelation 5:9, Revelation 7:9, Revelation 10:11, Revelation 11:9, Revelation 13:7, Revelation 14:6 and Revelation 17:15. Also note Revelation 5:13 and Revelation 11:15.

Revelation 7:9, At this moment I saw a massive throng of people, impossible to count, standing tall and innocent; everyone of them dressed in white with palm branches in their hands; they had escaped everything that could possibly define them as a non-Jewish, Gentile world. In fact, every sphere of society was there - including the entire spectrum of people-groupings; all tribal identities with their unique language-specific dialect preferences; they were all present facing the throne and the Lamb as the people of the planet. *(Amazing how, in the previous verses of this chapter, the tribes of Israel are associated with a very specific "number", emphasizing the prophetic detail of the entire Jewish nation. But here, John sees a massive throng of people, impossible to count. In Israel there is a prophetic voice of God's intention to release the blessing of the single SEED of God's faith through Abraham and bless all the nations of the earth. "Count the stars, count the sand."*

The word **stolay***, is the white outer garment worn by kings, priests, and persons of rank. The palm branches and the white robes are signs of the celebration of victory and joy. The Preposition* **ek***, points to source or origin; mankind was delivered out of their national, geographical and historical identities.) (See Extended Notes on Israel at the end of Revelation 20.)*

THE THEME OF THE BOOK: Revelation 1:9, I am John, your brother and companion in tribulation in the midst of which we are equally participating in the authority of the kingdom and the steadfastness of Jesus Christ. I was on the Isle of Patmos because of the word of God and because of the testimony of Jesus Christ. *(See Extended Notes at the end of Revelation 20.)*

Revelation 1:17, Observing all this, I fell at his feet like a dead man; then, kneeling down, he ordained me with his right hand upon me and said, Do not be afraid. I am the origin and the conclusion *[eschatology]* of all things.

Revelation 1:18, I am also the Living One; I died and now, see, here I am alive unto the ages of the ages and I have the keys wherewith I have disengaged

INTRODUCTION TO REVELATION

the gates of ¹Hades and death." *(This profound statement of Jesus in verses 17 & 18 is the platform, theme and focus of the entire book. To distract from these words of Jesus is to miss the point of the Revelation. ¹See commentary note in verse 20 and Revelation 2:7 on the gates of Hades.)*

Revelation 2:23, The offspring of these 'mindsets', conceived in your licentious idolatry has no future. I will cause it ¹to utterly perish. And every ekklesia shall ²know that I scrutinize the hidden thoughts of the heart. And I will expose every single work of your own doing as judged in my work. *(See verse 26 - my works vs your works. To ¹kill in death is a very strong expression,* **apokteuno en thanato**. *The symbolic significance of killing the children of the ekklesia's idolatrous adultery in death can only be understood in the context of the unveiling of Jesus the Christ who already died mankind's death and in that death brought final closure to the offspring of mankind's guilt-ridden mindsets that we have inherited from our world systems which were founded in the fruit of the "I-am-not tree system". He thus broke the spell of the claim of judgment and death over the Adamic race. This signifies the death of death. The significance of the implications of Jesus' death cannot be exaggerated. It reaches into the entire past, present and future of human history. The word* ²**ginosontai** *is the future ingressive punctiliar middle of* **ginosko**, *'we shall certainly come to know', this confirms the theme of the book of Revelation. The unveiling of Jesus Christ and his finished work will most definitely complete God's purpose of redeeming mankind's lost sense of sonship, value, innocence, identity and royalty in the earth.)*

THE TEXT: Revelation was clearly a book that needed to circulate with much commentary and explanations. In many cases the text represented by the commentary is older than the (most often very late) manuscript in which it is found.

Deliberate changes to the wording of the Book of Revelation itself were made to improve and clarify the force of its message. One of many examples can be found in the note on Revelation 20:5. The words, "But the rest of the dead lived not again until the thousand years were finished" were added at a time when the ekklesia claimed to be fulfilling the thousand-year reign of Christ. The Sinaitic manuscript - remarkable as for being the oldest as well as for its completeness and accuracy - is the only Greek authority on Revelation antedating the fifth century: and it does not contain the clause. Most minuscule manuscripts of Revelation are accompanied by a commentary; and these represent an unusually high proportion of witnesses. *"Text appears to have been added first as an explanatory note, and in the process of time crept into the text. Adam Clarke"*

We have no original manuscript - the thousands of manuscripts we do have are handwritten copies of copies for centuries and what happened was that, from time to time, a scribe's notes became text. The majority of these do not alter the meaning of the text though. But some do, which makes it an important observation.

The first edition of the New Testament with a Greek text was prepared by Erasmus and published in 1516. For Revelation, he based his Greek text on a single manuscript, minuscule 1r. (now numbered 2814 according to the new Gregory-Aland number). This manuscript, however, lacks the final verses of the book of Revelation, and in order to have

INTRODUCTION TO REVELATION

a complete text, Erasmus re-translated these verses into Greek from Latin. Elements of his translation survive in every edition of the so-called Textus Receptus, which were the standard text of the printed Greek New Testament until the nineteenth century.

Codex Sinaiticus [Aleph B 33] and the Codex Vaticanus are considered amongst most current scholars to be the best Greek texts of the New Testament. These were extensively used by Westcott and Hort in their edition of The New Testament in the Original Greek in 1881. Aleph is the famous Sinaiticus, the great discovery of Constantine von Tischendorf, the only surviving complete copy of the New Testament written prior to the ninth century. Also note that The oldest Greek manuscripts were all written in uncials - [pronounce ansials] all upper case letters. See Revelation 22:14 ΠΛΥΝΟΝΤΕΣ ΤΑΣ ΣΤΟΛΑΣ ΑΥΤΩΝ – wash their robes vs Textus Receptus ποιοῦντες τὰς ἐντολὰς αὐτοῦ - do his commandments.)

In his Textual Commentary on the Greek New Testament, Bruce Metzger writes, "Theodore Beza published no fewer than nine editions of the Greek Testament between 1565 and 1604, and a tenth edition appeared posthumously in 1611. The importance of Beza's work lies in the extent to which his editions tended to popularize and stereotype what came to be called the Texus Receptus. The translators of the Authorized King James Bible of 1611 made large use of Beza's editions of 1588-89 and 1598 The Byzantine form of the Greek text, reproduced in all early printed editions, was disfigured by the accumulation over the centuries of myriads of scribal alterations, some minor significance but others, often of considerable consequence.

It was the corrupt Byzantine form of text that provided the basis for almost all translations of the New Testament into modern languages down to the nineteenth century. During the eighteenth century scholars assembled a great amount of information from many Greek manuscripts, as well as from versional and patristic witnesses. But, except for three or four editors who timidly corrected some of the more blatant errors of the Textus Receptus, this debased form of the New Testament text was reprinted in edition after edition. It was only in the first part of the nineteenth century (1831) that a German classical scholar, Karl Landman, ventured to apply to the New Testament the criteria that he had used in editing texts of the classics. Subsequently other critical editions appeared, including those prepared by Constantin von Tischendorf, whose eighth edition (1869-72) remains a monumental thesaurus of variant reading, and the influential edition prepared by two Cambridge scholars, B.F. Westcott and F.J.A. Hort (1881). It is the latter edition that was taken as the basis for the present United Bible Societies' edition. During the twentieth century, with the discovery of several New Testament manuscripts much older than any that had hitherto been available, It has become possible to produce editions of the New Testament that approximate even more closely to what is regarded as the wording of the original documents."

There are more than 500,000 variants in the 5300 manuscripts of the New Testament we have access to. These are not necessarily "errors" but variant readings, the vast majority of which are strictly grammatical; but according to the warning you dare not add or take away any word, in Revelation 22:18 &19, the question arises, any of which manuscripts are we talking about?! See my notes at the end of Revelation 22.

INTRODUCTION TO REVELATION

It is also significant to note the difference between the Masoretic Text and the Septuagint of the Old Testament. The Scriptures in Jesus' and New Testament times were the Septuagint, since Greek was the academic language, though Aramaic was the spoken language. *[The Roman letters for 72, LXX is used to name the Septuagint which was translated by 72 Jewish scholars - 6 from each of the 12 tribes of Israel - 300 to 200 BC]* The discovery of the Dead Sea Scrolls in 1947, confirms that the Septuagint is based on a different, and older Hebrew text than the Masoretic text. *[The Dead Sea scrolls are multiple copies of the Hebrew Scriptures along with other literary works of the time untouched from as early as 300 BC.]*

For example, one of the main Jewish apologist arguments against the Messianic interpretation of Isaiah 53 is that all the references to the suffering 'servant', so they say, are in the plural, making him a symbol of Israel. But in the LXX they are singular.

See my commentary note in Revelation 8:1, *(Isaiah 52:13 in the Septuagint reads,* **Behold my boy.** *The word, "servant" is only in the Masoretic Hebrew text which dates a thousand years later than the LXX.*

Also Isaiah 53:4 Surely he has borne our griefs and carried our sorrows; **yet we esteemed him stricken, smitten by God, and afflicted**. *Then, Isaiah 53:10 in the Septuagint. No. It did not "please the Lord to bruise him.." The Lord desires to cleanse his wounds - and in the offering of his life as sacrifice he shall see his seed afar off. See verse 11 - the joy that is set before him. The offspring is the fruit of the travail of his soul. Hebrews 12:2, for the joy that was set before him endured the cross, despising the shame.*

See also my commentary on Hebrews 1:6 and Hebrews 10:5; this reveals an important change in the text.

I believe that, just like gold-containing ore, so the Bible contains the Word. Though the ore is a most important pointer to the gold, it cannot be confused with the gold. Jesus is the Word unveiled - He studied scripture with a different intent; he knew that he was reflected there. Familiar with the text, he brought context. Psalm 40:7 and Hebrews 10:7; also, John 5:39.

I deal more intensively with this in my introduction to the Mirror Bible - Understanding the Bible - The Incarnation Code.

Also, in my notes on the Word of God and the Testimony of Jesus - at the end of Revelation 20.

REVELATION Chapter 1

Revelation - a lifting of the veil to bring into view what is already there.

1:1 Jesus Christ ¹unveiled. This is the revelation of God's ²gift which was wrapped up ³in him, in order to clearly illustrate to his bond-servants that, which according to prophetic pointers, ⁴inevitably ⁵was to have happened in a brief moment of time. This message was ⁶vividly portrayed in symbolic pictures by his ⁷celestial prophetic-messenger, commissioned to communicate its mystery to his bond-servant John. *(The word, ¹**apokalupsis** means an uncovering. The word ²**didōmi** means to give; to furnish; to extend; to present. The word ³**autoo** is the Personal Pronoun in the Dative case, indicating location in. The word ⁴**dei** is from **deoo**, to bind; thus predictably, necessarily, inevitably. John employs the verb, ⁵**ginomai**, to beget, in the Aorist Infinitive tense, **genesthai**, which indicates prior completion of an action in relationship to a point in time. Greek Infinitives could have either a present or Aorist form. The contrast between the two forms was not necessarily one of time, it is a difference of aspect. The Present Infinitive was used to express progressive or imperfective aspect. It pictures the action expressed by the verb as being in progress. The Aorist Infinitive however does not express progressive aspect. It presents the action expressed by the verb as a completed unit with a beginning and end. The word ⁶**sēmainō**, to give a symbolic sign; signify; to picture; to portray. Symbolism and imagery play a significant role throughout the book. John would employ pictures that his mostly Jewish audience was already familiar with in their own prophetic writings. A bond-servant is one who cleaves to his master out of no other obligation but total loving devotion. The word often translated as angel, ⁷**aggelos,** has two components, **agō** to lead as a shepherd leads and **agele** a herd of cattle or company. This word carries the idea of a messenger both in the shepherd as well as the prophetic context.)*

1:2 John gave accurate evidence to the Word of God and the Testimony of Jesus Christ, exactly as he saw it. *(The Testimony of Jesus Christ is the context of the prophetic word. See Notes at the end of Chapter 20. Colossians 3:4, The unveiling of Christ, as defining our lives, immediately implies that which is now evident in him, is equally mirrored in you.)*

1:3 Blessed is the one who ¹reads and those in his audience who hear with understanding the words of this ²Prophetic Enlightenment and treasure what is recorded in this writing; its ³time has ⁴come. *(To read, ¹**anaginosko**, from **ana**, upward and **ginosko**, to know upward; thus to draw knowledge from a higher reference; from above; to recognize; to read with recognition. The word, ²**prophēteia**, prophecy, from **pro**, before, with the idea of face to face, [see **pros** in John 1:1] and **phemi**, to make known one's thoughts; **phos** light, and **phainō**, to shine. The word ³**kairos** implies particular time; as related to some event, a convenient, appropriate time; absolutely, a particular point of time, or a particular season, like spring or winter; ⁴**engus** pointing to that which is imminent.)*

1:4 I, John, address this writing to the seven ¹churches in Asia: I invite you to tap into the heavenly download of grace and peace from him who ²is I am, who always ³was and ⁴will continually be the Accompanying One. And from the seven Spirits who are in the throne room , in constant ⁵eye contact with him. *(The word ¹**Ekklesia**, ekklesia, from **ek**, pointing to origin or

REVELATION Chapter 1

*source and **klesia** from **kaleo**, to surname to identify by name. In the context of Matthew 16 where Jesus introduces this word, he reveals that the son of man is indeed the son of God, "I say to you Simon, son of Jonah, you are **petros** [Rock] and upon this **petra** I will build my **ekklesia**." [See note on Romans 9:33]. The word [4]**erchomenos**, to come or go, to accompany; to appear; here used in the Present Participle which describes an action thought of as simultaneous with the action of the main verb, [2]**ho hoon**, who is, which is also the Present Active Participle of **eimi**, the one who is I am; then John uses the Active Indicative Imperfect form of the verb [3]**eimi**, namely **ho aen [ἦν]** who continues to be. The Imperfect is the past tense, yet denoting continuous action. [See John 1:1, in the beginning 'was' the Word etc...] which conveys no idea of origin for God or for the Logos, but simply continuous existence, "I am." This phraseology is purely Jewish, and taken from the Tetragrammaton. The Four Letters referring to the unpronounceable Name of God - **YHVH** - יהוה - Jahweh "Existing" יהוה includes in itself all time, past, present, and future. Hidden in this word are three words, היה hajah, was, הוה havah, is, and יהיה jahjah, shall be. But they often use the phrase of which the Greek, **ho hoon, kai ho aen, kai ho erchomenos,** of the apostle, is a literal translation. [Adam Clark]*

The entire Revelation is set against the backdrop of the One who is and was and is to come, or, the ever unfolding one. Him who is I am; who always was and will continually be the accompanying one. It is impossible to interpret the Book, without seeing the prophetic significance of the Old Testament and its people.

*The word [5]**enopion** suggests eye to eye contact within the closest possible proximity of one another.* **See extended notes** *on the number 7 at the end of the chapter.)*

1:5 May this grace and peace of Jesus Christ overwhelm you. He is the first born from the dead and embodies the evidence and testimony of everything that God believes about you. He heads up the authority in which [1]we reign as kings on the earth. His crown endorses our crown. He always [2]loves us and [3]loosed us once and for all from the dominion of [4]sin in the shedding of his blood. *(We are the [1]kings of the earth - see the next verse. Note the change of tense. Christ [2]**loves us always**, [Present] and [3]**loosed us once for all**, λυσαντι [Aorist]. In his blood he brought closure to an incompetent sacrificial system in its attempt to manage mankind's sinfulness and their sin-consciousness. See 1 Peter 1:18,19. Jesus Christ who is fully God and fully man, represents the entire human race; by becoming our distortedness in his death, and raising us together with him in his resurrection as first born from the dead, he re-birthed us and redeemed his image and likeness within us. The word for sin, [4]**hamartia** from **ha**, negative and **meros**, portion or form, thus to be without your allotted portion or without form; pointing to a disoriented, distorted or bankrupt identity; the word **meros**, is the stem of the word **morphe**, as in 2 Corinthians 3:18 where the word **metamorphe**, with form, [transform] is the opposite of **hamartia** - without form. Sin is to live out of context with the blueprint of one's design; to behave out of tune with God's original harmony. Colossians 1:18 He is the principal rank of authority who leads the triumphant procession of our new birth out of the region of the dead. He is the first-born from the dead (" ... leading the resurrection parade" —Msg.) Also Ephesians 4:8,9.*

We are crowned with the triumph of Jesus' resurrection. See 1 Peter 1:3.

REVELATION Chapter 1

Psalm 103:1-5, A Psalm of David. Bless Jahweh יהוה *YHVH, Oh my soul; and all that is within me, bless his holy name. Bless Jahweh, Oh my soul, and forget not all his benefits, who forgives all your iniquity, who heals all your diseases,* **He redeems your life from the Pit and weaves a crown for you** *out of loving-kindness and tender mercies. He satisfies you with good as long as you live so that your youth is renewed like the eagle's.)*

1:6 He fashioned us into a kingdom of priests unto his God and Father. The glory and the ruling authority of the ages belong to him for all time and eternity. Amen. *(Again the revelation is contained within its familiar context of Scripture. See Exodus 19:6: ...and you shall be to me a kingdom of priests and a holy nation. Also 1 Peter 2:9: You are proof of the authentic [**eklego**] generation; you give testimony to the original idea of the royalty of true priesthood [the order of Melchizedek] you are a perfect prototype of the mass of the human race. You are the generation of people who exhibit the conclusion [**eis**] of the prophetic, poetic thought of God which has come full circle. You publish the excellence of his elevation and display that your authentic identity has been rescued out of obscurity and brought into his spectacular light.)*

1:7 Behold he comes with a ¹large dense multitude; an innumerable throng of people, united as one, like the particles of water in a cloud. Every eye will see him, not merely as observers, but they will perceive him for who he really is - even those who participated in his murder, when they pierced his hands and his side. Every single tribe of the earth will see him and weep greatly at the thought of their foolish rejection of him. This will surely be. *(The word **nephos** is a cloud, a large dense multitude, a throng. 1 Thessalonians 4:16, The Lord will personally step out of the invisible heavenly realm into our immediate visible horizon with an inciting shout, announcing his triumphant reign in the trumpet-like billowing voice of God. Even the dead will rise from their sleep, since they too are included in Christ. 1 Thessalonians 4:17, In the wake of their arising we will all be gathered into a large dense multitude; an innumerable throng of people, united as one, like the particles of water in a cloud, and we will encounter the Lord in the very air we breathe and so shall we continually celebrate our I-am-ness in our union with him. (This is the moment which redemption declares, where Deity and humanity are married. The Bride and her Groom are united.) 1 Thessalonians 4:18, The fact that we are all deeply connected in the same source of our 'beingness' causes us to be constantly engaged in this conversation with one another.)*

1:8 The God who is Lord over all things says: I am the Alpha and the Omega - my I-am-ness defines time - I am present, past and future. *(The union of **Alpha** and **Omega**, in Greek, makes the verb αω, I breathe. And in Hebrew the union of the first and last letter in their alphabet, **Aleph** [bull's head] and **Tav** [the cross] makes* ✝𐤀 *in Ancient Hebrew or* את *in modern Hebrew - **et**, which the Rabbis interpret as the first matter out of which all things were formed, [see Genesis 1:1]. The particle **et**, is untranslatable in English but, says Rabbi Aben Ezra, "it signifies the substance of the thing." Jesus is the* ¹**Alpha** *and* **Omega** *in whom we live, and move, and have our being. He is indeed closer to us than the air we breathe. Don't waste a day waiting for another day.*

The clause, "the commencement and completeness; the genesis and conclusion of everything", is wanting in almost every MS and version of importance. It appears to have been added first as an explanatory note, and in the process of time crept into the text [Adam Clarke].

Even though this does not distract from the context of the thought, it is an example of how commentary notes, in time, could become part of the text. We have no original manuscript - the thousands of manuscripts we do have are handwritten copies of copies for centuries and, unlike my own commentary notes where I have used italics and brackets, there were no such thing in those days which means this could easily have happened where a scribe's notes became text. See also another example in Luke 6:1 on the 1st 2nd Sabbath. The majority of these do not alter the meaning of the text however, but some do, which makes it an important observation.)

1:9 I am John, your brother and companion in tribulation in the midst of which we are equally participating in the authority of the kingdom and the steadfastness of Jesus Christ. I was on the Isle of Patmos because of the word of God and because of the testimony of Jesus Christ. *(See Extended Notes at the end of Revelation 20.)*

1:10 I was in a spiritual trance where I witnessed the ^{1}Day of the Lord. I heard a loud voice ^{2}behind me, clear and distinct, like the sound of a trumpet. *(The ^{1}Day of the Lord is the very day to which the prophetic voice of the Spirit of Christ pointed - Jesus the Messiah, is the fulfillment of this day. The word ^{2}***opiso*** *points to that which is behind in place and time. The fact that John hears a word* **behind him** *is so significant. It means that what he hears already happened within its prophetic context. This reminds of the incident recorded in Genesis 22:7 & 8 where Abraham was asked by Isaac, "We have the fire and the wood; but where is the lamb for a burnt offering?" Abraham answered, "God will provide a lamb for the burnt offering, Son." Then, in Genesis 22:13, we read that Abraham lifted up his eyes and looked, and behold,* **behind him** *was a ram, caught in a thicket by its horns. Jesus refers to this in John 8:56-58 when he says, "Abraham saw my day." And, "Before Abraham was, I am." [See Extended notes on the Day of the Lord in the Introduction to Revelation as well as at the end of Revelation 17.])*

1:11 This is what I heard the voice say, "Write what you see in a book and send it to the seven churches, to Ephesus, Smyrna, Pergamum, Thyatira, Sardis, Philadelphia and to Laodicea."

1:12 Having ^{1}turned about to face the source of the sound, I saw seven lampstands made out of gold. *(^{1}John's attention is drawn back to the prophetic context of the OT Scriptures. Exodus 25:36, "The entire lampstand was fashioned from one piece of hammered, pure gold." Exodus 25:37, "Make seven of these lamps for the table. Arrange the lamps so they throw their light out in front." [prophetic light.] Exodus 25:34, "The lampstand itself is to have four flower cups shaped like almond blossoms, with buds and petals." The almond tree is the prophetic tree; of all the trees, its blossoms awaken first after its winter sleep. It also pictures the resurrection, the first born from the dead. Jeremiah 1:11,12, "Jeremiah, what do you see?" I answered, "I see a branch of an almond tree." Then the LORD said to me, I* am *awake over my word to perform it. The Hebrew word* שָׁקַד *shaqad, means awake; it is also the word for an almond tree.*

The table in the temple is a significant theme in the Revelation of Jesus Christ. It clearly points to the New Covenant, the Bridal-banquet of the Marriage feast of the Lamb.)

1:13 And encircled by the lampstands there was one who appeared to be of human offspring, a son of man. He was wearing a long robe with a golden girdle round his chest. *(Revelation 2:18 and the extended notes on* **The Son of Man is the Son of God** *at the end of Revelation 2.)*

1:14 His head of hair was luminous white, like wool covered in fresh, shiny snow and his eyes were ablaze with fire. *(Resembling the Ancient of days. See Daniel 7:9 and Daniel 10:6. His body also was like beryl, and his face as the appearance of lightning, and his eyes as lamps of fire, and his arms and his feet alike in color to polished brass, and the voice of his words like the voice of a multitude.)*

1:15 His feet looked like brilliant bronze fashioned in a furnace and his voice was like the sound of many cascading waterfalls. *(Triumphant in the fiery furnace of the altar/cross.)*

1:16 In his right hand he held seven stars and his words were like a sharp two-edged sword proceeding from his mouth. His face shone like the sun in its full strength. *(See my comments in Revelation 2:16 on the imagery of the two edged sword. Also Hebrews 4:12 and Revelation 19:21. Hebrews 1:1 Throughout ancient times God spoke in many fragments and glimpses of prophetic thought to our fathers. Now, this entire conversation has finally dawned in sonship. In these last days* **(eschatos)** *God has spoken to us in the radiance of our redeemed sonship and innocence. Suddenly, what seemed to be an ancient language, falls fresh and new like the dew on the tender grass. [See Deuteronomy 32:1-4] He is the sum total of every utterance of God. He is whom the Prophets pointed to and we are his immediate audience. What God said about 'you-manity' and their redeemed sonship and innocence in Jesus, defines* **eschatology.***)*

1:17 Observing all this, I fell at his feet like a dead man. Then, [1]kneeling down, he ordained me with his right hand upon me and said, "Do not be afraid. I am the origin and the [2]conclusion of all things. *(See Isaiah 44:6. The word [1]***tithemi** *from* **theo***, to kneel down, lay down, to ordain, purpose, put, set forth. See John 15:16, I have* **ordained** *you - I have strategically positioned you. Also 1 Timothy 2:7 I am an "ordained" preacher.*

*Again the word, [2]***eschatos***; Jesus, as the Alpha and Omega, defines eschatology.)*

1:18 I am also the Living One; I died and now, see, here I am alive unto the ages of the ages and I have the keys wherewith I have disengaged the gates of [1]Hades and death. *(This profound statement of Jesus in verses 17 & 18, is the platform, theme and focus of the entire book. To distract from these words of Jesus is to miss the point of the Revelation. [1]See commentary note in verse 20 and Revelation 2:7 on the gates of Hades. Multitudes are in hell on this side of the grave; we have the keys to unlock a door that was already opened when Jesus went* *there as a man to free the human race from Adam to Noah, to now. Wow, what joy to introduce people to the freedom of sonship. Let's not make the other brother in Luke 15 our reference when we can know the Father's heart.)*

1:19 **¹Now therefore, ²without delay, give an accurate account in documenting everything that you have seen; both as they are and also what their immediate, ³intentional context has ⁴brought about. It is important to see the relevance in ⁵mirror-matching all these things, both in their prophetic context as well as in their fulfillment.** *(The word, ¹oun, certainly, accordingly, truly, then, therefore, verily. With direct reference to what was said in the previous statement. Then the word ²grapson, to document in writing, is used in the Aorist Imperative and employed here very intentionally, emphasizing once and for all, to get it over and done with. The idea was never to document a mystery in symbolic language that would in any way confuse or distract from the theme of the revelation of the triumph of the Lamb of God. The symbolic would purely be to picture the powerful parallels between the prophetic in the Jewish Scriptures, pointing to the Symbolic Lamb of God as the Redeemer of the world, and its complete fulfillment in the day of the Lord. Jesus is the fullness of time. The word ³mello, speaks of anticipated intent; expectation.*

*John again, as in verse 1, employs the verb, **ginomai**, to beget, in the Aorist Infinitive tense, ⁴**genesthai**, which indicates prior completion of an action in relationship to a point in time. Unfortunately many of the later texts changed the **e** for an **i**, which makes genesthai, ginesthai, which is the Present Infinitive, expressing progressive or imperfective aspect. Thus, not what is to follow hereafter, but, what their immediate, ³intentional context has ⁴brought about; I have translated the words **meta tauta**, as mirror-matching; **meta** - together with and **tauta**, all these things.)*

1:20 Here is the ¹significance of the seven stars that you saw in my right hand, and the seven lampstands that are made of gold: the seven stars are the ²celestial shepherd-messengers, representing the entire conclusion of the message of the ekklesia-ekklesia and the seven golden lamps are the seven churches in their complete prophetic context." *(The word ¹**musterion** suggests the inner meaning of a symbolic vision. The number seven speaks of completeness in its entire context. The stars are the carriers of light, the celestial shepherd-messengers. The word often translated as angel, ²**aggelos** has two components, **agoo** to lead as a shepherd leads and **agele** a herd of cattle or company. This word carries the idea of a messenger both in the shepherd as well as the prophetic context.*

The golden candlestick is the prophetic light - soon to be replaced by the Morning Star when the day dawns for everyone.)

Revelation Chapter 1 Extended Notes:

Significance of the Number Seven
The Day of the Lord
The Ekklesia

NOTES ON THE NUMBER SEVEN - REV 1

Significance of the Number Seven

The number seven is most significant in the context of its reference to the seventh day. The Sabbath [from שבע *Shva* -7 *Rest, wholeness, completeness, being ripe*], both in its prophetic shadow throughout the OT Scriptures and now in its substance in the person of Jesus Christ, is a constant reminder of God's celebration of perfection and completeness - behold, everything that he made, was very good.

Thus the number seven was regarded by the Hebrews as a sacred number, and it is throughout Scripture the covenant number, the sign of God's covenant relation to mankind. "Seven is the number of every grace and benefit bestowed upon Israel; which is thus marked as flowing out of the covenant, and a consequence of it. All the feasts are ordered by seven, or else by seven multiplied into seven, and thus made more even intense. Thus it is with the Sabbath, the Passover, the Feast of Weeks, of Tabernacles, the Sabbath-year, and the Jubilee." Vincent's Word Studies

In the book of Revelation the prominence of the number is marked. To a remarkable extent the structure of this book is molded by the use of numbers, especially of the numbers seven, four, and three. There are seven spirits before the throne; seven churches; seven golden candlesticks; seven stars in the right hand of him who is like unto a son of man; seven lamps of fire burning before the throne; seven horns and seven eyes of the Lamb; seven seals of the book; and the thunders, the heads of the great Dragon and of the Beast from the sea, the celestial messengers with the trumpets, the plagues, and the mountains which are the seat of the mystic Babylon, - are all seven in number.

See also **Isaiah 45:23 I have [1]sworn by myself; the word of my mouth has [2]begotten righteousness; this cannot be reversed. Every knee shall bow to me and every tongue shall echo my oath.** *(The Hebrew word,* שבע *Shaba means [1]to seven oneself, that is, swear - thus in the Hebrew mind, by repeating a declaration seven times one brings an end to all dispute. See Hebrews 6:13.16,17. See also Philippians 2:10 & 11. Extended notes on the Oath at the end of Revelation 10. The Hebrew word* יצא *Yatsa can be translated, begotten like in Judges 8:30. Thus, speak with the same certainty, sourced in me.*

The word שְׁבוּעָה *Shebuah, oath is used 7 times in scripture. A famous oath was made by Abraham and Abimelech where Abraham reinforced and substantiated the oath with a gift of seven lambs. The oath was to testify for Abraham's ownership of a well of water. Abraham named the place where the oath was taken 'Beersheba,' today a major city in Israel. This name means: 'the well of the seven' (Genesis. 21:22-32).)*

NOTES ON THE DAY OF THE LORD - REV 1

The Day of the Lord

John 1:9 A new day for mankind has come. The authentic light of life that illuminates everyone was about to dawn in the world.

Revelation 1:10 I was in a spiritual trance where I witnessed the ¹Day of the Lord. I heard a loud voice ²behind me, clear and distinct, like the sound of a trumpet. *(The ¹Day of the Lord is the very day to which the prophetic voice of the Spirit of Christ pointed - Jesus the Messiah, is the fulfillment of this day. The word ²opiso points to that which is behind in place and time. The fact that John hears a word **behind him** is so significant. It means that what he hears already happened within its prophetic context. This reminds of the incident recorded in Genesis 22:7 & 8 where Abraham was asked by Isaac, "We have the fire and the wood; but where is the lamb for a burnt offering?" Abraham answered, "God will provide a lamb for the burnt offering, Son." Then, in Genesis 22:13, we read that Abraham lifted up his eyes and looked, and behold, **behind him** was a ram, caught in a thicket by its horns. Jesus refers to this in John 8:56-58 when he says, "Abraham saw my day." And, "Before Abraham was, I am." [See Extended notes on the Day of the Lord in the Introduction to Revelation as well as at the end of Revelation 17.]*

The day of the Lord is the very day to which the prophetic voice of the Spirit of Christ pointed - Jesus the Messiah, is the fulfillment of the day. See 1 Peter 1:10 and 11 where Peter specifically makes mention of the fact that throughout Scripture the Prophets mentioned the day of the Lord as pointing to the sufferings of the Christ and the consequent glory. Their urgent quest was to search out when this would happen and who the Messiah would be. Also in Acts 17:31 Paul addresses the Greek Philosophers and reminds them of their own ancient writings and he quotes two of their well-known philosophers: in 600BC Epimenedes wrote a song saying, "We live and move and have our being in God" then Aratus wrote in 300BC that we are indeed God's offspring. Paul then announces to them that the God whom they worship in ignorance is not far from each one of us. He is not more Immanuel to the Jew than what he is to the Gentile. Then, in the context of his Jewish background and personal encounter with Jesus Christ, Paul declares to them the Good News of mankind's redeemed innocence. "God has overlooked the times of ignorance and now is calling all of mankind, whoever and wherever they are, to a radical mind-shift, since he has prophetically fixed a day on which he would judge the world in righteousness by a man whom he has appointed, and of this [righteous judgment] he has given proof to all by raising him from the dead." Acts 17:30,31. See also Romans 4:25 where, in Paul's understanding, the resurrection of Jesus from the dead includes mankind's co-resurrection and seals their acquittal and redeemed innocence.)

John 5:25 Oh how I desire for you to get this. The prophetic hour has come. This is the moment for the dead to hear the voice of the Son of God - C'mon. Hear and live.

Luke 4:19 I announce that the Jubilee year of the Lord has come. This is the liberation celebration of the Lord, embracing humanity home. *(Isaiah 61. The Jubilee year is connected with the 50th day of* שָׁבוּעוֹת *Shavuot - Sabbaths;*

NOTES ON THE DAY OF THE LORD - REV 1

*Πεντηκοστή Pentecost - 50 days. Shavuot is called the "Festival of Weeks" [originally tied to an ancient grain festival. See Luke 4:4] because it is held fifty days [seven Sabbaths plus one day] from the first Shabbat after Passover. Lev. 25,10 "You will declare this fiftieth year sacred and proclaim the liberation [Greek **aphesis**] of all the inhabitants of the land. This is to be a jubilee for you". In the Greek translation of the Old Testament the relation between jubilee and liberation is even closer because the Hebrew term יובל **jubel** is not translated into Greek as it was in the Latin of the Vulgate [jubilaeus] and in other languages, it has been translated as "liberation [**aphesis**; see my commentary of this word in the previous verse]" [Lev 25,13], or "year of liberation" [Lev 25,10)] or again "sign of liberation" [Lev 25,11-12]In Hebrew, יובל or in Ancient Hebrew ⌐⌐Y⌐⌐ to shepherd someone safely and securely home. See Lev 25:10 in the LXX "...and each of you shall return to his home." Luke 15. The prodigal son came to himself when he returned home. Back to his true I-am-ness.)*

Luke 4:20 Jesus then rolled up the scroll and gave it back to the attendant and sat down, while everyone's eyes were fixed on him. *(They knew that the Messianic expectation hinges on this Scripture; the big question was, when?.)*

Luke 4:21 He announced emphatically, Today this scripture is fulfilled in your hearing. *(This, "one-liner message", contains the weight of the entire prophetic, messianic and jubilee significance. Now, it is no longer a waiting game; it's all about your hearing. See Romans 10:8, "The Word is extremely close to you. It spills over from your heart and becomes a dynamic conversation in your mouth." [Deuteronomy 30:11-14.] Pentecost is the outpouring of Holy Spirit - "from your innermost being flow rivers of living water. John 7:37-39.)*

2 Corinthians 1:14 To some extent you have already understood that our joy is mirrored in one another. The day of the Lord Jesus Christ is no longer a distant promise but a fulfilled reality. *(The word, **kathaper**, comes from **kata**, meaning according to and **per**, which is an enclitic particle significant of abundance and thoroughness which comes from the word, **peiro**, meaning to pierce. The use of the Latin enclitic relates to a word that throws an accent back onto the preceding word, which is here translated as mirrored.)*

Zechariah 3:9 For behold, upon the stone which I have set before Joshua, upon a single stone with seven facets, I will engrave its inscription, says the LORD of hosts, I will remove the guilt of the earth in a single day.

Isaiah 66:8 Who has heard such a thing? Who has seen such things? Shall a land be born in one day? Shall a nation be brought forth in one moment?

Hosea 6:2 After two days he will revive us; on the third day he will raise us up, that we may live before him. *(Acts 17:31, Romans 4:25, 1 Peter 1:3.)*

*See my notes on the Day of the Lord in the introduction to Revelation. Also on **End Times** at the end of Chapter 17.)*

NOTES ON EKKLESIA - REV 1

The Ekklesia

Revelation 1:20 Here is the significance of the seven stars that you saw in my right hand, and the seven lampstands that are made of gold: the seven stars are the celestial shepherd-messengers, representing the entire conclusion of the message of the ekklesia-ekklesia and the seven golden lamps are the seven churches in its complete prophetic context. *(The golden candlestick is the prophetic light - soon to be replaced by the Morning Star when the day dawns for everyone. Note Peter's reference to his, James' and John's encounter with Jesus on the mount of transfiguration [Matthew 17] 2 Peter 1:16 We are not con-artists, fabricating fictions and fables to add weight to our account of his majestic appearance; with our own eyes we witnessed the powerful display of the illuminate presence of Jesus the Master of the Christ-life. [His face shone like the sun, even his raiment was radiant white.] 2 Peter 1:17 He was spectacularly endorsed by God the Father in the highest honor and glory. God's majestic voice announced, "This is the son of my delight; he completely pleases me." 2 Peter 1:18 For John, James, and I the prophetic word is fulfilled beyond doubt; we heard this voice loud and clear from the heavenly realm while we were with Jesus in that sacred moment on the mountain. 2 Peter 1:19,* **For us the appearing of the Messiah is no longer a future promise but a fulfilled reality.** *Now it is your turn to have more than a second-hand, hearsay testimony. Take my word as one would take a lamp at night; the day is about to dawn within you, in your own understanding. When the Morning Star appears, you no longer need the lamp; this will happen shortly on the horizon of your own hearts." Remember the significance of Matthew, 16:13-19, which records the remarkable unveiling of the answer to the most important question in the Bible and in life, "Who am I, the son of man.?" This happened just 6 days before the event referred to above in Matthew 17. The question Jesus asks here, in Matthew 16 underlines the focus of his mission; he is about to redeem mankind's lost sense of sonship and identity. Simon, by heavenly revelation realizes that the son of man is indeed the son of God. Jesus immediately endorses him, Simon, the flesh and blood son of Jonah, as Petros, Mr. Rock, the Chip off the old Block. We have forgotten the Rock from which we were hewn. Deuteronomy 32:18. "You who seek God and pursue righteousness, here is your clue. "Look to the Rock from which you were hewn." Isaiah 51:1. Then Jesus makes this remarkable statement, that on this Rock [the revelation of mankind's true sonship redeemed], he would build his* **ekklesia** *[from* **ek**, *origin and* **kaleo**, *to surname; original identity] and the gates of* **Hades** *[from the negative particle,* **ha**, *and* **eido** *to see] The blindfold mode of the human race will not prevail against the revelation of the son of man as the offspring of God - this is the triumph of the ekklesia. Revelation 2:7.)*

Revelation 2:18 Write also to the leader of the ekklesia in Thyatira; the Son of God with eyes ablaze and feet shining like burnished bronze, says, *(Here Jesus introduces himself as the son of God. John sees him as the son of man in Revelation 1:13. Haha. The Rock foundation of the ekklesia that Jesus is both the Architect and Master-builder of, is the unveiling of the Father. The son of man is the son of God. Blessed are you, Simon, son of Jonah. Flesh and blood did not reveal this to you, but My Father.. I say, you are Rock, a chip [***petros***] of the old Block [***petra***]. And upon this* **petra**, *I will build my ekklesia and the gates of Hades [not to see] will not prevail against it. Matthew 16:13-19.*

NOTES ON EKKLESIA - REV 1

See Deuteronomy 32:18 You were unmindful of the Rock that begot you, and you forgot the God who gave you birth. Isaiah 51:1 Look to the Rock from which you were hewn, the quarry from which you were dug.

Here, as in Revelation 1:15, his feet looked like brilliant, burnished bronze fashioned in a furnace. As the Lamb of God who presented his body in sacrifice on the Bronze Altar, he descended into mankind's deepest darkness and triumphantly led mankind out into a place where the enemy of the human race [the Satanas-System] was made our footstool. See Hebrews 1:13 "You are the extension of my right hand, my executive authority; take your position and witness how I make your enemies a place upon which you may rest your feet." Also 1 Corinthians 15:25 His dominion is destined to subdue all hostility and contradiction under his feet. ("The Lord said to my Lord, Sit at my right hand until I make your enemies your footstool." [Psalm 110:1] Jesus is Lord of Lords; in his victory mankind is restored to lordship; "I say you are gods, all of you are sons of the Most High" [Psalm 82:6 RSV].) Matthew 22:42-45.)

Ephesians 1:19 I pray that you will be overwhelmed with an understanding of the magnitude of his power in the finished work of Christ. This is what results in the dynamic of your faith. *(The Preposition **eis**, speaks of a point reached in conclusion. The word **pisteuontas** is the Present Participle in the Accusative case of **pisteuo** [to be certain; to be persuaded] which describes an action thought of as simultaneous with the action of the main verb, which, in this case is **energeken**, "which he has wrought"... [see v 20] which is the Perfect tense of **energeo**, to energize; to work dynamically. The Perfect tense denotes an action which is completed in the past, but the effects of which are regarded as continuing into the present. Paul is desiring to establish a basis for our faith that exceeds our attempts to believe.)*

Ephesians 1:20 Do you want to measure the mind and muscle of God? Consider the force which he unleashed in Jesus Christ when he raised him from the dead and forever seated him enthroned as his executive authority in the realm of the heavens. Jesus is God's right hand of power. He was raised up from the deepest dungeons of human despair to the highest region of heavenly bliss. *(See Ephesians 2:5,6 & 4:8,9.)*

Ephesians 1:21 Infinitely above all the combined forces of rule, authority, dominion or governments; he is ranked superior to any name that could ever be given to anyone of this age or any age still to come in the eternal future.

Ephesians 1:22 I want you to see this: he subjected all these powers under his feet. He towers head and shoulders above everything. He is the head;

Ephesians 1:23 the ekklesia is his body. The completeness of his being that fills all in all resides in us. God cannot make himself more visible or exhibit himself more accurately. *(The word, **ekklesia**, comes from **ek**, a Preposition always denoting origin, and **klesia** from **kaleo**, to identify by name, to surname; thus the "ekklesia" is his redeemed image and likeness in human form.)*

Ephesians 2:20 Your lives now give tangible definition to the spiritual structure, having been built into it by God upon the foundation that the

Prophets and Apostles proclaimed. The first evidence of this building was Jesus Christ himself being the chief cornerstone. *(He is the visible testimony to the restored image and likeness of God in human form.)*

Ephesians 2:21 In him everyone of us are like living Lego blocks fitted together of the same fabric (conversation), giving ever increasing articulation to a global mobile sanctuary intertwined in the Lord. *(The word, **sunarmologeo**, comes from **sun**, meaning union, **harmo** meaning harmony, and **logeo** meaning conversation. The word, **auxano**, means expanding with growth. The word, **naos**, is translated as the most sacred dwelling space.)*

Ephesians 2:22 In him you are co-constructed together as God's permanent spiritual residence. You are God's address.

In the next two chapters of Revelation, seven churches in Asia are addressed, *The seven Churches were Ephesus, Smyrna, Pergamos, Thyatira, Sardis, Philadelphia, and Laodicea.*

The seven symbolize the entire Ekklesia.

The geographic location of these churches signifies the rising sun - the new day that has come for mankind to re-discover their forgotten identity.

Asia - meaning East, or Orient - its origin is late Middle English: via Old French from Latin orient- 'rising or east', from *oriri* 'to rise'.

The Orient, literally the countries of the East, especially East Asia. Also referring to the treasures including pearls of the finest quality of the Orient.

East as in the pointer to the rising sun, being the most prominent point of reference in order to 'orientate' oneself; which means to align or position oneself or something relative to the points of a compass or other specified positions. Which is exactly the intent of the book of Revelation, to re-align the mindsets of the entire human race, mirrored in the ekklesia as the sons of God.

Anatolia, Greek: Ἀνατολία, from Ἀνατολή Anatole, "a rising above [the horizon]," from ***anatellein*** "to rise," from ***ana*** "up" + ***tellein*** "to accomplish, perform."

Turkish: Anadolu "east" or "sunrise", also known as Asia Minor.

REVELATION Chapter 2

Addressing the Shepherd Messengers of the 7 churches.

*(The word often translated as angel, ¹aggelos has two components, **agō** to lead as a shepherd leads and **agele** a herd of cattle or company.)*

2:1 Write to the celestial shepherd-messenger of the ekklesia of Ephesus: The One who holds the seven stars in his right hand and who walks between the seven golden lampstands, would say this to you:

2:2 I see how hard you work and all your exhausting efforts; also your unyielding commitment to the task and how you cannot stand the wicked. You have made it your business to scrutinize some so-called Apostles and judge them to be false.

2:3 You have applied great diligence and have relentlessly pushed yourself beyond limits - and all along you did it in my Name as if you were representing me.

2:4 Here is my problem, you have divorced me and abandoned your first love. *(A repeat of the Garden of Eden. Where Adam and Eve preferred the fruit of the tree of their own toil and labor to become like God rather than to rest in the conviction of the likeness and union they already enjoyed by design.)*

2:5 Now, I implore you to call to mind that place where you have fallen from. Remember our intimate romance. The poetry of this union is the driving force of your life. It is so different from being duty- or guilt-driven. It is in your ¹entwining with my thoughts that you are most ²strategic and effective. *(The word often wrongfully translated, repent as in the Latin penance, is the word ¹**metanoia** - with thought. The idea of the ²lampstand suggests a strategic location of influence. See notes on Isaiah 40:31 in James 1:5.)*

2:6 I must say to your credit that we both have a common disregard for those who want to abuse their position to ¹control people. *(The business of the ¹**nikolaitoon** - from **nikao**, to conquer, and **laos**, people.)*

2:7 Now listen up with your inner ears. Hear with understanding what the Spirit is saying to the ¹ekklesias: ²to the individual who continues to see their triumph mirrored in mine *[their co-seatedness with me in the throne room]* I will give to feast from the fruit of the tree of life in the ³paradise of God. *(The word ¹**ekklesias** [churches] plural of **ekklesia**, from **ek**, source and **kaleo**, to surname - thus their identity is sourced in me. The same word, **nikao** to conquer, as in the previous verse. This time it's not lording it over people to abuse them but discovering the lordship of the Christ-life within you. Here, it is νικωντι **nikoonti**, which is the Present Active Participle Dative, form of the verb **nikao**, to emphasize a continual or habitual victory. This reminds of the 2 trees in the garden, the knowledge of good and evil- [**poneros**] tree and the tree of life. The **poneros** tree is the tree representing labors annoyances and hardships in human efforts to become by their own doing what they already are by design and by redemption. The word ³**paradise** from **para**, closest possible union, and **eido**, to see; thus to see from a place of our co-seatedness - This is the opposite of the word **Hades** - not to see. See notes on 1 John 3:12, Why the other Tree?)*

REVELATION Chapter 2

2:8 Write the following to the messenger of the ekklesia in Smyrna; tell him that the One who is the origin and conclusion of all things, who died and was restored to life, says:

2:9 I see your hard work and the tight claustrophobic spaces that you are facing; also the beggarly state that you're convinced you're trapped in when in fact you are super rich. I know about the hurtful slander of those who pretend to defend Jewish culture against your influence, but are actually, part and parcel of the [1]satanic synagogue-system of accusation. *(From the Hebrew* שׂטן *sawtan,* [1]*to attack, to accuse, oppose.)*

2:10 You have no need to fear anything you might suffer at any time. Know that [1]this "Outcast-system" is about to cast some of you out of your comfort-zone of fellowship into a place of confinement and imprisonment where you will be examined and severely pressured for a period of [2]ten days. I desire for you to be fully persuaded even in the face of death and be crowned like a champion athlete with my victory over death - behold in death I will personally crown you with life. *(The* [1]*diabolos [from dia, because of and ballo, to cast down] represents the system of religion which is the typical fruit of the same tree of temptation in the garden of Eden; the Tree of legalistic rule and performance that would want to squeeze people into its mold to make them conform to their structures of control. It is the system empowered by the "I am-not-Tree."*

The significance of the [2]*10th day:* **the Passover lamb was selected on the 10th day of the 1st month.** *Exodus 12:3 also 12:5, "Your lamb shall be examined and proved to be without blemish, a year old male; you shall take it from the sheep or from the goats."*

So when faced with severe contradiction, remember how the Lamb was scrutinized and faced our death in his broken body.

FB Meyer comments, "This epistle has a new pathos and significance if we connect it with "the blessed Polycarp," who almost certainly was the chief minister of the ekklesia in Smyrna. He was the disciple of John. Irenaeus who lived a generation later, tells how, in early boyhood, he had heard from the lips of Polycarp what John had told him of our Lord's person, converse, and earthly ministry. How sweet the comfort of this epistle must have been to him in the closing scene of his life, when, at eighty-six, he was sentenced to be burned.")

2:11 Now, listen up with your inner ears. Hear with understanding what the Spirit is saying to the ekklesia: the individual who [1]continues to see their triumph mirrored in mine *[their co-seatedness with me in the throne room]*, is [2]most certainly not threatened by any [3]contradiction to their true likeness; there is nothing to fear [4]in the second death. *(The word* [1]*nikoon, is the Present Active Participle Nominative, form of the verb* **nikao,** *to emphasize a continual or habitual victory. Then the double negative,* οὐ μή ἀδικηθῇ [2]***ou mey**, plus the verb,* [3]***adikeō**, meaning unrighteous; out of sync with likeness - with* **a**, *negative and* **dikeo**, *two parties sharing likeness -* **adikeythey** *is the Aorist Subjunctive form, meaning a definite outcome that will happen as a result of another stated action. The Preposition,* ἐκ *[*[4]***ek**, mostly pointing to source, but here used for the agent or instrument]* τοῦ θανάτου τοῦ δευτέρου *the second death.*

REVELATION Chapter 2

So, in context of the previous verse [Revelation 2:10], "You have no need to fear anything you might suffer at any time", the Second Death is not to distract from the once and for all death that Jesus died, but to endorse it. In the lake of fire, Death and Hades are eradicated from memory. The first death is the once and for all death that Jesus died, representing the global death of humankind. Jesus' death took mankind's death in Adam, out of the equation. The idea of the Second Death has to do with the fact that the revelation of the full extent of everyone's inclusion in the death of Jesus, has not yet dawned on some - so it will take a crisis, even their own death, to immediately engage them with the symbolic cleansing [from their doubts, ignorance and unbelief] represented by the lake of burning sulphur, purifying like in a furnace, separating the gold from the dross-mindsets. This is the ultimate awakening to the success of the cross - the realizing that even Death and Hades itself died in Jesus' death. It is indeed the death of Death. Revelation 20:14. See my notes on **The Lake of Fire and the Second Death** *at the end of Revelation 19.*

But here, specifically in Smyrna's case, the intensity of their persecution is neutralized by their realizing that gold is never threatened by fire.

Remember the One talking is he who said, I am the Living One; I died and now, see, here I am alive unto the ages of the ages and I have the keys wherewith I have disengaged the gates of Hades and death. Revelation 1:18. Also Hebrews 9:25-28.

He thus broke the spell of the supposed claim of judgment and death over the Adamic race. The significance of the implications of Jesus' death cannot be exaggerated. It reaches into the entire past, present and future of human history.

As representative of the human race, Jesus Christ fulfilled mankind's destiny with death and judgment. *[1 Corinthians 15:3-5, Romans 4:25, Acts 17:30, 31.] Note: Jesus did not come to condemn the world. The Father judges no one for he has handed over all judgment to the Son, who judged the world in righteousness.)*

2:12 And to the messenger of the ekklesia in Pergamos write: these are the words of him with the swift double-edged sword: *(Pergamos means united by marriage)*

2:13 I see where you reside, in the very headquarters, as it were, of the [1]Accuser, yet you remain strong in your association with my Name and have not [2]contradicted my belief in you. Even during those difficult times when my faithful witness Antipas was murdered in your midst; right there where severe satanic accusation seems to have taken up permanent residence. *([1]From the Hebrew שטן sawtan, [1]to attack, to accuse, oppose. The word [2]arneomai means to contradict.)*

2:14 My concern is that you are compromising the ekklesia by tolerating those who encourage idol worship and sexual perversion, forgetting how Balaam seduced Balak back in the day and sabotaged Israel's pilgrimage.

2:15 So in the same way that Israel had the wiles of Balaam, you now entertain the ideas of the Nicolaitans. *(The [1]nikolaitoon - from nikao, to conquer, and laos, people. The business of those who wish to abuse their position to [1]control people.)*

REVELATION Chapter 2

2:16 I urge you to come to your senses immediately. The ¹sword of my mouth will swiftly wage war against this type of conversation. *(Cutting to the division of soul and spirit - see Hebrews 4:12 Also Revelation 1:16. Engaging the deepest longings of the heart. See Luke 2:35 for **rhomphaia**.*

*The Sword, ¹**rhomphaia** [LXX] would always point back to mankind's original identity. The Hebrew word in Genesis 3:24, הפך **hâpak** is a primitive root; meaning to turn about; by implication to change, to return, to be converted, turn back. Also in the Septuagint the same thought is communicated in the Greek word, **strephō**, which is the strengthened from the base of **tropay**; to turn around or reverse: - convert, turn again, back again, to turn self about. In Luke 15 the prodigal son returns to himself - Plato is quoted by Ackerman [Christian Element in Plato] as thinking of redemption as coming to oneself. See Notes on the splendor of the Gates Revelation 21.)*

2:17 Your victory is secured in your hearing the word of the Spirit addressing the ekklesias - feast on the revelation of the hidden manna in the Ark. *[This prophetically pointed to the Messiah - the mystery that was hidden for ages and generations is Christ in you.]* **I also give you a little white pebble used in the courts of justice, signifying your acquittal - take it as your secret source of strength in the midst of accusation - it has your new name on it. No one knows you by this name, until you ¹realize your own identity reflected in it.** *(The golden pot of manna was "laid up before God in the ark". Exodus 16:23. It was believed that Jeremiah hid the ark, before the destruction of Jerusalem, where it would not be discovered till Israel was restored. 2 Macc. 2:5ff. Robertson's Word Pictures. See Matthew 16:13 on Simon discovering his new name.)*

2:18 Write also to the leader of the ekklesia in ¹Thyatira: The ²Son of God with eyes ablaze and ³feet shining like burnished bronze says, *(Also interesting to note that ¹Thyatira means sacrifice. Here Jesus introduces himself as the ²**Son of God**. See Extended notes on **The Son of Man is the Son of God** at the end of Revelation 2.)*

2:19 I know your hard work and how you love what you're doing - also that you are absolutely convinced that you are doing the right thing and how relentlessly you've exerted yourselves - even more so now than ever before.

2:20 It disturbs me that you accommodate the typical Jezebel influence, a self-appointed Prophetess who teaches and seduces my ¹devoted friends into participating in an ²idolatrous sacrificial system by eating food offered to ³idols and fornicating with her foreign ideas about God. *(The word ¹**doulos**, bond-servant or slave; also a devoted friend, from **deo**, to be bound to another in friendship or marriage. The word ²**eidōlothuton**, from **eidolon** and **thuo**, to slay in sacrifice. The word ³**eidolon** where we get the word idol from means image or likeness - this is the theme of the Bible and redemption; the image and likeness of God revealed and redeemed in human form. See **Extended Notes on Food Offered to Idols** at the end of this chapter.)*

2:21 I gave her opportune time ¹to see with my eyes, to know my heart and to wake up out of the sway of her adultery but she had no inclination to yield to my thoughts. *(The word ¹**metanoia** means to realize God's thoughts.*

*Like most Greek words, μετάνοια metanoia is a compound word, from **meta**, with νοιέω **noieō**, to perceive with the mind. It describes the awakening of the mind to that which is true; it is a gathering of one's thoughts, a co-knowing. Faith is not a decision; it is a discovery. It has nothing in common with the Latin word **paenitentia** - where the idea of penance and repentance stems from. Sadly the word repentance became the popular English translation of **metanoia**.)*

2:22 The bed of your adultery will become you and your lovers' [1]**confinement to great anguish. Even then will I continue to invite you to awaken from your deception.** *(The word* [1]***thlipsis*** *means a narrow claustrophobic space of intense pressure. The very platform of the man-made 'ekklesia' institution from where you have run your religious business will become your prison and punishment- the scene of the sin is also the scene of the inevitable consequence. "But where sin increased grace superseded it." Romans 5:20)*

2:23 The offspring of these 'mindsets', conceived in your licentious idolatry has no future. I will cause it [1]**to utterly perish. And every ekklesia shall** [2]**know that I scrutinize the hidden thoughts of the heart. And I will expose every single work of your own doing as judged in my work.** *(See verse 26 - my works vs your works. To* [1]*kill in death is a very strong expression,* **apokteuno en thanato***. The symbolic significance of killing the children of the ekklesia's idolatrous adultery in death can only be understood in the context of the unveiling of Jesus the Christ who already died mankind's death and in that death brought final closure to the offspring of mankind's guilt-ridden mindsets that we have inherited from our world systems which were founded in the fruit of the "I-am-not tree system". He thus broke the spell of the claim of judgment and death over the Adamic race. This signifies the death of death. The significance of the implications of Jesus' death cannot be exaggerated. It reaches into the entire past, present and future of human history. The word* [2]***ginosontai*** *is the future ingressive punctiliar middle of* **ginosko***, 'we shall certainly come to know', this confirms the theme of the book of Revelation. The unveiling of Jesus Christ and his finished work will most definitely complete God's purpose of redeeming mankind's lost sense of sonship, value, innocence, identity and royalty in the earth.*

Hebrews 4:12, The message God spoke to us in Christ, is the most life giving and dynamic influence in us, cutting like a surgeon's scalpel, sharper than a soldier's sword, piercing to the deepest core of human conscience, to the dividing of soul and spirit; ending the dominance of the sense realm and its neutralizing effect upon the human spirit. In this way a person's spirit is freed to become the ruling influence again in the thoughts and intentions of their heart. The scrutiny of this living Sword-Logos detects every possible disease, discerning the body's deepest secrets where joint and bone-marrow meet. Hebrews 4:13, The entire person is thoroughly exposed to his scrutinizing gaze. (Psalm 139:2, You know the deepest impulse of my thoughts.))

2:24 I would urge those of you in Thyatira who do [1]**not embrace this Jezebel influence, as well as the ones who perhaps feel that they might be missing out on something by not studying the so-called 'deep things of Satan', to embrace what your hearts resonate with. I'm not giving you anything that will burden you in any way.** *(The words* [1]***ou echo***, *not in echo;*

REVELATION Chapter 2

*not in sync with her distorted teachings. Sin-consciousness is the seat of ²**satanas** - the accuser. The word ³**loipoi** from **leipo**, to be left out - those who feel that they are excluded from certain practices or privileges. The word ⁴**baros**, weight or burden is also used in Galatians 6:2, "Bear one another's burdens, and so fulfill the law of Christ." And in the Mirror it reads, "The law of the Christ-life distinguishes your spirituality; taking the weight off someone's shoulders is fulfilling the law of Christ. The message of grace removes all law-related burdens such as guilt, suspicion, inferiority, shame and sin-consciousness.)*

2:25 ¹Lay hold of that which your hearts ²bear witness to ³until you fully grasp the scope and understand the most conclusive significance of ⁴my coming. *(The word ¹**kratesate** from **krateo** is in the Aorist Imperative suggesting, "get it over and done with." Again the word ²**echo** is used, to hold, to resonate. The word ³**achri**, until, from **akron**, the farthest bounds, uttermost parts, end, highest, extreme - related to the word **akmen**, extremity, climax, acme, highest degree. The verb ⁴**hekso** from **heko** to have come, is the Aorist Active subjunctive which is the mood of probability. The time of the action of the subjunctive mood is relative to the time of the main verb, which in this case is - **echete**, Present Active Indicative of **echo**, "that which your hearts resonate with." Heart resonance is certain. As in 2 Corinthians 3:2 "...known and read by all." Or in the Mirror, "You are our Epistle written within us, an open letter speaking a global language; one that everyone can read and recognize as their mother tongue." If the subjunctive mood is used in a purpose or result clause, then the action should not be thought of as a possible result, but should be viewed as a definite outcome that will happen as a result of another stated action.)*

2:26 Seeing my victory as your victory makes you the overcomer. By embracing the ¹completeness of my works as your ²treasure, you realize my authority in you to possess the nations. *(See verse 23 - the ¹success of my works is to your credit. The words, αχρι τελους **achri telous** suggest, taking my words to its full conclusion. The word ²**tereo** means to value, to treasure, to guard with great care. See Psalm 2: 7,8 [also verse 9 as referenced in the next verse, 27] You are my son, today I have begotten you. Ask of me, and I will make the nations your heritage, and the ends of the earth your possession. Paul quotes Psalm 2 in Acts 13:33 when he preaches the resurrection of Jesus and in Ephesians 2:5,6 and Colossians 3:1-3 he celebrates our co-begottenness. Also Peter announces that we were born anew when Jesus was raised from the dead. 1 Peter 1:3. The word ²**exousia**, often translated as authority has two components, **ek**, out of, source and **eimi**, I am. The Preposition ³**epi** suggests continuous influence upon, from a position of authority.)*

2:27 You will ¹shepherd the nations with a royal scepter and shatter ²their 'alienated mindsets' like a potter's vessel of clay. *(He quotes Psalm 2:9, "You shall break them with a rod of iron, and dash them in pieces like a potter's vessel." Sadly, the Hebrew Masoretic Text uses the word רעע **RAA** - to be bad, be evil; to be displeasing; to be injurious; to be wicked; to do an injury or hurt; to be mischief; instead of the same sounding word, ¹ רעה **RA'AH** with a **Hay** at the end and not an **Ayin**, which means **to shepherd**. Also in the Septuagint, the Greek word ποιμανεῖς ¹**poimaneis**, shepherd is used. You shall feed them as a shepherd* *nurtures his flock. With reference to the ²alienated mindsets that ruled the nations see Numbers 24:17, "A scepter shall rise out of Israel; it shall crush the forehead of Moab." (mindset.) The shepherd's staff was never intended to beat up the sheep but to protect and free them from any possible threat. See Revelation 19:15.*

See Extended Notes on The Rod of Iron at the end of the Chapter.)

2:28 In the same way that my shepherding mission is ³sourced in the Father I have extended it to you. I also give you the ²Morning Star. *(I've attached part of the previous verse here; the Greek word, ¹**para**, with the Genitive, indicating source or origin, close and immediate proximity, intimate connection, union. See 2 Peter 1:19, "Take my word as one would take a lamp at night; the day is about to dawn for you in your own understanding. When the ²Morning Star appears, you no longer need the lamp; this will happen shortly on the horizon of your own hearts." Revelation 22:16 I am Jesus. I sent my celestial messenger to be witness of these things to you before the churches; confirming to them that I am the Root and offspring of David, the radiant Morning Star. See my notes on **The "Fallen Star" is The bright Morning Star**, at the end of Revelation 9.)*

2:29 Now listen up with your inner ears. Hear with understanding what the Spirit is saying to the ekklesia. *(See 1 Corinthians 2:13, "The impact of our words are not confined to the familiar wisdom of the world taught by human experience and tradition, but communicated by seamless spirit resonance, combining spirit with spirit.")*

Revelation Chapter 2 Extended Notes:

The Son of Man is the Son of God
Food Offered to Idols
The Rod of Iron

The Son of Man is the Son of God

Revelation 1:13 And encircled by the lampstands there was one who appeared to be of human offspring, a son of man. He was wearing a long robe with a golden girdle round his chest.

Revelation 1:14 His head of hair was luminous white, like wool covered in fresh, shiny snow and his eyes were ablaze with fire. *(Resembling the Ancient of days. See Daniel 7:9 and Daniel 10:6. His body also was like beryl, and his face as the appearance of lightning, and his eyes as lamps of fire, and his arms and his feet alike in color to polished brass, and the voice of his words like the voice of a multitude.)*

Revelation 1:15 His feet looked like brilliant bronze fashioned in a furnace and his voice was like the sound of many cascading waterfalls. *(Triumphant in the fiery furnace of the altar/cross.)*

Revelation 2:17 Your victory is secured in your hearing the word of the Spirit addressing the ekklesia - feast on the revelation of the hidden manna in the Ark *[which prophetically pointed to the Messiah - the mystery that was hidden for ages and generations is Christ in you.]* **I also give you a little white pebble used in the courts of justice, signifying your acquittal - take it as your secret source of strength in the midst of accusation - it has your new name on it. No one knows you by this name, until you [1]realize your own identity reflected in it.** *(This beautifully reminds of Simon's encounter in Matthew 16 - "Blessed are you Simon, son of Jonah for flesh and blood has not known that the son of man is indeed the son of God. Now that you know who I am, allow me to introduce you to you. Your real name, as son of God, is* **Petros** *- little stone - son of* **Petra** *[the Rock] - yes, Mr Rock, you're a chip off the old Block! See my notes on John 1:12 - Our grasping [[1]lambano] is simply the awakening to the fact that our genesis is already completed in the* **Logos**. *[See John 1:3] The* **Logos** *is the source; everything commences in him. He remains the exclusive Parent reference to their genesis. There is nothing original, except the Word. We are his offspring. [see Acts 17:28]. "He has come to give us understanding to know him who is true and to realize that we are in him who is true." [1 John 5:20].)*

The white stone - **psēphon leukēn**, *is an old word for pebble - from* **psaō**, *to rub - which was used in courts of justice; black pebbles for condemning, white pebbles for acquitting. The only other use of the word in the N.T. is in Acts 26:10, where Paul speaks of "depositing his pebble" -* **katēnegka psēphon** *- or casting his vote. The white stone with one's name on it was used to admit one to entertainments and also as an amulet or charm. In this instance it could also refer to the Lord's name written on it - see Revelation. 3:12. There is also an allusion here to conquerors in the public games, who were not only conducted with great pomp into the city to which they belonged, but had a white stone given to them, with their name inscribed on it; which badge entitled them, during their whole life, to be maintained at the public expense. See Pind., Olymp. vii. 159, and the Scholia there; and see the collections in Wetstein, and Rosenmuller's note. These were called tesserae among the Romans, and of these there were several kinds.*

Revelation 2:18 Write also to the leader of the ekklesia in Thyatira; the [1]Son of God with eyes ablaze and [2]feet shining like burnished bronze

says, *(Here Jesus introduces himself as the Son of God. John sees him as the son of man in Revelation 1:13; And encircled by the lampstands there was* **one who appeared to be of human offspring, a son of man.** *Clothed with a long robe and with a golden girdle round his chest." See Notes on The ekklesia at the end of Chapter 1.*

Here, as in Revelation 1:15, his feet looked like brilliant, burnished bronze fashioned in a furnace. As the Lamb of God who presented his body in sacrifice on the Bronze Altar, he descended into mankind's deepest darkness and triumphantly led mankind out into a place where the enemies of the human race was made our footstool. See Hebrews 1:13; "You are the extension of my right hand, my executive authority; take your position and witness how I make your enemies a place upon which you may rest your feet." Also 1 Corinthians 15:25; His dominion is destined to subdue all hostility and contradiction under his feet. ("The Lord said to my Lord, Sit at my right hand until I make your enemies your footstool." [Psalm 110:1] Jesus is Lord of Lords; in his victory mankind is restored to lordship; "I say you are gods, all of you are sons of the Most High". [Psalm 82:6 RSV] Matthew 22:42-45.)

See John 5:18 This was fuel for the fire of Jewish zeal in their determination to execute Jesus. Not only did he break their Sabbath, but now he has gone beyond all extremes. He calls God his own Father - who does he think he is - God's equal?

John 5:19 Jesus explained to them with utmost certainty that whatever they see the Son does, mirrors the Father - he does not act independent of his Father - the Son's gaze is fixed in order to accurately interpret and repeat what he sees his Father does. The one reveals the other without compromise or distraction. *(The incarnation does not interrupt what the Word was from the beginning - face to face with God.)*

John 5:20 For the Father and the Son are [1]best of friends. They have no secrets; the Father gladly lets his Son in on everything he does and will continue to show him works of most significant proportions, which will astound you. *(The Father loves [[1]phileo] the Son with fondness.)*

John 5:21 For just as the Father awakens people from their death-sleep and revitalizes them with Zoe-life, even so it pleases the Son to awaken people to life.

John 5:22 For the Father judges no-one but has given all judgment to the Son.

John 5:23 The Father's desire is that all may value the son with the same honor wherewith they esteem him - there is no distinction - to dishonor the Son is to dishonor the Father.

John 5:24 Most certainly do I say unto you that this is the vital transition from dead religion into the very life of the ages - embrace the Son's word with the same persuasion as you would the Father's and you will not know any judgment - the Son gives voice to the Father. *(He is the Father's Word made flesh.)*

THE SON OF MAN IS THE SON OF GOD - REV 2

John 5:25 Oh how I desire for you to get this. The prophetic hour has come. This is the moment for the dead to hear the voice of the Son of God - C'mon. Hear and live.

John 5:26 The [1]very self existence within the Father is what he has bestowed upon the Son in order for the Son to [2]radiate the same Zoe-life. *(The word [1]hosper from hos, in that manner; and per, an enclitic particle significant of abundance [thoroughness], that is, emphasis; much, very or ever. The word [2]echo, to have possession of, reminds of the English word echo; thus to resonate, radiate.)*

John 5:27 The Father has also given the Son of man [1]authentic authority to execute judgment on mankind's behalf. *(The word [1]exousia, often translated as authority has two components, ek, out of, source and eimi, I am.)*

John 5:28 Do not be alarmed by this, but the hour is coming when those in the [1]graves will hear his voice. *(No-one who ever lived will escape the extent of his righteous judgment. Those who have [1]forgotten who they are will hear his incarnate voice. The word for grave, [1]__mnēmeion__, memory, suggests a remembrance - to bring something from memory into the here and now! Like David prophecies in Psalm 22 when he sees the cross-crisis [__krisis__ - judgment, means the 'decisive moment' or, turning point] a thousand years before it happens. His conclusion in verse 27 sums up the triumph of God's resolve. "All the ends of the earth shall [1]remember and turn to the LORD; and all the families of the nations shall worship before him." See 1 Corinthians 15:21,22 The same mankind who died in a man was raised again in a man. In Adam all died; in Christ all are made alive.)*

Food Offered to Idols

Revelation 2:20 It disturbs me that you accommodate the typical Jezebel influence, a self-appointed Prophetess who teaches and seduces my [1]devoted friends into participating in an [2]idolatrous sacrificial system by eating food offered to [3]idols and fornicating with her foreign ideas about God.

*([1] The word [1]doulos, bond-servant or slave; also a devoted friend, from **deo**, to be bound to another in friendship or marriage.*

*[2] The word [2]eidōlothuton, from **eidolon** and **thuo**, to slay in sacrifice.*

[3] The word [3]eidolon where we get the word idol from means image or likeness - this is the theme of the Bible and redemption; the image and likeness of God revealed and redeemed in human form. **Idolatry is a projection of an image of one's own making.** *Idolatry is the crux of religion - it is an expensive business since your idol is like a slot machine at the casino. It remains hungry and it is wired to bite and bankrupt you.*

To appreciate this statement, "eating food offered to idols", one needs to understand the significance of meals in NT context. **Your mind consumes thoughts like you eat food - just as food becomes flesh so do words become incarnate.**

By teaching pagan philosophies to the ekklesia where they feast on food offered to idols there is a direct rejection of the New Covenant symbolized in our every meal as a celebration of the incarnation. Jesus as the Lamb of God introduced the New Covenant meal where his incarnate body and shed blood turns the prophetic word of God into our true sustenance.

> See **1 Corinthians 11:23-34** in the Mirror: Your every meal makes the mandate of his coming relevant and communicates the meaning of the New Covenant. "This cup holds the wine of the New Covenant in my blood; you celebrate me every time you drink with this understanding."
>
> From now on our meals are meaningful. We celebrate the fact that the incarnation reveals our redemption; the promise became a person. He redeemed our original value, identity, and innocence; he died our death and defines the life we now live. He fulfills the theme of Scripture: the sufferings of the Messiah and the subsequent glory. [**1 Peter 1:10, 11**])

In John's gospel chapter 6 he reminds us about the economy of Jesus' ministry; he knew very well the pivotal significance of his appointment with the ultimate Passover where he would lay down his life as the Lamb of God to be slaughtered by his own creation for their salvation.

John 6:5 when Jesus saw the multitude arrive, he said to Philip, How do you think we are going to feed all these people?

John 6:6 This wasn't a trick question, but simply to engage their faith; he already knew exactly what he was going to do. Jesus was not about to be distracted by the enormity of his mission where his body would be broken at the highest price in order to feed the multitudes of mankind with the true bread from heaven. Just like in Chapter 24 of Luke - the picture of a meal always translates into incarnation language - bread becomes flesh.

John 6:7 *Philip immediately concluded that this was impossible to do and far beyond a budget of any reasonable calculation; two hundred days wages could never buy enough for each person in the crowd to even get a little morsel of bread. Mankind cannot redeem themselves. Again, Jesus leads the conversation into a different dimension - like with Nicodemus and the Samaritan woman - he points to a different source; not related to external reasoning or challenges to be met with personal contributions of our own toil or labor to define or defend ourselves but simply accessing the Father's limitless resources within. He has come to free our minds from the restrictions of a dimension that could never truly define us. He dramatically and very intentionally disengages us with every effort of our own to save ourselves. Our salvation is beyond our budget. BUT WAIT.. What about the little lad.? For unto us a child is born remember.)*

John 6:31 How do you compete with Moses? Our fathers ate the manna in the wilderness - as it is written - He gave them bread from heaven to eat.

(The rabbis quoted Psalm 72:16 to prove that the Messiah, when he comes, will outdo Moses with manna from heaven. Robertson's Word Pictures.

Psalm 72:16 *"There shall be a handful of corn in the earth upon the top of the mountains; the fruit thereof shall shake like the cedars of Lebanon: and they of the city shall flourish like grass of the earth. KJV [A handful of corn - five loaves here and in the following year's Passover Jesus' own body would be the bread broken on the mount of Golgotha.]*

Deuteronomy 8:3 *And he treated you gently in the wilderness of your unbelief and fed your hunger there with manna, which you did not know, nor did your fathers know; that he might make you know that man does not live by the bread of their own labor, but that the life of our design hungers to be completely sustained by that Word which proceeds out of the mouth of the LORD. [Some translations say, "humbled you" but in **2 Samuel 22:36** the Hebrew word ענוה anavah is translated, "Thou hast given me the shield of thy salvation, and thy **gentleness** made me great." The Hebrew word בל KOL, often translated, "every" actually means the whole; the word in its most complete context - which clearly points to the incarnation.]*

He delivered them from that which does not satisfy. "You freed us from our slavery and led us gently like a shepherd through the wilderness of our own unbelief and made known to us our authentic hunger not for the bread we labor for but for the word which mirrors our joint-genesis and eternal oneness.")

John 6:32 Jesus reminded them that it wasn't Moses who gave them the bread from heaven - My Father is the one who gives the real bread from heaven.

John 6:33 For the bread from God that comes down from heaven is that which gives life to the entire world.

John 6:34 They said, Oh Lord, this is the bread we crave. Give us this bread.

FOOD OFFERED TO IDOLS - REV 2

John 6:35 Jesus said, I am the bread of life. He that comes face to face with me shall never hunger and he who finds his faith resting in me shall never thirst.

1 Corinthians 10:16 When we share a meal together we declare our association in Christ. Every time we drink from the same cup, we communicate the language of the covenant of grace, which is what our fellowship is all about. The wine we drink is our participation in what the blood of Christ represents. *(You know that you were ransomed from the futile ways inherited from your fathers, not with perishable things such as silver or gold, but with the precious blood of Christ, like that of a lamb without blemish or spot [1 Peter 1:18, 19]. He redeemed our original value and transparent innocence. The bread we break celebrates our participation in the incarnation. The prophetic promise became flesh in his person; we are jointly declaring that in the revelation of our inclusion in his death and resurrection we are now the visible body of Christ.)*

1 Corinthians 10:17 The single loaf of bread that we all partake of represents the fact that although there are many of us, there is only one Christ. By eating together from that one bread we are declaring that we are one body in Christ and that he is incarnated in each one of us. *(Our "many-ness" becomes "one-ness;" Christ doesn't become fragmented in us. Rather, we become unified in him. — The Message)*

1 Corinthians 10:18 Let us consider the context of the prophetic type of the sacrificial system of Israel; those who ate the sacrificed animals were partners in the same altar.

1 Corinthians 10:19 Now by this I am not saying that there is any magical power in a sacrifice made to an idol; an idol is nothing more than a mere figment of the imagination. The meat offered to an idol is just meat like any other barbecue.

Corinthians 1 10:20 The difference between Israel and the Gentile nations is in the prophetic type that Israel's sacrifices pointed to; a sacrifice offered to demons points to nothing and holds no advantage to you. I mean why would you associate with anything that reduces you to less than what you are. *(The only significance in the Jewish sacrificial system was in its pointing to the Messiah; both the promise and the person of the Messiah points to the redemption of mankind's original identity and innocence.)*

1 Corinthians 10:21 You cannot celebrate the Lord in one meal and then devote yourselves to pagan worship the next time you eat. Every time you drink and eat you ¹co-echo your union in Christ. *(In our every communion, even in our daily meals, we co-echo "I am." To partake comes from ¹**metecho**; with **meta** meaning together with, and **echo** meaning to echo what God spoke to us in Christ; like the word **metanous**, NOT repentance [re-penance]; but to join thoughts about something; to co-know with God; to agree with God about you.)*

1 Corinthians 10:22 God is not in a tug of war with demons or our obsession with religious rituals. He has no competition. He is I am. *(Even the Jews, who continued their sacrificial rituals after Christ was sacrificed as God's*

FOOD OFFERED TO IDOLS - REV 2

Passover Lamb, were presenting their offerings to pagan gods and not to God. There remains no further spiritual relevance in the practice of Jewish rituals, including the Sabbaths and the annual feasts.)

1 Corinthians 8:1 You have also asked me questions about whether believers are free to eat food offered to idols. We are free to hold to our own convictions about what to eat and what not to eat; but ultimately it is not about who wins the diet debate, but about sincerely loving people.

1 Corinthians 8:2 Let love define your convictions and not mere head knowledge.

1 Corinthians 8:3 Loving God *[and your fellow human]* is so easy when you understand that he knows you. Let God's knowledge of you inspire your love for him and your fellow human.

1 Corinthians 8:4 By making a fuss about eating food offered to idols gives idols undue prominence; they are nothing so why make something out of nothing. We know that there is only one God and that he has no competition.

1 Corinthians 8:5 There is a lot of talk about other gods and demonic powers operating on earth as well as in the heavenly realm; obviously they seem to be empowered by people's belief in them and conversation about them; so there seem to be many gods "lording" it over people.

1 Corinthians 8:6 This does not make them competition to God; we know that for us there is only one God who is the source of all things; there is only one authority, the Lord Jesus Christ. All things exist because of him; we owe our very being to him. He alone gives context and reference to our lives.

1 Corinthians 8:7 However not everyone realizes this; there are some believers who are convinced that idols are real, so for them to hear that we say that it's okay to eat food offered to idols presents a massive problem to their conscience.

1 Corinthians 8:8 Your diet preference certainly does not improve your standing before God; whether you eat meat or not.

1 Corinthians 8:9 The point is not about how justified you feel in your freedom to eat what you like, but how considerate you are not to be a stumbling block to someone else.

Revelation 14:15 Another celestial messenger appeared out of the most holy place of the temple and with a loud voice addressed the One seated upon the cloud, saying, "Thrust forth your pruning hook, your hour has come - this is your moment to reap for the earth's harvest is ready."

> John 4:31 In the mean while his disciples were urging him to take some food.

> John 4:32 But he said, "I am feasting on food you cannot see."

John 4:33 His disciples were baffled, "Who brought him anything to eat?"

John 4:34 Jesus told them, "My food is to fulfil the desire of him who commissioned me and to leave no detail undone."

John 4:35 The bread you labor for takes four months from the day you sow the seed until it ripens in the ear, doesn't it? This is not the food that I am talking about. The fruit of your own toil and performance will never satisfy permanently; from now on, look at yourselves and everyone else differently; see them through your Father's eyes and you will know that they too are ripe and ready to discover how fully included they are in my finished work. They are perfectly mirrored in me. *(A harvest is ripe when the seed in the ear matches the seed that was sown. My mission is to reveal and redeem the image and likeness of God in human form.)*

John 4:36 This harvest reveals how both he who sows and he who reaps participate in the same joy of the life of the ages.)

NOTES ON THE ROD OF IRON - REV 2

The Rod of Iron

Revelation 2:26 Seeing my victory as your victory makes you the overcomer. By embracing the ¹completeness of my works as your ²treasure, you realize my authority in you to possess the nations. *(See Revelation 2:23 - the ¹success of my works is to your credit. The words, αχρι τελους **achri telous** suggest, taking my words to its full conclusion. The word ²**tereo** means to value, to treasure, to guard with great care. See Psalm 2: 7,8 [also verse 9 as referenced in the next verse, 27] You are my son, today I have begotten you. Ask of me, and I will make the nations your heritage, and the ends of the earth your possession. Paul quotes Psalm 2 in Acts 13:33 when he preaches the resurrection of Jesus and in Ephesians 2:5,6 and Colossians 3:1-3 he celebrates our co-begottenness. Also Peter announces that we were born anew when Jesus was raised from the dead. 1 Peter 1:3. The word ²**exousia**, often translated as authority has two components, **ek**, out of, source and **eimi**, I am. The Preposition ³**epi** suggests continuous influence upon, from a position of authority.)*

Revelation 2:27 You will ¹shepherd the nations with a royal scepter and shatter ²their 'alienated mindsets' like a potter's vessel of clay. *(He quotes Psalm 2:9, "You shall break them with a rod of iron, and dash them in pieces like a potter's vessel." Sadly the Hebrew Masoretic Text uses the word רעע **RAA** - to be bad, be evil; to be displeasing; to be injurious; to be wicked; to do an injury or hurt; to be mischief; instead of the same sounding word, ¹ רעה **RA'AH** with a **Hay** at the end and not an **Ayin**, which means **to shepherd**. Also in the Septuagint, the Greek word ποιμανεῖς ¹**poimaneis**, shepherd is used. You shall feed them as a shepherd nurtures his flock. With reference to the ²alienated mindsets that ruled the nations see Numbers 24:17, "A scepter shall rise out of Israel; it shall crush the forehead of Moab." [mindset.] The shepherd's staff was never intended to beat up the sheep but to protect and free them from any possible threat.*

*To appreciate its prophetic context, see LXX [Septuagint] rendering of Psalm 2:2, The rulers of the world-order have set themselves up against the Christ; Psalm 2:3, "Let us break apart their chains and cast off their yokes." From the heavens, however, the LORD breaks out in laughter and says [6- 9], "I was appointed under him as King on Zion, my holy hill. Announcing the decree of the LORD: He said to me, You are my son, **today I have begotten you. Ask of me, and I will make the nations your heritage, and the ends of the earth your possession.** You shall shepherd them with a rod of iron, and dash them ['their distorted mindsets'] in pieces like a potter's vessel."*

In Acts 13, Luke records the launch of Paul's missionary journeys from Antioch. This is where he and Barnabas established the first ekklesia. He gives powerful context to Psalm 2 in recording the impact of the gospel in Paul and Barnabas' ministry into the Gentile world. Paul clearly sees the prophetic context of Psalm 2 as pointing to mankind's co-begottenness in the resurrection of Jesus from the dead. This revelation will conquer the nations. He preaches the resurrection of Jesus and quotes Psalm 2:9.

Also in his discourse with the Greek Philosophers in Acts 17, Paul reminds them that their own writings record the fact that we live and move and have our being in God and that we are indeed his offspring.

NOTES ON THE ROD OF IRON - REV 2

See Isaiah 9:2-4 The people who walked in darkness have seen a great light; those who dwelt in a land of deep darkness, on them light shone. Thou hast multiplied the nation, thou hast increased its joy; they rejoice before thee as with joy at the harvest, as men rejoice when they divide the spoil. For the yoke of his burden, and the staff for his shoulder, the rod of his oppressor, thou hast broken **as on the day of Midian.** *Remember Gideon's strategy of hiding lamps in clay jars when they defeated the mighty Midians who out-numbered them by far. Bonsai mindsets have trapped the nations of the world for centuries. But this is the day where the mystery that was hidden in clay pots for ages and generations shall be revealed. Christ in the nations is the hope and desire of the nations. He is what heaven and earth were waiting for. All flesh shall see it together. Haggai 2:6,7; Colossians 1:27; Isaiah 40:5 In Acts 13:47 Paul quotes Isaiah 49:6 in the context of his ministry, "For so the Lord has commissioned us, saying, 'I have set you to be a light for the nations, that you may bring salvation to the uttermost parts of the earth.'" For unto us a child is born. .... Father of the ages, Prince of peace. ... And of the increase of his government and of peace there will be no end, upon the throne of David, and over his kingdom, to establish it, and to uphold it with justice and with righteousness from this time forth and for evermore. The zeal of the LORD of hosts will do this. Isaiah 9:6,7. Revelation 11:15, "The kingdom of the world has become the kingdom of our Master and of his Anointed, and he shall reign forever and ever.")*

Revelation 19:15 And from his mouth proceeds a sharp sword - the words of his utterance cut to the core of the heart of the nations and he shall shepherd them with an iron scepter. And on his own he will tread out the winepress of the [1]**intensity of the passion of the sovereign God of the universe.** (*See my comments in Revelation 2:16 on the imagery of the Sword.*

The words, **tou thumou tes orges tou theo**, *speaks of the intensity of the passion of God, with the word thumos, passion, and the word often translated wrath,* **orge**, *meaning strong desire - as a reaching forth or excitement of the mind, from the word,* **oregomai**, *meaning to stretch one's self out in order to touch or to grasp something.*

See my commentary notes in Revelation 2:26,27 **at the end of Revelation chapter 2** *with reference to Psalm 2:7,8,9 on* **the Rod of Iron**.

See commentary notes at the end of chapter 19, on **The shepherd-King of the Nations.**

Commentary notes at the end of this chapter 19, on **the winepress of the passion of God.**

Also my further commentary at the end of Revelation 22:16,21 on **the Root Of Jesse** *Isaiah 11:1-10.)*

REVELATION Chapter 3

3:1 And to the messenger of the ekklesia in Sardis write: he who holds the seven Spirits of God and the seven stars in resonance says, I see your toil, but there is a big difference between dead works and vibrant life.

3:2 [1]Awake from your slumber. [2]Get a firm grip on what little life you have left in you. Your work does not [3]mirror my finished work. *(The word [1]gregoreuo, to be vigilant from egeirō to arouse from sleep. The word [2]steiritzo, means to turn resolutely in a certain direction; to confirm with steadfast resolve. The word [3]eponopion, in full view - face to face as in a mirror.)*

3:3 [1]Remember therefore what it felt like when you first heard and [2]embraced the word as your own. It was like discovering a priceless [3]treasure. Now [4]make up your mind once and for all. [5]Why would I surprise you like a thief, and break into your space whilst you are fast asleep and you're not even anticipating my [6]intimate intent; as if you are not at all acquainted with my visitation and still do not [7]realize the significant relevance *[now-ness]* of this hour?

*([1] Here, the word, μνημονεύω **mnēmoneuō** to remember, is the Present Active Imperative, μνημονευε, [1]mnemoneue, to keep something constantly in mind.*

[2] The word [2]eilephas from lambano is in the Perfect tense, meaning, what you received as a permanent deposit.

[3] The word [3]tereo means to treasure - [where our English word stems from.]

[4] The word, metanoia, is in the Aorist Active Imperative [4]metanoeson, - meaning, "Engage your thoughts with my thoughts once and for all - get it over and done with." Now make this mindshift your permanent reference, once and for all! The word metanoia means to realize God's thoughts. Like most Greek words, μετάνοια [3]metanoia is a compound word, from meta, together with and νοιέω noieō, to perceive with the mind. It describes the awakening of the mind to that which is true; it is a gathering of one's thoughts, a co-knowing. Faith is not a decision; it is a discovery. It has nothing in common with the Latin word paenitentia - where the idea of penance and repentance stems from. Sadly the word repentance became the popular English translation of metanoia.

[5] The word [5]ean suggests, in case you were not alert; if perhaps you would not anticipate the intimacy of my presence...

[6] The word [6]heko means to be present - to approach one with intimate intent.

*[7] The, οὐ μὴ γνως **gnoōs**, is the strong double negative **ou mē** with the second Aorist Active Subjunctive of **ginōsko** γινώσκω, to be acquainted with; to know. The strong double negative with the Aorist Subjunctive, expresses a wish with emphatic assertion. The Mood of the Greek verb expresses the mode in which the idea of the verb is employed; here, the definite outcome that will happen as a result of another stated action. The Hebrew idiom, like a thief in the night, refers to the surprise element; this is in reference to one of the traditions of the Jewish marriage practices as celebrated in the 1st century, where the Groom comes to "retrieve" his Bride at an unexpected moment. This is to be looked for with joyful expectation. [Revelation 3:20]*

*See extended **Thoughts on "Thief in the Night"** at the end of the chapter.)*

3:4 Yet you do have a few [1]individual names in Sardis who have not forgotten their true identity and [2]soiled their garments - they are those who walk with me in [3]innocence and who mirror the reference of their [4]worth to be equal to my estimate of them. *([1]Individual names - see significance of a name in John 1:41. He immediately fetched his own brother Simon, telling him, "We've found the Messiah" which in Greek means, "the Christ." [Aramaic was the spoken language and Greek the academic language in which the New Testament was written.] John 1:42 When he introduced him to Jesus, he gazed intently at him and said, you are Simon the son of Jonah; you will be known as Mr. Rock. [The Hebrew word יונה **yona**, means dove. The word **kaleo** means surname, to identify by name. **Kefas** is the Aramaic for **Petros**, a stone or chip of rock - a chip off the old block. See Matthew 16:13 - 18. This conversation beautifully reminds of the Song of Songs in chapter 2:14 "Oh my dove [**yona**], in the clefts of the rock, in the crevice of the cliff, let me see your face, let me hear your voice, for your voice is sweet, and your face is comely. The crevice of the cliff is the address and home of the rock pigeon. The birds have nests...]*

*The word [2]**moluno**, from **melas**, black ink; to soil, suggests a garment soiled with the stains of their own attempts to define their own worth and identity through personal effort and religious discipline. Isaiah 64:6 We have all become like one who is unclean, and all our righteous deeds are like filthy rags.*

*The word, [3]**leukos** means, light, bright, brilliant from whiteness, dazzling white - a display of innocence. The word [4]**axios** means having the weight of another thing of like value, worth as much. See Extended Thoughts on **"Your God-identity"** at the end of the chapter.)*

3:5 Everyone who sees their victory in me, I will clothe in white [3]garments - and they will realize that I am not in the business of fulfilling their law and performance based fears by [1]blotting out their names from the Book of Life. Instead, I am the one who endorses their identity face to face before my Father and his [2]celestial shepherd-messengers. *(This language is taken from the [1]custom of registering the names of persons in a list, roll, or catalogue. In Jewish tradition there was a prevailing fear that your name might be blotted out of the Book of Life if your behavior did not please God. The word often translated, angel, [2]**aggelos** from **agō** to lead as a shepherd leads and **agele** a herd of cattle or company of people.*

*[3]Garments: **himation** the upper garment, the cloak or mantle. See **Extended Notes on the Lamb's Book of Life** at the end of Chapter 17. Also **Extended Notes on our God-identity** at the end of this chapter.)*

3:6 Now listen up with your inner ears. Hear with understanding what the Spirit is saying to the ekklesias.

3:7 And to the messenger of the ekklesia of [1]Philadelphia write: I am the Holy and True One. I hold the key of David as prophesied in [1]Isaiah 22:22. Yes, I [2]unlock the mysteries of the heavenly dimension and no one can shut the door. And I lock the entrance and none *(of the old mindsets)*

REVELATION Chapter 3

can access it. (*¹Philadelphos, from philos, fondness; friendship, and adelphos, the same womb; immediate family; kinsfolk; household. ²Isaiah 22:22 And I will place on his shoulder the key of the house of David; he shall open, and none shall shut; and he shall shut, and none shall open. The word ²anoigo from ana upward and agoo, to lead. Also Ezekiel 34:23 Then I will place one shepherd over them, my servant David, and he will take care of them and be their shepherd.*)

3:8 I am fully aware of your efforts in doing the work of the ministry. I want you to see something, I ¹have given you a doorway right in front of you that has been fully opened into the heavenly dimension. Nothing can possibly close it again. Even when you had very little strength you have treasured my word and have not contradicted my name. (*I have given you, ¹dedoka, Perfect Active Indicative of didomi, denotes an action that has been completed in the past and the results of the action are continuing on in this moment, in full effect. Revelation 4:1 I want you to see something. Oh wow. What I see takes my breath away. A wide-open door in the heavenly realm. The first thing I heard was this voice addressing me. It was distinct and clear like the sound of a trumpet; it captured my attention, inviting me to enter. "Come up here and I will show you how everything coincides with what you have already seen."*)

3:9 Behold, the Jewish disguise will be exposed to be the synagogue of Satanas. They have ¹sourced their ²gatherings in ³accusation but now ⁴I give them to you and will cause them to come ⁵face to face with you in fellowship in acknowledgment of my love which I have bestowed upon you. (*The Preposition ¹ek always points to source or origin; the ²synagogue, [gathering] of ³satanos [accuser]. "⁴I give them to you." In the language of Isaiah 45:14 and Isaiah 60:14. The word often translated worship, ⁵proskuneo, from pros, face to face and kuneo, which I would like to believe to be a derivation of koinonia, joint-participation; rather than kuon which means dog. I know, some tried to connect the idea of a dog licking its master's hand, which then became a possibility of kissing. I prefer a divine face to face koinonia encounter to define true worship. Although, I do believe that dogs, often referred to as man's best friend because of the very nature of their devotion to their master, has its Greek root connected - koinonia is a friendship word to begin with and it is therefore possible to see its etymological link. See Extended commentary on the word proskuneo at the end of the Mirror.*)

3:10 You have greatly ¹valued the prophetic word which came to fulfillment in what ²I endured. I will also ¹guard you with great care, empowering you to stand strong ³in the midst of the troubled times that are about to come upon the ⁴inhabited world to scrutinize the ⁵dwellers of the earth. (*The word ¹tereo means to value, to treasure, to guard with great care; ton logon tes hupomones mou, the word of my patience. "For the joy that was set before him, he endured the cross and despised the shame." Hebrews.12:2; Isaiah 53:11. The Preposition ³ek here implies, not a keeping from temptation, but a keeping in temptation, as the result of which they shall be delivered out of its power. The words ⁴oikoumene and ⁵katoikeo both suggest the established society of the day versus the habitation of God where the lordship of the life of our design will reign under the King of kings and the Lord of lords.*)

REVELATION Chapter 3

3:11 Do not let tough times make me seem distant from you. I am at hand - see my nearness, not my absence. And don't let temporal setbacks diminish your own authority either. Remember that you call the shots; you wear the crown. My crown endorses your crown. (Lit. Let nothing take your crown. Revelation 1:5; He is the King of kings and Lord of lords. Not the King of slaves. Revelation 19:16. See Psalm 103:4 He redeems his life from the Pit and weaves a crown for him out of loving-kindness and tender mercies.)

3:12 It is in your individual, continual association with your [1]victory in me that I will make you to be like a [2]strong pillar in the inner shrine of God's sanctuary, supporting the entire structure of my God-habitation within you. A place to be your permanent abode 'from whence you will never have to depart. And I will engrave upon you [3]the name of my God, also the name of the [4]city [the bride.] **of my God, the new Jerusalem that descends from heaven; as well as [5]my own new Name.** (The word [1]nikoon, is the Present Active Participle form of the verb **nikao** to emphasize a continual or habitual victory. Participles are verbal adjectives; nearly a third of Greek verbal forms are participles. The Present Stem of the Greek Verb has the sense of continuous or repeated action. For the Present Participle this implies that the action of the Participle is going on at the same time as the action of the main verb in the sentence Philadelphia was a city of earthquakes - the [2]strong column or pillar in the temple structure resembles the strength of God's habitation in the midst of conflict and challenging times.

[3]My Father's Name, John 5:43, I have come in my Father's Name. John 12:28, Father, glorify your Name. **Abba Father.**

Revelation 21:2 And I saw the holy [4]**city**, new Jerusalem, coming down out of heaven from God, **prepared as a bride adorned for her husband.** In John 7:37,38 when Jesus speaks of waters gushing forth out of your innermost being, he says that you are the city. You are the bride. God's redeemed society.

Psalm 87:3 Glorious things are spoken of you, Oh **city** of God - "This one and that one were born in her" Psalm 87:7 Singers and dancers together say, "All my springs of joy are in you. There is no greater glory to pursue but to know that all my springs of joy are in you.

Revelation 19:16 On his robe and on his thigh **he has a name inscribed,** [5]**King of kings and Lord of lords.** My crown endorses your crown. Revelation 1:5

Of all the seven churches Philadelphia had the longest duration of prosperity as a Christian city. It still exists as a Turkish town under the name of Allah Shehr, City of God. One of the mosques is believed by the native Christians to have been the gathering-place of the ekklesia addressed in Revelation. One solitary pillar of high antiquity remains. Vincent.

See Extended Thoughts on the City-Bride at the end of the chapter.)

3:13 Now listen up with your inner ears. Hear with understanding what the Spirit is saying to the ekklesia.

REVELATION Chapter 3

3:14 And to the celestial shepherd-messenger of the ekklesia in ¹Laodicea write: he who speaks is ²the amen; he is the ultimate ³evidence and the one who defines ⁴faith; he personifies the ⁵truth; ⁶she is the very ⁷source of God's creation. (*¹Laodikeia from laos and dikea, thus the righteousness of the people - their claim to fame was their self-righteousness. See verse 17. The word ²amen is from a Hebrew word,* אמן *âman meaning support, confirmation, faithful, certainty, reliable, uphold, nourish; foster-parent, nurse; also a word used for pillars, supporters of the door. This one is the sustainer and fulfillment of all that God has spoken. Literally, "The one who speaks is the ²Amen, the ³Testimony, the ⁴Faith, the ⁵Truth, and the ⁶Source of Creation." The two components of the word translated truth,* **alethinos** *are ha, negative and* **lanthano***, hidden, thus unveiled. ⁶While the rest of the sentence is masculine, the phrase, "Source of Creation," ἡ ἀρχὴ τῆς κτίσεως is in the Feminine Gender.*

The word ⁷arche, suggests commencement or beginning, from **archomai***, to rehearse from the beginning. See John 1:1 To go back to the very beginning is to find the Word already present there; face to face with God. The Word is I am; God's eloquence echoes and concludes in him. The Word equals God. John 1:2 The beginning mirrors the Word face to face with God. John 1:3 The Logos is the source; everything commences in him. He remains the exclusive Parent reference to their existence. There is nothing original, except the Word. The Logic of God defines the only possible place where mankind can trace their genesis.*

See also Isaiah 40:18, To whom then will you liken God, or what likeness compares with him? Isaiah 40:19, The idol. a workman casts it, and a goldsmith overlays it with gold, and casts for it silver chains. Isaiah 40:21, Have you not known? Have you not heard? Has it not been told you **from the beginning***? The Septuagint reads, ἐξ ἀρχῆς - eks arches - sourced in the beginning.)*

3:15 I am familiar with your works and you remind me of the typical situation in Laodicea. How I wish that your lives were like the cold, refreshing waters of Colossae or like the waters of the healing thermal springs of Hierapolis. But they are neither cold nor hot. (*By the time the waters arrive via the aqueducts in Laodicea.*)

3:16 This is what really disappoints: when you anticipate a refreshing cool drink but instead get a mouthful of lukewarm sulphur-tasting water, you would naturally spit it out. (*There is no substitute for living from the source. Compromise could never suffice. This metaphor has been drawn from the water supply of the city, which was lukewarm, in contrast to the hot springs at nearby Hierapolis - [6 miles north] and the cold, refreshing waters from Colossae [11 miles east]. Laodicea had aqueducts connecting it to these sources. The imagery of the Laodicean aqueduct suggests not that "hot" is good and "cold" is bad, but that both hot and cold water are useful, whereas lukewarm water is emetic. Hierapolis became a healing center where doctors used the thermal springs as a treatment for their patients. Laodocea is called by Ramsay "the City of Compromise." This again highlights the danger of a mixed message, not drawn directly from the source but, en-route, mingled with one's own ideas, efforts and performance - just like Paul warning the Galatians about a little leaven, leavening the entire lump of dough.*)

REVELATION Chapter 3

3:17 As your name suggests, you are experts in [1]justifying yourselves, you are convinced that you have all your ducks in a row - your plumbing is sorted, your trade and economy are thriving industries - you think that you are completely independent. Yet you have no idea of how bankrupt you really are. Your entire economy is flawed since you are trading with "Monopoly money". It is fake currency - your [2]scales are [3]rigged. If only you knew how desperately in need you are of someone to show you tender compassion and mercy. I mean, look at you. On the outside you may appear to be standing tall and proud in your self-righteousness but in reality you are in a pitiful state. You are like a [4]crouching, cringing beggar. Your [5]smoke-screen has blinded your view. You think you're hiding in your fancy brand-name clothes but you don't realize how [6]naked and exposed you are. *([1]Laodikeia from laos and dikea, thus the righteousness of the people. Their claim to fame was their self-righteousness. The word [2]talaipōros occurs only twice in the New Testament - Romans 7:24, Revelation 3:17 - and both times it is translated wretched.? It has two components, **talanton**, which is the word for the scale of a balance; that which is weighed, a talent, and **poros** which is a trade word. See **emporos**, [en + poros] a merchant, trader. The word **poros** derives from **peira**, to examine closely; a test to determine the hidden value of something. A talent of silver weighed about 100 pounds (45 kg) and a talent of gold weighed about 200 pounds (91 kg) The Hebrew word for a scale of balances is the word, אזן **azan** which literally means to broaden out the ears with cupped hands, weighing words; to give undivided attention to. From אזן 'ôzen ear. [3]Rigged scales ie. gold not thoroughly refined - see v 18. Two of their most famous and successful products were an ear ointment from spice nard and eye-salve made from "Phrygian powder" mixed with oil. They seem to have the monopoly on this strategic trade-route; yet, while their ear salve and eye ointment medicines were in unique demand they themselves suffered from hearing and seeing wrong. The word [4]**ptochos** means to cringe or crouch like a beggar. The word [5]**tuphlos**, smoky eyes, blind, from **tuphoo,** to envelop with smoke. The word [6]**gumnos** means naked. See Isaiah 64:6 all our righteous deeds are like a polluted garment. They fade like a leaf, instead of covering our nakedness they emphasize our shame. Revelation 3:4.*

*Situated near Colossae and Hierapolis, the great road from the coast to the inner country passed through the middle of Laodicea - the city was the doorkeeper to the great eastern highway and central trade-route of the Roman Empire from Ephesus to the east. The city was renowned for three main industries: a **banking center** for the province of Asia Minor, including a gold exchange; then, the **textile center** where glossy, black wool was woven into garments called trimata that were prized in the Roman world; it was also the location of a **major medical school** known worldwide and where an eye salve called Phyrigian powder was made from a local stone. It was the leading city in the valley during the first century, Laodicea was destroyed by an earthquake in AD 60. According to Roman writer Tacticus, Rome offered to pay for the city to be rebuilt, but the people declined, saying that they were wealthy enough to restore their own city; this coincides with John's writing.)*

3:18 I invite you to talk business with me. Come, [1]let us resolve this together. I want to make you really rich. I advise you [2]to buy gold [3]from me.

REVELATION Chapter 3

Gold that is thoroughly refined in the fire - not the flawed currency of your own trade. We're not talking a mixture here. No dross. And from now on, buy your clothing from me; white garments - not the blended brand of your own making. Clothe yourself completely with these and there will be not even a [4]hint of shame. For your eyes, buy [5]eye-salve from me to [6]anoint your eyes so that you may clearly see yourself in Christ. *(The word [1]sumbouleo from sun, jointly, together and bouleo to reason, to resolve. [2]Come and buy from me. Heaven's currency is to "pay" attention. To cup your ears. See commentary in verse 17. This transaction reminds of Isaiah 55:1 "Ho, everyone who thirsts, come to the waters; and he who has no money, come, buy and eat. Come, buy wine and the finest wheat without money and without price. Isaiah 55:2 Why do you spend your money for that which is not bread, and your labor for that which does not satisfy? [In Hebrew the word for grain and buying or selling is the same - שׁבר shâbar - crushed grain.] Hearken diligently to me, and eat what is good, and delight yourselves in fatness. Isaiah 55:3 Incline your ear, and come to me; hear, that your soul may live; and I will make with you an everlasting covenant, my steadfast, sure love for David. [3]"From me, 'par' emou - para closest possible proximity of nearness.*

[4]**No shame.** *See Genesis 3:7 Then the eyes of both were opened, and they knew that they were naked; and they sewed fig leaves together and made themselves aprons. Genesis 3:9 GOD called to the Man: "Where are you?" Genesis 3:10 He said, "I heard you in the garden and I was ashamed because I was naked. And I hid. [Note, God wasn't hiding from them.]*

*The word [5]**kollourion** is the name for a famous Phrygian powder for the eyes made in Laodicea. To anoint, [6]**enchrisai**, from en, in and chriō, Christ.)*

3:19 It is with [1]affection that I address everyone of you, whoever you are. I would [2]earnestly persuade you as a parent would [3]instruct and nurture their children: [4]eagerly [5]acquaint yourselves with all that I have in mind for you. *(The word [1]**phileo**, is a friendship word and suggests fondness and affection; [2]**enlencho** means to encourage, convince, to persuade. This is a quote from Proverbs 3:12 for the LORD reasons convincingly with whom he loves, as a father communicates with the son in whom he delights. Here the Hebrew word, יכח yâkach is used, which in this context suggests to reason together; see Isaiah 1:18. The word [3]**paideuo** means to nurture and trother 480 ain a child; [4]**tzeleuo** from zelos - means to be fervently eager; to have strong feelings of excitement. The word often translated 'repentance' is actually [5]**metanoeo** which has nothing to do with penance. It means to join thoughts about something; to co-know.)*

3:20 You have shut me out in your self-righteousness [Laodicea], but behold, here I stand knocking at the door. Oh, that every single one of you may [1]recognize my voice and let me in; I am so ready to join you for a feast. Yes, I will dine with you and you with me. *(Song of Songs 5:2 I was asleep, but my heart was awake. **It is the voice of my beloved who knocks**: "Open to me, my sister, my love, my dove, my undefiled; for my head is filled with dew, and my hair with the dampness of the night." Revelation 3:3 Remember therefore what it felt like when you first heard and embraced* the word as your own. It was like discovering a priceless treasure. Now make up your mind once and for all. Why should I surprise you like a thief and break into your space whilst you are fast asleep and not even anticipating my intimate intent, not knowing the moment of my visitation? See John 10:2, The shepherd of the sheep enters by the door. [In the context of Jesus' conversation he emphasizes the fact that the Shepherd-Messiah would surely only enter by the door; which is [1]**the familiar voice of the prophetic word**. Hebrews 1:1-3; Hebrews 4:12]

See John 6:58 and Revelation 2:20 on the significance of meals as well as the extended commentary at the end of Luke 11 and Revelation 2.

It is characteristic of John to note the sayings of Christ which express the reciprocal relations of himself and his followers. "I will dine with you and you with me." See John 6:56,"you in me and I in you; John 10:38, "the Father is in me and I am in him"; John 14:20, "I am in my Father, you are in me and I am in you"; John 15:4, "you in me and I in you"; John 15:5 "in your seamless abiding in me and I in you, fruit-bearing is as natural as it is inevitable!"; John 17:21 "That they all may be one, exactly as you Father are mirrored in me and I in you, that they also will be exactly mirrored to be one in us"; John 17:26 "...understanding to know that the same love wherewith you have loved me is in them even as I am in them."; Also, John 14:23 "this is about someone's passionate, loving desire, finding its rest in me; they will treasure my words and encounter my Father's love reflecting in them, and my Father and I will appear face to face to them, and make our abode with each one individually.". Vincent's Word Studies.)

3:21 *[Through this door of my death as your death, and my resurrection as your resurrection]* **- we now dine together in the throne room, [1]celebrating your victory mirrored in mine. This is my gift to you; it is on exactly the same basis of [2]my victory celebration and my joint-seatedness with my Father in his throne-room.** *(The word [1]nikoon, is the Present Active Participle, form of the verb nikao, to conquer; to emphasize a continual or habitual victory. Note the words, hōs kagō enikēsa where [2]enikesa is the first Aorist Active Indicative of the same verb, nikaō, looking back on the victory as over in the past. A.T. Roberston compares this to John 16:33 where before the Cross Jesus says egō nenikēka ton kosmon which is in the Perfect Active tense of the same verb nikao, emphasizing the abiding effect of the victory.)*

3:22 Now listen up with your inner ears. Hear with understanding what the Spirit is saying to the ekklesia. *(Paul prays in Ephesians that the eyes of our understanding will be flooded with light so that we may see our co-seatedness.)*

Revelation Chapter 3 Extended Notes:

Like a Thief in the Night
Our God-identity
The City-Bride

NOTES ON THE THIEF IN THE NIGHT - REV 3

Like a Thief in the Night

Revelation 3:3 Remember therefore what it felt like when you first heard and ¹embraced the word as your own. It was like discovering a priceless ²treasure. Now ³make up your mind once and for all. ⁴Why should I surprise you like a thief and break into your space whilst you are fast asleep and not even anticipating my ⁵intimate intent; not knowing the moment of my ⁵visitation? *(The word ¹eilephas from lambano is in the Perfect tense, meaning, what you received as a permanent deposit. The word ²tereo means to treasure. The word metanoia means to realize God's thoughts. Like most Greek words, μετάνοια ³metanoia is a compound word, from meta, together with and νοιέω noieō, to perceive with the mind. It describes the awakening of the mind to that which is true; it is a gathering of one's thoughts, a co-knowing. Faith is not a decision; it is a discovery. It has nothing in common with the Latin word paenitentia - where the idea of penance and repentance stems from. Sadly the word repentance became the popular English translation of metanoia. Here ³metanoesan, is in the Aorist Imperative - meaning, "Engage your thoughts with my thoughts once and for all - get it over and done with." The word ⁴ean suggests, if perhaps, in case you were not alert, you would not anticipate the intimacy of my presence. The word ⁵heko means to be present - to approach one with intimate intent. The Hebrew idiom, like a thief in the night, refers to the surprise element; this is in reference to one of the traditions of the Jewish marriage practices as celebrated in the 1st century, where the Groom comes to "retrieve" his Bride at an unexpected moment. This is to be looked for with joyful expectation.)*

Revelation 3:19 It is with ¹affection that I address everyone of you, whoever you are. I would ²earnestly persuade you as a parent would ³instruct and nurture their children: ⁴eagerly ⁵acquaint yourselves with all that I have in mind for you. *(The word ¹phileo, is a friendship word and suggests fondness and affection; ²enlencho means to encourage, convince, to persuade. This is a quote from Proverbs 3:12 for the LORD reasons convincingly with whom he loves, as a father communicates with the son in whom he delights. Here the Hebrew word, יכח yâkach is used, which in this context suggests to reason together; see Isaiah 1:18. The word ³paideuo means to nurture and train a child; ⁴tzeleuo from zelos - means to be fervently eager; to have strong feelings of excitement. The word often translated 'repentance' is actually ⁵metanoeo which has nothing to do with penance. It means to join thoughts about something; to co-know.)*

Revelation 3:20 You have shut me out in your self-righteousness [Laodicea], but behold, here I stand knocking at the door. If anyone ¹recognizes my voice and lets me in, I am so ready to join you for a feast. Yes, I will dine with you and you with me. *(Song of Songs 5:2 I was asleep, but my heart was awake.* **It is the voice of my beloved who knocks:** *"Open to me, my sister, my love, my dove, my undefiled; for my head is filled with dew, and my hair with the dampness of the night." Revelation 3:3. See John 10:2, The shepherd of the sheep enters by the door. [In the context of Jesus' conversation he emphasizes the fact that the Shepherd-Messiah would* *surely only enter by the door; which is* ¹*the familiar voice of the prophetic word. Hebrews 1:1-3; Hebrews 4:12]*

See John 6:58 and Revelation 2:20 on the significance of meals as well as the extended commentary at the end of Luke 11 and Revelation 2.

It is characteristic of John to note the sayings of Christ which express the reciprocal relations of himself and his followers. See John 6:56; John 10:38; John 14:20; John 15:4, John 15:5; John 17:21, John 17:26. Compare John 14:23. Vincent's Word Studies.)

Revelation 3:21 *[Through this door of my death as your death, and my resurrection as your resurrection]* **- we now dine together in the throne room, ¹celebrating your victory mirrored in mine. This is my gift to you; it is on exactly the same basis of ²my victory celebration and my joint-seatedness with my Father in his throne-room.** *(The word* ¹***nikoon****, is the Present Active Participle, form of the verb* ***nikao****, to conquer; to emphasize a continual or habitual victory. Note the words,* ***hōs kagō enikēsa*** *where* ²***enikesa*** *is the first Aorist Active Indicative of the same verb,* ***nikaō****, looking back on the victory as over in the past. A.T. Roberston compares this to John 16:33 where before the Cross Jesus says* ***egō nenikēka ton kosmon*** *which is in the Perfect Active tense of the same verb* ***nikao****, emphasizing the abiding effect of the victory.)*

1 Thessalonians 5:1 I do not need to speculate about ¹specific prophetic moments or even mention ²significant dates. *(The word* ¹***xronos****, speaks of a specific space or portion of time, an individual opportunity, or season;* ²***kairos****, a fixed and definite time, the decisive epoch waited for.)*

1 Thessalonians 5:2 You know for yourselves from experience how the day of the Lord suddenly dawns like a thief in the night. *(Acts 9:3 Now as he journeyed he approached Damascus, and suddenly a light from heaven flashed about him. 2 Corinthians 4:6 For it is the God who said, "Let light shine out of darkness," who has shone in our hearts to give the light of the knowledge of the glory of God in the face of Christ. Isaiah 9:2 The people who walked in darkness have seen a great light; those who dwelt in a land of deep darkness, have been illuminated with light. John 1:9 A new day for mankind has come. The authentic light of life that illuminates everyone was about to dawn in the world.)*

1 Thessalonians 5:3 The systems of this world of darkness and unbelief, which held the masses under their pseudo-sway of make-belief peace and security shall suddenly be broken into, like travail upon a woman with child, and none of their captives shall remain under their claim. *(The gates of Hades shall not prevail. Hades from* ***ha + eido****, not to see. In a walled city, the gates are the most strategic point - if the gates are disengaged, the city is taken. Thus, the blindfold mode of mankind's forgotten identity, will not prevail against you.)*

1 Thessalonians 5:4 You are no longer in darkness; there are no daunting surprises waiting for you like a thief in the night.

1 Thessalonians 5:5 All of you are begotten of light, the Day of the Lord is your true parent. Neither night nor darkness have any claim on you.

NOTES ON THE THIEF IN THE NIGHT - REV 3

1 Thessalonians 5:6 Live alert and you will not become intoxicated by the indifference of others.

1 Thessalonians 5:7 Sleeping and drunkenness are typical things people do at night, but now the day of the Lord has dawned within us and has put an end to the slumbering effect and intoxication of the practices of darkness.

1 Thessalonians 5:8 So let us clothe ourselves with day-garments, protecting our sober seeing by having our hearts fully guarded by the breastplate of love-inspired faith, and having our minds encircled, like a helmet, with an expectation which is consistent with what salvation declares.

1 Thessalonians 5:9 For God did not set us up for disappointment; he is not teasing us with [1]desires that we desperately reach for but cannot attain. He has brought us to a place where we are surrounded by the poetry of what salvation communicates in the lordship of Jesus Christ. *(The word often translated, wrath, is the word [1]orge, from oregomai which means to stretch oneself out with strong and passionate desire.)*

1 Thessalonians 5:10 The fact that he died our death is equally valid to those who are awake to its effect or still fast asleep in their indifference to it; we are together destined to live entwined in the [1]closest possible association with him. *(The word [1]hama is a particle of union denoting close association. See Galatians 2:20.)*

Our God-identity

Revelation 3:4 Yet you do have a few ¹individual names in Sardis who have not forgotten their true identity and ²soiled their garments - they are those who walk with me in ³innocence and who mirror the reference of their ⁴worth to be equal to my estimate of them. *(¹Individual names - see significance of a name in **John 1:41** He immediately fetched his own brother Simon, telling him, "We've found the Messiah" which in Greek means, "the Christ." (Aramaic was the spoken language and Greek the academic language in which the New Testament was written.) **John 1:42** When he introduced him to Jesus, he gazed intently at him and said, you are Simon the son of Jonah; you will be known as Mr. Rock. (The Hebrew word יונה **yona**, means dove. The word **kaleo** means surname, to identify by name. **Kefas** is the Aramaic for **Petros**, a stone or chip of rock - a chip off the old block. See Matthew 16:13 - 18. This conversation beautifully reminds of the Song of Songs in chapter 2:14 "Oh my dove [יונה **yona**], in the clefts of the rock, in the crevice of the cliff, let me see your face, let me hear your voice, for your voice is sweet, and your face is comely. The crevice of the cliff is the address and home of the rock pigeon. The birds have nests.*

*The word ²**moluno**, from **melas**, black ink; to soil, suggests a garment soiled with the stains of their own attempts to define their own worth and identity through personal effort and religious discipline. Isaiah 64:6 We have all become like one who is unclean, and all our righteous deeds are like filthy rags. The word, ³**leukos** means, light, bright, brilliant from whiteness, dazzling white - a display of innocence.*

*The word ⁴**axios** means having weight, having the weight of another thing of like value, worth as much.)*

1 John 3:9 To discover one's authentic sonship in God, is to discover true freedom from sin. We are born of him and his seed remains in us; this is the only possible reference to sober up the mind from the intoxicating influence of deception. *(The incorruptible seed of our Father carries the exact pattern of the authentic life of our design. Jesus calls the Devil [**diabolos** - through the fall; from **dia** and **ballo**, a mindset defined by the fall - "I am not who God says I am", the voice of the father of lies.)*

John 8:31 Jesus then said to those Jews who were believing in him, "To take my word to its complete conclusion and then to abide in seamless union with its logic is to truly be my disciples. *(Here, he is not referring to some future "red-letter-edition Bible" highlighting his "words"; Jesus is speaking about the Logos defining his "I-am-ness", face to face with God before time was, then documented in prophetic language in ancient Scripture and now unveiled in incarnate human form, as in a mirror.)*

John 8:32 In this abiding you will fully know the truth about who you are and this knowing will be your freedom.

John 8:35 The difference between the slave and the son is that the slave only works there; for the son the father's house is home. *(John 14:2 What makes my Father's house home, is your place in it. If this was not the ultimate* *conclusion of my mission, why would I even bother to do what I am about to do if it was not to prepare a place for you? I have come to persuade you of a place of seamless union where you belong. What Jesus is about to accomplish in his death and resurrection will forever shift the idea of religious works and pretense and performance from the typical slave-mentality to the freedom and reality of sonship.)*

John 8:36 With the freedom found in sonship there is ¹no pretense. *(Free indeed. The word, ¹**ontoos**, indeed, is the opposite to that which is pretended.)*

John 8:44 You are the offspring of a ¹fallen mindset and you desire to prove its diabolic parenthood in your willingness to execute its cravings. This "cast down" mindset is what kills the ²anthropos since the beginning - *[it violently opposes the idea of the image and likeness of God in human form.]* **The diabolos mindset cannot abide the truth. There is no connection with truth - lying is its ³language; in fact, the diabolos is the father of lies. The intention was to kill mankind's awareness of their god-identity.** *(The word, ¹**diabolos**, Devil, has two components, **dia**, because of or through, and **ballo**, to cast down; thus referring to the cast down condition mankind suffered in association with Adam's fall. The diabolos is a man-slayer, ²**anthrōpoktonos** from **anthropos** and **kteinoo** to kill. The word for the human species, male or female is **anthropos**, from **ana**, upward, and **tropos**, manner of life; character; in like manner. See John 1:51, 2:25. The word ³**lalia** means dialect or language.)*

John 8:56 Your father Abraham was leaping with joy to see my day. What he saw made him exceedingly glad.

John 8:57 Then the Jews said, "Ha. You're not even fifty years old and you claim to have seen Abraham."

John 8:58 "Most certainly do I say unto you that before Abraham was born, I am." *(See note on John 1:1 Three times in this sentence John uses the imperfect of **eimi**, namely **aen**, to be, which conveys no idea of origin for God or for the Logos, but simply continuous existence, "I am." Quite a different verb **egeneto**, "became," appears in John 1:14 for the beginning of the Incarnation of the Logos. The incarnation is not the origin of Jesus, neither of us.. See the distinction sharply drawn in John 8:58, "before Abraham was [born, **genesthai** from **ginomai**] I am." The word **eimi**, I am; the essence of being, suggesting timeless existence. See 1 Peter 1:16.)*

Two chapters later Jesus addresses the same audience again:

John 10:30 My Father and I are one."

John 10:31 This filled the Jews with renewed rage and they picked up stones to stone him.

John 10:32 Then Jesus questioned them saying, "I have openly shown you many good works confirming my union with my Father; for which one of these works do you stone me?"

John 10:33 They said, "We are not stoning you for something that you have done but for what you have just said. You blasphemed God. You

are a mere man and you make yourself equal with God? *(The penalty for blasphemy was death by stoning - Leviticus 24:16.)*

John 10:34 Jesus said, "Is it not written in your law, 'I said you are gods?' *(Here Jesus quotes from Psalm 82:6 I say, "You are gods, sons of the Most High, all of you."*

What does it mean to build your house upon the rock? "Son of man, I say you are Rock; you're a chip off the old block - the son of man is the son of God." Dig deep = Gaze deeply, intently into the mirror likeness of the face of your birth. Luke 6:48; James 1:18,23-25; Isaiah 51:1; Deuteronomy 32:18 Living your life from who you are in Christ [Grace] beats living your life from who you are in Adam [law of works] by far. Plus it is storm-proof.)

See **Romans 9:33** The conclusion of the prophetic reference pointed towards the rock as the spirit identity of human life. In Messiah, God has placed his testimony of mankind's identity in front of their eyes, in Zion, the center of their religious focus, yet, blinded by their own efforts to justify themselves, they tripped over him. But those who recognized him by faith, as the Rock from which they were hewn, are freed from the shame of their sense of failure and inferiority. *(See Deuteronomy 32:18, "you have forgotten the Rock that birthed you…", and in Isaiah 51:1, "Look to the Rock from which you were hewn." It is only in him that mankind will discover what they are looking for. "Who is the son of man?" Mankind's physical identity is defined by their spiritual origin, the image and likeness of God, "I say you are Petros, you are Rock, and upon this rock - the revelation that the son of man is the son of God, I will build my ekklesia. [See Matthew 16:13-19]. Mankind's origin and true identity is preserved and revealed again in the Rock of ages. The term "rock" in those days represented what we call the "hard drive" in computer language; the place where data is securely preserved for a long time. Rock fossils carry the oldest data and evidence of life.)*

Galatians 1:19 During this time I did not see any of the other Apostles except James, the younger brother of Jesus. *(Saul [Paul], Peter [Kefas] and James shared a vital revelation; all three of them discovered their original identity beyond their natural birth: "From now on, we no longer know anyone according to the flesh", says Paul in 2 Corinthians 5:16. "Simon son of Jonah, flesh and blood did not reveal to you that as the son of man, I am the Christ, the Son of God; now that you know who I am, allow me to introduce you to you. I say that you are Rock, a chip off the old block. [Matthew 16:17, 18] James speaks about the effect of the Word as discovering the reflection of the face of our birth as in a mirror there. Rescuing us from our forgetfulness. "We have forgotten what manner of people we are.")*

In David's dramatic account of the cross in Psalm 22, a thousand years BC, he concludes with this most significant statement, "The ends of the earth shall remember, and turn to the Lord; and all the families of the nations shall worship before him. " And again in the next Psalm, 23, he says, "By the waters of reflection, my soul remembers who I am." Now I can go through the valley of the shadow of death and fear no evil.

One of the greatest teachers in the Celtic world, John Scotus Eriugena in ninth-century Ireland, also taught that Christ is our memory. We suffer from the "soul's forgetfulness," he says. Christ comes to re-awaken us to our true nature. He is our epiphany. He comes to show us the face of God. He comes to show us also our face, the true face of the human soul. This leads the Celtic tradition to celebrate the relationship between nature and grace. Instead of grace being viewed as opposed to our essential nature or as somehow saving us from ourselves, nature and grace are viewed as flowing together from God. They are both sacred gifts. The gift of nature, says Eriugena, is the gift of "being"; the gift of grace, on the other hand, is the gift of "well-being." Grace is given to reconnect us to our true nature. At the heart of our being is the image of God, and thus the wisdom of God, the creativity of God, the passions of God, the longings of God. Grace is opposed not to what is deepest in us but to what is false in us. It is given to restore us to the core of our being and to free us from the unnaturalness of what we are doing to one another and to the earth.

Genesis 3:22 *does not say, "he has now become like one of us." It says, "Behold, the man, who was already created like one of us, now also partook of the knowledge of evil; [the Greek word 'evil' is* **poneros** *- full of labors, hardships and annoyances - which describes the system which tries to manage the fruit of the "I am not-Tree" - I am not good enough, I am not this- or that-enough, etc etc.] and now, lest he puts forth his hand, and take also of the tree of life, only to continue to live in this "lost identity" state..." [See note on Genesis 3:24 below.]*

The original Hebrew and the most authentic versions use the Perfect tense, היה *hayah, which is the Qal Stem, masculine, third person, Active, and in the Perfect form, and signifies was, not is. The Perfect tense denotes an action which is completed in the past, but the effects of which are regarded as continuing into the present.*

The Samaritan text, the Syriac, and also the Septuagint, have the same tense. The Greek verb, γέγονεν, is the Perfect Active Indicative tense of ginomai.

See my commentary notes on 1 John 3:12 Thoughts on, "Why the other tree and why the temptation in the Garden?")

The Hebrew word in **Genesis 3:24**, הפך *hâpak is a primitive root; meaning to turn about; by implication to change, to return, to be converted, turn back. Also in the Septuagint the same thought is communicated in the Greek word,* **strephō***, which is the strengthened from the base of* **tropay***; to turn around or reverse: - convert, turn again, back again, to turn self about. The Sword would always point back to mankind's original identity. In Luke 15 the prodigal son returns to himself -* **Plato** *is quoted by Ackerman [Christian Element in Plato] as thinking of redemption as coming to oneself.*

Garments of identity

Revelation 3:5 Everyone who sees their victory in me will I clothe in white garments - and they will realize that I am not in the business of fulfilling their law and performance based fears by blotting out their names from the Book of Life. Instead I am the one who endorses their identity face to face before my Father and his celestial messengers.

*See extended notes at the end of Revelation 17 on **The Lamb's Book of Life** and Mankind's Redeemed Identity.*

Notes on Garments: himation - upper garment, cloak or mantle.

Romans 4:21 Abraham's confidence was his dress-code; he knew beyond doubt that the power of God to perform was equal to his promise. *(**plerophoreo**, from **plero** to be completely covered in every part, + **phoreo**, to wear garments or armor; traditionally translated to be completely persuaded. His faith was his visible identity and armor; he wore his persuasion like he would his daily garments.)*

Colossians 3:9 That old life was a lie, foreign to our design. Those garments of disguise are now thoroughly stripped off us in our understanding of our union with Christ in his death and resurrection. We are no longer obliged to live under the identity and rule of the robes we wore before, neither are we cheating anyone through false pretensions. *(The garments an actor would wear define his part in the play but cannot define him.)*

Colossians 3:10, We stand fully identified in the new creation renewed in knowledge according to the pattern of the exact image of our Creator.

Colossians 3:11, The revelation of Christ in us gives identity to the individual beyond anything anyone could ever be as a Greek or a Jew, American or African, foreigner or famous, male or female, king or pawn. From now on everyone is defined by Christ; everyone is represented in Christ.** *(In seeing him not just recorded in history but revealed in us, we discover the face of our birth as in a mirror. James 1:18)*

Colossians 3:12, You are the product of God's love; he restored you to his original thought. You belong to him exclusively. It is like changing garments. Now that you have gotten rid of the old, clothe yourselves with inner compassion, kindness, humility, gentleness and patience, *(Just like you were once identified by your apparel, the characteristics of these qualities define you now.)*

Colossians 3:13, upholding one another in positive expectation. If anyone finds fault with another, restore that person to favor, remembering how the Lord's forgiveness has transformed our lives.

Colossians 3:14, Wear love like a uniform; this is what completes the picture of our oneness.

1 Thessalonians 5:8 So let us clothe ourselves with day-garments, protecting our sober seeing by having our hearts fully guarded by the breastplate of love-inspired faith, and having our minds encircled, like a helmet, with an expectation which is consistent with what salvation declares.*)*

The City-Bride

Just like Babylon is not a city in the symbolic language of Revelation, it is a fallen-mindset society; so the New Jerusalem is not a city but the redeemed society of mankind. The Bride of Christ. In John 7:37,38 when Jesus speaks of waters gushing forth out of your innermost being, he says that you are the city. You are the bride. God's redeemed society.

Revelation 3:12 It is in every individual's continual association with their victory in me that I will make them to be like a strong pillar in the Inner Shrine of God's sanctuary supporting the entire structure of my God-habitation within you. A place to be your permanent abode where you will never depart from. And I will engrave upon them the name of my God, also the name of the city [the Bride.] of my God, the new Jerusalem that descends from heaven; as well as my own new Name.

Revelation 21:2 And I saw her, in spotless magnificence, the Holy City, the New Jerusalem, descending out of the heavens; having been fully prepared as a bride and beautifully adorned for her husband.

Psalm 87:3 Glorious things are spoken of you, Oh city of God - "This one and that one were born in her"

Psalm 87:7 Singers and dancers together say, "All my springs of joy are in you." *(There is no greater glory to pursue but to know that all my springs of joy are in you.)*

Revelation 19:16 On his robe and on his thigh he has a name inscribed, ^{5}King of kings and Lord of lords.

Revelation 1:5 His crown endorses our crown.

John 7:37 On the final day, the crescendo of the eight-day Feast of Tabernacles, Jesus stood up and proclaimed with a loud voice, "If anyone is thirsty, let him come and stand face-to-face with me and drink. *(John again employs the word pros in order to emphasize the face-to-face fellowship we are invited into.)*

John 7:38 In your realizing that I am what the Scriptures are all about you will discover uniquely for yourself, face to face with me, that I am what you are all about and rivers of living waters will gush out of your innermost being." *(Jesus addresses the individual; you singular. Here John records how Jesus witnessed the eighth day, the great and final day of the Feast of Tabernacles, when, according to custom, the High Priest would draw water from the Pool of Siloam with a golden jar, mix the water with wine, and then pour it over the altar while the people would sing with great joy from Psalm 118:25-26, See also the entire Psalm 118 which was obviously what Jesus reminded himself of and also Isaiah 12:3; "Therefore with joy shall we draw water from the wells of salvation." Then, Jesus, knowing that he is the completeness of every prophetic picture and promise, cried out with a loud voice: "If anyone is thirsty, let him come to me and drink. If you believe that I am what the Scriptures are all about, you will discover that you are what I am all about, and rivers of living waters will gush from your innermost being." The Siloam tunnel – a winding tunnel carved into the rock,* *leading from the spring of Gihon to the Pool of Siloam in the city of Jerusalem. Dating from the time of Hezekiah [800 BC] or earlier, it was an aqueduct that effectively replaced the Middle Bronze Age channel. Gihon derives from the Hebrew, גיח Giha which means **gushing forth**; like in an eruption. The pool of Siloam as the source in the city of Jerusalem and mirrors your innermost being. You are the city. See Luke 13:34,35.)*

Revelation 5:11 Then I saw ¹wave upon wave of innumerable celestial messengers ¹engulfing the throne and the elders and the Living Beings and I heard singing. It was a mass choir of ²multiple millions. *(The word ¹kuklo, encircle, from **kuma**, a swelling wave; which also connects with the etymological value of the word **muriades**, from **meu**, like in waves of the sea. Countless ²myriads - literally ten thousands times ten thousands and thousands of thousands. The largest number named in Ancient Greek was the myriad, myriad [written MM] or hundred million. In his Sand Reckoner, Archimedes of Syracuse used this quantity as the basis for a numeration system of large powers of ten, which he used to count grains of sand.*

According to PIE, the etymology of the word myriad has been variously connected to meu- "damp" in reference to the waves of the sea and to Greek myrmex μύρμηξ, "ant", in reference to their swarms. Proto-Indo-European [PIE] is the linguistic reconstruction of the common ancestor of the Indo-European languages, the most widely spoken language family in the world.)

Revelation 5:12 In their full capacity they exploded in song, proclaiming in unison, "The Lamb's worth is now fully ¹realized. ²Having been slain in sacrifice, the power, wealth, wisdom, strength, honor, glory, and blessing belong to him." *(The word ¹labein, to have taken/realized, from **lambano**, to take, to grasp, to receive; here in the Aorist Infinitive tense, which indicates prior completion of an action in relationship to a point in time. The word ²**esphagmenon** is the Perfect Passive Participle of the verb, **sphazō**, to slay in sacrifice. It is used to describe a state that exists at the time coincident with that of the leading verb as a result of action completed prior to the time of the main verb. The basic thought of the Perfect tense is that the progress of an action has been completed and the results of the action are continuing on, in full effect. In other words, the progress of the action has reached its culmination and the finished results are now in existence.)*

Revelation 5:13 At that point the entire universe burst out in praise. I heard every created being in the heavenly realm and upon the earth and under the earth and upon the ocean and everything within all these spheres, declaring to the One seated upon the throne and to the Lamb: "The most ¹articulate language, the admiration, the supreme magnificence, the might until the ages of the ages." *(The word ¹eulogia, from **eu**, good, well done, and **logos**; thus, polished language; such language which is artfully adapted to captivate the hearer: fair speaking, fine speeches.)*

Revelation 5:14 To which the four Living Beings added their endorsement and the elders prostrated themselves before the throne in silent worship.

(This is the conclusion of the ages and the theme wherein the entire book of Revelation unfolds.)

Revelation 7:9 At this moment I saw a massive throng of people, impossible to count, standing tall and innocent - all of them [1]dressed in white with palm branches in their hands; they had [1]escaped everything that could possibly define them as a non-Jewish, Gentile world. In fact, every sphere of society was there - including the entire spectrum of people-groupings; all tribal identities with their unique language-specific dialect preferences, they were all present facing the throne and the Lamb as the people of the planet. *(Amazing how, in the previous verses of this chapter, the tribes of Israel are associated with a very specific "number", emphasizing the prophetic detail of the entire Jewish nation. But here, John sees a massive throng of people, impossible to count. In Israel there is a prophetic voice of God's intention to release the blessing of the single SEED of God's faith through Abraham and bless all the nations of the earth. "Count the stars, count the sand."*

*The word [1]**stolay**, is the white outer garment worn by kings, priests, and persons of rank. The palm branches and the white robes are signs of the celebration of victory and joy. The Preposition [1]**ek**, points to source or origin; mankind was delivered out of their national, geographical and historical identities. Seven times in the book of Revelation human society is addressed in the most all-inclusive fashion, with a similar grouping of words. Revelation 5:9, here in Revelation 7:9, Revelation 10:11, Revelation 11:9, Revelation 13:7, Revelation 14:6 and Revelation 17:15. Also note Revelation 5:13 and Revelation 11:15. See Extended Notes on Israel at the end of Revelation 20.*

I looked again and saw a huge crowd, too huge to count. Everyone was there—all nations and tribes, all races and languages. And they were standing, dressed in white robes and waving palm branches, standing before the throne and the Lamb. The Message)

Revelation 7:10 Then I heard the masses shouting as if with one thundering voice saying, "Our salvation is secure in our God who is seated upon the throne and endorsed in the Lamb's doing."

Revelation 19:6 Then I heard the voice of an innumerable mass of people exploding like a thunderous torrent of mighty cascading waterfalls, bellowing, Hallelujah. The Lord our God has claimed his kingdom and established his sovereign rule over everything.

Revelation 19:7 This is the climax of the ages. Celebrate his glory with ecstatic joy and extreme delight, for the wedding feast of the Lamb has come. The day didn't catch her by surprise. His bride has prepared herself appropriately. She is ready and fully [1]fit for the occasion. *(The word, [1]**hetoimasen**, is in the Aorist Active Indicative tense pointing to what has already happened. This word derives from an old word, **heteos**, fitness. She has gotten herself ready. Verse 8 tells us how she did it. See my extended notes on **the City-Bride** at the end of Revelation 19.)*

Revelation 19:8 She [1]was given the finest linen to clothe herself; there she stands, wrapped in radiant white - dressed in [2]spotless, saintly innocence. *(The verb, **edothe** from **didomi**, was given, Aorist Passive Indicative. The word innocence, [2]**dikaiōma** stems from the word **dike**, two parties finding likeness in each other. Dike is also the root for the word **dikaiosune**, righteousness. Sadly, many translations have it completely wrong here. This is not the righteous "deeds" of the saints.*

*Our redeemed innocence gives testimony to the merits of the Redeemer. Paul says in Philippians 3:9, "And be found in him, not having my own righteousness, which is of the law, but what is through the faith of Christ, the righteousness which is of God by faith." Zechariah 3:4 And the celestial messenger said to those who were standing before him, "Remove the filthy garments from him." And to him he said, "Behold, I have taken your iniquity away from you, and I will clothe you with righteousness." Aramaic Targum. See my extended notes on **the City-Bride** at the end of Revelation 3.)*

Revelation 19:9 And he instructed me to record this in writing: Oh the [1]blessedness of this bliss which is the supreme celebration of the union of the ages. You have individually been [2]identified by name and invited to the Lamb's supper, concluding in the ultimate wedding feast. This is the Grand Finale in the [3]unveiling of God's word. *(This is not a wedding where you are invited simply because you're a friend of a friend of the Groom or the Bride - or a distant second cousin to a relative of a relative on someone's mother's side. No. You're the Bride.*

*The word, [1]**makarios**, usually translated, blessed, suggests a special intensity of delight. It is another beatitude [**makarioi**] like that in Revelation 14:13 [fourth of the seven in the book]*

*The verb, κεκλημενοι [2]**kekelemenoi** is a Perfect Passive Participle of **kaleo**, to identify by name, to surname. The Passive Participle describes a state that exists at the time coincident with that of the leading verb as a result of action completed prior to the time of the main verb, [in previous verse] **edothe** from didomi, was given [v8] which is in the Aorist Passive Indicative. The Perfect Participle endorses the fact that this is a standing invitation. See the extended notes on **ekklesia** at the end of chapter 1. The word, [3]**alethinos**, from **alethes**; from the negative particle, **a** and **lanthanō**, to lie hidden; thus, that which is unveiled truth.*

*Just like Babylon is not a city in the symbolic language of Revelation, it is a "fallen", distorted-mindset-society; so the New Jerusalem is not a city but the redeemed society of mankind. The Bride of Christ. Revelation 17:18. See my extended notes on **the City-Bride** at the end of Revelation 19.)*

Revelation 19:10 I was so overwhelmed that I fell down at his feet to worship him; he immediately asked me to see him as a fellow bond-servant and a fellow brother, jointly echoing the testimony of Jesus. Worship God, he said, the testimony of Jesus is the spirit of prophecy. This wedding is the entire culmination of the prophetic word.

Revelation 19:11 Then, in my vision, heaven opened and I saw a white horse appear; the Name of the one seated upon the horse is Faithful and True. Righteousness spans the range of his judgment and warfare. *(See notes on the **Open heaven** at the end of Revelation 13.)*

Revelation 19:12 And his eyes were like flashing flames of fire. His head was adorned with many royal diadems. He has a Name written upon him which he alone understands; no one recognizes him by that name. *(The Jews knew God as the "unpronounceable Name, and therefore called him, **HaShem** - השם The Name. See my commentary on Revelation 1:4.*

They could not connect this most sacred Name to the Messiah-Christ, JESUS, born in Bethlehem, condemned and crucified by them."

John 1:11 *It was not as though he arrived on a foreign planet; he came to his own, yet his own did not recognize him. [The Jews should have been the first to recognize him.]*

Isaiah 7:14 *Therefore the Lord himself will give you a sign. Behold, a virgin shall conceive and bear a son, and shall call his name Immanuel. See Luke 1:28,31.*

"...and you shall call his Name Jesus, for he will save his people from their sins." See Jeremiah 23:6 "In his days Judah will be saved, [yâsha`, a primitive root; properly to be open, wide or free, that is, [by implication] to be safe; causatively to free or succor, defend, deliver [-er], help, preserve, rescue, be safe, bring [having] **salvation,** *get victory.] And Israel will dwell securely. And* **this is his Name** *by which he will be called:* יהוה צדקנו *- Jahweh Tzadeknu -* **Jahweh our righteousness."**

The One with eyes ablaze as in Revelation 1:14 and Revelation 2:17,18, also Revelation 3:12...And I will engrave upon them the name of my God, also the name of the city [the bride.] of my God, the new Jerusalem that descends from heaven; as well as my own new Name.

See extended **notes on the hidden Name at the end of Revelation 19.)**

Revelation 19:13 The robes he wore were dipped in blood and his ¹Name has always been the Word of God. *(He is the Logos that was before time was; the completeness of prophecy, the Incarnate One. See John 1:1-3,14. See* **Notes on the Hidden Name** *at the end of Revelation 19.)*

Isaiah 54:5 For your Maker is your husband, the LORD of hosts is his Name; and the Holy One of Israel is your Redeemer, the God of the whole earth he is called.

The Prostitute becomes the Bride.

In Hosea 3:1, after Gomer had left Hosea and was living in immorality, the Lord commanded Hosea to find her and buy her back.

Hosea 1:2, "The LORD said to Hosea, 'Go, take to yourself a wife of whoredom and have children of whoredom.'"

Hosea 2:14, Therefore, behold, I will allure her, and bring her into the wilderness, and speak tenderly to her.

Hosea 2:15, And there I will give her vineyards, and make the Valley of Achor a door of hope. And there she shall answer as in the days of her youth, as at the time when she came out of the land of Egypt.

Hosea 2:16, "And in that day, says the LORD, you will call me, 'My ¹husband,' and no longer will you call me, 'My Boss.' [Baal בעל *- also husband but more in an owner/manager context, rather than ¹my man,* אישי *- ishi, my man. My intimate spouse/companion. From "slave-driver" to soul mate.)*

Hosea 2:17 For I will remove the names of the Baals from her mouth, and they shall be mentioned by name no more.

Hosea 2:18 And I will make for you a covenant on that day with the beasts of the field, the birds of the air, and the creeping things of the

ground; and I will abolish the bow, the sword, and war from the land; and I will make you lie down in safety.

Hosea 2:19 And I will betroth you to me forever; I will betroth you to me in righteousness and in justice, in steadfast love, and in mercy.

Hosea 2:20 I will betroth you to me in faithfulness; and you shall know the LORD.

Hosea 2:21 "And in that day, says the LORD, I will answer the heavens and they shall answer the earth;

Hosea 2:22 and the earth shall answer the grain, the wine, and the oil, and they shall answer Jezreel;

Hosea 2:23 and I will sow him for myself in the land. And I will have pity on Not pitied, and I will say to Not my people, 'You are my people'; and he shall say, 'Thou art my God.'"

Isaiah saw the new Jerusalem-Bride in the context of the powerful prophetic salvation poetry recorded in Isaiah 52,53 and 54.

Isaiah 52:1 Awake, awake; put on thy strength, O Zion; put on your beautiful garments, O Jerusalem, the holy city. (*Addressing the city of Jerusalem in the feminine singular in Hebrew. Through the feminine form of the command 'awake.'* **uri. uri.** עורי *and livshi.* לבשי *'put on', as well as the feminine singular possessive and objective pronoun endings on the words, izek,* עזך *'your strength', **tifartek**,* תפארתך *'your beauty' and* בך *bak, 'in you'.*)

Eve was not an afterthought! Adam was put into a deep sleep; then God took her out of the word that was already made flesh! Mankind redeemed, the Bride, began the same way! Co-quickened, co-raised we are!

When Adam awoke from his sleep, Eve was there! Behold, Bone of my bone, flesh of my flesh! She shall be called woman...

*See Isaiah 11:1 Then a shoot will come out from the stump of Jesse, and a branch from its roots will bear fruit. See notes on Jesse in Luke 3:32 Son of **Jesse** ישי Jahweh is my husband - from* שיאי *from* שי *yêsh/yaysh. From an unused root meaning to stand out, or exist; entity; used adverbially or as a copula for the substantive verb* היה *hâyâh H1961 to breathe; to be; to exist; from the core of the name of Jahweh,* הוהי *"existing". Thus, the root word for Jesse,* היה *hajah, in the Ancient Hebrew is,* 𐤉𐤄 *- the pictograph* 𐤄 *represents one who is looking at a great sight with his hands raised. In David's father, Jesse, it is the one looking at the other in mirror likeness. See Acts 13:22, Romans 15:12, And further Isaiah says, "The root of Jesse shall come, he who rises to rule the Gentiles; in him shall the Gentiles hope." Also, hidden in the name Jesse is the prophetic picture of the incarnation - Jahweh embracing man. The word for man,* שיא *ish and woman, adding the* ה *breath-sound, hey,* **ishah** *השא - Thus, Jesse also includes the jod connecting Jahweh with **ish**, man - Jahweh, the incarnate man.*

See notes on the root of Jesse at the end of Revelation 22.)

REVELATION Chapter 4

4:1 [1]Talking about our co-seatedness, I want you to see something. Oh wow. What I see takes my breath away. A [2]wide-open door in the heavenly realm. The first thing I heard was this voice addressing me. It was distinct and clear, like the sound of a trumpet; it captured my attention, inviting me to enter. "Come up here and I will show you how everything [3]coincides with what you have already seen." *(I saw [eidon] second Aorist Active Indicative of horaō. Behold [idou] exclamation of vivid emotion as John looked, "With this I saw."Most translations would translate **meta tauta** with, "after this" The word [1]**meta** however refers to, with this; coinciding with this. [Our co-seatedness and enjoying feasting together with him. Revelation 3:20 and Revelation 3:21, And everyone's personal triumph will be celebrated together with me, by being jointly seated together in my Kingship. On exactly the same basis of my victory celebration and my joint-seatedness with my Father in his throne.] Robertson suggests that it is a change in the panorama, not chronology.*

*The word [2]**eneogmene** is the Perfect Passive Participle of **anoigō** to open, from **ana**, upward and **agō**, to lead; as in Revelation 3:8 [door of opportunity] and Revelation 3:20 [door of the heart]. A dimension of limitless possibilities open, right in front of my eyes. The Passive Participle describes a state that exists at the time coincident with that of the leading verb as a result of action completed prior to the time of the main verb, behold. Thus John witnessed the opening of the door. The Perfect tense denotes an action which is completed in the past, but the effects of which are regarded as continuing into the present. The verb [3]**genesthai** is not the future of the verb to be; it is the Aorist Infinitive where the thought is not the prophetic, but the necessity of the inevitable consequence as a result of the crucified and risen Christ. John again employs the verb, **ginomai**, to beget, in the Aorist Infinitive tense, **genesthai**, which indicates prior completion of an action in relationship to a point in time. Greek Infinitives could have either a Present or Aorist form. The contrast between the two forms was not necessarily one of time, it is a difference of aspect. The Present Infinitive was used to express progressive or imperfective aspect. It pictures the action expressed by the verb as being in progress. The Aorist Infinitive however does not express progressive aspect. It presents the action expressed by the verb as a completed unit with a beginning and end.)*

4:2 So here I am, immersed in this unrestricted space of spirit ecstasy. As the vision opens I immediately notice the throne and One seated upon it. *("Having accomplished purification for sins he sat down." His throne is proof of mankind's redeemed innocence. This unveiling is central to the throne-theme. See Hebrews 1:1-4 in the Mirror. The bold imagery is linked to the following familiar passages in Jewish Scriptures, 1Kings 22:19; Isaiah 6:1; Ezekiel 1:26-28; Daniel 7:9.)*

4:3 The One seated upon the throne appeared to reflect multi earthy-color patterns like that of a Jasper stone and the blood-red color of sardion, with the entire throne wrapped in a rainbow radiance of emerald greens. *(Gr. **sardion**, from a root meaning "red", a gem of a blood-red color. It was called "sardius" because it came from Sardis in Lydia. It was also one of the precious stones in the high priest's breastplate [Exodus. 28:17; 39:10]. "A radiance of emerald" - **smaragdinos** is a transparent precious stone noted especially for its light green color.)*

4:4 And coiled into a complete circle around the throne were twenty four thrones with twenty four ¹presbyterians seated upon the thrones. They were enwrapped in white with ²victor's wreaths of gold crowning their heads. Their minds were co-enthroned in the authority of the throne engulfing them in their co-seatedness. *(In the symbolic language of Revelation, we have a circle of people representing the entire human race. ¹Typo drawn again from the Jewish **suneidron** - a co-seatedness around the throne - the 24 **presbuterians** or ¹Elders picture the twelve prophetic Patriarchs and the twelve Apostles, here as two dispensations merged into one, now fully representing the entire ekklesia. The word **kuklothen** is the adverb from **kuklo**; to form a circle, that is, all around; from **kuliō**, rolling together. From the base of **kuma**, from **kuō**, to swell [with young], that is, bend, curve; a billow, as bursting or toppling: - thus, a wave; through the idea of circularity. The word ²**stephanos**, is a victor's wreath.*

Much of what John saw, reflected in the Jewish mind as familiar prophetic pointers and symbols. See the prophetic imagery in Ezekiel 1:1-28. The symbolic pictures John sees of judgment would immediately remind his typical Jewish audience of their prophets imaginary of judgment. This time the slaughtered and risen Lamb brings brand new context. Israel's unfaithfulness is met and eclipsed by God's faithfulness. The Lamb's death and resurrection confronts every idea of judgment that was mankind's due.)

4:5 And ¹proceeding out of the throne, there were flashes of lightning and the sound of thunderous voices. Also the seven Spirits of God, with their ²gazes fixed upon the throne appeared to be like flaming torches ablaze with light. *(Proceed ¹**ekporeuontai**. Graphic historical Present tense. The word ²**enopion** suggests eye to eye contact within the closest possible proximity of one another. Revelation 1:4 Ezekiel 1:13,14.)*

4:6 The throne was located in what appeared to be a sea of transparent glass, like crystal. And as if ¹fused into one with the throne and ²engulfing it from all sides, I saw four Living Beings, all eyes, gazing ahead and behind. *(See Exodus 24:10 and they saw the God of Israel; and there was under his feet as it were a pavement of sapphire stone, like the very heaven for clearness. The word, ¹**mesos** in the midst of; from **meta** - suggests an immediate closeness as in an inseparable union. The word ²**kuklō**, encircle. Ezekiel 1:4 and a fire infolding itself, and a brightness was about it, and out of the midst thereof as the colour of amber.)*

4:7 The first Living Being resembled a Lion and the second a ¹Young Animal, the third Living Being had the countenance of a ²Human, and the fourth looked like an Eagle in full flight. *(The word ¹**moschos**, a tender juicy shoot, a sprout; a delicate young animal - typically of a young animal for sacrifice - the idea was that the younger the sacrifice the more its innocence was emphasized. Hebrews 9:12, Hebrews 9:19.*

*The word for the ²human species, male or female is **anthropos**, from **ana**, upward, and **tropos**, manner of life; character; in like manner. See John 1:51.*

These four faces beautifully picture the completeness of salvation. The Lion who becomes the Scapegoat-Sacrifice in a Human face now ascends in resurrection language on Eagle wings. See Isaiah 40:30,31.)

REVELATION Chapter 4

4:8 And the four Living Beings each had six wings pointing upward, these wings were rotating continually in a full circle. They had eyes everywhere, engaging with their complete horizon within and without. Day and night they continued without pause to proclaim, Holy. Holy. Holy is the God whose Lordship is the supreme authority over all things, whose I-am-ness defines time - present, past and future. *(See my commentary note on Revelation 1:4. The origin of the word **hagios**, translated, holy, can be connected to the ancient **yagios** having the Hindo-European root **yag-**, that means, to give honor.)*

4:9 And [1]whenever the Living Beings would [2]repeat their [3]esteem of his glorious reputation and worth and the [4]inexhaustible goodness of the grace of the One seated upon the throne, the One whose life spans across the [5]perpetuity of the ages, *(The indefinite temporal clause **hotan**, meaning whensoever and the Future Active Indicative [2]**dōsousin** - to give, to present - rather than the more common second Aorist Active Subjunctive **dōsin**, communicate the notion of repetition rather than unbroken continuance, "whenever they give." [Robertson] The word [3]**doxa** implies esteem, reputation; from **dokeo**, to form an opinion. The word often translated thanksgiving, [4]**eucharistia** from **eucharistos** - is a word that again has 2 components, **eu**, good; well done and **charis**, benevolence, grace. The [5]perpetuity of the ages - **eis tous aionas toon aionoon**.)*

4:10 then the twenty four representatives of the entire co-enthroned, co-seated ekklesia would descend from their thrones and prostrate themselves in the awesome presence of him who [1]forever sits enthroned; the One whose life spans the perpetuity of the ages. And they would worship him and cast their crowns before the throne saying, *(The tense of the word, [1]**kathemenon**, the seated one, suggests the one who forever owns the throne. Present, Participle, Genitive - possession, "of"; also origin)*

4:11 "Our Lord and our God. You are worthy to take the glory and the honor for the dynamic competence displayed in every detail of all of creation. Yes, everything owes their existence to your resolve and for your pleasure we were created." *(See Colossians 1:16, Everything that is begins in him whether in the heavenly realm or upon the earth, visible or invisible, every order of justice and every level of authority, be it kingdoms or governments, principalities or jurisdictions; all things were created by him and for him.*

John 1:3, All things were made by him; and without him was not any thing made that was made. KJV

Hebrews 2:10, He towers in conspicuous prominence far above all things. He is both their author and their conclusion.)

REVELATION Chapter 5

5:1 And I saw the One seated upon the throne holding a scroll in the open palm of his right hand; it was written on both sides and sealed with seven signet stamps. *(See Ezekiel 2:9. These seals were typical signet stamps in clay or wax to authenticate a document.)*

5:2 Then I saw a very powerful ¹celestial shepherd-messenger, heralding with a loud voice, "Is there anyone anywhere who would claim the right to open the scroll and break its seven seals.?" *(The word often translated as angel, ¹aggelos has two components, agō to lead as a shepherd leads and agele a herd of cattle or company.)*

5:3 And no-one in the heavenly realm or upon the earth or in the underworld was eligible to open the scroll or even see a hint of what was written therein. *(See 1 Corinthians 2:7-9.)*

5:4 I felt terribly heartbroken and cried inconsolably at the thought that there seemed to be no-one entitled to open the scroll in order to interpret it.

5:5 Then one of the elders said unto me, "You need not weep anymore. Look. The Lion has conquered. He who is of the tribe of Judah, the root of David. His victory qualifies him to open the scroll and to break its seven seals." *(Idou enikesen Behold. He has conquered. ho leon, ho ek tes phules Jodah, he ritza David, The Lion who is out of the tribe of Judah, the root of David. Revelation 3:7 I hold the key of David as prophesied in Isaiah 22:22.*

*See Genesis 49:9, Judah is a lion's whelp; Genesis 49:10, The scepter shall not depart from Judah, nor the ruler's staff from between his feet, until he comes to whom it belongs; and to him shall be the obedience of the peoples. Genesis 49:11, Binding his foal to the vine and his ass's colt to the choice vine, he washes his garments in wine and his vesture in the blood of grapes. See my comments on **The Root of Jesse** Revelation 22:16.)*

5:6 So I looked to see the Lion, and there - as if fused into one with the throne and in unison with the four Living Beings - taking center stage in the midst of the elders, I saw a little Lamb, alive and standing - even though it seemed to have been violently butchered in sacrifice. It had seven horns and seven eyes which are the seven Spirits of God having been sent out to accomplish his bidding in all the earth. *(You cannot see the Lion until you see the Lamb. Mankind's redeemed innocence is the authority of the throne of the Kingdom of God. "Having made purification for sins, he sat down." Hebrews 1:3.*

The word ¹mesos, in the midst; from meta - suggests an immediate closeness as in an inseparable union. The word ²arnion, is the diminutive from aren; thus a lambkin. The verb ³esphagmenon, indicates violence, butchery - also the sacrificial word. Exodus 12:6.

Interesting prophetic pointer to the slain Lamb of God. The Lion of Judah. See Genesis 49:6 Oh my soul, come not into their council; Oh my spirit, be not joined to their company; for in their anger they slay men, as if they are slaying an animal in their wantonness. And then 3 verses on, Genesis 49:9 Judah is a lion's whelp; and :10 The scepter shall not depart from Judah.

Isaiah 52:10 The LORD has bared his holy arm before the eyes of all the nations; and all the ends of the earth shall see the salvation of our God. Isaiah 52:14 As many were astonished at him—his appearance was so marred, beyond human semblance, and his form beyond that of the sons of men— Isaiah 52:15 so shall he startle many nations; kings shall shut their mouths because of him; for that which has not been told them they shall see, and that which they have not heard they shall understand. Psalm 22:27 All the ends of the earth shall remember and turn to the LORD; and all the families of the nations shall worship before him.)

5:7 The Lamb ¹came and ²at once took it out of the right hand of the One seated upon the throne. *(The use of the Greek tenses create a vivid dramatic picture of the actual scene; ¹**elthen** [Aorist] and ²**eilephen** which is in the Perfect tense of the verb, **lambano**, to take, receive, grasp. Alternating the Perfect tense with the Aorist, is very graphic. [Vincent] Then in the next verse it is back to the narrative Aorist tense.)*

5:8 The moment he ¹took the scroll, the four Living Beings and the twenty four elders bowed down in worship in their priestly offices before the little Lamb. Each one had a ²stringed instrument and a typical temple ³vessel, a broad shallow saucer of pure gold, filled with incense - in the context of this imagery their praise represented the prayers and worship of the masses of saints - and every single one realized how sanctified they were because of the Lamb. *(Here John again resumes the narrative Aorist tense, ¹**elaben**. The imagery is from the typical tabernacle and temple service. The word ²**kitharos** [guitar] harp was a triangular shaped stringed instrument with 7 and later 10 strings traditionally associated with joy and gladness in worship [Psalm 33:2; Psalm 98:5] Then each one of the elders also had a ³**phialas chrusas**, a golden fire-pan specifically designed to receive the sweet smelling frankincense which was lighted with coals from the brazen altar, where the sacrifice has just been presented in the outer court and then proceeded to offer it on the golden altar before the veil. See Luke 1:10 And the whole multitude of the people were praying outside at the hour of incense.)*

5:9 And they sang a new ¹song saying, "We proclaim your excellent worth. You are the only one in the universe entitled to open the scroll and break its seals, since you were slaughtered in sacrifice and ²in your blood redeemed mankind's authentic identity ³in God. You rescued them ⁴from everything that could possibly define society before and brought them out of the confines of their dwarfed mindsets. This includes the entire spectrum of people-groupings: our ⁵tribal identities, our ⁶language-specific dialect preferences, our ⁷political and religious associations, as well as every form of ⁸racial identity. *(An ¹**ode** is poem praising or glorifying an individual, describing their nature intellectually as well as emotionally. Greek odes were originally poetic pieces performed with musical accompaniment.*

*In the sentence, "in your blood" John uses the Preposition ²**en**, in. It is used Hebraistically of the price; the value of the thing purchased being contained in the price. [Vincent] And redeemed ²in God; τῷ Θεῷ - the Dative case also points to location "in" [the words τῷ Θεῷ, **tō Theo**, in or to God, are most likely added by copyist] Textual Commentary by Bruce Metzger.*

Jesus said in Matthew 13:44, that the man who found the treasure in the agricultural field, sold all he had and bought the entire field. He did not buy from the thief - a thief never becomes an owner; his priceless blood was shed to persuade mankind of their worth. Hebrews 6:16,17.

*The word, **hemas**, "us", in "He redeemed **us**", is not in the original text. Thus, we are not a select group of individuals that are redeemed; this is mankind redeemed out of whatever it was that defined them before. The Preposition **ek**, is used here; thus, ⁴out of everything tribal, dialect-related, political etc. - ⁴ek pases ⁵phules kai ⁶gloosses kai ⁷laou kai ⁸ethnous. The word ⁵phule from phuo to beget - tribe - immediate family-ties; blood relatives; ⁶glōssa, mother-tongue dialect; ⁷laos, a people group, any specific segment of society; ⁸ethnos, race; Hebrew גוי goy, non-Jewish, in the racial Jewish mind it included the masses of the heathen nations.*

Seven times human society is addressed in the most all-inclusive fashion, with a like grouping of words for all mankind of all races and nations; - here in Revelation 5:9, then also Revelation 7:9, Revelation 10:11, Revelation 11:9 Revelation 13:7; Revelation 14:6 and Revelation 17:15.)

5:10 And you have made ¹them unto God a realm of royalty to reign upon the earth as priests. *(Again, not, ἡμᾶς, us; but αὐτούς, them. Also, not, we shall reign (βασιλεύσομεν basileusomen), but, βασιλεύουσιν **basileuousin**, they reign. They are the redeemed human race as a whole - redeemed to reign as kings and priests, after the order of Melchizedek. The Christ-life rules. See Psalm 110:4; Hebrews 7:14-24)*

5:11 Then I saw ¹wave upon wave of innumerable celestial messengers ¹engulfing the throne and the elders and the Living Beings and I heard singing. It was a mass choir of ²multiple millions. *(The word ¹kuklo, encircle, from **kuma**, a swelling wave; which also connects with the etymological value of the word **muriades**, from **meu**, like in waves of the sea. Countless ²myriads - literally ten thousands times ten thousands and thousands of thousands. The largest number named in Ancient Greek was the myriad, myriad [written MM] or hundred million. In his Sand Reckoner, Archimedes of Syracuse used this quantity as the basis for a numeration system of large powers of ten, which he used to count grains of sand.*

According to PIE, the etymology of the word myriad has been variously connected to meu- "damp" in reference to the waves of the sea and to Greek myrmex μύρμηξ, "ant", in reference to their swarms. Proto-Indo-European [PIE] is the linguistic reconstruction of the common ancestor of the Indo-European languages, the most widely spoken language family in the world.)

5:12 In their full capacity they exploded in song, proclaiming in unison, "The Lamb's worth is now fully ¹realized. ²Having been slain in sacrifice, the power, wealth, wisdom, strength, honor, glory, and blessing belong to him." *(The word ¹labein, to have taken/realized, from **lambano**, to take, to grasp, to receive; here in the Aorist Infinitive tense, which indicates prior completion of an action in relationship to a point in time. The word ²esphagmenon is the Perfect Passive Participle of the verb, **sphazō**, to slay in sacrifice. It is used to describe a*

REVELATION Chapter 5

state that exists at the time coincident with that of the leading verb as a result of action completed prior to the time of the main verb. The basic thought of the Perfect tense is that the progress of an action has been completed and the results of the action are continuing on, in full effect. In other words, the progress of the action has reached its culmination and the finished results are now in existence.)

5:13 At that point the entire universe burst out in praise. I heard every created being in the heavenly realm and upon the earth and under the earth and upon the ocean and everything within all these spheres, declaring to the One seated upon the throne and to the Lamb: "The most [1]articulate language, the admiration, the supreme magnificence, the might until the ages of the ages." *(The word [1]eulogia, from eu, good, well done, and logos; thus, polished language; such language which is artfully adapted to captivate the hearer: fair speaking, fine speeches.)*

5:14 To which the four Living Beings added their endorsement and the elders prostrated themselves before the throne in silent worship.

(This is the conclusion of the ages and the theme wherein the entire book of Revelation unfolds.)

REVELATION Chapter 6

6:1 When I saw the little Lamb open one of the seals, the [1]first Living Being roared with a thunderous voice, [2]Come forth. *([1]The one with the appearance of a lion. The word, [2]erchou, "Come." is the Present Middle Imperative of erchomai, but with exclamatory force. In the mighty roar of the Lion, the victory of the slain and risen little Lamb is announced.)*

6:2 I looked and saw a white horse, mounted by an archer. And a victor's wreath was given to him. He arrived as [1]Conqueror and [2]to establish his victory. *(In Zechariah 6:1-8 we have red, black, white, and grizzled bay horses like the four winds of heaven, ministers to do God's will. White seems to be the color of victory - the white horse of the Persian Kings - like the white horse typically ridden by the Roman conqueror in a triumphant procession.*

Conquering -[1]nikōn - Present Active Participle of nikaō. And to conquer - [2]kai hina nikēsēi - purpose clause with hina and the first Aorist Active subjunctive of nikaō. The Aorist tense here points to certain victory. A Participle is considered a "verbal adjective". A Participle can be used as a 'substantive' to take the place of a noun. The subjunctive mood indicates probability or objective possibility. The action of the verb will possibly happen, depending on certain objective factors or circumstances. It is oftentimes used in conditional statements [i.e. 'If...then...' clauses] or in purpose clauses. However if the subjunctive mood is used in a purpose or result clause, then the action should not be thought of as a possible result, but should be viewed as a definite outcome that will happen as a result of another stated action.)

6:3 When the Lamb opened the second seal I heard the [2]second Living Being say, "Proceed." *(This time it is the voice of the [2]young animal of sacrifice.)*

6:4 And a flame-red horse appeared and its rider had been given the mission to remove peace from the earth - resulting in people scapegoating and butchering one another - he was given a large knife. *(Addressing mankind's political structures. Here the little Lamb willingly faces the butcher's knife to be murdered by his own creation. Reminding of the Levitical priesthood of sacrifice; also representing the political crisis that mankind plunged into. See Genesis 49:5 Simeon and Levi are brothers; weapons of violence are their swords. Genesis 49:6 Oh my soul, come not into their council; Oh my spirit, be not joined to their company; for in their anger they slay a man, and in their wantonness they hamstring oxen. In John 14:27 Jesus says, "My peace I give unto you; not the kind of peace the world gives." In the brutal murder of Jesus on the cross, the slaughtered Lamb collided victoriously with every principality of darkness and accusation sourced in the fallen mindset-system of mankind's societies and religions, and in his death and resurrection, he disengaged the very basis of their fragile, pseudo-peace, founded on compromised and corrupt values as represented in their political and religious agendas. The Prince of peace established a peace based on mankind's redeemed identity, innocence and value and not on hidden agenda-driven, performance-based laws of shame and accusation.)*

6:5 When he opened the third seal the Living Being with the Human face said, "Proceed." And this is what I saw, behold, this time it is a black horse and its rider held the beam of a scale of balances in his hand. *(Addressing mankind's poverty stricken economy.)*

6:6 What I heard sounded like the four Living Beings were speaking with one voice saying, one denarius *[a day's wage]* will buy a [1]measure of wheat or three measures of barley and ²no restrictions will be placed on wine and oil. *(A measure, a **choenix** of corn for a man's daily supply. Barley was the food of the poor. No restrictions will be placed on wine and oil - μὴ ἀδικήσῃς. The word ²**adikea** from **a**, not and **dikay**, two parties finding likeness in each other - the stem for righteousness, **dikaiosune** - where **dikay** reminds of the Greek goddess of Justice typically portrayed holding a scale of balances in her hand. In Lamb's death and resurrection, even the poorest of the poor must have equal access to bread and wine. In times of poverty the first things that cannot be afforded would be the luxury of wine and oil. And here, in the face of death, the eternal covenant is celebrated. The covenant currency is not affected by the economy of the world-system.)*

6:7 And when the little Lamb opened the fourth seal I heard the fourth Living Being, the Eagle in full flight, announce, "Proceed." *(The Eagle reminds of the resurrection - the one who has fallen, exhausted, will entwine with the Lord and mount up with eagle wings, run and not be weary, walk and not faint. Isaiah 40:31.)*

6:8 I looked and saw a horse which appeared to have the color of tender green grass; its rider's name was Death and Hades was its close companion. And they were given the authority to destroy a quarter of the earth by sword, famine, disease, and wild beasts. *(Addressing mankind's appointment with death and Hades. Four possible causes of death are mentioned, war, famine, disease or wild beasts. Each one of these could be responsible for one quarter of the world's population to die which suggests the death of the entire human race. See 2 Corinthians 5:14 - I am convinced that if one has died for all - then all have died. See Hebrews 9:26 But Jesus did not have to suffer again and again since the fall of the world; the single sacrifice of himself in the fulfillment of history now reveals how he has brought sin to nought. [God's Lamb took away the sins of the world.] Hebrews 9:27 The same goes for everyone: a person dies only once, and then faces judgment. Hebrews 9:28 Christ died once and faced the judgment of the entire human race. His second appearance [in his resurrection] has nothing to do with sin, but to reveal salvation for all to fully embrace him.)*

6:9 And when he opened the fifth seal I saw underneath the altar the souls of those slain in sacrifice because of the word of God and their testimony. *(Addressing the murdered prophets. Matthew 23:37 "Jerusalem, Jerusalem, who kills the prophets and stones those who are sent to her. How often I wanted to gather your children together, the way a hen gathers her chicks under her wings, and you were unwilling.")*

6:10 Their voices were loud and urgent. How long, our holy and true ¹Husband, will you not judge and balance the scales of justice in the shedding of innocent blood? Are we mere scapegoats in the futile sacrificial system of the rest of the earth-dwellers.? *(The word **despotes** from **deo**, binding as in wedlock and **posis**, husband. The word **ekdikea** from **ek**, source and **dikay**, two parties finding likeness in each other - the stem for righteousness, **dikaiosune** - where **dikay** reminds of the Greek goddess of Justice typically portrayed holding a scale of balances in her hand.)*

6:11 Then white robes were given to each and everyone of them. Mankind's redeemed innocence is about to be announced. "Whilst you briefly rest with your ¹faces turned upward in expectation, you will be rejuvenated in

the awareness of the ²fulfillment of the prophetic word. Your fellows, co-included in the sufferings of the Christ *[even his murderers]* **are about to be revealed as your friends; they too are equally included in the slain Lamb of God."** *("And there was given to each one white robes, and it was said to them that they may rest themselves yet a little time, till may be fulfilled also their fellow-servants and their brethren, who are about to be killed—even as they. Young's Literal Translation."*

One has died for all, therefore all have died. 2 Corinthians 5:14. "While you briefly rest with your faces turned upward" [¹***anapauō****, **ana**, upward and **pauo**, rest; also refresh, far more than mere rest, rejuvenation. The English expression "rest up" is close to the idea of the Greek compound **anàpauō**.] This suggests a resting in the awareness of the significance of their lives and death in prophetic context; the word of your testimony pointing to my day. The word, ²**pleroo** is in the Aorist Passive Subjunctive, suggesting the inevitable fulfillment of that which the prophetic word pointed to. In the slaughtered Lamb's death, God dramatically brings closure to every definition of sacrifice - he takes mankind's appointment with death and judgment out of the equation and introduces resurrection life to be our true portion. See 1 Peter 1:10,11 In all of their conversation there was a constant quest to determine who the Messiah would be, and exactly when this would happen. They knew with certainty that it was the spirit of Christ within them pointing prophetically and giving testimony to the sufferings of the Christ and the subsequent glory. Revelation 7:9)*

6:12 When he opened the sixth seal, there was a massive earthquake, the sun was in mourning, wearing black sackcloth and the entire moon became like blood. *(Just like it was during the crucifixion. A lunar eclipse is possible at Passover - lunar eclipse of April 3, AD 33 was a fulfillment of Joel's prophecy of the moon being turned to blood quoted by the Apostle Peter at Pentecost [Acts 2:15–21] - a totally eclipsed moon often has a red appearance, and hence could be called a blood moon.)*

6:13 And the stars of heaven fell on the earth just like the figs of a winter tree which a strong wind scatters to the ground to ripen. *(The word, **olunthos**, "winter-figs" or, such as grow under the leaves and do not ripen at the proper season, but hang upon the trees during the winter and falls off the tree in Spring - good intentions under the system of the law of works will fall to the ground like unripe fruit.*

*Jesus used the fig tree [**Mark 13:28**] as a sign of the end of the world's long winter. "Yet once, it is a little while, and I will shake the heavens and the earth, and the sea, and the dry land, and I will shake all nations, **and the desire of all nations shall come**; and I will fill this house with glory, says the Lord of hosts." **Haggai 2:6-7**.*

Isaiah 34:4 *All the host of heaven shall rot away, and be rolled up like a scroll. All their host shall fall, as leaves fall from the vine, like leaves falling from the fig tree. [RSV]*

*See **Colossians 2:15** In him dying mankind's death, he defused every possible claim of accusation against the human race and thus made a public spectacle of every rule and authority in God's brilliant triumph, demonstrated in him. The voice of the cross will never be silenced. [The horror of the Cross is now the eternal trophy of God's triumph over sin. The cross stripped religion of its authority to* *manipulate mankind with guilt. Every accusation lost its leverage to blackmail the human race with condemnation and shame.])*

6:14 The sky was split apart and rolled up like a scroll. *(History was split in a before and after Christ. He is the fullness of time. The prophetic scroll was fulfilled. And every geographic location was challenged to re-align.*

Albert Barnes suggests that thrones and dynasties long established would be overthrown; institutions that seemed to be fixed and permanent were abolished; a new order of things would rise...)

6:15 And all the kingdoms of the earth were suddenly on equal terms. The great and most influential people, the highest ranked military commanders, the wealthiest business personalities, the high and mighty; everyone from the freeborn down to the lowest ranked slave were all equal. They all ran for cover into the dens and caves,

6:16 pleading with the mountains and the hills to cover and protect them. "Hide us from the face of the One seated upon the throne and from the ¹reach of the Lamb." *(The word, ¹orge, means excitement of mind, from the word, orgeomai, meaning to stretch one's self out in order to touch or to grasp something, to reach after or desire something. See Hebrews 4:3, Hear the echo of God's cry through the ages, "Oh. If only they would enter into my rest." [Some translations read, "As I have sworn in my wrath" derived from orge, meaning passionate desire, any strong outburst of emotion. "Oh. If only they would enter into my rest."] Just like Adam and Eve who went into hiding to escape their perceptions of Papa's judgment.*

Psalm 139:7 Where shall I go from Your Spirit? Or where shall I flee from Your face? Psalm 139:8 If I go up to heaven, You; if I make my bed Sheol, behold, You. [Literal translation by Jay P. Green Sr.]

Hosea 10:8 *Also, the high places of Aven, the sin of Israel, shall be destroyed. The thorn and the thistle shall come up on their altars. [Their sacrificial system has failed them.] And they shall say to the mountains, "Cover us." and to the hills, "Fall on us.")*

6:17 For the great day of his ¹passion ²has already arrived and who would have imagined it would be possible for anyone ³to have been restored and positioned in a place of innocence? *(The word orgay to desire [as a reaching forth or excitement of the mind], that is, [by analogy] passion and only by implication often translated punishment: - anger, indignation, vengeance, wrath. The word ²elthen, Aorist Active Indicative of erchomai, to come. The word ³stathenai is the Aorist Passive Infinitive tense of histēmi, [this tense, is not referring to a future event; it presents the action expressed by the verb as a completed unit with a beginning and end], to stand, also to be placed in a balance, to weigh; in the presence of others, in the midst, before judges, before members of the Sanhedrin, to cause a person or a thing to keep his or its place, be kept intact [of family, a kingdom], to escape in safety, to establish a thing, cause it to stand, to uphold or sustain the authority or force of anything, to set or place in a balance, to weigh: money to one [because in very early times before the introduction of coinage, the metals used to be weighed] continue safe and sound, stand unharmed, of quality, one who does not hesitate, does not waiver.)*

7:1 In this setting I saw four celestial messengers ¹positioned on the four corners of the earth and they restrained the four winds - so that the wind would not blow upon the earth, the sea or even a single tree. *(The perception of all earth dwellers of the time was that the planet was flat and square. So the four corners of the earth were not factual but merely to communicate a symbolic picture and principle within their perceptions - as also the idea of an underworld. See the four spheres already referenced in Genesis 1:2, and the earth being without form and empty, and darkness on the face of the deep, [abussos - LXX] and the Spirit of God moving gently on the face of the waters. Also in Psalm 135:6 Whatever the LORD pleases he does, in heaven and on earth, in the seas and the Abyss. Or in the LXX it is Psalm 134:6.*

*The word, ¹estotas is the Perfect Participle of **histemi**, to stand, also, to set or place in a balance, to weigh. Ezekiel 43:2 And behold, the glory of the God of Israel came from the east; and the sound of his coming was like the sound of many waters; and the earth shone with his glory. Matthew 24:31 and he will send out his celestial messengers with a loud trumpet call, and they will gather his blueprint likeness from the four winds, from one end of heaven to the other. The word, **eklegomai**, traditionally associated with the idea of election, has two components, **ek**, a Preposition that indicates source or origin and **lego**, meaning to communicate ideas; thus, the original blueprint-word, the **logos**; see John 1:1-3 and 12. The word becomes flesh in the fruit you eat. The many are called, [**kaleo**] but few are "chosen" **eklegomai** thus, The masses are defined by my name but few realize their origin in me. Matthew 22:14.)*

7:2 And I saw another celestial messenger ascending from the east with the rising sun - *[Every daybreak is a picture of the resurrection - coming up out of the region of the night of "the under-world".]* **he had the signet ring of the living God and cried out with a loud voice addressing the four celestial messengers who had been given the task of ¹disrupting the harmony of the earth and sea.** *(The word, ¹hadikeo from **ha**, as a negative particle and **dikeo** which speaks of that which engages two parties in likeness. Thus, with the negative it suggests a disruption of harmony. Note Revelation 7:2 **anabainonta** ascending - compare Revelation 10:1 **katabainonta**, descending.)*

7:3 Commanding them not to disrupt the harmony of the earth, sea or trees until the bond-servants of God are ¹sealed between the eyes. *(To seal between the eyes, **sphragizō** to make an inscription or impression by a seal, a signet ring; between the eyes - the focus of attention; **epi tōn metōpōn** - old word meta, ōps.)*

7:4 And I heard the number of those embossed with the impression of God's signet ring; one hundred and forty four thousand - representing the entire tribal system of Israel; they were all sealed with God's signet ring between their eyes. *(This sealing is an act of God's mercy in signifying salvation for all of Israel to see and understand what happened in the death, descent into the underworld and the resurrection of Jesus Christ, the enthroned Lamb of God. The number 12 is a symbol for totality; then it is squared and multiplied by one thousand for more emphasis The number 144,000 is a positive integer - Latin,* *integer, literally, "untouched," whole, entire, i.e. a whole number. As a reminder to his Jewish audience of the prophetic significance of their escape from slavery and how they were protected from the plagues in Egypt - so now they are protected.)*

7:5 Of the tribe of Judah twelve thousand were sealed; of the tribe of Reuben twelve thousand were sealed; of the tribe of Gad twelve thousand were sealed;

7:6 of the tribe of Asher twelve thousand were sealed; of the tribe of Naphtali twelve thousand were sealed; of the tribe of Manasseh twelve thousand were sealed;

7:7 of the tribe of Simeon twelve thousand were sealed; of the tribe of Levi twelve thousand were sealed; of the tribe of Issachar twelve thousand were sealed;

7:8 of the tribe of Zebulun twelve thousand were sealed; of the tribe of Joseph twelve thousand were sealed and of the tribe of Benjamin twelve thousand were sealed.

7:9 At this moment I saw a massive throng of people, impossible to count, standing tall and innocent - all of them [1]dressed in white with palm branches in their hands; they had [1]escaped everything that could possibly define them as a non-Jewish, Gentile world. In fact, every sphere of society was there - including the entire spectrum of people-groupings; all tribal identities with their unique language-specific dialect preferences, they were all present facing the throne and the Lamb as the people of the planet. *(Amazing how, in the previous verses of this chapter, the tribes of Israel are associated with a very specific "number", emphasizing the prophetic detail of the entire Jewish nation. But here, John sees a massive throng of people, impossible to count. In Israel there is a prophetic voice of God's intention to release the blessing of the single SEED of God's faith through Abraham and bless all the nations of the earth. "Count the stars, count the sand."*

The word [1]stolay, is the white outer garment worn by kings, priests, and persons of rank. The palm branches and the white robes are signs of the celebration of victory and joy. The Preposition [1]ek, points to source or origin; mankind was delivered out of their national, geographical and historical identities. Seven times in the book of Revelation human society is addressed in the most all-inclusive fashion, with a similar grouping of words. Revelation 5:9, here in Revelation 7:9, Revelation 10:11, Revelation 11:9, Revelation 13:7, Revelation 14:6 and Revelation 17:15. Also note Revelation 5:13 and Revelation 11:15. See Extended Notes on Israel at the end of Revelation 20.

I looked again and saw a huge crowd, too huge to count. Everyone was there—all nations and tribes, all races and languages. And they were standing, dressed in white robes and waving palm branches, standing before the throne and the Lamb. The Message)

7:10 Then I heard the masses shouting as if with one thundering voice saying, "Our salvation is secure in our God who is seated upon the throne and endorsed in the Lamb's doing."

7:11 And the multitude of celestial messengers engulfing the throne together with the elders and the four Living Beings fell on their faces before the throne and they worshiped God. *(Revelation 5:11 Then I saw wave upon wave of innumerable celestial messengers engulfing the throne and the elders and the living beings and I heard singing. It was a mass choir of multi millions. Revelation 5:12 In their full capacity they exploded in song, proclaiming in unison, "The Lamb's worth is now fully realized. Having been slain in sacrifice, the power, wealth, wisdom, strength, honor, glory, and blessing belong to the Lamb." Revelation 5:13 At that point the entire universe burst out in praise. I heard every created being in the heavenly realm and upon the earth and under the earth, and upon the ocean and everything within all these spheres, declaring to the One seated upon the throne and to the Lamb: "The most [1]articulate language, the admiration, the supreme magnificence, the might until the ages of the ages." [The word [1]eulogia, from eu, good, well done, and logos; thus polished language; such language which is artfully adapted to captivate the hearer: fair speaking, fine speeches.] Revelation 5:14 To which the four Living Beings added their endorsement and the elders fell down in silent worship.)*

7:12 They added their Amen to confirm everything declared by the masses of mankind, they then proclaimed in the most reverent adoration, *[this time voicing each of the seven attributes of their admiration of God in separate feminine articles, thus acknowledging her Majesty, the Holy Spirit]* **her [1]most eloquent language, her [2]magnificence, her [3]unveiling of wisdom's mysteries, her [4]extravagant generosity, her [5]preciousness and infinite worth, her [6]dynamic and her [7]strength are [8]located in our God, spanning across the ages of eternity.** *(The word [1]eulogia, from eu, good, well done, and logos; thus polished language; such language which is artfully adapted to captivate the hearer: fair speaking, fine speeches; the [2]doxa - in the sacred writers always of a good or favorable opinion, the admiration, the supreme magnificence; the [3]sophia, wisdom, clarity; extravagant generosity, [4]eucharistia - from eu, well and charitsomai, to give freely; the word [5]timay, speaks of honor, preciousness and worth; [6]dunamis, dynamic, power; ischus strength, ability and might. Located in God - [8]to theo hemoon - Dative - indirect object, "to"; also location "in")*

7:13 Then one of the elders asked me if I knew who these masses of people all [1]dressed in white were. *(The word [1]stolay, is the white outer garment worn by kings, priests, and persons of rank.)*

7:14 I said, "No Mister, I don't; would you please explain this to me?" He answered, "This is [1]co-raised mankind, brought out of their [2]extreme claustrophobic spaces that they were trapped in. They have [3]plunged their stained priestly garments in the blood of the Lamb and they were made white." *(The verb [1]erchomenoi is the Present Passive Participle of erchomai - to come - in the nominative case - the brought out ones. Traditionally translated the great tribulation but literally, their extreme claustrophobic spaces - [2]tes thlipseos tes megales - in the Genitive case, possession, "of"; also origin or separation, "from." The word [3]pluō is a prolonged form of an obsolete pluō, to "flow"; to "plunge", that is, launder clothing: - wash. Note, it was not their suffering that gave them their standing or their white garments - it was the suffering of the Lamb.)*

REVELATION Chapter 7

7:15 Standing free and forgiven in their redeemed innocence and union, face to face before the throne of God, they are fully engaged, day and night in their priestly service of worship in the inner sanctuary. The One seated upon the throne is their tabernacle; he shelters them with his presence.

7:16 Here there is no memory of hunger or thirst nor a scorching sun to plague them. *(Isaiah 49 is fulfilled. See Isaiah 49:6 "I will give you as a light to the nations, that my salvation may reach to the end of the earth." The tribes of Judah as a prophetic pointer to the entire population of the planet are gathered as one in worship." Isaiah 49:10 "They shall not hunger or thirst, neither scorching wind nor sun shall smite them, for he who has pity on them will lead them, and by springs of water will guide them.")*

7:17 For the little Lamb who occupies the center stage of the throne will shepherd them and lead them beside living springs of water and God shall [1]blot out every hurtful memory of the tears they have cried. *(The word, [1]exaleipho, comes from ek, out of, and aleipho, with a, as a particle of union, and liparos, to grease, to leave a stain; scars of hurtful experiences were like grease stains stored in memory.*

A similar scene is set here to mirror the historical deliverance of Israel out of slavery in the build-up to the first prophetic Passover - this time the dramatic symbolic pictures reflect on the final Passover and the slain Lamb on the throne addressing, and bringing closure and conclusion to the many ideas of judgment so deeply entrenched in Jewish consciousness. **Their stories and symbolic prophetic pictures are repeated again and again, waging war against their perceived reasonings and philosophies portrayed in their own historic priesthood and altar services.**

The number seven brings out the varied forms as well as their essential oneness; whether the "seven Spirits of God"; the "seven churches," the "seven horns" and "seven eyes" of the Lamb, the "seven seals," the "seven trumpets", and the "seven bowls.")

8:1 When he opened the seventh seal there was a solemn pause; a silence in the heavens which lasted for half an hour. *(In sharp contrast to the thundering voices of praise and adoration there is a sudden silence. As if all of heaven is holding their breath. The word silence **siōpaō** from **sigē** and **pao** to rest/pause.*

*See Isaiah 52:13 in the LXX [Septuagint], Ἰδοὺ **Idou** - Behold. συνήσει **suniesei** from suniemi, to understand; as in two rivers flowing together. [Carrying in it the idea of the Incarnation - the word made flesh - "In the Scriptures it is written about me."] Thus, he shall be full of understanding; ὁ παῖς μου ho pais mou - my boy - kai **hupsothesetai** he shall be exalted/elevated [proclaiming his resurrection.], kai doxasthesetai sphorda, and decorated with exceedingly great esteem. Note the LXX reads, **my boy** and not "servant" which is only in Masoretic Hebrew text. The Masoretic Text dates a thousand years later than the LXX. Isaiah 52:14 As many were astonished at him—his appearance was so marred, beyond human semblance, and his form beyond that of the sons of men— Isaiah 52:15 so shall he startle many nations; kings shall shut their mouths because of him; for that which has not been told them they shall see, and that which they have not heard they shall understand.*

Habakkuk 2:20 The Lord is in his temple; let all the earth be silent before his face.

There is here, and in the following verses, a strong allusion to different parts of the temple worship. The silence here refers to this fact - while the priest went in to burn incense in the holy place, all the people continued in silent prayer without till the priest returned. See Luke 1:10. The angel mentioned here appears to execute the office of priest. Adam Clarke

The symbolic significance of half an hour gives emphasis to this specific moment - Jesus often made reference to his hour when he spoke about the culmination of his mission. The silence in prayer and contemplation here was to allow the impact of the moment to reinforce and impress the awareness of the worshipper.)

8:2 And my eyes were fixed on the seven celestial messengers before the face of God and they were given seven trumpets. *(Probably the same as those called the seven Spirits which are before his throne, Revelation 1:4)*

8:3 Then another celestial messenger arrived with a golden ¹censer for frankincense and ²took charge of the ³altar in priestly fashion. Much ⁴perfume was given to him and this would be burned as a sweet smelling fragrance upon the golden altar of incense [in the Holy Place]**, before the throne** [now, unveiled within the Most Holy place - See Hebrews 9:4]**, to represent the ⁵prayers of every single saint.**

*(The word ¹**libanōtos** refers to the gum exuding from a frankincense tree; also the censer for burning the frankincense with the coals from the brazen altar of sacrifice. The verb ²**estathē** is the ingressive first Aorist Passive of **histēmi** [intransitive], "took his place." - was positioned; **epi tou** ³**thusiastēriou** - took up his priestly position over the altar.*

> This was a preparation peculiar to the day of expiation. On other days it was the custom of the priest to take fire from the brazen altar in a silver censer, but on the great Day of Atonement the high priest took the fire from the bronze altar in a

*golden censer; and when he was come down from the brazen altar in the outer court, he took **incense** from one of the priests, who brought it to him, and went with it to the golden altar of incense in the Holy place, and then, within the veil before the Ark of the Covenant in the Most Holy Place, worship before God. Sir Isaac Newton.*

*The following words are all connected to the idea of sacrifice - **thusiastērion** - the place of sacrifice - altar - from **thusia**, sacrifice, from **thuo**, to slay and burn the sacrifice; **thumiama**, the smoke or in the Greek mind, the soul of the sacrifice; **thumos** passion. All the Romansch languages derive their word for smoke, or smoking, **fumar** from **thumos**. Also the word perfume originates from the same idea. Much perfume was given him, [4]**thumiamata**, again the sweet smelling, favorable fumes from the sacrifice is implied.*

*The word translated prayer is [3]**proseuchomai**, from **pros**, face to face and **eu**, well done, good and possibly **echo**, to hold or echo - thus, face to face resonance of that which is good.)*

8:4 And thus the smoke of the fragrant perfume infused with the silent prayers of the entire community of saints, rose before God out of the hand of the priestly ministry of the celestial messenger.

8:5 Then the celestial messenger took the golden censer for frankincense and filled it with burning coals from the altar and cast it upon the earth. And the burning coals became thunder and voices and lightning shaking the earth like an earthquake. *(The altar is central in the vision of the Lamb that was slain - the triumph of the cross is unveiled, in redeeming mankind's innocence. This reminds of Isaiah 6:6 when one of the seraphs flew to me with a live coal in his hand, snatched with tongs from the altar. Then flew one of the seraphim to me, having in his hand a burning coal which he had taken with tongs from the altar. Isaiah 6:7 And he touched my mouth, and said: "Behold, this has touched your lips; your guilt is taken away, and your sin forgiven."*

*The fire from the altar is the source to all the symbolic fiery pictures of the extent of the judgment that the Lamb faced as scapegoat of the human race. In the following scenes where the seven trumpets are sounded, every known sphere of the universe is pictured: the **earth** with its green trees and fields of grass; then the **ocean** both with its hidden life within as well as the trade ships upon the seas. Then the burning star falling from heaven upon the rivers and their sources - from where their waters gush forth - [waters gushing from innermost being.] Then the sun moon and stars in the **heavenly sphere** are struck and darkness ensues upon the earth. Every external source of light is taken away in order to usher in the new day dawning within. Revelation 21:23 "The city doesn't need any sun or moon to give it light because the glory of God gave it light. The Lamb was its lamp." Even the smoke rising from the **bottomless pit** [under-world] clearly reveals that the fire from the altar had its effect there. The Lamb descended into the lowest parts of the earth when he set the captives free and led them as his trophies in his triumphant procession on high. Ephesians 4:8-10. The entire known world is addressed in the slain and risen Lamb. The old things have passed away, behold everything has become new.*

"An earthquake takes place because of fault lines - a great shifting is taking place along the fault-lines of people's thinking", says Dr. Kay Fairchild. See also Isaiah 55:9,10,11.)

8:6 And the seven celestial messengers with the trumpets got ready to blow them.

8:7 The first trumpeted and it became hail which fell on the earth like fireballs dipped in blood. And a third of the earth and a third of the trees and every green blade of grass were consumed in the fire. *(Like the plague of hail and fire in Exodus 9:24. The first four trumpets are very much like the plagues in Egypt, this one like a semitropical thunderstorm [Swete] with blood like the first plague. Exodus 7:17, Exodus 9:24. Robertson.*

As it was in Pharaoh's day, stubborn minds that were set in their perceptions had to be convinced - the 144,000 were sealed and therefore protected from harm - yet they were witnesses of the prophetic/historic fate of Pharaoh, now repeated in dramatic fashion in front of their eyes to persuade them of the prophetic picture of deliverance from slavery which was now concluded in the Lamb's death burial and resurrection to be celebrated for ages upon ages by the entire universe. Revelation 5:13.)

8:8 The second celestial messenger trumpeted and a volcanic fiery mass the size of a big mountain was flung into the sea and a third of the ocean became blood. *(Like the Nile in the first plague - Exodus 7:20.*

Mountain, in prophetic language, signifies a kingdom Jeremiah 51:25 also Zechariah 4:7 What are you, Oh great mountain? Before Zerubbabel you shall become a plain; and he shall bring forward the top stone amid shouts of 'Grace, grace to it.'"; I will stretch out my hand against you, and roll you down from the crags, and make you a burnt mountain; Revelation 17:15 And he said to me, "The waters that you saw, where the harlot is seated, are peoples and multitudes and nations and tongues.

The third part is a symbolic expression of a representative portion of the whole. As within the Triune God, the Son fully represents the Father and the Holy Spirit - so every individual member of the trinity is fully represented and reflected in the other.)

8:9 And a third of all the living creatures in the ocean died. And a third of the ships perished.

8:10 And the third celestial messenger trumpeted and a great burning star, like a lamp, fell out of heaven and it fell upon the third part of the rivers, including their sources.

8:11 And the name of the star was "Loathsomely Bitter" and a third of the waters became intoxicated and bitter and caused many to die. *(The bitter taste that sin leaves was dealt with on the cross where Jesus felt our thirst and tasted the vinegar mixed with gall. Also reminds of the prophetic Jewish custom by eating matza and bitter herbs during Passover to commemorate the conclusion of their bitter slavery. See Exodus 12:8, That same night they are to eat the meat roasted over the fire, along with bitter herbs, and bread made without yeast. They* *were to eat the whole lamb. Wormwood - ἄψινθος - Hebrew,* לענה *la`ănâh, gall bitter, associated with judgment. Compare these Scriptures, Matthew. 27:34; Psalm 69:21 They also gave me gall for food, and for my thirst they gave me vinegar to drink. With reference to Deuteronomy 29:18; Jeremiah 9:15; Jeremiah 23:15; Lam 3:15; Lam 3:19; Amos 5:7; Amos 6:12.)*

8:12 When the fourth celestial messenger blew his trumpet, one-third of the sun, the moon and the stars were struck so that there was no light for one-third of the day and one-third of the night. *(The eclipse here is only partial and relates to the ninth Egyptian plague. Exodus 10:21.)*

8:13 Then I saw an eagle fly in the heavenly sphere and heard it announce with a loud voice to the earth dwellers that three more woes were about to be revealed in the sounding of the remaining three trumpets. *(The purpose of these woes was to uncover the crisis in people's lives and lead them to **metanoia** - to see what God saw in the Lamb's triumph. Where every woe is turned into praise and rejoicing. Psalm 30:11 You have turned my mourning into dancing for me. You have removed my sackcloth, and girded me with gladness.)*

9:1 When the ¹fifth celestial messenger blew his trumpet, I saw a ²star that had fallen to earth from the sky. The star was given the key to the shaft into the fathomless depths of the Abyss. *(The ¹symbolic value of the number five is divine grace. Jesus is the bright ²Morning Star Revelation 2:28 and Revelation 22:16 I am Jesus. I sent my celestial messenger to be witness of these things to you before the churches; confirming to them that I am the Root and offspring of David, the radiant Morning Star. Also 2 Peter 1:19 For us the appearing of the Messiah is no longer a future promise but a fulfilled reality. Now it is your turn to have more than a second-hand, hearsay testimony. Take my word as one would take a lamp at night; the day is about to dawn for you in your own understanding. When the Morning Star appears, you no longer need the lamp; this will happen shortly on the horizon of your own hearts. In his death, Jesus conquered the underworld and he has the keys; no-one else does. Revelation 1:18. See Philippians 2:6-10 His being God's equal in form and likeness was official; his Sonship did not steal the limelight from his Father. Neither did his mankind distract from the deity of God. Philippians 2:7 His mission however, was not to prove his deity, but to embrace our mankind. Emptied of his reputation as God, he fully embraced our physical human form; born in our resemblance he identified himself as the servant of the human race. His love enslaved him to us.*

See Notes on **The Fallen Star is The Morning Star** *at the end of this chapter.)*

9:2 He opened the shaft of the bottomless pit, and smoke came out of the shaft like the smoke from a large ¹furnace. The smoke darkened the sun and the atmosphere. *(The smoke is evidence of the fire from the altar of worship which was lit by the coals from the brazen altar - the prophetic picture of the cross where the Lamb of God was slaughtered - Revelation 8:5. The word ¹***kaminos*** *is an old word for a smelting-furnace; Revelation 1:15, "His feet were like a brilliant bronze fashioned in a furnace." In contrast to the feet of mingled iron and clay of the image Daniel saw in Daniel 2:38. The army of God is set to swallow up the consciousness of good and evil in people's minds.*

The natural light was veiled and even the atmosphere was filled with smoke for the moment while the effect of Jesus' presence in our hell was released.

Notes on **The bottomless pit** *at the end of this chapter.)*

9:3 And locusts with the sting of scorpions came out of the smoke. *(OT imagery to remind of how God brought Israel out of slavery in Egypt to now take the slave-mindset of "Egypt" out of us. Also Joel 2. Revelation 16 - the seven vessels line up with seven of the ten plagues.)*

9:4 They were not allowed to ¹disrupt the vegetation but only target the people whose foreheads were not marked - those whose thoughts were not synced with God's thoughts about them. *(To emphasize the symbolic meaning of these apparent locusts it is clearly stated that, unlike normal grasshoppers, these do not go for vegetation, their mission was to conquer the mindset of unbelief in the people - Numbers 13:33 - "we were like grasshoppers in our own eyes." This is a dangerous and destructive mindset. Although appearing to be locusts they were armed for battle. The "hurting" is the word,* **adikeo** *which suggests a disruption - out of sync with the life of one's design - so the "army" coming out of*

REVELATION Chapter 9

*the Abyss now enforces the victory of the Lamb upon those who couldn't see or believe it before. The word **metopon** - the space between the eyes; forehead - focus.)*

9:5 They were not to kill these, but would ¹harass and test them for five months with the annoying pain of a scorpion sting. *(The word ¹**basanizō**, old verb, to test metals from **basis** - to get to the bottom of a thing; to torment. The interval from Passover to Tabernacles is five months. Where Passover is the graphic picture of total deliverance out of slavery, the Feast of Tabernacles is a reminder of a forty year, detour journey of unbelief in the wilderness where an entire generation died in unbelief by not possessing the promised land because their leaders taught them to believe a lie about themselves. See Numbers 13:33 and Joshua 2:11. Although they were rescued from slavery they remained slaves in their estimate of themselves - the typical grasshopper-mentality. Now this mindset has turned on them and becomes their own worst nightmare. Acts 26:14 And I heard a voice speaking to me, and saying in the Hebrew dialect, Saul, Saul why do you persecute Me? It is hard for you to kick against the prods.)*

9:6 This would drive them so mad that they would wish to die but there would be no escape, death was nowhere to be found. *(Their own unbelief seemed to haunt them and made them feel trapped in their own minds. Their own death would not deliver them.)*

9:7 The locusts had the appearance of trained battle horses; their faces seemed almost human and it looked like they were wearing golden crowns.

9:8 Their antennae compared to a woman's long hair and they had teeth like a lion. *(There is an Arabic proverb in which the antennae of locusts are compared to a girls' hair.)*

9:9 They wore metal armor - their wings made a fearful sound - like countless horses and chariots at full charge.

9:10 Their tails were like a scorpion's tail with its ¹sting giving them the ability to disorient people for five months. *(This reminds of Paul's conversion encounter - "it hurts to kick against the goads." Same Greek word, ¹**kentron** - also 1 Corinthians 15:55 Oh death where is your sting? Oh grave, where is your victory? 15:56 The sting of death is sin; the strength of sin is the law. [It was sin that made death so frightening and law-code guilt that gave sin its leverage. — The Message])*

9:11 Their reigning king was the celestial shepherd-messenger of the bottomless pit; his name in Hebrew was ¹Abaddon and in Greek, Apollyon - the One who breaks the bonds. *(¹Abaddon אבדון from **abad**, to wander away, - we all like sheep have gone astray. He found us and delivered us from our abandonment. He left no stone unturned in seeking and finding every single lost sheep. He went into the most extreme depths of our lost-ness and hell. He is called the Searcher of those who have wandered away. See 2 Corinthians 2:15, This parade of victory is a public announcement of the defeat of the religious systems and structures based on the law of works. Just like it is in any public game where the victory celebration of the winning team is an embarrassment for the losing team. The death of evil is announced in resurrection life. The word, **apollumi**, is derived from **apo**, away from, and **luo**, to loosen, to undo, to dissolve. The message we communicate* *is a fragrance with an immediate association; to darkness, it is the smell of doom [the death of death] See also my comment on John 3:16. Also 1 John 3:8, Sin's source is a fallen mindset, from the beginning. For this purpose the son of God was revealed. His mission was to undo [apollumi] the works of the Devil. The word, **diabolos**, from **dia**, because of and **ballo**, to cast down. Isaiah 54:16)*

9:12 This was the conclusion of the first of three painfully powerful initiatives to persuade those whose thoughts were not sealed and in sync with God's belief in them. Two more were on their way. *(Revelation 11:14)*

9:13 Then the sixth celestial messenger blew his trumpet and I heard what seemed like one voice proceeding out of the four horns of the golden altar before the face of God. *(The altar of incense positioned before the now, torn veil of the most holy place between the table of the bread and the golden lampstand with the blossoming almonds.)*

9:14 The voice from the four horns of the altar instructed the sixth celestial messenger to release the four messengers from their confinement to the great Euphrates river. *(The number four represents the entire universe - the so-called four "corners" of the earth, the earth itself, the oceans, the under-world and then the heavenly sky-dimension. The meaning of the Euphrates is sweet water; the good and abounding river.)*

9:15 And the four celestial messengers were released from their confinement and time of preparation to bring to a conclusion the death of one third of mankind. This all pointed to the specific hour which was prophetically contained in the Jewish calendar. Zooming out into their holy days, months and years. *(Every annual prophetic picture in their feasts, repeated on a monthly basis in the new moons, then on a weekly basis in every Sabbath, all culminated in the hour of the Lord. The only relevant death that contains and represents every other death was the one where Jesus died mankind's death - 2 Corinthians 5:14 / Hebrews 9:28.)*

9:16 And I heard the number of the armies of the cavalry which amounted to two myriads of myriads which is two hundred million horsemen. *(This is an immense and unparalleled number of horsemen. Ten thousand x ten thousand is one hundred million; consequently the number here referred to would be 200 million. The Japanese also have a highest value of ten thousand and their next highest would be ten thousand times ten thousand which is a hundred million. Countless - 2 myriads - literally ten thousands times ten thousands and thousands of thousands. The largest number named in Ancient Greek was the myriad-myriad [written MM] or hundred million. In his Sand Reckoner, Archimedes of Syracuse used this quantity as the basis for a numeration system of large powers of ten, which he used to count grains of sand. According to PIE, the etymology of the word myriad has been variously connected to meu- "damp" in reference to the waves of the sea and to Greek myrmex (μύρμηξ, "ant") in reference to their swarms. Proto-Indo-European (PIE) is the linguistic reconstruction of the common ancestor of the Indo-European languages, the most widely spoken language family in the world.)*

9:17 In my vision of the unparalleled number of horsemen and their horses, they appeared to be engulfed as if with breastplates of fire. It looked like the deep blue color of a [1]hyacinth flower or a jacinth gem stone or the

REVELATION Chapter 9

blue flame of ²burning sulphur and the horses had heads of lions. Fire, smoke and sulphur issued from their mouths. *(In the Greek mind, the Hyacinth flower speaks of resurrection. Vincent writes in his word studies, ¹Ὑάκινθος - hyacinth is the name of a flower and also of a precious stone. The noun occurs only in Revelation 21:20, and the adjective only here. According to classical Greek mythology, the flower sprang up from the blood of Hyacinthus, a beautiful Spartan youth, who was accidentally killed during a game of quoits. [When Hyacinth died, Apollo did not allow Hades to claim the youth; rather, he made a flower, the hyacinth, spring up from his spilled blood. Hyacinth was the tutelary deity of one of the principal Spartan festivals, the Hyacinthia, held every summer. The festival lasted three days, one day of mourning for the death of Hyacinth, and the last two celebrating his rebirth as Apollo Hyakinthios. - Wikipedia] It was thought by some that the letters AI, AI, ai ai - the exclamation of woe, could be traced on the petals, while others discovered the letter Υ, the initial letter of Ὑάκινθος. The story of the slaying of Hyacinthus is told by Ovid.*

"Lo, the blood

Which, on the ground outpoured, had stained the sod,

Is blood no more. Brighter than Tyrian dye,

Like to the lily's shape a flower appears,

Purple in hue as that is silvery white.

Nor yet does such memorial content

Phoebus Apollo at whose word it rose.

Upon its leaves he writes his own laments,

And on the flower forever stands inscribed

AI, AI - ai ai"

"Metamorphoses," x., 175 sqq.

²θειώδεις *theiōdēs, from **theios** and **eidos**, from **theion** godlike [neuter as noun, divinity]: - divine, godhead. Also the word for sulphur; a yellow inflammable mineral substance found in quantities on the shores of the Dead Sea. This was also known as divine incense, because burning brimstone was regarded as having power to purify, and to ward off disease. Its medicinal values are well known even today. See notes on **the lake of fire** at the end of Revelation 19.)*

9:18 These three plagues proceeding from their mouths were what caused the third of humans to die, by the fire, and by the smoke, and by the brimstone coming out of their mouths.

9:19 Their inherent authority was located in their mouths and also in their tails which looked just like serpents, complete with heads. If the bite wasn't deadly enough they had a venomous back-up in the tail. *(The word often translated, authority is the word **exousia** from **ek**, denoting origin and **eimi**, I am - thus the seat of inherent I-am-ness. The horses had heads like lions - a lion's tail has a fluff of hair at the end which could make the tail look like a serpent. The serpent was the symbol of wisdom. These visions were all connected* *with the heavenly revelation of the lion of Judah who conquered mankind's crisis or judgment as the Lamb of God. Only a third of mankind was struck - the man Jesus the Christ represents the third party of the Triune God who dies mankind's death in his incarnate human body - the two thirds of mankind, symbolizing the majority initially not responding to the revelation of the Lamb in co-knowing their salvation unveiled in the genius of God.)*

9:20 The death of a third of the human race seemed to have had no effect on the rest of the peoples - they continued to create [1]their own gods and [2]demons of their imagination with any material they could afford, be it gold, silver, bronze, stone or wood - it didn't matter to them that these images couldn't see or hear or move. *(See Deuteronomy 32:17 "They sacrificed to demons which were no gods, to gods they had never known, to new gods that had come in of late, whom your fathers had never dreaded. Deuteronomy 32:18 You were unmindful of the Rock that begot you, and you forgot the God who gave you birth."*

Worshipping ideas of your own imagination and invention, is the fruit of the wrong Tree. The thought that I'm not God's idea. The extreme graphic visions of judgment portrayed in the book of Revelation deals with layer after layer of mankind's hardened hearts and stubborn resistance to see the completeness of their redemption from the lies they believed about themselves and God. In this specific account of the 200 million strong cavalry on a mission to slay the human race, there seems to be no chance for anyone to escape. Yet two thirds of mankind remains totally indifferent to the judgment that fell on their fellows. [1]They seem to be inseparably attached to worshipping a distorted image of themselves - which is what idolatry is all about - an image of their own imagination, projecting their ideas of the g.o.d. of their own making - no mind shift taking place - no understanding that their own worst fears of judgment was thoroughly dealt with in the crucified Lamb of God who died their death and went into their hell and was gloriously raised into the embrace of the Father of the human race.)

9:21 Neither was there any change in their views on murder, witchcraft, adultery or stealing. *(There is no alternate salvation. Mankind's philosophies and their willpower-driven, performance and fear-based life styles will never suffice. Even their witnessing every form of judgment that their law-based systems can imagine, cannot successfully convert their minds or behavior. See Isaiah 55:9,10 Your behavior reflects the fact that your thoughts contradict God's thoughts. The Incarnation will unveil how my Word saturates all flesh; just like the rain and the snow descend from heaven and saturate the soil, making it bring forth and sprout, so shall my Word be.)*

Revelation Chapter 9 Extended Notes:
The "Fallen Star" is The bright Morning Star
The Abyss
Idols and Demons

THE FALLEN STAR IS HE BRIGHT MORNING STAR - REV 9

The "Fallen Star" is The bright Morning Star

Revelation 9:1 When the [1]fifth celestial messenger blew his trumpet, I saw a [2]star that had fallen to earth from the sky. The star was given the key to the shaft into the fathomless depths of the Abyss. *(The [1]symbolic value of the number five is divine grace. Jesus is the bright [2]Morning Star Revelation 2:28 and Revelation 22:16 I am Jesus. I sent my celestial messenger to bear witness of these things to you before the churches; confirming to them that I am the Root and offspring of David, the radiant Morning Star. Also 2 Peter 1:1:19 For us the appearing of the Messiah is no longer a future promise but a fulfilled reality. Now it is your turn to have more than a second-hand, hearsay testimony. Take my word as one would take a lamp at night; the day is about to dawn for you in your own understanding. When the Morning Star appears, you no longer need the lamp; this will happen shortly on the horizon of your own hearts.*

In his death, Jesus conquered the underworld and he has the keys; no-one else does. Revelation 1:18. See Philippians 2:6-10 His being God's equal in form and likeness was official; his Sonship did not steal the limelight from his Father. Neither did his mankind distract from the deity of God. Philippians 2:7 His mission however, was not to prove his deity, but to embrace our mankind. Emptied of his reputation as God, he fully embraced our physical human form; born in our resemblance he identified himself as the servant of the human race. His love enslaved him to us. Philippians 2:8 And so we have the drama of the cross in context: the man Jesus Christ who is fully God, becomes fully man to the extent of willingly dying mankind's death at the hands of his own creation. He embraced the curse and shame of the lowest kind in dying a criminal's death. (Thus through the doorway of mankind's death he descended into our hellish darkness.) Philippians 2:9 From this place of utter humiliation, God exalted him to the highest rank. God graced Jesus with a Name that is far above every other name. The name of Jesus endorses his mission as fully accomplished. He is the Savior of the world. Titus 2:1. Philippians 2:10 What his name unveils will persuade every creature of their redemption. Every knee in heaven and upon the earth and under the earth shall bow in spontaneous worship. Ephesians 1:20 Do you want to measure the mind and muscle of God? Consider the force which he unleashed in Jesus Christ when he raised him from the dead and forever seated him enthroned as his executive authority in the realm of the heavens. Jesus is God's right hand of power. He was raised up from the deepest dungeons of human despair to the highest region of heavenly bliss. [See Ephesians 2:5,6 & 4:8,9] Ephesians 1:21 Infinitely above all the combined forces of rule, authority, dominion or governments; he is ranked superior to any name that could ever be given to anyone of this age or any age still to come in the eternal future.

Numbers 24:17 I see him, but not here and now. I perceive him, but far in the distant future. A star will rise from Jacob; a scepter will emerge from Israel. It will crush the foreheads of Moab - [mindsets] Also Isaiah 9:2-4 For the yoke of his burden, and the staff for his shoulder, the rod of his oppressor, thou hast broken **as on the day of Midian.** *Remember Gideon's strategy of hiding lamps in clay jars when they defeated the mighty Midians who out-numbered them by far. Bonsai mindsets have trapped the nations of the world for centuries. But this is the day* *where the mystery that was hidden in clay pots for ages and generations shall be revealed. Christ in the nations is the hope and desire of the nations.*

Revelation 22:16 I am Jesus. I sent my celestial messenger to bear witness of these things to you before the churches; confirming to them that I am the Root and offspring of David, the radiant Morning Star. *(Revelation 5:5 Then one of the elders said unto me, "You need not weep anymore. Look. The Lion has conquered. He who is of the tribe of Judah,* **the root of David.** *His triumph qualifies him to open the scroll and its seven seals." Revelation 5:6 So I looked to see the Lion, and there, as if fused into one with the throne and in unison with the four living beings, taking center stage in the midst of the elders, I saw a little Lamb, alive and standing even though it seemed to have been violently butchered in sacrifice. It had seven horns and seven eyes which are the seven Spirits of God having been sent out to accomplish his bidding in all the earth.*

*In Jesus, the prophetic word, which shone all along like a lamp in the night, became the radiant Morning Star, rising in our hearts, announcing the full unveiling of the day. When the Morning Star [**phōsphoros**] appears, you no longer need the lamp; this will happen shortly on the horizon of your own hearts. In his death Jesus conquered the underworld and he has the keys; no-one else does. Revelation 1:17 Observing all this I fell at his feet like a dead man; then he laid his right hand on me and said, "Do not be afraid. I am the origin and conclusion of all things. Revelation 1:18 And the Living One; I died and now, see, here I am alive unto the ages of the ages and I have the keys wherewith I have disengaged the gates of Hades and Death. See Isaiah 14:12,* הילל *heilel, means "shining one" In the Greek,* **phōsphoros** *- bearer of light - LXX Septuagint. Which translates, Lucifer in Latin. Here, in Isaiah 14, Babylon's rule is compared to the bright morning star - ushering in the rule of its day - which is the counterfeit image - Isaiah 14:14 "I will make myself like the Most High." The fallen mindset-system is based on the idea that we are not image bearers of God - the Ophis lie in Genesis 5 - we have to eat the fruit of the tree of the knowledge of good and evil [**poneros** - hardships labor and annoyances] in order to become like God.*

The incarnate Jesus, the only true Morning Star descended into the deepest pits of mankind's hellish darkness and despair in their lost identity on his rescue mission to lead us out as God's trophies in his triumphant procession on high. Ephesians 4:8-10. See Ephesians 2:5,6. Also, Revelation 12:7-10 and Revelation 17:8,14.)

THE ABYSS - REV 9

The Abyss

Revelation 9:1 When the [1]fifth celestial messenger blew his trumpet, I saw a [2]star that had fallen to earth from the sky. The star was given the key to the shaft into the fathomless depths of the Abyss.

([1] The [1]symbolic value of the number five is divine grace.

[2] Jesus is the bright [2]Morning Star. Revelation 2:28 and Revelation 22:16, "I am Jesus, I sent my celestial messenger to bear witness of these things to you before the churches; confirming to them that I am the Root and offspring of David; I am the radiant Morning Star.

*Also **2 Peter 1:1:19**, For us the appearing of the Messiah is no longer a future promise but a fulfilled reality. Now it is your turn to have more than a second-hand, hearsay testimony. Take my word as one would take a lamp at night; the day is about to dawn for you in your own understanding.*

When the Morning Star appears, you no longer need the lamp; this will happen shortly on the horizon of your own hearts.

In his death, Jesus conquered the underworld and he has the keys; no-one else does. Revelation 1:18.

> ***Philippians 2:6*** *His being God's equal in form and likeness was official; his Sonship did not steal the limelight from his Father. Neither did his mankind distract from the deity of God.*
>
> ***Philippians 2:7*** *His mission however, was not to prove his deity, but to embrace our mankind. Emptied of his reputation as God, he fully embraced our physical human form; born in our resemblance he identified himself as the servant of the human race. His love enslaved him to us.*
>
> ***Philippians 2:8*** *And so we have the drama of the cross in context: the man Jesus Christ who is fully God, becomes fully man to the extent of willingly dying mankind's death at the hands of his own creation. He embraced the curse and shame of the lowest kind in dying a criminal's death. (Thus, through the doorway of mankind's death, he descended into our hellish darkness. Revelation 9:1 and Ephesians 4:8-10.)*
>
> ***Philippians 2:9*** *From this place of utter humiliation, God exalted him to the highest rank. God graced Jesus with a Name that is far above every other name. (Ephesians 1:20 Do you want to measure the mind and muscle of God? Consider the force which he unleashed in Jesus Christ when he raised him from the dead and forever seated him enthroned as his executive authority in the realm of the heavens. Jesus is God's right hand of power. He was raised up from the deepest dungeons of human despair to the highest region of heavenly bliss. [See Ephesians 2:5,6 & 4:8,9]*
>
> *Ephesians 1:21 Infinitely above all the combined forces of rule, authority, dominion or governments; he is ranked superior to any name that could ever be given to anyone of this age or any age still to come in the eternal future. The name of Jesus endorses his mission as fully accomplished. He is the Savior of the world.*
>
> *Titus 2:11 The grace of God shines as bright as day making the salvation of mankind undeniably visible. See also Ephesians 3:15, Every family in heaven and on earth originates in him; his is mankind's family name and he remains the authentic identity of every nation.)*
>
> ***Philippians 2:10*** *What his name unveils will persuade every creature of their redemption. Every knee in heaven and upon the earth and under the earth shall bow in*

THE ABYSS - REV 9

spontaneous worship. (See Isaiah 45:23 "My own life is the guarantee of my conviction, says the Lord, every knee shall freely bow to me in worship, and every tongue shall spontaneously speak from the same God-inspired source.")

Philippians 2:11 *Also every tongue will voice and resonate the same devotion to his unquestionable Lordship as the Redeemer of life. Jesus Christ has glorified God as the Father of creation.*

This is the ultimate conclusion of the Father's intent.)

Revelation 9:2 He opened the shaft of the bottomless pit, and smoke came out of the shaft like the smoke from a large ¹furnace. The smoke darkened the sun and the atmosphere. *(The smoke is evidence of the fire from the altar of worship which was lit by the coals from the brazen altar - the cross where the Lamb of God was slaughtered - Revelation 8:5. The word ¹**kaminos** is an old word for a smelting-furnace; Revelation 1:15, "His feet were like a brilliant bronze fashioned in a furnace." In contrast to the feet of mingled iron and clay of the image Daniel saw in Daniel 2:38. The army of God is set to swallow up the consciousness of good and evil in people's minds.*

The natural light was veiled and even the atmosphere was filled with smoke for the moment while the effect of Jesus' presence in our hell was released.)

Revelation 11:7 In the conclusion of their testimony the "Beast" shall ascend out of the Abyss and shall overcome the two witnesses and kill them in battle. *(Jesus' death seemed an initial defeat to the prophetic purpose and significance sustained in the law and the Prophets.)*

Revelation 11:8 And their dead bodies shall lie in the street of the great city which spiritually represents Sodom and Egypt where our Lord was crucified. *(Clearly the city of Jerusalem is implicated here. The future Bride-city, the new Jerusalem [Revelation 21:2] was just like Sodom and Egypt during the rule of the Prostitute/Beast of Babylon and in the genius of God's wisdom, their murder of Jesus became the salvation of the entire human race.)*

Revelation 11:9 And those [*religious institutions*] **representing all the peoples in their various groupings, their tribes and cultures and languages of all the multitudes of the nations shall gaze upon the dead bodies of the two witnesses for three and a half days and they will not allow their bodies to be buried.**

Revelation 11:10 And these earth dwellers [*earth-ruled mindsets*] **shall rejoice over them with great jubilation celebrating their deliverance from these two prophetic voices who challenged and frustrated their religious indulgences and beliefs. They will even send gifts to one another celebrating their apparent victory.**

Revelation 11:11 With the eyes of all earth dwellers fixed upon them for three and a half days, suddenly, Spirit of life issuing out of God entered them and they stood upon their feet and great awe struck the earth dwellers as they beheld these things. *(In the resurrection of Jesus the prophetic significance of Jewish Scripture, represented by Moses and Elijah, is powerfully endorsed.)*

THE ABYSS - REV 9

Revelation 20:1 And I witnessed a celestial messenger descending out of the heavenly sphere and he had the key of the bottomless Abyss and a great chain over his hand. *(Ephesians 4:8, He who ascended in also he who descended into the lowest parts of the earth. Ephesians 4:9 The fact that he ascended confirms his victorious descent into the deepest pits of human despair.)*

Revelation 20:2 And he overpowered the Dragon, in its every disguise as the old Serpent in the garden in Genesis, also called the Devil, or going under the name, Satan, and chained him up for a thousand years. *(From David to Jesus is a thousand years.* **Revelation 3:7 I hold the key of David** *as prophesied in* **Isaiah 22:22.** *Yes, I unlock the mysteries of the heavenly dimension and no one can shut the door. And I lock the entrance and none [of the old mindsets] can access it.* **The links in the chain,** *are the prophetic words in the mouth of David and the Prophets till John the Baptist. These words already chained Satanas to the irreversible intention of God. Matthew 12:29 Or how can one enter a strong man's house and plunder his goods, unless he first binds the strong man? Then indeed he may plunder his house. See John 5:28 Do not be alarmed by this, but the hour is coming when those in the graves will hear his voice. [No-one who ever lived will escape the extent of his righteous judgment. Those who have forgotten who they are will hear his incarnate voice. The word for grave, mnēmeion, memory, suggests a remembrance - to bring something from memory into the here and now! Like David prophecies in Psalm 22 when he sees the cross-crisis [The Greek word ²**krisis**, means the 'decisive moment' or, turning point] a thousand years before it happens. His conclusion in verse 27 sums up the triumph of God's resolve. "All the ends of the earth shall remember and turn to the LORD; and all the families of the nations shall worship before him." See 1 Corinthians 15:21,22 The same mankind who died in a man was raised again in a man. In Adam all died; in Christ all are made alive.]*

Thus, in **prophetic language**, *every definition of the Satanas-system is already chained by the prophetic significance in Scripture recorded in the Psalm and the Prophets. The Spirit of Christ within them pointed to and concluded in the cross and resurrection of Jesus Christ. His death was the doorway into the very domain wherein mankind was held captive, to be freed and led out triumphantly as the Lamb's trophies. In* **symbolic language**, *the effect of Jesus' victory is compared to a thousand years. Against the very brief 3 days of his cross, descent into hell and resurrection, on the one hand as well as the very "brief" time of the Devil's apparent release on the planet.* **See Extended Notes on The Thousand Years at the end of chapter 20.**)

Job 11:7 "Do you think you can explain the mystery of God? Do you think you can diagram God Almighty?

Job 11:8 God is far higher than you can imagine, far deeper than the depths of Sheol,

Job 11:9 Stretching farther than earth's horizons, far wider than the endless ocean.

Job 26:5 "The souls of the dead tremble beneath the water, and so do the creatures living there.

Job 26:6 Sheol is naked in God's presence, and Abaddon has no clothing.

Job 26:7 He stretches out his heavens over empty space. He hangs the earth on nothing whatsoever.

Job 28:22 Abaddon and Death say, 'We have heard a rumor of it with our ears.'

Job 31:12 for that would be a fire which consumes unto Abaddon, and it would burn to the root all my increase.

Proverbs 15:11 Sheol and Abaddon lie open before the LORD how much more the hearts of men.

Genesis 1:1 In the beginning God created the heavens and the earth;

Genesis 1:2 and the earth being without form and empty, and darkness on the face of the deep, *[abussos]* and the Spirit of God moving gently on the face of the waters. *(The word ἄβυσσος abussos - Abyss, the fathomless Deep.)*

Psalm 134:6 Whatever the LORD pleases he does, in heaven and on earth, in the seas and the abyss.

Romans 10:5 Moses is the voice of the law; he says that a person's life is only justified in their doing what the law requires.

Romans 10:6 Faith finds its voice in something much closer to a person than their most disciplined efforts to obey the law. Faith announces that the Messiah is no longer a distant promise; neither is he reduced to a mere historic hero. He is mankind's righteousness now. The revelation of what God accomplished in Christ, births a new conversation. The old type of guess-talk has become totally irrelevant; Christ is not hiding somewhere in the realm of heaven as a future hope; so, to continue to say, "Who will ascend into heaven, to bring Christ down", makes no sense at all. *(The nearness of the Word in incarnation-language is the new conversation. The word has become flesh, so that all flesh may witness the glory of God, reflected in the radiance of their own illuminated understanding.)*

Romans 10:7 Faith-conversation understands the resurrection-revelation *(and mankind's co-inclusion in it. Hosea 6:2).* The Messiah is not roaming around somewhere in the region of the dead. Someone asks, "Oh, but what about the pit? Where does the abyss fit into this? Who will descend into the abyss to bring Christ back from the dead?" This revelation takes the abyss out of the equation. *(Those who deny the resurrection of Jesus would wish they could send someone down there and confirm their doubts, and bring back final proof that Jesus was not the Messiah. Faith announces a righteousness that reveals that mankind has indeed been co-raised together with Christ. See Ephesians 4:8 Scripture confirms that he arrested every possible threat that held mankind hostage. ["he took captivity captive"] And in his resurrection, he led us as trophies in his triumphant procession on high. Consider the genius of God, in the incarnate Christ, he repossessed what belonged to us by design, in human form; this is his grace-gift to us. Ephesians 4:9 The fact that he ascended confirms his victorious descent into the deepest pits of human despair. See Luke 9:27 You don't have to wait till you're dead to see the kingdom of God; some of you standing here*

THE ABYSS - REV 9

*with me right now, are about to dramatically witness the kingdom of God with your own eyes. [The word, ὁράω **horaoo**, to stare; to gaze with wonder; to encounter; to see for yourselves. Then, in the next verse, [Luke 9:28], Peter James and John join Jesus in prayer on the mountain, where his appearance is spectacularly changed by the radiance of God's glory bursting through his skin; even his clothes became dazzling white like light. Then, the voice of his Father confirms that his beloved son is the conclusion of the conversation represented in both Moses, [the law] and Elijah, [the prophets] - "Hear him." - Jesus is the conversation of God - he is the Logos - See John 1:1,2,5,9 To go back to the very beginning, is to find the Word already present there; face to face with God. The Word is I am; God's eloquence echoes and concludes in him. The Word equals God. The beginning mirrors the Word face to face with God. [Nothing that is witnessed in the Word distracts from who God is. "If you have seen me, you have seen the Father."] The darkness was pierced and could not comprehend or diminish this light. A new day for mankind has come. The authentic light of life that illuminates everyone was about to dawn in the world. At the end of his life Peter reminds us that, 2 Peter 1:16 We are not con-artists, fabricating fictions and fables to add weight to our account of his majestic appearance; with our own eyes we witnessed the powerful display of the illuminate presence of Jesus the Master of the Christ-life. 2 Peter 1:17 He was spectacularly endorsed by God the Father in the highest honor and glory. God's majestic voice announced, "This is the Son of my delight; he completely pleases me." 2 Peter 1:18 For John, James, and I the prophetic word is fulfilled beyond doubt; we heard this voice loud and clear from the heavenly realm while we were with Jesus in that sacred moment on the mountain. 2 Peter 1:19 For us the appearing of the Messiah is no longer a future promise but a fulfilled reality. Now it is your turn to have more than a second-hand, hearsay testimony. Take my word as one would take a lamp at night; the day is about to dawn within you, in your own understanding. When the Morning Star appears, you no longer need the lamp; this will happen shortly on the horizon of your own hearts. 2 Peter 1:20 It is most important to understand that the prophetic word recorded in Scripture does not need our interpretation or opinion to make it valid. 2 Peter 1:21 The holy men who first spoke these words of old did not invent these thoughts, they simply voiced God's oracles as they were individually inspired by the Holy Spirit.)*

Revelation 5:13 At that point the entire universe burst out in praise. I heard every created being in the heavenly realm and upon the earth and under the earth, and upon the ocean and everything within all these spheres, declaring to the One seated upon the throne and to the Lamb: "The most articulate language, the admiration, the supreme magnificence, the might until the ages of the ages."

IDOLS AND DEMONS OF MAN'S IMAGINATION - REV 9

Idols and Demons

Revelation 9:16 And I heard the number of the armies of the cavalry which amounted to two myriads of myriads which is two hundred million horsemen. *(The extreme graphic visions of judgment portrayed in the book of Revelation deals with layer after layer of mankind's hardened and stubborn resistance to see the completeness of their redemption from the lies they believed about themselves and God. In this specific account of the 200 million strong cavalry on a mission to slay the human race, there seems to be no chance for anyone to escape. Yet two thirds of mankind remains totally indifferent to the judgment that fell on their fellows. They seem to be inseparably attached to worshipping a distorted image of themselves - which is what idolatry is all about - an image of their own imagination, projecting their ideas of the g.o.d. of their own making - no mind shift taking place - no understanding that their own worst fears of judgment was thoroughly dealt with in the crucified Lamb of God who died their death and went into their hell and was gloriously raised into the embrace of the Father of the human race.)*

Revelation 9:20 The death of a third of the human race seemed to have had no effect on the rest of the peoples - they continued to create their own gods and demons of their imagination with any material they could afford whether it be gold, silver, bronze, stone or wood - it didn't matter to them that these images couldn't see or hear or move. *(Daniel 5:23 You have praised the gods of silver and gold, of bronze, iron, wood, and stone, which do not see or hear or know, but the God in whose hand is your breath, and whose are all your ways, you have not honored.)*

See Paul's discourse at the Areopagus, **Acts 17:23 For as I passed along, and observed the objects of your worship, I found also an altar with this inscription, 'To an unknown god.' Whom therefore you worship as unknown, him I proclaim to you.**

Acts 17:24 The God who made the world and everything in it, being Lord of heaven and earth, does not live in shrines made by man,

Acts 17:25 nor is he served by human hands, as though he needed anything, since he himself gives to all men life and breath and everything.

Acts 17:26 And he made from one every nation of men to live on all the face of the earth, having determined allotted periods and the boundaries of their habitation,

Acts 17:27 that they should seek God, in the hope that they might feel after him and find him. Yet he is not far from each one of us;

Acts 17:28 for 'In him we live and move and have our being', as even some of your poets have said; 'For we are indeed his offspring.'

Acts 17:29 Being then God's offspring, we ought not to think that the Deity is like gold, or silver, or stone, a representation by the art and imagination of man. *(Paul reminds them of their own ancient writings and he quotes two of their well known philosophers: in 600BC Epimenedes wrote a song saying, "We live and move and have our being in God" and Aratus wrote in 300BC that we are indeed the offspring of God. Paul then announces to them* *that the God whom they worship in ignorance is not far from each one of us. He is not more Immanuel to the Jew than what he is Immanuel to the Gentile. Then, in the context of his Jewish background and personal encounter with Jesus Christ Paul declares to them the Good News of mankind's redeemed innocence. "God has overlooked the times of ignorance and now is calling all of mankind everywhere to a radical mind-shift since he has prophetically fixed a day on which he would judge the world in righteousness by a man whom he has appointed, and of this [righteous judgment] he has given proof to all mankind by raising him from the dead." In Paul's understanding, the resurrection of Jesus from the dead includes mankind's co-resurrection and seals their acquittal and redeemed innocence.)*

Psalm 135:15 The idols of the nations are silver and gold, the work of men's hands;

Psalm 135:16 they have mouths, but they say nothing; they have eyes, but they see nothing;

Psalm 135:17 they have ears, but they hear nothing; yea, there is no breath in their mouths.

Psalm 135:18 Those who make them are like them, everyone who is trusting in them.

*According to these statements, demons too are the invention and idea of man's own making. The word translated demon, **daimōn**; from **daiō**, means to distribute fortunes. The Greeks gave the word **daímōn** the same meaning as god. What they meant by the word; however, is still a conjecture. They may have related a demon with **daemmonas**, knowing or being experienced in a thing, or they may have derived the word from **daíomai**, meaning to assign or award one's lot in life [**diaítētai kai dioikemtai tōn ánthrōpōn**], the arbitrators or umpires and governors of mankind. They conceived of them as those who ruled and directed human affairs, not as a personality, but primarily as a destructive power. Thus they called the happy or lucky person **eudaímōn**, one who is favored by this divine power. The adjective, **daimónios**, was used for one who demonstrated power irrespective of whether it was saving or destructive. The Tragic Poets use **daímōn** to denote fortune or fate, frequently bad fortune, but also good fortune if the context represented it as such. Thus, **daímōn** is associated with the idea of a gloomy and sad destiny independent of a person, coming upon and prevailing over them. Consequently, **daímōn** and **túchē**, luck, are often combined, and the doctrine of demons developed into signifying either a beneficent or evil power in the lives of people. — Zodhiates Complete Word Study Lexicon)*

Isaiah 40:18 To whom then will you liken God, or what likeness compares with him?

Isaiah 40:19 The idol. A workman casts it, and a goldsmith overlays it with gold, and casts for it silver chains.

Isaiah 40:20 He who is impoverished chooses for an offering wood that will not rot; he seeks out a skilful craftsman to set up an image that will not move.

Isaiah 40:21 Have you not known? Have you not heard? Has it not been told you from the beginning?. Genesis 1:26,27.

Revelation 2:20 It disturbs me that you accommodate the typical Jezebel influence, a self-appointed Prophetess who teaches and seduces my [1]devoted friends into participating in an [2]idolatrous sacrificial system by eating food offered to [3]idols and fornicating with her foreign ideas about God. *(The word [1]doulos, bond-servant or slave; also a devoted friend, from deo, to be bound to another in friendship or marriage. The word [2]eidōlothuton, from eidolon and thuo, to slay in sacrifice. The word [3]eidolon where we get the word idol from means image or likeness - this is the theme of the Bible and redemption; the image and likeness of God revealed and redeemed in human form.* **Idolatry is a projection of an image of one's own making.** *Idolatry is the crux of religion - it is an expensive business since your idol is like a slot machine at the casino. It remains hungry and it is wired to bite and bankrupt you.)*

Revelation 13:14 Deceiving the earth-dwellers, dazzling them with signs, whilst operating like a puppet on a string under the watchful eye of the Beast. The instruction was for the earth-dwellers to make an [1]idol-image of the "lamb" who was slain with a [1]knife and then revived again. *(The word [1]eikon means image or likeness - this is the theme of the Bible and Redemption; the image and likeness of God revealed and redeemed in human form. Idolatry is a projection of an image of one's own making. Idolatry is the crux of religion - it is an expensive business since your idol is like a slot machine at the casino. It remains hungry and it is wired to bite and bankrupt you. The word, **machaira** is used for a large knife, used for killing animals typically in the slaying of a sacrifice. Religion has a life of its own - the idea was that since the Dragon has lost its accusation against the human race in the heavenlies, [Revelation 12:8,9,10] it now had to find a pseudo, make-belief future existence in the icons of man's imagination.)*

1 John 5:19 We know that we have our origin in God; yet the whole world [1]lies trapped in the blindfold-mode of a lost identity; intoxicated by the poneros system of a futile mentality of hardships labors and annoyances. *(The word [1]keimai means to lie prostrate, outstretched; buried.)*

1 John 5:20 This is what has become distinctly clear to us: the [1]coming of the Son of God is God's mission accomplished. He is the incarnate Christ. The moment all of Scripture pointed to has arrived. The Son is [1]present. In him God has given us the greatest gift, [2]a mind whereby we may know him who is true; and in the same knowing, to find ourselves there in him who is true. Mankind is fully included and located in him, in his Son Jesus Christ; this means that whatever Jesus is as Son, we are. This is the true God; this is the life of the ages. *(The word [1]heko means to have come, to have arrived, to be present. John uses the word [2]dianoian; deep thought; with dia relating to the means by which we may know; a mind to know; compare metanoia, to know together with; an entwining of thought; the mind of Christ.*

Jesus said, you will know the truth as it is unveiled in me, and that will set you free.

The culmination of the gospel according to John is summed up in these verses: John 14:20 "In that day you will know that we are in seamless union with one another.

IDOLS AND DEMONS OF MAN'S IMAGINATION - REV 9

I am in my Father, you are in me and I am in you." Also 1 John 2:7 & 8, "what is true of him, is equally true of us. 1 John 4:17 "As he is, so are we in this world. Our lives are mirrored in him" as well as here in 1 John 5:20)

1 John 5:21 This defeats every image of our imagination that could possibly compete with the authentic likeness of our design. Darling children, distance yourselves from every substitute image, which is what idolatry is all about. *(The word [1]eidolon, often translated idol, refers to image or likeness.)*

In the symbolic language of the book of Revelation, the judgment of the Dragon, the Beast and the Whore; the counterfeit Trinity, is not a judgment against an entity, but against a corrupt mindset-system. A virus doesn't have a life of its own - it needs a host.

Microbiology Professor, Vincent Racaniello writes, "Life is 'an organismic state characterized by capacity for metabolism, growth, reaction to stimuli, and reproduction.' Viruses are not living things. Viruses are complicated assemblies of molecules, including proteins, nucleic acids, lipids, and carbohydrates, but on their own they can do nothing until they enter a living cell. Without cells, viruses would not be able to multiply. Therefore, viruses are not living things."

1 Corinthians 8:4 By making a fuss about eating food offered to idols gives idols undue prominence; they are nothing so why make something out of nothing. We know that there is only one God and that he has no competition.

1 Corinthians 8:5 There is a lot of talk about other gods and demonic powers operating on earth as well as in the heavenly realm; obviously they seem to be empowered by people's belief in them and conversation about them; so there seem to be many gods "lording" it over people.

1 Corinthians 8:6 This does not make them competition to God; we know that for us there is only one God who is the source of all things; there is only one authority, the Lord Jesus Christ. All things exist because of him; we owe our very being to him. He alone gives context and reference to our lives.

See my notes on Armageddon at the end of chapter 16.

REVELATION Chapter 10

10:1 Then I saw another super strong celestial messenger descending out of the heavenly realm clothed in a cloud. His head was crowned in a rainbow, his face was shining like the sun and his legs were like pillars of fire. *(The rainbow immediately reminds of the promise of God in Genesis 9:13, I have set my rainbow in the cloud, and it shall be a sign of the covenant between me and the earth. Jesus is the fulfillment of every promise.)*

10:2 He held a ¹small ²open scroll in his hand. His right foot was on the sea and his left foot on land. *(The word, ¹biblaridion is the diminutive of biblarion (papyri), itself a diminutive of biblion. Again, like in Revelation 9:15, where the hour contains the entire prophetic thought that pointed for generations to the specific year, month week and moment, now concluded in the Lamb. The slain and risen Lamb redeeming God's, image in incarnate, human form, is the theme, context and conclusion of Scripture. The verb ηνεωγμενον, eneogmenon is the Perfect Passive Participle of anoigō, to open; thus, having been fully opened; from ana, upward and agoo, to lead.)*

10:3 And he cried with a great voice which sounded like the roar of a lion. When he cried, the seven thunders spoke. *(Now, in the light of what the Lamb accomplished, the Lion of Judah's voice is heard.)*

10:4 I was about to record what I heard but was told by another voice from heaven not to, but rather to seal their sayings in silence. *(The prophetic picture sealed the mystery, anticipating the incarnation moment. Revelation 10:11)*

10:5 Then I saw the celestial messenger standing victoriously on the sea and land lifting his hand to heaven.

10:6 He made a ¹solemn oath in him whose life spans the ages; in him who created the heaven, the earth and the sea – and everything in them: this is the conclusion of prophetic time. *(To swear an oath, ¹omnuō - [shoulder omohyoid] - the lifting of the hand [a shoulder action] signifying a higher authority. See Genesis 14:22; also Deuteronomy 32:40, in which God is described as swearing by himself, compare Isaiah 45:23; Hebrews 6:13, 16-18. God, having no one greater to swear by, swore by himself, thus bringing an end to all dispute. Create ²ktizo, to form from ktaomai, to marry a wife. See **Extended notes on the solemn Oath** at the end of the chapter.)*

10:7 In the days when the sounding of the seventh messenger's trumpet commences, the mystery of God will be fully realized in exact accordance with the ¹good news he announced to his servants the Prophets. *(Revelation 11:15 ¹euengelisen - having announced good news - Aorist tense of ευαγγελίζω with eu, well done; and aggelos, announcement - Good News.)*

10:8 And again I heard the voice addressing me out of heaven, telling me to go and take the little book that ¹was opened. *(This is of the narrative of Ezekiel, Ezekiel 2:9-10; Ezekiel 3:1-3. The little book - the broken morsel of bread - condensed into bite-size -the entire prophetic relevance of Scripture is fulfilled in this one man and this one act of righteousness. Jesus Christ and Him crucified and raised.*

*The word ⁷eneogmenon is the Perfect Passive Participle of **anoigo**, from **ana**, upward and **oigo** to open; thus having been opened. Its effect is constant.)*

10:9 I went and faced the messenger and asked him to hand me the little book; he instructed me to take it and devour it entirely. It would be bitter in the belly but sweet as honey in the mouth. *(Just like Jonah was 3 days and 3 nights in the belly of the whale, so the son of man....*

*The word, **kataphage**, is the Aorist Active Imperative [get it over and done with immediately] of the verb **katesthiō** to devour entirely. This reminds of Exodus 12:8, That same night they are to eat the meat roasted over the fire, along with bitter herbs, and bread made without yeast. They were to eat the whole lamb.)*

10:10 So I took the little book out of the celestial messenger's hand and ate it up entirely and it was indeed sweet in my mouth and became bitter in my belly. *(The eating of the word celebrates the incarnation.)*

10:11 And he said to me, "Necessity is laid upon you to now disclose with new insight the prophetic word again - this prophecy's time has come and is now relevant. You will declare it before many peoples and different nations and their kings in their specific mother-tongue language." *(This list of peoples occurs seven times in Revelation - See Revelation 5:9.)*

Revelation Chapter 10 Extended Notes:

The Solemn Oath - Revelation 10:6

The Solemn Oath - Revelation 10:6

Revelation 10:6 And made a ¹solemn oath in him whose life spans the ages. The one who ²created the heaven, and everything in it; the earth and everything in it and the sea and everything in it - this is the conclusion of prophetic time. *(To swear an oath, ¹omnuō - [shoulder omohyoid] - the lifting of the hand [a shoulder action] signifying a higher authority. See Genesis 14:22; also Deuteronomy 32:40, in which God is described as swearing by himself, compare Isaiah 45:23; Hebrews 6:13, 16-18. God, having no one greater to swear by, swore by himself, thus bringing an end to all dispute. Create ²ktizo, to form from ktaomai, to marry a wife.*

Hebrews 6:16 It is common practice in human affairs to evoke a higher authority under oath in order to add weight to any agreement between parties, thereby ¹silencing any possibility of quibbling. *(The word ¹peras, means the end of all dispute; the point beyond which one cannot go.)*

Hebrews 6:17 In the same context we are confronted with God's eagerness to go to the last extreme in his dealing with us as heirs of his promise, and to cancel out all possible grounds for doubt or dispute. In order to persuade us of the unalterable character and finality of his resolve, he confined himself to an oath. The promise which already belongs to us by heritage is now also confirmed under oath. *[The prophetic Word is the promise; the Incarnate, crucified and risen Christ is the proof.]*

Hebrews 6:18 So that we are now dealing with two irreversible facts which make it impossible for anyone to prove God wrong. *(The promise of redemption sustained throughout Scripture and the fulfillment of that promise in Jesus. For many years we have 'window-shopped' the promises of God. Even the most diligent students of Scripture became so pre-occupied with the future that they missed the Messiah in their midst. John 5:39, 40. Jesus is the central theme of Scripture; He is the fullness of time; we are no longer dealing with a post-dated promise. Luke 4:21, Luke 24:27, 44-46.*

See also **Isaiah 45:23 I have sworn by myself; the word of my mouth has ²begotten righteousness; this cannot be reversed. Every knee shall bow to me and every tongue shall echo my oath.** *(See Romans 1:17. The Hebrew word יצא Yatsa can be translated, begotten like in Judges 8:30] [Thus, speak with the same certainty sourced in me.] The Hebrew word, שבע Shaba means to seven oneself, that is, swear - thus in the Hebrew mind, by repeating a declaration seven times one brings an end to all dispute. See also Philippians 2:10 & 11.)*

REVELATION Chapter 11

11:1 I was handed a measuring reed resembling a royal scepter and instructed to arise and measure the ¹inner sanctuary of God and the altar *[of incense]* **as well as those who worshiped in there.** *(He first introduces the Jewish believers to the new order: The royal scepter as measure speaks of the Melchizedek anointing upon the worshipper as the inner sanctuary of God. A temple, not made with hands. The mystery of the ages is Christ in you. The word ¹***naos***, inner sanctuary; the most holy place - see there the table and the daily bread, the golden lampstand, the golden altar of incense, the torn veil, the ark of covenant - the intimate, incarnate embrace in our eternal, redeemed union - we are measured in the Messiah. The order of Melchizedek, the reign of righteousness by faith, replaced the old Levitical order of righteousness by performance. The royal scepter of the Melchizedek-order is the measure of the new Covenant. See Revelation 21:17*

The root of the word Messiah also means to measure. Aramaic משח ***misah*** *stem for Messiah* משיח *to anoint; to measure. Also the word,* ***xristos****, the Anointed one, from* χρίω ***chriō****, to smear or rub with oil, to anoint; to draw the hand over, to measure; from* χείρ ***cheir****, hand. [We still measure the height of horses by hand - ie. "A seventeen hand horse."]*

The verb to smear, anoint - משח *- late Hebrew, originally probably as Arabic to wipe or stroke with the hand [compare RS Semitic i. 215; 2nd ed., 283], anoint, Aramaic anoint; in Aramaic inscription see CISii.1. No.145, C, 1; Palmyrene oil VogNo.16; Ethiopic anoint, feast, dine DiLex 176; Assyrian mašâ—is measure; Aramaic id.; Arabic measurement, compare DlProl. 178 Frä282])*

11:2 This measuring shall not include the outer court since it was given to the multitudes of Gentile nations who would be treading around the outskirts of the holy city for forty-two months. *(Before the Lamb was slain and raised, in the duration of the time of the unfolding of the prophetic word in the mouths of the two witnesses [Moses and Elijah] represented in the ministry of Jesus - the multitudes of mankind were outside the covenants of Israel.*

See Notes on the Measure of the temple within the context of the 42 Months at the end of this chapter.)

11:3 I will appoint my two witnesses, dressed in sackcloth, to make known my thoughts for one thousand, two hundred and sixty days. *(1260 days equals 42 months or 3 and a half years, mirroring the prophetic extent of Jesus' ministry, from his baptism to his resurrection and ascension.*

Moses and Elijah represent the law and the prophets - they are the two witnesses Jesus points to in Luke 24:26,27. Also on the mount of transfiguration in Matthew 17, Moses and Elijah appear and speak to Jesus about his death.)

11:4 These are the two olive trees and the two lampstands which stand before the Lord of the earth. *(Romans 11:17, Romans 11:24. In Zechariah 4:2, Zechariah 4:3, Zechariah 4:14 See the prophetic significance of the golden lampstand - the budding almond blossoms - Jeremiah 1:12.)*

11:5 And every form of ¹unrighteous dispute coming against them will be consumed as with fire by the authority of their utterance. Any conversation

that would promote unrighteousness will be silenced. *(The word **adikeo**, out of sync; from **ha**, negative particle and **dikay**, two parties in harmony.)*

11:6 Their authority to stop the rain and turn water into blood and every other plague reminds of Elijah and Moses. *(The 2 witnesses are the law and the Prophets - no rain and every plague as witnessed under Moses in forcing Pharaoh's hand to release the slaves.)*

11:7 At the conclusion of their testimony the "Beast" shall ascend out of the Abyss and shall overcome the two witnesses and kill them in battle. *(Jesus' death seemed an initial defeat to the prophetic purpose and significance sustained in the law and the Prophets.)*

11:8 And their dead bodies shall lie in the street of the great city which spiritually represents Sodom and Egypt where our Lord was crucified. *(Clearly the city of Jerusalem is implicated here. The future Bride-city, the new Jerusalem [Revelation 21:2] was just like Sodom and Egypt during the rule of the Prostitute-Beast of Babylon and in the genius of God's wisdom, their murder of Jesus became the salvation of the entire mankind.)*

11:9 And those [religious institutions] **representing all the peoples in their various groupings, their tribes and cultures and languages of all the multitudes of the nations shall gaze upon the dead bodies of the two witnesses for three and a half days and they will not allow their bodies to be buried.**

11:10 And these earth dwellers [earth-ruled mindsets] **shall rejoice over them with great jubilation celebrating their deliverance from both of these prophetic voices who challenged and frustrated their religious indulgences and beliefs. They will even send gifts to one another celebrating their apparent victory.**

11:11 After three and a half days with the eyes of all earth dwellers fixed upon them, the Spirit of Life, which issues out of God, suddenly entered them and they stood upon their feet. Great awe struck the earth dwellers as they beheld these things. *(In the resurrection of Jesus the prophetic significance of Jewish Scripture, represented by Moses and Elijah, is powerfully endorsed.)*

11:12 And they heard a great voice out of heaven bidding them to come up and they ascended into heaven transported in a cloud while their enemies looked on. *(In the ascension of Jesus the entire prophetic word, represented here by the two witnesses, endorsed mankind's co-resurrection and co-ascension. See Hosea 6:2, after two days he will revive us; on the third day, he will raise us up. Also Ephesians 2:6, We are co-included in his resurrection. We are also co-elevated in his ascension to be equally present in the throne room of the heavenly realm where we are now co-seated with him in his executive authority.)*

11:13 And in that same hour there was a massive earthquake which caused a tenth of the city to collapse. Seven thousand names were killed. *(In symbolic language a tenth represents the entire city [one died for all] and 7000 names representing all the Jewish families - the entire Jewish population were represented in their two prophetic voices, Moses and Elijah, in the death and resurrection* *of Jesus the Messiah. See Revelation 3:12...And I will engrave upon them the name of my God, also the name of the city [the Bride.] of my God, the new Jerusalem that descends from heaven; as well as my own new Name. Also Ephesians 3:15, Every family in heaven and on earth originates in him; his is humanity's family name and he remains the authentic identity of every nation.)*

11:14 Thus the second dramatic symbolic scene departed from view; the third was about to follow. *(Revelation 9:12 This was the conclusion of the first of three painfully powerful initiatives to persuade those whose thoughts were not sealed and in sync with God's belief in them. Two more were on their way.)*

11:15 When the seventh celestial messenger sounded his trumpet, there was a massive crescendo of voices in the heavenly realm, saying, "The kingdom of the ¹cosmos has become the kingdom of our Lord and of his Christ, and he will reign as king for all the ages of the ages." *(The word, ¹**kosmos** in the NT refers to the entire human family. Remember Revelation 10:7 In the days when the sounding of the seventh messenger's trumpet commences, the mystery of God will be fully realized in exact accordance to the Good News he announced to his servants the Prophets. Already in Revelation 7 we see the eventual outcome of what is portrayed here in chapter 11 etc.*

> ***Revelation 7:9** At this moment I saw a massive throng of people, impossible to count, standing tall and innocent; everyone of them ¹**dressed** in white with palm branches in their hands; they had ²**escaped** everything that could possibly define them as a non-Jewish, Gentile world. In fact, every sphere of society was there - including the entire spectrum of people-groupings; all tribal identities with their unique language-specific dialect preferences; they were all present facing the throne and the Lamb as the people of the planet. (Amazing how, in the previous verses of this chapter, the tribes of Israel are associated with a very specific "number", emphasizing the prophetic detail of the entire Jewish nation. But here, John sees a massive throng of people, impossible to count. In Israel there is a prophetic voice of God's intention to release the blessing of the single SEED of God's faith through Abraham and bless all the nations of the earth. "Count the stars, count the sand."*
>
> *The word ¹**stolay**, is the white outer garment worn by kings, priests, and persons of rank. The palm branches and the white robes are signs of the celebration of victory and joy. The Preposition ²**ek**, points to source or origin; mankind was delivered out of their national, geographical and historical identities. See Extended Notes on Israel at the end of Revelation 20.*
>
> *[I looked again and saw a huge crowd, too huge to count. Everyone was there—all nations and tribes, all races and languages. And they were standing, dressed in white robes and waving palm branches, standing before the throne and the Lamb. The Message]*
>
> ***Revelation 7:10** Then I heard the masses shouting as if with one thundering voice saying, "Our salvation is secure in our God who is seated upon the throne and endorsed in the Lamb's doing.")*

11:16 At that moment, the twenty four elders who were seated on their thrones face to face with God, fell down prostrate before him in adoration

11:17 and exclaimed: Our hearts are flooded with gratitude and the affection of your favor. We salute your Lordship oh God. You are the Supreme Authority over all things; your I-am-ness defines time - present, past and

future. The ¹due dynamic of your ²Royal-reign is forever established. *(The word translated due, ¹eilepsas from **lambano** is in the Perfect Active tense which suggests the continual effect of an action already completed in the past. The word **lambano** means to take what is one's own, one's due. Then the word **esbasileusas** from **basileuo**, to reign, is the Aorist Active tense which speaks of a completed act. Both these tenses emphasize the permanence of God's rule. There was never a time where God's royal rule was in question. Giving himself as scapegoat to be murdered by his own creatures assumes a weakness that does not compromise his authority at all. In the genius of his wisdom he defeats the entire system of judgment under the law of performance, governing the tree of the knowledge of good and evil. The seeming frailty of the slain Lamb never compromised the authority of the Lion of Judah. 1 Corinthians 1:25 It seems so foolish that God should die mankind's death on the cross; it seems so weak of God to suffer such insult; yet mankind's wisest schemes and most powerful display of genius cannot even begin to comprehend or compete with God in his weakest moment on the cross.)*

11:18 The culmination of mankind's wrath collided with your passion oh God - this is the critical moment where judgment is met in death. *(Jesus said, "When I am lifted up on the cross, I will draw all judgment unto me.")* **This is the anticipated moment and prize of your bond-friends, the Prophets, the saints and everyone who were awed by your Name - both the insignificant and the prominent - this is the destruction of the corrupting virus in the earth.** *(In the symbolic language of the book of Revelation, the judgment of the Dragon, the Beast and the Whore; the counterfeit Trinity, is not a judgment against an entity, but against a corrupt mindset-system. A virus doesn't have a life of its own - it needs a host.*

Microbiology Professor, Vincent Racaniello writes, "Life is 'an organismic state characterized by capacity for metabolism, growth, reaction to stimuli, and reproduction.' Viruses are not living things. Viruses are complicated assemblies of molecules, including proteins, nucleic acids, lipids, and carbohydrates, but on their own they can do nothing until they enter a living cell. Without cells, viruses would not be able to multiply. Therefore, viruses are not living things."

See my notes on Armageddon at the end of chapter 16.)

11:19 And the innermost sanctuary of God's heavenly temple was laid bare, where the ark of the covenant was fully unveiled to be gazed upon with insight - and there were lightning and thunderous voices and an earthquake and great hailstones. *(See my notes on the Inner Shrine at the end of the chapter.)*

Revelation Chapter 11 Extended Notes:

The Measure of the Temple - Revelation 11:1,2
Two Witnesses Dressed in Sackcloth - Revelation 11:3,4
The Inner Shrine - Revelation 11:19

THE MEASURE OF THE TEMPLE - REV 11

The Measure of the Temple - *Revelation 11:1,2*

The Incarnate Messiah is the measure of the temple. The Human Body is the sanctuary of God. See also 1 Peter 2:5+6.

Revelation 11:1 I was handed a measuring reed resembling a royal scepter and instructed to arise and measure the ¹inner sanctuary of God and the altar [of incense] **as well as those who worshiped in there.** *(He first introduces the Jewish believers to the new order: The royal scepter as measure speaks of the Melchizedek anointing upon the worshipper as the inner sanctuary of God. A temple, not made with hands. The mystery of the ages is Christ in you. The word ¹naos, inner sanctuary; the most holy place - see there the table and the daily bread, the golden lampstand, the golden altar of incense, the torn veil, the ark of covenant - the intimate, incarnate embrace in our eternal, redeemed union - we are measured in the Messiah. The order of Melchizedek, the reign of righteousness by faith, replaced the old Levitical order of righteousness by performance. The royal scepter of the Melchizedek-order is the measure of the new Covenant.*

The root of the word Messiah also means to measure. Aramaic משח *misah stem for Messiah* משיח *to anoint; to measure. Also the word,* **xristos,** *the Anointed one, from* χρίω **chriō,** *to smear or rub with oil, to anoint; to draw the hand over, to measure; from* χείρ **cheir,** *hand. [We still measure the height of horses by hand - ie. "A seventeen hand horse."]*

The verb to smear, anoint - משח *Late Hebrew, originally probably as Arabic to wipe or stroke with the hand [compare RS Semitic i. 215; 2nd ed., 283], anoint, Aramaic anoint; in Aramaic inscription see CISii.1. No.145, C, 1; Palmyrene oil VogNo.16; Ethiopic anoint, feast, dine DiLex 176; Assyrian mašâ—is measure; Aramaic id.; Arabic measurement, compare DlProl. 178 Frä282])*

Revelation 11:2 This measuring shall not include the outer court since it was given unto the multitudes who would be treading around the outskirts of the holy city for forty-two months. *(Before the Lamb was slain and raised, in the duration of the time of the unfolding of the prophetic word in the mouths of the two witnesses [Moses and Elijah] represented in the ministry of Jesus - the multitudes of mankind were outside the covenants of Israel.)*

Ephesians 2:12 During that time you were distanced from the Messianic hope; you had nothing in common with Israel. You felt foreign to the covenants of prophetic promise, living a life with nothing to look forward to in a world where God seemed absent.

Ephesians 2:13 But now, oh wow. Everything has changed; you have discovered yourselves to be located in Christ. What once seemed so distant is now so near; his blood reveals your redeemed innocence and authentic genesis.

Ephesians 2:14 It is in him that we are one and at peace with everyone; he dissolved every definition of division.

Ephesians 2:15 In his incarnation, he rendered the entire Jewish system of ceremonial laws and regulations useless as a measure to justify human life and conduct. In that he died mankind's death all grounds for tension

and hostility were entirely removed. The peace he proclaims reveals one new human race, created and defined in Christ, instead of two groups of people separated by their ethnic identity and differences.

Ephesians 2:16 Both parties are fully represented and equally reconciled to God in one human body through the cross. He reinstated the former harmony; all opposing elements were thus utterly defeated.

Ephesians 2:17 On that basis he made his public appearance, proclaiming the Good News of peace to the entire human race; both those who felt left out in the cold *[as far as the promises and covenants were concerned]*, as well as to those who were near all along *[because of their Jewish identity]*.

The measuring of the temple reminds of Ezekiel 40-43 and Zechariah 2. In John 2:19, referring to his murder on the cross and his glorious resurrection, Jesus says, "Tear down this temple and in three days I will raise it up." His death and resurrection concludes the prophetic significance of the temple and shifts the focus to the human person as the temple-address of God. He does not dwell in buildings made by human hands. Psalm 74:2; Jeremiah 10:16; Jeremiah 51:19. We are the rod [the measure] of God's inheritance.

Colossians 1:26 Mankind's most sought after quest, the mystery which has remained elusive and concealed for ages and generations, is now fully realized in our redeemed innocence.

Colossians 1:27 Within us, God is delighted to exhibit the priceless treasure of this glorious unveiling of Christ's indwelling in order that every person on the planet, whoever they are, may now come to the greatest discovery of all time and recognize Christ in them as in a mirror. He is the [1]desire of the nations and completes their every expectation. *(He is not hiding in history, or in outer space nor in the future, neither in the pages of Scripture, he is merely mirrored there to be unveiled within you. Matthew 13:44, Galatians 1:15, 16, 2 Corinthians 3:18, 2 Corinthians 4:4,7. This is huge. What God was now able to disclose in the saints is immediately equally relevant in the nations. Christ in the nations is the hope of glory. This is the mystery of the ages. This is what we were waiting for [[1]Haggai 2:6,7])*

John 2:19 To which Jesus responded, "Tear down this temple and in three days I will raise it up."

John 2:21 They did not understand that the temple Jesus was pointing to, was the human body. *(In him, the only true address of God was to be redeemed in human life in his resurrection. See Hosea 6:2 "After two days he will revive us, on the third day he will raise us up." Also Ephesians 2:5,6 and 1 Peter 1:3; Acts 7:47-50 But it was Solomon who built a house for him. Yet the Most High does not dwell in houses made with hands; as the Prophet says, 'heaven is my throne, and earth my footstool. What house will you build for me, says the Lord, or what is the place of my rest? Did not my hand make all these things?'*

The word **hieros** *speaks of the greater temple building including its outer court, whereas the word Jesus uses here is* **naos**, *referring to the inner sanctuary - this is also the word Paul uses in 1 Corinthians 6:19 "Do you not realize that your body by design is the sacred shrine of the Spirit of God." This is the most sacred place in*

THE MEASURE OF THE TEMPLE - REV 11

the universe. There is nowhere in eternity that can match this. See John 1:14 *"And the Word became flesh and now resides within us. And 14:20 In that day you will know that I am in my Father and you in me and I in you."*

John 2:22 These words of Jesus as well as their significant prophetic connection with Scripture gave such clear context to the disciples when they later, after his resurrection, recalled all these things.

Colossians 1:19 The full measure of God's [1]happy delight in human life indwells him. *(Delightful intent, [1]eudokeo.)*

Colossians 2:9 All of [1]Deity [2]resides in him, in a human body. He proves that human life is tailor-made for God. *(The word, [1]theotes, godhead/deity, is feminine. Jesus gives detailed expression of what the Father, Son and Spirit is like, in human form. The word [1]katoikeō means to dwell in, to inhabit. While the expanse cannot measure or define God, their exact likeness is displayed in human skin. See Colossians 1:19, God is fully at home in him. Jesus exhibits God's [1]happy delight to be human.)*

Colossians 2:10 And you are in him. He is the [1]chief authority and [2]fountainhead of your being, [3]endorsing your completeness. *(The word, [1]arche, means chief in rank. The head - [2]hē kaphalē. God packaged completeness in "I am". The word, [3]exousia, is often translated as authority; from, **ek** + **eimi**, originating out of "I am." The days are over where our lives were dictated to under the rule of the law of performance and an inferior identity.)*

Ephesians 4:7 The gift of Christ measures the extravagant dimensions of grace; where everyone is equally advantaged.

Ephesians 4:11 What God has in us is gift-wrapped to the world...

Ephesians 4:13 ...Standing face-to-face in equal stature to the measure of the [1]completeness of Christ. *(The word, [1]pleroma, means a life filled to the brim with Christ, like a freight ship carrying its cargo.)*

Zechariah 2:1 And lifting up my eyes, I saw a man with a measuring-line in his hand.

Zechariah 2:2 And I said to him, Where are you going? And he said to me, To measure Jerusalem, to see how wide and how long it is. *(In Hebrew, **madad**, מדד measure et [untranslated] את - Aleph Tav the first and last letters of the Hebrew alphabet - like Alpha and Omega of the Greek alphabet. ירושלם Jerusalem. Jesus, the Aleph Tav or, Alpha and Omega is the true measure of the Bride, Jerusalem. In the Ancient Hebrew Alphabet the bull's head is Aleph and the cross is the Tav. †⌒)*

Zechariah 2:3 And the angel who was talking to me went out, and another angel went out, and, meeting him,

Zechariah 2:4 Said to him, Go quickly and say to this little boy, [נער na'ar] Jerusalem will be as open country villages without walls, because of the great number of people and cattle in her.

Zechariah 2:5 For I myself will be a wall of fire around her, and I will be the glory inside her, says the Lord.

Two Witnesses Dressed in Sackcloth - Revelation 11:3,4
Moses & Elijah

Luke 24:27 And beginning with Moses and all the prophets, he interpreted to them in all the Scriptures the things concerning himself.

Deuteronomy 19:15 At the mouth of two witnesses, a matter shall be established.

Revelation 11:3 I will appoint my two witnesses, dressed in sackcloth, to make known my thoughts for one thousand, two hundred and sixty days. *(1260 days equal 42 months or 3 and a half years, mirroring the prophetic extent of Jesus' ministry, from his baptism to his resurrection and ascension.*

Moses and Elijah represent the law and the prophets - they are the two witnesses Jesus points to in Luke 24:26,27. Also on the mount of transfiguration in Matthew 17, Moses and Elijah appear and speak to Jesus about his death.)

Revelation 11:4 These are the two olive trees and the two lampstands which stand before the Lord of the earth. *(Romans 11:17, Romans 11:24. See Zechariah 4:2, Then I said to him, "What are these two olive trees on the right and the left of the lampstand?" Zechariah 4:14 Then he said, "These are the two anointed ones, who stand by the Lord of the whole earth." The Lampstand is the prophetic light - the almond blossoms - the awake tree. See the prophetic significance of the golden lampstand - the budding almond blossoms - Jeremiah 1:12. [Also, my notes on Hebrews 9:2-4.])*

In symbolic language, in his High Priestly role [Joshua/Zechariah 3] - the Incarnate Jesus himself is the second witness - the one, who mirror-fulfills the prophetic word represented in the law and the prophets. Hebrews 6:13-20.

Hebrews 6:13 *Since God had no one greater by whom to swear, he swore by himself. He could give Abraham no greater guarantee but the integrity of his own Being; this makes the promise as sure as God is.*

Hebrews 6:14 *Saying, "I will continue to speak well of you. I will confirm my intention always only to bless you, and to multiply you beyond measure." (In blessing I will bless you, and in multiplying I will multiply you.)*

Hebrews 6:15 *And so Abraham continued in patience and secured the promise.*

Hebrews 6:16 *It is common practice in human affairs to evoke a higher authority under oath in order to add weight to any agreement between parties, thereby ¹silencing any possibility of quibbling. (The word ¹peras, means the end of all dispute; the point beyond which one cannot go.)*

Hebrews 6:17 *In the same context we are confronted with God's eagerness to go to the last extreme in his dealing with us as heirs of his promise, and to cancel out all possible grounds for doubt or dispute. In order to persuade us of the unalterable character and finality of his resolve, he ¹confined himself to an oath. The promise which already belongs to us by heritage is now also ¹confirmed under oath. (The word ¹mesiteo is used, interposed or mediated. Compare mesites, mediator, from mesos, midst. In the incarnation, God has positioned himself in the midst, of his creation. See Galatians 3:20 With Abraham there was no middleman; it was just God.*

TWO WITNESSES DRESSED IN SACKCLOTH - REV 11

[The Mosaic law sopke the language of "the fallen mind" and required mediators - the Levitical priesthood - because it was an arrangement whereby mankind had a part and God had a part. Mankind's part was to obey the commandments and God's part was to bless. God's covenant with Abraham was a grace covenant pointing to the man Jesus Christ, in whom God himself would fulfil mankind's part and therefore needed no mediator apart from himself.

In the incarnation Jesus fulfills both the proposal and the "I do." M. Perez]

The Word is the promise; the Incarnate, crucified and risen Christ is the proof. He desires to show more convincingly to the heirs of the promise the unchangeable character of his purpose. RSV .

Mankind was not redeemed from the Devil; a thief never becomes an owner; neither did Jesus do what he did to change his Father's mind about us. It was our minds that needed persuasion. God was not to be reconciled to his creation; God was in Christ when he reconciled the world to himself. 2 Corinthians 5:18-20)

Hebrews 6:18 *So that we are now dealing with two irreversible facts which make it impossible for anyone to prove God wrong; thus our persuasion as to our redeemed identity is powerfully reinforced. We have already escaped into that destiny; our expectation has come within our immediate grasp. (The promise of redemption sustained throughout Scripture and the fulfillment of that promise in Jesus. See John 8:13-18. Also, Revelation 10:6 See notes on the Oath at the end of Revelation 10 also the Notes on the Testimony of Jesus at the end of Revelation 20.])*

Hebrews 6:19 *Our hearts and minds are certain; anchored securely within the innermost courts of God's immediate Presence; beyond the (prophetic) veil.*

Hebrews 6:20 *By going there on our behalf, Jesus pioneered a place for us and removed every type of obstruction that could possibly distance us from the promise. In him we are represented for all time; he became our High Priest after the order of Melchizedek. We now enjoy the same privileged access he has. (He said, "I go to prepare a place for you so that you may be where I am. On that day you will no longer doubt that I and the Father are one; you will know that I am in the Father and you in me and I in you."[John 10:30, 14:3, 20]))*

John 8:15 *You form your own judgment according to the flesh; I judge no-one.*

John 8:16 *And even if I do make a judgment, it is true since I am not making it up in my imagination or on my own accord, my record reflects the testimony of the Father who sent me.*

John 8:17 *That should settle it for you since it is written in your law that the testimony of two, is true. (This combined witness of two is not true just because they agree, unless true in fact separately. But if they disagree, the testimony falls to the ground. Deuteronomy 17:6; and Deuteronomy 19:15. - Robertson's Word Pictures)*

John 8:18 *I am witness to who I am and my Father himself also bears witness to me.*

Revelation 11:6 Their authority to stop the rain and turn water into blood and every other plague reminds of Elijah and Moses.

(The 2 witnesses are the law and the Prophets - no rain and every plague as witnessed under Moses in forcing Pharaoh's hand to release the slaves.)

Revelation 11:7 At the conclusion of their testimony the "Beast" shall ascend out of the Abyss and shall overcome the two witnesses and kill them in battle. *(Jesus' death seemed an initial defeat to the prophetic purpose and significance sustained in the law and the Prophets.)*

Dressed in Sackcloth - the prophetic word in the law and prophets points to Jesus who took our mourning upon himself on the cross and in our hellish darkness. And having loosed our bonds he raised us in his triumphant joy.

Isaiah 58:5 Is such the fast that I choose, a day for a man to humble himself? Is it to bow down his head like a rush, and to spread sackcloth and ashes under him? Will you call this a fast, and a day acceptable to the LORD?

Isaiah 58:6 "Is not this the fast that I choose: to lose the bonds of wickedness, to undo the thongs of the yoke, to let the oppressed go free, and to break every yoke?

Isaiah 58:7 Is it not to share your bread with the hungry, and bring the homeless poor into your house; when you see the naked, to cover him, and not to hide yourself from your own flesh?

Isaiah 58:8 Then shall your light break forth like the dawn, and your healing shall spring up speedily; your righteousness shall go before you, the glory of the LORD shall be your rear guard.

Isaiah 58:9 Then you shall call, and the LORD will answer; you shall cry, and he will say, Here I am. "If you take away from the midst of you the yoke, the pointing of the finger, and speaking wickedness,

Isaiah 58:10 if you pour yourself out for the hungry and satisfy the desire of the afflicted, then shall your light rise in the darkness and your gloom be as the noonday.

Isaiah 58:11 And the LORD will guide you continually, and satisfy your desire with good things, and make your bones strong; and you shall be like a watered garden, like a spring of water, whose waters fail not.

Isaiah 58:12 And your ancient ruins shall be rebuilt; you shall raise up the foundations of many generations; you shall be called the repairer of the breach, the restorer of streets to dwell in.

Psalm 30:11 You have turned my mourning into dancing; thou hast loosed my sackcloth and girded me with gladness.

The Inner Shrine - Revelation 11:19

The Inner Shrine is the innermost being of human life, now redeemed to be the most sacred and intimate place of spirit encounter.

Revelation 11:1 I was handed a measuring reed resembling a royal scepter and instructed to arise and measure the ¹inner sanctuary of God and the altar [of incense] **as well as those who worshiped in there.** *(He first introduces the Jewish believers to the new order: The royal scepter as measure, speaks of the Melchizedek-anointing upon the worshipper as the inner sanctuary of God. A temple, not made with hands. The mystery of the ages is Christ in you. The word ¹***naos***, inner sanctuary; the most holy place - see there the table and the daily bread, the golden lampstand, the golden altar of incense, the torn veil, the ark of covenant - the intimate, incarnate embrace in our eternal, redeemed union - we are measured in the Messiah. The order of Melchizedek, the reign of righteousness by faith, replaced the old Levitical order of righteousness by performance. The royal scepter of the Melchizedek-order is the measure of the new Covenant.*

The root of the word Messiah also means to measure. Aramaic משה *misah stem for Messiah* משיח *- to anoint; to measure.)*

Revelation 11:18 The culmination of mankind's wrath collided with your passion oh God - this is the critical moment where judgment is met in death. *(Jesus said, "When I am lifted up on the cross, I will draw all judgment unto me.")*

Revelation 11:19 And the innermost sanctuary of God's heavenly temple was laid bare where the ark of the covenant was fully unveiled to be gazed upon with insight - and there were lightning and thunderous voices and an earthquake and great hailstones.

Revelation 15:4 Who will not be awestruck by you oh Lord as they recognize their identity in your glorious name? All your work confirms the truth of who you are. You have no competition. Therefore all the nations will arrive at the same conclusion and they will worship you since your righteousness has been openly shown. *(Sing unto the Lord a new song, for he has done marvelous things. His right hand and his holy arm have gotten him the victory. The Lord has made known his salvation, his righteousness has he openly shown and all the ends of the earth shall see the salvation of our God. Psalm 98:1)*

Revelation 15:5 And coinciding with this, I saw the inner shrine of the skin-tabernacle of testimony, with the veil wide open in the heavenly dimension. *(The prophetic skin-tabernacle, the Tent of Meeting is now redeemed in the Incarnation - the human body hosts this place of intimate encounter. See Exodus 33:7 the tent of meeting* מועד *the moyed which is the Niphal [reflexive] of* עד *- od, with Ayin ⊙ as a picture of the eye in the Ancient Hebrew alphabet, the Dalet* ד *is a picture of the ᴛ door; combined, these mean "see the door". As coming to a tent of meeting and entering in. A place, time or event that is repeated again and again - in the reflexive form; signifying a place of mirror-encounter. In the Septuagint the Greek word* **marturion** *is used - that which gives evidence - testimony. So the tent of meeting is the tent of testimony. Revelation 11:19.)*

Here is the context:

Hebrews 9:3 The second veil led to the inner tent known as the Most Holy Place.

Hebrews 9:4 The golden [1]cencer *["fire-pan"]* **of incense was taken there once a year on the day of atonement. The heart of the entire sanctuary was represented in the [2]ark of the covenant, also called the ark of testimony. It was a wooden chest, covered in pure gold, both inside and out. In it were kept the [3]golden jar with a sample of the miracle manna from the wilderness, as well as the [4]budding staff of Aaron, as also the [5]two engraved tablets of stone with the ten commandments of the Covenant.** *([1] A golden "fire-pan" was for the purpose of carrying fire, in order to burn incense on the day of Atonement [at-one-ment] once a year in the ultimate place of worship. Exodus 37:25-29.)* **Leviticus 16:12,13.** *[2] The word, [1]kibotos, the wooden box, is the same word used for Noah's ark; the container of mankind's redemption. Genesis 6:14. [3] The [3]manna prophetically pictured the true bread from heaven, not the bread that mankind's labor produces. John 4:35, 38. [4] Moses' staff - but here referred to as Aaron's - when they first met with Pharaoh Aaron's staff turned into a snake - the symbol of Pharaoh's rule, and swallowed the snake staffs of the Egyptian magicians. [5] The two engraved tablets of stone, pointing prophetically to the rebooted life of our design where the law of agape is inscribed in our inner consciousness.)*

Hebrews 9:5 Hovering above and over the ark of the Covenant were the two cherubim, images of glory, intent upon the mercy seat that covered the box on which the blood was sprinkled once a year by the High Priest to cover the sins of the people. Every detail is significant but cannot be discussed at length in this writing. *(The Hebrew word, רפב **kopher**, means to cover [specifically with bitumen], figuratively to cover by legal and equal exchange in order to restore a previously disturbed balance. The legal requirement according to human tradition and mythology, was an eye for an eye, etc. Jesus urges his followers to turn the other cheek: You have heard that it was said, "An eye for an eye and a tooth for a tooth." But I say to you...*

The ark represented a place of mercy where atonement would be made. Innocence had to be achieved at a cost equal to the replacement value of the peace sought between the different parties. See also Genesis 6:14, where the same word denotes the covering of Noah's ark with pitch. The Cross cannot be taken out of the equation of atonement.

See 1 Peter 1:18,19 how God speaks the most radical scapegoat language of the law of judgment, and brings final closure to a dead and redundant system. In Psalm 40:6,7, it is clearly stated that God does not require sacrifices or offerings. Jesus is the Lamb of God. He collides victoriously with the futile sacrificial system)

Hebrews 9:6 In the context of this arrangement the priests performed their daily duties, both morning and evening. *(The daily duties included their dress and preparations, washings, sacrificial offerings, lighting and trimming, then, on every Sabbath, replacing the old showbread with 12 fresh loaves, and sprinkling the blood of the sin offerings on the golden altar of incense before the veil of the sanctuary.)*

Hebrews 9:7 The routine was interrupted only once a year, when the High Priest alone would enter the second tent, the most sacred place of worship, with the blood sacrifice for his own and the people's accumulated errors.

Hebrews 9:8 Already in this arrangement the Holy Spirit indicated that there was a yet more sacred way, beyond the first tent, that was still to be opened. While the first pattern was still being upheld, its fulfillment in truth could not yet commence.

Hebrews 9:9 The tabernacle pattern of that time was an analogy of the hitherto imperfect system in which the gifts and sacrifices presented failed completely to cleanse the conscience of the worshipper.

Hebrews 9:10 All these external rituals pertaining to food and drink and the various ceremonial baptisms and rules for bodily conduct were imposed upon them until the anticipated time of restoration; the foretold moment when ¹all that was crooked would be made straight and restored to its natural and original condition. *(This word, ¹diothosis, is only used in this one place in the New Testament; what was crooked will be made thoroughly straight, restoring to its natural and normal condition something which in some way protrudes or has gotten out of line, as broken or misshapen limbs.)*

Hebrews 9:11 But now Christ has made his public appearance as High Priest of a perfect tabernacle. The good things that were predicted have arrived. This new tabernacle is not a compromised replica of its shadow type, man-made one. This is the real deal. *(The restoration of God's original dwelling place in human life is again revealed.)*

Hebrews 9:12 As High Priest, his permission to enter the Holy Place was not secured by the blood of beasts. By his own blood he obtained access on behalf of the human race. Only one act was needed for him to enter the most sacred place of grace and there to institute a ransom of perpetual consequence. *(The perfection of the redemption he secured needs no further sacrifice. There are no outstanding debts; there is nothing we need do to add weight to what he has accomplished once and for all. The only possible priesthood activity we can now engage in is to continually bring a sacrifice of the fruit of our lips, giving thanks to his Name; no blood, just fruit, even our acts of self-sacrifice, giving of time and money, etc. are all just the fruit of our constant gratitude.)*

Hebrews 9:13 The blood of beasts and the ashes of the burnt sacrifice of a heifer could only achieve a very temporal and surface cleansing by being sprinkled on the guilty. *(The word for heifer, is damalis, from damatzo, to tame; this was the most dear and expensive sacrifice. She was a strong, pristine, spotless female calf, she was raised as a family pet; "A Little Princess." This was the best that the law-system could present; yet, no inner purging of conscience was possible; only the sense of temporal relief; whilst knowing that the entire process would have to be repeated again and again. In this arrangement, God addressed the dilemma of our sin consciousness; the deep-seated stain that it had left needed to be thoroughly exposed, and then brought to closure. The shadow system with its imperfections, as a possible means of obtaining a lasting and meaningful sense of innocence, had to be exhausted; ultimately proving that no sacrifice that anyone can bring at any expense of their own, could possibly match the sacrifice of God giving himself as scapegoat to the human race in order to persuade us that his love for us would go to the scandalous extreme, where we are finally confronted with the fact that it is not in a sacrifice that we bring where God's mind is favorably influenced towards us; but* *in the shocking sacrifice of himself, where he forever, in the most radical language, impact our ideas and thoughts about the Father, Son and Spirit's estimate of us. There is nothing dearer in the universe to them, but our redeemed innocence and our individual value realized. See Colossians 2:14,15 in the Mirror Bible.)*

Hebrews 9:14 How much more effective was the blood of Christ, when he presented his own flawless life through the eternal Spirit before God, in order to purge your conscience from its frustration under the cul-de-sac rituals of the law. There is no comparison between a guilt and duty-driven, dead religious system, and the vibrancy of living your life free from a sin-consciousness. This is what the new testament priesthood is all about. *(Dead works, nekros ergon. A dead, religious-routine system can never compete with the resurrected Christ now realized in you.)*

Hebrews 9:15 As fully representing mankind, Jesus's death brought an end to the old, and introduced the New Testament. He thus redeemed us from the transgressions recorded under the first Covenant and identified us as heirs; qualifying us to participate in the full inheritance of all that he obtained on our behalf. *(The concept of a mediator, mesites, in this analogy, is not a go-between, as if Jesus had to change the Father's mind about us; it was our minds that needed to be persuaded. Jesus did not save us from God; he is fully God and fully man, and in him mankind is most completely represented. See Galatians 3:20; also Hebrews 6:16-20)*

Hebrews 9:16 For a will to take effect the person who made it must be dead.

Hebrews 9:17 Before the testator dies the will is merely a future promise with no immediate benefit to anyone.

Hebrews 9:18 Even the first Covenant required a death for its actualization; the blood of the animal sacrifice represented that death.

Hebrews 9:19 After Moses uttered the detailed requirements of the law in the hearing of all the people, he would take the blood of calves and of goats, mix it with water and, dipping a bunch of hyssop bound with scarlet wool into the blood-basins, sprinkle the blood on the book and upon the people.

Hebrews 9:20 While performing this cleansing ritual, Moses would solemnly declare, "This is the blood of the covenant which God has made binding upon you."

Hebrews 9:21 The same blood was then also sprinkled on the tabernacle, and on all the furniture and ministry utensils.

Hebrews 9:22 Thus, according to the law, all purging was by means of blood; forgiveness was specifically associated with the shedding of blood. *(The idea of closure to the particular case was communicated in the death of an innocent victim. The blood symbolizes this currency. The word translated forgiveness, or remission is the word **aphiemi**, from **apo**, away from, and **hieimi** an intensive form of **eimi**, I am; thus forgiveness is in essence a restoring to your true 'I-am-ness.' The injury, insult, shame, hostility or guilt would no longer define the individual.)*

Hebrews 9:23 If the methods of the law were only a shadow prefiguring the heavenly reality, the fulfillment of these examples surely requires a stronger and more efficacious sacrifice.

Hebrews 9:24 In Christ we have so much more than a type reflected in the tabernacle of holy places set up by human hands. He entered into the heavenly sphere itself, where he personally represents mankind face to face with God.

Hebrews 9:25 Neither was it necessary for him to ever repeat his sacrifice. The High Priests under the old shadow system stood proxy with substitute animal sacrifices that had to be offered every year.

Hebrews 9:26 But Jesus did not have to suffer again and again since the ¹fall of the world; the ²single sacrifice of himself in the fulfillment of history now reveals how he has brought sin to nought. *(The word, ¹katabole, means cast down. ²God's Lamb took away the sins of the world.)*

Hebrews 9:27 The same goes for everyone: a person dies only once, and then faces judgment.

Hebrews 9:28 Christ died once and faced the judgment of the entire human race. His second appearance *[in his resurrection]* has nothing to do *with sin,* but to reveal salvation for all to ¹fully embrace him. *(To fully embrace, ¹apekdechomai, from apo, away from [that which defined me before] and ek, out of, source; and dechomai, to take into one's hands to accept wholeheartedly, to fully embrace. In his resurrection he appeared as Savior of the world. Sin is no longer on the agenda, for the Lamb of God has taken away the sins of the world. Jesus Christ fulfilled mankind's destiny with death. [1 Corinthians 15:3-5, Romans 4:25, Acts 17:30, 31.])*

Hebrews 10:19 So, fellow family, what the blood of Jesus communicates, seals our immediate access into this ultimate place of sacred encounter, with unashamed confidence.

Hebrews 10:20 This is the official inauguration of a brand new way of life. The torn flesh of Jesus opened the veil for us. Our own flesh can no longer be a valid excuse to interrupt the expression of the life of our design from within our innermost shrine.

Hebrews 10:21 We have a High Priest in the house.

Hebrews 10:22 We are free to approach God with absolute confidence, fully persuaded in our hearts that nothing can any longer separate us. We are invited to draw near now. We are thoroughly cleansed, inside and out, with no trace of sin's stains on our conscience or conduct. The sprinkled blood purges our inner thought-patterns; our bodies also are bathed in clean water.

1 Corinthians 6:19 Do you not realize that your body is the sacred shrine of the Spirit of God, echoing within you. You do not own your life.

1 Corinthians 6:20 You are bought and paid for. All of you are his. Live your life conscious of how irreplaceable priceless you are. You host God in your skin.

REVELATION Chapter 12

12:1 Suddenly a spectacular symbolic image appears in the sky. A woman clothed in sunlight with a shining moon under her feet and a crown of twelve stars on her head. *(The day the Prophets pointed to has dawned, clothed with the sun, reigning over the night - about to give birth to the child. Song of Songs 6:10 [The chorus of young women] Who is this young woman? She looks like the dawn. She is beautiful like the moon, pure like the sun, awe-inspiring like those heavenly bodies.)*

12:2 She was in the agony of labor; crying out with birth pangs. *(Such vivid imagery of the prophetic Word, the Logos, as a woman, about to give birth to Jesus, who now faces the cross also in the agony of fulfilling his mission - knowing that he has come for this hour. His victorious death and descent into hell and glorious resurrection would re-boot mankind into newness of life. "We were born anew when he was raised from the dead." John 12:27 My soul is exceedingly perplexed right now. What shall I say, "Father. Rescue me ¹out of the clutches of this hour." No. This hour is the very culmination of my destiny.*

Isaiah 9:6 For to us a Child is born, to us a Son is given; and the government shall be upon his shoulder, and his name shall be called Wonderful Counselor, Mighty God, Everlasting Father, Prince of Peace. Isaiah. 9:7. Of the increase of his government and of peace there shall be no end, upon the throne of David and over his kingdom, to establish it and to uphold it with justice and with righteousness from the latter time forth, even forevermore. The zeal of the Lord of hosts will perform this.)

12:3 Then another sign showed up in the sky - a monster sized red Dragon with seven heads and ten horns. The heads were wrapped in royal diadems. *(The picture of a multi headed Dragon appearing to devour the woman's seed is a typical prophetic narrative where the Messianic promise of salvation would crush the serpent's head as declared in Genesis 3:15)*

12:4 And with his tail he dragged a third of the stars and flung them upon the earth. He then positioned himself in front of the woman and threatened to devour the child as soon as it was born. *(The tail represents the false Prophets Isaiah 9:15, 16... the tail for those who lead this people lead them astray, and those who are led by them are swallowed up. See also Daniel 8:10 The stars are the celestial messengers. Revelation 1:20, but here they are the shepherds of Israel who led Israel into rejecting the child. The third part is a symbolic expression of a representative portion of the whole. Man is also a triune being, spirit, soul and body - the third part referenced here could mean the soul part which would include the mindset, which would then suggest that the Jewish leadership were entangled by the multi-headed Dragon into a mindset of a lower fallen order. Not realizing or acknowledging that Jesus was indeed the child to be born as the savior of the world. Ezekiel 34.)*

12:5 And she gave birth to a boy who was about to shepherd all the nations with a royal scepter of steel. And immediately the child was raptured to be face to face with God and his throne. *(See Revelation 2:27 - also my commentary note there. You will shepherd them with a royal scepter and that [mindset which ruled the nations] shall be shattered like a potter's vessel of clay. Remember a shepherd's staff was to defend the sheep against thieves and wild animals - it wasn't used to hurt the sheep.*

More literally, "that when she was delivered he might devour her child." Professor Milligan says: "In these words we have the Dragon doing what Pharaoh did to Israel [Exodus 1:15-22], and again and again, in the Psalm and the Prophets, Pharaoh is spoken of as the Dragon [Psalm 74:13; Isaiah 27:1; Isaiah 51:9; Ezekiel 29:3]. Nor is it without interest to remember that Pharaoh's crown was wreathed with a Dragon [the asp or serpent of Egypt], and that just as the eagle was the ensign of Rome, so the Dragon was that of Egypt. Hence the significance of Moses' rod being turned into a serpent.")

12:6 And the woman escaped into the wilderness to a safe place prepared for her where she was nourished by ¹them for 1,260 days. *(The prophetic Word is protected and sustained for the entire duration of Jesus' ministry. The plural form points to the ¹triune God; Elohim, inseparably one with their Word. This is 42 months or three and one-half years. This verse again displaying various prophetic dimensions completes the story of Mary going to Egypt with Joseph and baby Jesus and staying there approximately three and a half years until Herod was dead who was seeking to kill the child. Also the fact that Jesus' three and a half year ministry was a protected place - here the pregnant woman represents the prophetic, incarnate word as the womb bearing the Promise, pointing to his death, victorious descent into hell and glorious resurrection where he led mankind into the new birth. "We were born anew, when Jesus was raised from the dead. 1 Peter 1:3. See Hosea 6:2 "After two days he will make us alive; on the third day he will raise us up." Also Ephesians 2:5,6 and Ephesians 4:8,9.)*

12:7 Mikael and his celestial cohorts led the war in the heavenly realm against the Dragon and his cohorts. *(Mikael מיכאל means, "Who is like God?" The context of the onslaught against the human race has always been identity-related. The fruit of the "I-am-not tree system." Jesus faced this temptation on mankind's behalf, "If you are the Son of God..." See John 10:30-36. Also my comments in Revelation 17:8 and commentary at the end of Revelation 16.)*

12:8 The Dragon's influence was totally demolished and rendered powerless - not a trace of its presence was found in the heavens. *(Principalities and powers were completely disarmed on the cross. Colossians 2:14,15 "And their place was not found" see Daniel 2:35 - the little stone against whom the Gates of Hades shall not prevail - the Chip off the old Block demolished the pseudo man-made identity. There are numeral references to the same "once and for all war" in the heavens. It is however the same hour; the same event. Revelation 16:13,14; Revelation 17:13,14; 19:19; Revelation 20:8. Also **John 12:31,32** Now is the judgment of this world; now the ruler of this world shall be cast down. [When I am lifted up on the cross.])*

12:9 So the great Dragon, the ¹ancient ²ophis [serpent], also known as the Devil or Satan - whose sole mission was to lead the entire inhabited world astray - was cast down to the earth-dimension, together with all his cohorts. *(The word ¹archaios, ancient, of old; from arche, from the beginning. As Jesus said that the Devil was a murderer "from the beginning" The Greek word, ²ophis is translated serpent and comes from optomai, to gaze, in this case, to present a visual idea through illusion. John 8:44. He was stripped of his pseudo rank of authority see Colossians 2:14,15 he was made a public spectacle. Luke 10:18*

And Jesus said to them, I saw Satan falling out of heaven like lightning. These all represent mindsets that have blindfolded mankind since the fall of Adam.)

12:10 Then I heard a very loud voice in the heavens announcing, "This is the moment which the entire prophetic word pointed to and culminates in; it is the realization of mankind's salvation. The power of the kingdom of our God and its authority is endorsed in the I-am-ness of his Christ. The business of accusation is bankrupt. The 24/7 industry of condemning the brotherhood of mankind before the face of God has been annihilated."
*(The word [1]kategoros, a name given to the Devil by the Rabbis, the one whose business is accusation, from **kata**, downward and **agora**, to trade; a word used for all kinds of business in the public arena.*

John 12:27 My soul is exceedingly perplexed right now. What shall I say, "Father. Rescue me [1]out of the clutches of this hour." No. This hour is the very culmination of my destiny. [Greek Preposition, [1]ek, out of; source; origin.]

John 12:28 "Father. Glorify your name." And immediately there came a voice out of the heavenly realm saying, "I have glorified it, and I will glorify it again."

John 12:29 The crowd heard the voice and said that it had thundered; others thought it was the voice of a celestial messenger.

John 12:30 Jesus replied, "This voice was not for my sake but for yours. [Signs are for unbelievers. 1 Corinthians 14:22.]

John 12:31 Now is the judgment of this world; this is the moment where the authority of the world-system is cast out. (The serpent's head is about to be crushed. Genesis 3:15; Colossians 2:14,15. Luke 10:18. I saw Satan fall like lightning.)

*John 12:32 When I am lifted up from the earth, I will draw all of mankind and every definition of judgment unto me. (He would be lifted up on a cross, descend into the depths of our hell, then, according to the prophetic word in Hosea 6:2, after two days, the entire human race he represents, will be co-quickened and on the third day, be co-raised, out of the lowest parts of the earth and elevated to the highest heavens. Ephesians 4:8,9; see also Ephesians 2:5,6 and Colossians 3:1-3. 'All' includes all of mankind and every definition of judgment. The subject of the sentence, as from the previous verse, is the judgment of the world - thus the primary thought here is that in his death, Jesus would draw all judgment upon himself. John 3:14; John 8:28; Acts 2:33. 1 John 3:5 We have witnessed with our own eyes how, in the unveiling of the prophetic word, when he was lifted up upon the cross as the Lamb of God, he lifted up our sin and broke its dominion and rule over us. John 1:29 "Behold, the Lamb of God, who takes away [airo] the sin of the world. The word **airo** means to lift up.")*

John 12:33 This he said to point to the way in which he would die. [See John 19:15 - Lift him up. Lift him up. Crucify him."])

12:11 Mikael and his celestial messengers conquered the Dragon because of the blood of the little Lamb and the word of their testimony. They did not believe that the agape of life discovered in Christ can be threatened or [1]terminated in death. *(The blood of the Lamb brought closure to every possible accusation against the human race. This is the testimony of the prophetic word* *announcing the Good News throughout the ages. The word* ¹***achri** - the end; the idea of terminating. Mikael and his messengers represent the entire host of heaven - including all the multitudes previously mentioned. See* **Extended Notes on the Word of God and the Testimony of Jesus Christ** *at the end of chapter 20.)*

12:12 An ¹eruption of belly-laughter followed in the heavenlies and in all those inhabiting this realm. Woe to the land and sea for the Devil was cast down there in great embarrassment, seeing that his time had run out. *(The word, ¹**euphraino**, jubilant rejoicing, from **eu**, well done; extravagantly good; and **phren**, the midriff or diaphragm, the innermost parts of the heart. This makes Paul's appeal in Colossians 3:1-3 so relevant. Engage your minds with heavenly dimension realities and not with the earthbound soul realm. See Notes on Armageddon, Revelation 16.)*

12:13 As soon as the Dragon realized that he had lost his supposed position in the heavenlies and was now confined to the earth realm, he pursued the woman who birthed the male child.

12:14 But the woman was given very large eagle wings with which to fly away to her safe place in the wilderness where she would be pampered for a time and times and half a time out of sight of the serpent. *(Beyond the reach of Ophis. 1260 days; 3 and a half years which points to the uninterrupted extent of Jesus' ministry.)*

12:15 Then waters flooded out of the mouth of the serpent in an attempt to drown the woman [*the prophetic voice unveiling the Christ*] **in his devilish conversation.**

12:16 But the earth rescued the woman by opening its mouth and gulped down the entire river proceeding from the Dragon's mouth. *(In his death, burial and descent into the lowest parts of the earth. See Ephesians 4:8,9. Note, like in Revelation 12:9, the words for the Serpent-system are interchanged, including the Dragon, Satan, Devil and also in 12:10, the Accuser, Kategoros, whose business is the industry of accusation.)*

12:17 The fact that the woman escaped his pursuit extremely infuriated the Dragon, so he turned his attention to contend with the remnant of her seed who treasured ¹the completeness of God's fulfilled purpose echoing the ²testimony of Jesus. *(The word ¹**entole**, which is often translated commandment or precept, has two components: **en**, in and **telos**, from **tello**, to set out for a definite point or goal; the point aimed at as a limit, that is, by implication, the conclusion of an act or state, the result; the ultimate or prophetic purpose. Strong's 5056 See 1 John 2:3 Mirror Bible) The ²testimony of Jesus is the spirit of prophecy. Revelation 19:10. See* **Notes on the Testimony of Jesus Christ** *at the end of chapter 20.)*

Revelation Chapter 12 Extended Notes:

Notes on Ophis, the old Serpent

Notes on Ophis, the old Serpent

2 Corinthians 11:3 I am concerned for you that you might ¹pine away through the ²illusion of separation from Christ and that, just like Eve, you might become ³blurry-eyed and ⁴deceived into believing a lie about yourselves. The temptation was to exchange the truth about our completeness *[I am]* with the idea of incompleteness *[I am not]* and shame; thinking that perfection required your toil and all manner of wearisome labor. (*The word, ¹phteiro, means to pine or waste away, to wither . Any idea of separation causes one to wither away in loneliness. The word ²haplotes from hama, a particle of union, and pleko, to braid or plait together; sometimes translated, simplicity or unmixed. The Greek word, ³ophis is translated serpent, from optomai, to gaze, in this case, to present a visual idea through illusion. The word ⁴exapatao from ek, source + apateo, apathy is the source of deception, to be without faith, believing a lie about yourself. Hebrews 4:6 Israel died in the wilderness because of their unbelief. [Both Adam and Israel believed a lie about themselves. Numbers 13:33, Joshua 2:11, 2 Corinthians 4:4.] The word ⁵panourgia, from the words, pas, all, and ergon, work or toil, where your entire existence is reduced to wearisome labor. This word is often translated, cunning or craftiness. See also 2 Corinthians 4:2 "We have renounced hidden agendas [employing a little bit of the law in an attempt to "balance" out grace]; we have distanced ourselves from any obscure craftiness to manipulate God's word to make it mean what it does not say.")*

Revelation 12:7 Mikael and his celestial colleagues led the war in the heavenly realm against the Dragon and his cohorts. (*Mikael* מיכאל *means, "Who is like God?" The context of the onslaught against the human race has always been identity-related. The fruit of the "I-am-not tree system ." Jesus faced this temptation on mankind's behalf, "If you are the Son of God?" See John 10:30-36 Also my comments on being "earthbound" in Revelation 17:8 and Revelation 16:16.)*

Revelation 12:8 The Dragon's influence was totally demolished and rendered powerless - not a trace of its presence was found in the heavens. (*Principalities and powers were completely disarmed on the cross. Colossians 2:14,15 "And their place was not found" see Daniel 2:35 - the little stone against whom the Gates of Hades shall not prevail - the Chip off the old Block demolished the pseudo man-made identity. There are numeral references to the same "once and for all war" in the heavens. It is however the same hour; the same event. Revelation 16:13,14; Revelation 17:13,14; 19:19; Revelation 20:8. Also **John 12:31,32** Now is the judgment of this world; now the ruler of this world shall be cast down. [When I am lifted up on the cross.])*

Revelation 12:9 So the great Dragon, the ¹ancient ²ophis *[serpent]*, also known as the Devil or Satan - whose sole mission was to lead the entire inhabited world astray - was cast down to the earth-dimension, together with all his cohorts. (*The word ¹archaios, ancient, of old; from arche, from the beginning. As Jesus said that the Devil was a murderer "from the beginning" The Greek word, ²ophis is translated serpent and comes from optomai, to gaze, in this case, to present a visual idea through illusion. John 8:44. He was stripped of his pseudo rank of authority see Colossians 2:14,15 he was made a public spectacle. Luke 10:18 And Jesus said to them, I saw Satan falling out of heaven like lightning. These all represent mindsets that have blindfolded mankind since the fall of Adam.)*

NOTES ON OPHIS THE OLD SERPENT - REV 12

Revelation 12:10 Then I heard a very loud voice in the heavens announcing, This is the moment which the entire prophetic word pointed to and culminates in; it is the realization of mankind's salvation. The power of the kingdom of our God and its authority is endorsed in the I-am-ness of his Christ. The business of accusation is bankrupt. The 24/7 industry of condemning the brotherhood of mankind before the face of God has been annihilated. *(The word [1]kategoros, a name given to the Devil by the Rabbis, the one whose business is accusation, from **kata**, downward and **agora**, to trade; a word used for all kinds of business in the public arena.*

Luke 10:18. Also John 12:27 My soul is exceedingly perplexed right now. What shall I say, "Father. Rescue me [1]out of the clutches of this hour." No. This hour is the very culmination of my destiny. [Greek Preposition, [1]ek, out of; source; origin.]

John 12:28 "Father. Glorify your name." And immediately there came a voice out of the heavenly realm saying, "I have glorified it, and I will glorify it again.")

Revelation 12:13 As soon as the Dragon realized that he had lost his supposed position in the heavenlies and was now confined to the earth realm, he pursued the woman who birthed the male child.

Revelation 12:14 But the woman was given very large eagle wings with which to fly away to her safe place in the wilderness where she would be pampered for a time and times and half a time out of sight of the serpent. *(Beyond the reach of Ophis. 1260 days; 3 and a half years which points to the uninterrupted extent of Jesus' ministry.)*

Revelation 12:15 Then waters flooded out of the mouth of the serpent in an attempt to drown the woman *[the prophetic voice unveiling the Christ]* in his devilish conversation.

Revelation 12:16 But the earth rescued the woman by opening its mouth and gulped down the entire river proceeding from the Dragon's mouth. *(In his death, burial and descent into the lowest parts of the earth. See Ephesians 4:8,9. Note, like in Revelation 12:9, the words for the Serpent-system are interchanged, including the Dragon, Satan, Devil and also in 12:10, the Accuser, **kategoros**, whose business is the industry of accusation.)*

John 3:14 *(This is my mission: See the prophetic relevance - this is how the veil will be removed.)* **Remember how Moses lifted up the [1]serpent in the wilderness even so the son of man will be lifted up.** *(John 12:31 Now is the judgment of this world, now shall the ruler of this world be cast out; John 12:32 and I, when I am lifted up from the earth, will draw all of mankind and every definition of judgment unto me. John 12:33 He said this to show by what death he was to die. Revelation 12:9. John 3:13 and 14 are most significant since they point to the very essence of the Mission of Jesus - the co-begotteness of the human race now redeemed in our co-crucifixion and co-resurrection on the third day into newness of life. 1 Peter 1:3. The word serpent in the Greek is [1]**ophis**.)*

John 3:15 In the same prophetic pattern, I will be lifted up for all to see and be equally persuaded in the echo of the life of the ages now redeemed within them.

Revelation 20:2 And he overpowered the Dragon, in its every disguise as the old Serpent in the garden in Genesis, also called the Devil, or going under the name, Satan, and chained him up for a thousand years. *(From David to Jesus is a thousand years. Revelation 3:7 I hold the key of David as prophesied in Isaiah 22:22. Yes, I unlock the mysteries of the heavenly dimension and no one can shut the door. And I lock the entrance and none [of the old mindsets] can access it.* **The links in the chain**, *are the prophetic words in the mouth of David and the Prophets till John the Baptist. These words already chained Satanas to the irreversible intention of God. Matthew 12:29 Or how can one enter a strong man's house and plunder his goods, unless he first binds the strong man? Then indeed he may plunder his house.*

See Extended Notes on The Thousand Years at the end of chapter 20.)

REVELATION Chapter 13

13:1 As I stood upon the sand of the seashore, I saw a ferocious Beast emerging out of the waters. It had ten horns and seven heads and every horn was wrapped in royal diadems. And written upon its heads were slanderous, blasphemous names. *(Have you ever wondered why the name Jesus, not Buddha, Mohammed or Elvis Presley or any other influential name in history or modern times, is the name that is most commonly used as a swear word? See Ephesians 3:15 Every family in heaven and on earth originates in him; his is mankind's family name and he remains the authentic identity of every nation. Also Ephesians 1:21, God has given Jesus a Name that is beyond comparison above any other name in the heavenly realm or upon the earth for all time and eternity. The salvation that he accomplished is the greatest source of frustration and embarrassment to the religious systems of this world. What the Name of Jesus represents puts religion out of business.*

The imagery reminds of Daniel 7:3. See also Revelation 17:8. This "wild Beast from the sea," as in Daniel 7:17, Daniel 7:23)

13:2 This wild animal looked like a leopard with the powerful paws of a ¹bear and the mouth of a lion. And the Dragon gave its assumed power to the Beast; also its throne and great authority. *(¹arktos, bear, from arkeo, to be possessed of great strength. throne, from **thrao** to sit; a stately seat. The Satanas-system is what empowers religion.)*

13:3 One of its heads appeared to be ¹slain then it miraculously revived and was restored to health again. The entire human race was mesmerized by this. *(Here the "Christian-Religion" is represented by the same multi-headed Beast - mimicking the slain and resurrected Lamb - Only John uses the word, ¹**sphatzo**, which speaks of a brutal slaying. Four times in the book of Revelation he employs this word with direct reference to the slain Lamb of God, and once in 1 John 3:12 in reference to Cain's ¹killing of his brother Abel. See my commentary notes there.*

There is no saving power or relevance in a death and resurrection-belief that fails to see mankind's co-inclusion in the same event. In the mind and belief of God, an inseparable association exists, where, together with Jesus, mankind died and the same human race was co-revived and co-raised. Hosea 6:2 After two days he will revive us on the third day he will raise us up. This happened while we were still dead in our sins and trespasses. Ephesians 2:5,6.)

13:4 They all worshiped both the Dragon who gave its power to the Beast as well as the Beast itself. Convinced that it had no equal and that it was invincible. *(The Dragon is the source-system of accusation empowering the Beast of the religion of performance and self-effort with its inevitable fruit of judgment and condemnation.)*

13:5 The Beast was given a loud, boastful and blasphemous mouth for the duration of forty two months. *(See v 2, The Dragon gave its assumed power to the Beast; also its throne and great authority. Forty and two months - **mēnas tesserakonta kai duo** - accusative of extent of time. This period is also mentioned in Daniel 7:25 and Daniel 12:7. It occurs in three forms in Revelation, forty-two months, here; **1260 days**, Revelation 11:3; Revelation 12:6; **time, times and half a time** or **3-1/2 years**, Revelation 12:14 and so also in Daniel. This symbolic period is is the duration of the sojourn of the woman in the wilderness, as well* *as the duration of the prophesying of the two witnesses, which is the culmination of the law and the prophets in the 3 and a half years of Jesus' ministry - from his baptism to his crucifixion. And he shall confirm the covenant with many for one week: and in the midst of the week he shall cause the sacrifice and the oblation to cease. Daniel 9:27. The middle of the week - 3 and a half days, again prophetically pointing to the 3 and a half years of Jesus' ministry.)*

13:6 It hurled its accusations [1]in God's face, while blaspheming his Name and tabernacle and [2]those dwelling in the heavenlies. *(The words, [1]pros ton theon positions the Accuser to now face God's image and likeness incarnate in human form, since there was no trace of accusation present in the heavenlies, having been thoroughly expelled from any further presence or relevance in the heavenly sphere. [Revelation 12:8-10] The significance of heaven endorsing the tabernacle of God on earth - in both its prophetic symbolism as well as its tangible unveiling in incarnate human life, is now the target of accusation and every blasphemous utterance of this Beast who takes its authority from Mr. Accusation himself.*

[2]Those dwelling in the heavenlies; **kai tous en tō ouranō skenountas** *- in contrast to those whose minds are still trapped in earthbound-mode. See verse 8.)*

13:7 And it was given the mission to wage war against [1]those who have discovered their wholeness in Christ in order to conquer them and to dominate the entire spectrum of people-groupings; every tribe, tongue and nation. *(The word, [1]hagios, saints, refers to the wholeness of body, soul and spirit - see 1 Corinthians 1:30. The words remind of Daniel 7:21,22,23. Where there seemed to be no escape from the Beast's rule. However, the fact that the Beast failed in its mission is already celebrated in Revelation 5:13 as well as in Revelation 7:9 At this moment I saw a massive throng of people, impossible to count, standing tall and innocent; everyone of them dressed in white with palm branches in their hands; they had [1]escaped everything that could possibly define them as a non-Jewish, Gentile world. In fact, every sphere of society was there - including the entire spectrum of people-groupings; all tribal identities with their unique language-specific dialect preferences; they were all present facing the throne and the Lamb as the people of the planet. [The Preposition [1]ek, points to source or origin; mankind was delivered out of their national, geographical and historical identities. Seven times in the book of Revelation human society is addressed in the most all-inclusive fashion, with a similar grouping of words. Revelation 5:9, Revelation 7:9, Revelation 10:11, Revelation 11:9, here in Revelation 13:7, Revelation 14:6 and Revelation 17:15. Also note Revelation 5:13 and Revelation 11:15.])*

13:8 The plan was to engage the entire [1]earthbound population of the planet to worship the Beast *[The counterfeit "slain and risen lamb"].* **This would endorse the idea** *[of the religious system],* **that there were individuals, since the [3]fall of the [4]cosmos, whose [2]names were not included in the [5]slain Lamb's Book of Life.** *(The word [1]katoikeō from kata, down and oikeo, to dwell or set up home - ἐπὶ τῆς γῆς upon the earth - thus, the earthbound population of the planet. In Colossians 3:1-3, Paul invites us to engage our thoughts with resurrection realities and to see ourselves co-raised and seated together with Christ in heavenly places. Revelation 17:8 also Revelation 16 extended notes: Armageddon - Earthbound vs. Heavenly Dimension.*

In the context of verse 6, clearly the target of the "blasphemy" was to insult and interrogate the ²Name and thereby question mankind's authentic identity. See Ephesians 3:15 Every family in heaven and on earth originates in him; his is mankind's Family Name and he remains the authentic identity of every nation. The entire industry of accusation is about the blatant blasphemy of the Name that reveals and redeems humanity's original identity.

"The Book of Life" - this language is taken from the custom of registering the names of persons in a list, roll, or catalogue. In Jewish tradition there was a prevailing fear that your name might be blotted out of the Book of Life if your behavior did not please God. See Exodus 32:32 Here the suggestion is that some names were not even written in the Lamb's Book of Life to begin with. See also Revelation 17:8, ...the ones whose names have not been written in the Book of Life from the fall of the world." This idea would obviously boost the Calvinistic deception of election, that if you're not "chosen", you're doomed - which is a ridiculous contradiction to the entire context and conclusion of the Gospel. See notes on The Book of Life at the end of chapter 17.

*The word ⁵**esphagmenou** is the Perfect Passive Participle of the verb, **sphazō**, to slay in sacrifice. The Perfect Participle is used to describe a state that exists at the time as a result of action completed prior to the time of the main verb. The basic thought of the Perfect tense is that the progress of an action has been completed and the results of the action are continuing on, in full effect. In other words, the progress of the action has reached its culmination and the finished results are now present. The word, ⁴**kosmos** in the NT refers to the entire human family and their social structures. The word often translated foundation, **kataballo**, from **kata** and **ballo**, meaning "to fall away, to put in a lower place," instead of **themelios**, meaning "foundation" [see Ephesians 2:20; also Revelation 21:14,19]; thus, I translated it "the fall of the world," instead of "the foundation of the world." The entire "Fall" was a falling away in our minds from our true identity as image and likeness bearers of Elohim. Just like Eve, were we all deceived to believe a lie about ourselves, which is the fruit of the "I-am-not-tree". We all, like sheep, have gone astray. [Isaiah 53:6]*

See 1 Peter 1:20 He was always destined in God's prophetic thought; God knew since the fall of the world order that his son would be the Lamb, to be made manifest in these last days, because of you. [You are the reason Jesus died and was raised.])

13:9 Now listen up with your inner ears.

13:10 Here is something for ¹those who have discovered their wholeness in me to patiently ponder and perceive by faith. Being taken ²captive by the spear and killed by the sword made death a doorway into the very domain in which mankind was held captive. (*The word, ¹**hagios**, saints, refers to the wholeness of body, soul and spirit - see 1 Corinthians 1:30 and Romans 1:7. The word ²**aichmalōtizō** from **aichme**, spear and **halosis**, to capture, thus, to arrest at spear point. See John 18:3, "Judas was given a Roman military cohort of about 600 soldiers to accompany him; they came together with temple officers from the chief priests and Pharisees with torches, lanterns and their weapons."*

This reminds of Paul's letter to the Ephesians. Being in prison himself at the time, he ponders and is obviously intrigued by the entire context of Psalm 67 [in the LXX] which celebrates God rescuing the prisoners from their captivity and even the wayward and stubborn, who already died and are stuck in their graves. See Psalm 67:7 in the LXX ...leading forth prisoners mightily, also the stubborn, even them that dwell in tombs. [Psalm 139:7,8 Wither shall I go from your Spirit? Or wither shall I flee from your presence? If I ascend to heaven, You. If I make my bed in Sheol, You.] Paul sees by revelation the relevance of Jesus dying our death and entering into our darkness and hell on a rescue mission. He then quotes Psalm 67:19 in Ephesians 4:8 Scripture confirms that he arrested every possible threat that held mankind hostage. ["he took captivity captive"] And in his resurrection, he led us as trophies in his triumphant procession on high. Consider the genius of God, in the incarnate Christ, he repossessed what belonged to us by design, in human form; this is his grace-gift to us. Psalm 67:19 continues with, καὶ γὰρ ἀπειθοῦντες τοῦ κατασκηνῶσαι - **kai gar apeithountes tou kataskenoosai,** *in order that even the backsliding, the headstrong, the wayward, the rebellious may rest; or may now inhabit -* ἀπειθοῦντες **apeithountes** *[the unbelieving/the ones resisting persuasion]* τοῦ **kataskenosai** *- to encamp within - again this word emphasizes the significance of the incarnation -* **kata,** *down and* **skenosai,** *from* **skenos** *- skin. [The gifts which Jesus Christ distributes to us he has received in us, in and by virtue of his incarnation. Commentary by Adam Clarke.] After two days he will revive us. On the third day he will raise us up. Hosea 6:2 We were born anew in his resurrection. 1 Peter 1:3. Also Ephesians 2:5,6. This is how grace rescued us: while we were yet in that state of deadness and indifference in our deviations, we were co-quickened together with Christ. Revelation 21:23-27.)*

13:11 Then I saw another wild animal; this one emerged out of the earth - it had two horns and resembled a young Lamb, yet it had a Dragon's voice. *(The counterfeit "trinity" emerges - the one mirroring the other - the Dragon Accuser, the seven-headed sea-monster of religion with its leading role player, the head that was slain but became alive again and now the Dragon clothed in a lamb's-disguise.)*

13:12 Even though it had the appearance of the Lamb, it operated under the same authority as the previous Beast - under the watchful eye of the Dragon. *[Counterfeit-Christianity as a religion is a wolf in sheep's clothing.]* **It is the same old Dragon in a Lamb's disguise. Its mission was to engage the [1]earthbound dwellers to worship the counterfeit - the slaughtered animal that was restored to life out of its death.** *(The historic relevance of the death and resurrection of the Lamb is in the revelation of mankind's co-inclusion - Jesus died our death and went into our hell and we were co-quickened in his resurrection and are co-seated together with him in heavenly places.*

Again John employs the word [1]katoikeō from **kata,** *down and* **oikeo,** *to dwell or set up home - thus to be earthbound. Revelation 13:8.*

Matthew 7:15 "Beware of false Prophets, which come to you in sheep's clothing, but inwardly they are ravenous wolves." Under the watchful eye of the dragon -In his sight - **enōpion autou.** *In the eye of the first Beast who gets his authority* *from the Dragon - Revelation 13:3. Their eyes engage in the same deception. See 2 Corinthians 11:3 The Greek word, **ophis** is translated serpent, from **optomai**, to gaze, in this case, **to present a visual idea through illusion**.)*

13:13 It had the power to mesmerise the masses with great signs - even fire falling out of the sky, *(Reminds of Pharaoh's magicians. 1 Corinthians 1:22 The Jews crave signs [to confirm their doubts] while the Greeks revel in philosophical debate. [Both groups are addicted to the same soul realm.] The supernatural is not proof of faith - Israel witnessed the supernatural for 40 years, day and night but an entire generation died in unbelief, failing to possess the promise, by believing a lie about themselves. See Numbers 13:33 and Joshua 2:11.)*

13:14 deceiving the earth-dwellers, dazzling them with their magic, whilst operating like a puppet on a string under the watchful eye of the Beast. The instruction was for the earth-dwellers to make an ¹idol-image of this "lamb" who was slain with a ²knife and then revived again. *(The word ¹**eikon** means image or likeness - this is the theme of the Bible and redemption; the image and likeness of God revealed and redeemed in human form. Idolatry is a projection of an image of one's own making. Idolatry is the crux of religion - it is an expensive business since your idol is like a slot machine at the casino. It remains hungry and it is wired to bite and bankrupt you. The word, ²**machaira** is used for a large knife, used for killing animals typically in the slaying of a sacrifice. Religion has a life of its own - the idea was that since the Dragon has lost its accusation against the human race in the heavenlies, [Revelation 12:8,9,10] it now had to find a pseudo, make-belief, future existence in the icons of man's imagination.)*

13:15 This lamb-like Beast *[resembling the typical counterfeit performance-based Christian religion]* **gave its man-made mirror image breath and a voice to speak and threaten to kill all who would not worship the image.**

13:16 Its mission was to mirror-imprint its ¹character upon everyone's hands and minds in order to manipulate what they think and do. *(So what is the mark of the Beast all about? The Greek word translated mark, is the word ¹**charagma** χαραγμα, closely related to the word, **charaktēr**, χαρακτηρ. From **charax** a tool used to engrave an express image or inscription. Either the character of the Father [I am], or the character of a distorted mindset [I am not] will influence our actions [hand] because it is what engages our thoughts [forehead]. See Hebrews 1:1-3, the son radiates the character of the Father. The only other place where this word is used is in Acts 17:29 Since we are the offspring of God then we already bear his image – God is not an image of our invention, artistically chiseled out of our imagination.*

See notes at the end of the chapter.)

13:17 The intent was clear: to control the world markets by manipulating people's minds and behavior with the same idea of the original sin, with its typical symptoms: "I am not defined by my being, I am defined by my doing. Therefore, I need to achieve this and buy that to endorse me." Failure- and sin-consciousness would be the currency of the entire religious industry. No one could buy or sell without being identified by the character, name and number-code *[password]* **of their idol, the Beast - the make-belief slain and raised to life lamb with the Dragon's voice.**

REVELATION Chapter 13

(The entire industry of religion was based on the currency of sin-consciousness. The business of accusation [Satanas] flourishes in an environment of sin-consciousness. See John 2:13 Jesus then went up to Jerusalem in time for the Jewish Passover. John 2:14 When Jesus went into the temple he was shocked to find scores of traders selling their sacrificial items, cattle, sheep and doves. Even their money brokers were comfortably set up in the sanctuary. (The business of sin-consciousness has taken over the mindset of religion - until Jesus arrives.) 2:15 Then with a whip that he plaited of small strands, he drove everyone with their sheep and oxen out of the temple and overturned the tables of the money brokers so that their money went flying all over the place. (Jesus dramatically reveals that his Father has no delight in our religious sacrificial systems and its sin-conscious currencies. The word σχοῖνος - schoinos, from skenos, tabernacle or skin - leather thongs - this is a profound prophetic picture of his own broken skin that would become the whip to drive out sin-consciousness from our minds - the ultimate cleansing of the temple - the sanctuary of God within us. 1 Peter 1:18,19.) 2:16 He also drove the dove traders out with, "How dare you turn my Father's house into a shopping mall?")

13:18 This riddle demands solving. Now put your mind to it, here is the clue: calculate the number of the Beast and see how it points directly to the number of mankind - it is a trinity of sixes. *(The numerical value of human life is 6 - Man-made religion is a mindset dominated by knowing oneself and others according to the flesh - the trinity of sixes is the mark of the counterfeit trinity that is defeated in the unfolding of the Lamb's triumph. In the imagery that follows, in the next chapter, John sees how the triune religious counterfeit system, the Dragon, the Beast and the False Prophet are thoroughly stripped of their influence and dominion and brought to nought.*

The name Ἰησοῦς Jesus is expressed by the number 888. Ι = 10; η = 8; σ = 200; ο = 70; υ = 400; σ = 200.

Written in full, heksakosioi, εξακοσιοι = 600, heksekonta, εξηκοντα = sixty and hex, εξ = 6 or, χ = 600; ξ = 60; ς' = 6 Thus χξς = 666

Vincent makes the following observation, χς' the name of Christ abridged, and ξ the emblem of the serpent, so that the sublimated sense is the Messiah of Satanas.)

Revelation Chapter 13 Extended Notes:

Counterfeit-Christianity - A wolf in sheep's clothing.
The Mark of The Beast - the currency of sin-consciousness
Notes on An Open Heaven

COUNTERFEIT CHRISTIANITY - REV 13

Counterfeit-Christianity - A wolf in sheep's clothing.

Counterfeit Christianity is not a specific denomination; its a veiled perception of mankind's authentic origin and redeemed identity and innocence. See Paul's take here in **2 Corinthians 4:3 If our message seems vague to anyone, it is not because we are withholding something from certain people. It is just because some are so stubborn in their efforts to uphold an outdated system that they don't see it. They are all equally found in Christ but they prefer to remain lost in the cul-de-sac language of the law.**

2 Corinthians 4:4 The survival and self-improvement programs of the [1]religious systems of this world veil the minds of the unbelievers; exploiting their ignorance about their true origin and their redeemed innocence. The veil of unbelief obstructs a person's view and keeps them from seeing what the light of the gospel so clearly reveals: the [2]glory of God is the image and likeness of our Maker redeemed in human form; this is what the gospel of Christ is all about. *(The god of this [1]aion, age, refers to the religious systems and governing structures of this world. The unbelief that neutralized Israel in the wilderness was the lie that they believed about themselves; "We are grasshoppers, and the 'enemy' is a giant beyond any proportion." [Numbers 13:33, Joshua 2:11, Hebrews 4:6] "They failed to possess the promise due to unbelief." The blueprint [2]doxa, glory of God, is what Adam lost on mankind's behalf. [See Ephesians 4:18])*

Revelation 13:3 One of its heads appeared to be [1]slain then it miraculously revived and was restored to health again. The entire human race was mesmerized by this. *(Here the "Christian-Religion" is represented by the same multi-headed Beast - mimicking the slain and resurrected Lamb - Only John uses the word, [1]sphatzo, which speaks of a brutal slaying. Four times in the book of Revelation he employs this word with direct reference to the slain Lamb of God, and once in 1 John 3:12 in reference to Cain's [1]killing of his brother Abel. See my commentary notes there.*

There is no saving power or relevance in a death and resurrection-belief that fails to see mankind's co-inclusion in the same event. In the mind and belief of God, an inseparable association exists, where, together with Jesus, mankind died and the same human race was co-revived and co-raised. Hosea 6:2 After two days he will revive us on the third day he will raise us up. This happened while we were still dead in our sins and trespasses. Ephesians 2:5,6.)

Revelation 13:11 Then I saw another wild animal; this one emerged out of the earth - it had two horns and resembled a young lamb; yet it had a Dragon's voice. *(The counterfeit "trinity" emerges - the one mirroring the other - the Dragon Accuser, the seven-headed sea-monster of religion with its leading role player, the head that was slain but became alive again and now the Dragon clothed in a lamb's-disguise)*

Revelation 13:12 Even though it had the appearance of the lamb, it operated in the same authority as the previous Beast - under the watchful eye of the Dragon. *[Counterfeit-Christianity as a religion is a wolf in sheep's clothing.]* **It is the same old Dragon in a lamb's disguise. Its mission was to engage the [1]earthbound dwellers to worship the counterfeit - the slaughtered animal that was restored to life out of death.** *(The historic relevance of the death and resurrection of the Lamb is in the revelation of mankind's* *co-inclusion - Jesus died our death and went into our hell and we were co-quickened in his resurrection and are now co-seated together with him in heavenly places. Our inclusion is the crux of the Gospel. It's what makes the good news, good news.*

*Again John employs the word ¹**katoikeō** from **kata**, down and **oikeo**, to dwell or set up home - thus to be earthbound. Revelation 13:8.*

*Matthew 7:15 "Beware of false Prophets, which come to you in sheep's clothing, but inwardly they are ravening wolves." In his sight - **enōpion autou**. In the eye of the first Beast who gets his authority from the Dragon - Revelation 13:3)*

Revelation 13:13 It had the power to mesmerise the masses with apparent great signs - even fire falling out of the sky. *(1 Corinthians 1:22 The Jews crave signs [to confirm their doubts] while the Greeks revel in philosophical debate. [Both groups are addicted to the same soul realm.] The supernatural is not proof of faith - Israel witnessed the supernatural for 40 years, day and night but an entire generation died in unbelief, failing to possess the promise, by believing a lie about themselves. See Numbers 13:33 and Joshua 2:11.)*

Revelation 13:14 Deceiving the earth-dwellers, dazzling them with signs, whilst operating like a puppet on a string under the watchful eye of the Beast. The instruction was for the earth-dwellers to make an ¹idol-image of the "lamb" who was slain with a ²knife and then revived again. *(The word ¹**eikon** means image or likeness - this is the theme of the Bible and redemption; the image and likeness of God revealed and redeemed in human form. Idolatry is a projection of an image of one's own making. Idolatry is the crux of religion - it is an expensive business since your idol is like a slot machine at the casino. It remains hungry and it is wired to bite and bankrupt you. The word, ²**machaira** is used for a large knife, used for killing animals typically in the slaying of a sacrifice. Religion has a life of its own - the idea was that since the Dragon has lost its accusation against the human race in the heavenlies, [Revelation 12:8,9,10] it now had to find a pseudo, make-belief future existence in the icons of man's imagination. See my notes on Armageddon at the end of Revelation 16 for, "earth-dwellers".)*

Revelation 13:15 This lamb-like Beast *[resembling the typical counterfeit performance-based Christian religion]* **gave its man-made mirror image breath and a voice to speak and threaten to kill all who would not worship the image.**

Revelation 13:16 Its mission was to mirror-imprint its ¹character upon everyone's hands and minds in order to manipulate what they think and do.

(The deception of the religious structures of the world engaged mankind with a counterfeit trinity, playing out in counterfeit "worship", based on a counterfeit identity, and an economy; built upon the business of fake, "what's-in-it-for-me-friendship" and adulterous fornication. Her harlotry intoxicated all the nations, even the kings of the earth have committed fornication with her; and the merchants of the earth became rich from the power of her make-belief luxury.

Mankind became snared in the perverted harlotry system of religion and by the Lamb's doing is now dramatically redeemed to the bliss of the romance of the ages.

Revelation 12:9 So the great Dragon, the ¹ancient ²ophis *[serpent]*, **also known as the Devil or Satan - whose sole mission was to lead the entire inhabited**

world astray - was cast down to the earth-dimension, together with all his ³celestial messengers. *(The word ¹archaios, ancient, of old; from arche, from the beginning. As Jesus said that the Devil was a murderer "from the beginning" The Greek word, ²ophis is translated serpent and comes from optomai, to gaze, in this case, to present a visual idea through illusion. John 8:44. He was stripped of his pseudo rank of authority see Colossians 2:14,15 he was made a public spectacle. Luke 10:18 And Jesus said to them, I saw Satan falling out of heaven like lightning. Also John 12:31 Now is the judgment of this world; now the ruler of this world shall be cast down. [When I am lifted up on the cross. John 12:32] The word often translated as angel, ³aggelos has two components, agō to lead as a shepherd leads and agele, a herd of cattle or company.)*

Revelation 12:10 Then I heard a very loud voice in the heavens announcing, This is the moment which the entire prophetic word pointed to and culminates in; it is the realization of mankind's salvation. The power of the kingdom of our God and its authority is endorsed in the I-am-ness of his Christ. The business of accusation is bankrupt. The 24/7 industry of condemning the brotherhood of mankind before the face of God has been annihilated. *(The word ¹kategoros, a name given to the Devil by the Rabbis, the one whose business is accusation, from kata, downward and agora, to trade; a word used for all kinds of business in the public arena.)*

Revelation 17:2 She engaged the kings of the earth with her harlotry intoxicating the earth dwellers with the wine of her passion and fornication.

Revelation 17:3 The messenger then carried me into a desert place *[in total contrast to the hustle and bustle of the busy trade routes of the oceans and the rivers]* I was transported there in spirit and saw a woman seated upon a ¹scarlet colored Beast; with ²blasphemous, insulting names written all over them like a label revealing the content of their ³cargo. The Beast had seven heads and ten horns. *(For reference to the same Beast, Revelation 13:1-10 and its second Partner in verse 11, 12, the Lamb with the Dragon's voice, later called the False Prophet and here, the Harlot. Together in their alliance with the Dragon they form the Counterfeit Trinity. Also Revelation 17:12.)*

Revelation 19:20 And the Beast and the miracle working Puppet Partner, the False Prophet were arrested and cast into the lake ablaze with sulphur. These two were the ones, empowered by the Dragon to amaze and deceive those who were tattooed in their heads and hands with the character of the Beast and paying religious homage to its image. *(The word ¹theion, sulphur, from theios, godlike [neuter as noun, divinity]: - divine, godhead. Sulphur is a yellow inflammable mineral substance found in quantities on the shores of the Dead Sea. This was also known as divine incense, because burning brimstone was regarded as having power to purify, and to ward off disease. Its medicinal values are well known even today.*

Revelation 14:8-20 In the imagery here, John sees how the triune religious counterfeit system, the Dragon, the Beast and the False Prophet are thoroughly stripped of their influence and dominion and brought to nought. The False Prophet is mentioned in Revelation 16:13 [KJV] "And I saw three unclean spirits like frogs come out of the mouth of the Dragon, and out of the mouth of the Beast, and out of the mouth of the False Prophet." Here in Revelation 19:20 and also in Revelation 20:10 The Devil, who led them astray will be hurled into the lake of fire and brimstone where his puppet partners, the Beast and the False Prophet have already been confined to. Day and Night they will be the subject of God's touchstone for the ages of the ages - the very atmosphere of the entire universe will be thoroughly fumigated from any evidence of Satanas. [See my notes on the Touchstone in Revelation 14:10] Revelation 13:11 Then I saw another wild animal; this one emerged out of the earth - it had two horns and resembled a young lamb; yet it had a Dragon's voice. [The counterfeit "trinity" emerges - the one mirroring the other - 1/ the Dragon-Accuser; 2/ the seven headed sea-monster of religion with its leading role player, the head that was slain but became alive again; 3/ and now, here, the Dragon clothed in a lamb's-disguise; later called, the false Prophet.] See extended **Notes on The lake of fire** *at the end of chapter 19.)*

Revelation 15:2 Then I saw something that looked like an ocean on fire; its liquid waters became a solid surface like transparent glass ¹molded in its heat. Standing tall in triumph on top of the glassy sea, with their God-harps, were the redeemed ones who ²emerged victorious ³out of the grasp and claim of the false trinity-system of religious indoctrination - the Beast, its image, its character imprint and its password name and number-code. *(The word ²**nikoontas** is the Present Participle of **nikao**, to conquer; the Present Participle describes an action thought of as simultaneous with the action of the main verb, ¹**memigmenen** - a victory having been forged in fire, which is the Perfect Passive Participle of **mignumi**, to mingle, to mix. The Perfect tense denotes an action which is completed in the past, but the effects of which are regarded as continuing into the present.*

A reminder of the prophetic picture of Israel walking as if it were on dry land through the ocean of waters when God led them out of Pharaoh's claim.

The Preposition **ek** *denotes origin - here, clearly pointing to the fact that these have escaped the tyranny of slavery to the corrupt religious system of a false identity.*

This is the transaction of the ages, where the Lamb that was slain enters the marketplace where slaves are sold and he redeems mankind – purchases us back out of the hands of the claim of accusation – **Satanas** *– the Dragon , the Beast of religion, the false Prophet – mankind is redeemed from the idolatry of centuries of devotion to an image of their own making, reflecting a lost identity. The transaction-idea is to persuade our minds of our redeemed value. Jesus didn't buy us back from the Devil. A thief never becomes an owner. Psalm 22:27 and Psalm 24:1.)*

Revelation 15:3 This song of the redeemed echoes the song of Moses, God's servant and the song of the Lamb, singing: "The things you do are spectacular and amazing, Lord God Almighty. Righteousness and truth are your trademarks. You are the King of the ages and of the Nations." *(See my commentary note to this verse.)*

In the genius of God, the scandal of the cross, revealed in the extremities of the Lamb's suffering as the scapegoat of the human race, disengaged every principality and pseudo mindset of opposition to the revelation of the Romance of the ages.

SIN-CONSCIOUS CURRENCY - REV 13

The Mark of The Beast - the currency of sin-consciousness

Revelation 13:15 This lamb-like Beast [*resembling the typical counterfeit performance-based Christian religion*] **gave its man-made mirror image breath and a voice to speak and threaten to kill all who would not worship the image.**

Revelation 13:16 Its mission was to mirror-imprint its ¹character upon everyone's hands and minds in order to manipulate what they think and do. (*So what is the mark of the Beast all about? The Greek word translated mark, is the word ¹**charagma** χαραγμα, closely related to the word, **charaktēr**, χαρακτηρ. From **charax** a tool used to engrave an express image or inscription. Either the character of the Father [I am], or the character of a distorted mindset [I am not] will influence our actions [hand] because it is what engages our thoughts [forehead]. See Hebrews 1:1-3, the son radiates the **character** of the Father. The only other place where this word is used is in Acts 17:29 Since we are the offspring of God then we already bear his image — God is not an image of our invention, artistically chiseled out of our imagination.*

Just like in Isaiah 55:8-11 where God says, "Your thoughts are not my thoughts; therefore your ways are not my ways. For as the heavens are higher than the earth, so are my ways higher than your ways and my thoughts than your thoughts..... but my word will incarnate, and saturate earth (flesh) just like the rain and the snow cancel the distance between heaven and earth. Instead of the thorn, the fir and instead of the brier, the myrtle. This explains the first part of Isaiah 55 - Ho. Everyone who is thirsty - disappointed in their own efforts to buy that which cannot be purchased with the currency of their own achievement; desperate to escape the sense of unworthiness, lack and condemnation; paying any price in the hope to become [what they in reality already are by design.] This is the basis of the mindset of the "I-am-not tree-system." Isaiah 55:1 Your thirst drives you to the waters but you have no money; I urge you to buy without your currency and drink priceless wine and eat the finest wheat [ἄνευ ἀργυρίου καὶ τιμῆς [perceived value] οἴνου καὶ στέαρ - Psalm 147:3 -Septuagint: He satisfies you with the finest of the wheat.]

Your painful and wearisome labor adds no value to your life. Hear me. Incline your ears. I want to honor and indulge you with that which truly satisfies. This is the bread your soul craves; this is your true sustenance.

Adam Clarke comments on Isaiah 55:2, "Why should ye be so zealously attached to a doctrine from which your souls derive neither comfort nor nourishment?")

Revelation 13:17 The intent was clear: to control the world markets by manipulating people's minds and behavior with the idea of the original sin, with its typical symptoms: "I am not defined by my being, I am defined by my doing. Therefore, I need to achieve this and buy that to define me." Failure- and sin-consciousness would be the currency of the entire religious industry. No one could buy or sell without being identified by the character, name and number-code [*password*] **of their idol, the Beast - the make-belief slain and raised to life lamb with the Dragon's voice.** (*The entire industry of religion was based on the currency of sin-consciousness. The business of accusation [Satanas] flourishes in an environment of sin-consciousness.*

See **John 2:13 Jesus then went up to Jerusalem in time for the Jewish Passover.**

John 2:14 When Jesus went into the temple he was shocked to find scores of traders selling their sacrificial items, cattle, sheep and doves. Even their money brokers were comfortably set up in the sanctuary. *(The business of sin-consciousness has taken over the mindset of religion - until Jesus arrives.)*

John 2:15 Then with a whip that he plaited of small strands, he drove everyone with their sheep and oxen out of the temple and overturned the tables of the money brokers so that their money went flying all over the place. *(Jesus dramatically reveals that his Father has no delight in our religious sacrificial systems and its sin-conscious currencies. The word σχοῖνος - schoinos, from skenos, tabernacle or skin - leather thongs - this is a profound prophetic picture of his own broken skin that would become the whip to drive out sin-consciousness from our minds - the ultimate cleansing of the temple - the sanctuary of God within us. 1 Peter 1:18,19.)*

John 2:16 He also drove the dove traders out with, "How dare you turn my Father's house into a shopping mall?")

Revelation 13:18 This riddle demands solving. Now put your mind to it, here is the clue: calculate the number of the Beast and see how it points directly to the number of mankind - it is a trinity of sixes. *(The numerical value of human life is 6 - Man-made religion is a mindset dominated by knowing oneself and others according to the flesh - the trinity of sixes is the mark of the counterfeit trinity that is defeated in the unfolding of the Lamb's triumph. In the imagery that follows, in the next chapter, John sees how the triune religious counterfeit system, the Dragon, the Beast and the False Prophet are thoroughly stripped of their influence and dominion and brought to nought.*

The name Ἰησοῦς Jesus is expressed by the number 888. Ι = 10; η = 8; σ = 200; o = 70; υ = 400; σ = 200.

Written in full, heksakosioi, εξακοσιοι = 600, heksekonta, εξηκοντα = sixty and hex, εξ = 6 or, χ = 600; ξ = 60; ς' = 6 Thus χξς = 666. Vincent makes the following observation, χς' the name of Christ abridged, and ξ the emblem of the serpent.

The Christ image in man is flawed by the veiled mind introduced by the Serpent's deception of the "I am not- idea".)

1 John 3:8 Sin's source is a ¹fallen mindset, from the beginning. For this purpose the Son of God was revealed. His mission was to undo the works of the Devil. *(The word, diabolos, from dia, because of and ballo, to cast down.)*

1 John 3:9 To discover one's authentic sonship in God, is to discover true freedom from sin. We are born of him and his seed remains in us; this is the only possible reference to sober up the mind from the intoxicating influence of deception. *(The incorruptible seed of our Father carries the exact pattern of the authentic life of our design. Jesus calls the Devil, the father of lies.)*

1 John 3:12 Cain's ¹killing of his brother Abel, is in such contrast to this. His motivation was clearly ²sourced in the ³poneros tree-system; his idea of Divine ⁴favor was to count on his own works as being superior to his

brother's faith righteousness. *(Immediately after the fall, [Genesis 3:20] Adam named the woman Elohim gave him, Eve, [in Hebrew חוה **Chawah**, and in Greek, ζωη **Zoe**.] He thus co-echoes and reinforces the prophetic word that **Elohim** gave him: Life in the face of death. "The seed of the woman, shall crush the deceiver's head." The fallen mindset shall be destroyed. So here, in their two sons, we have the first generation of fallen mankind confronted with their personal pursuit of a lost identity and a lost sense of value and favor. Caleb's motivation was clearly sourced [²ek, out of, origin] in the **diabolos** [cast down], which is so typical of the ³**poneros** tree-system. The tree of the knowledge of good and evil [**poneros**] represents mankind's lost sense of identity and righteousness, where the global pursuit of mankind would now be their constant effort to achieve righteousness by means of their own works. This inevitably leads to disappointment where shame replaces innocence, and union and fellowship are lost. The word evil, **poneros**, suggests to be full of hardships, labors and annoyances. Genesis 3:19 "In the sweat of your face shall you eat your bread." The sacrifice of Cain is exactly that. It represents his trust in the fruit of his own toil to gain him a ⁴favorable [**charin**] standing with God.*

We have the prophetic picture of a scapegoat repeated here in Genesis 4. Not only in the sacrifice that Abel brought; but also in him being murdered by his brother. Just like we would one day murder our brother Jesus. In Genesis 3, Elohim did not clothe Adam with the skin of an animal because of a divine need to be appeased, but because of their unconditional love for Adam; they spoke the language of Adam's own judgment: Adam, not Elohim, was embarrassed about his nakedness. The clothing was not to make Elohim look at Adam differently, but to make Adam feel better about himself. And ultimately it was to prepare Adam for the unveiling of the mystery of mankind's redemption in the incarnation. Here Deity would clothe themselves in human skin in a Son, and the Lion of Judah, would become the Lamb of God, in order to free our minds to re-discover his image and likeness in our skin. Revelation 5:5,6.

*Only John uses the word, ¹**sphatzo**, which speaks of a slaying. Four times in the book of Revelation he employs this word in the context of the slain Lamb of God.*

See also Hebrews 11:4, "It was faith that made the difference between the sacrifices of Abel and Cain, and confirmed Abel's righteousness. God bore witness to righteousness as a gift rather than a reward. Even though he was murdered, his faith still has a voice today."

Philo, a Hellenistic Jewish philosopher, says that in the dispute between Cain and Abel, Abel attributed all things to God, and Cain ascribed everything to himself; so that the controversy was about grace and works. [Philo lived c. 25 BCE – c. 50 CE]

The tree of the knowledge of good and evil represents a fallen identity; the thought that likeness with God could be earned through good intentions, rather than realizing the gift of life that already defines his image and likeness in us.)

Hebrews 8:12 This knowledge of me will never again be based on sin-consciousness. My act of mercy, extended in Christ as the new Covenant, has removed every possible definition of sin from memory. *(God's memory of our sins was not what needed to be addressed in the redemption of our innocence. God did not have a problem with sin-consciousness, we had. He wasn't hiding from Adam and Eve in the garden; they were hiding from him. What needed to* *be addressed were our perceptions of a judgmental God, which were the inevitable fruit of the I-am-not tree system and mentality.*

Revenge, judgment, guilt, condemnation, inferiority, shame, regret, suspicion etc. could not be treated lightly; they are the enemies of romance. If rules could do it, then the law would be our opportunity to save ourselves, simply by making the correct decisions. If willpower could save us, then Moses would be our savior. But, alas. "The good that I want to do I cannot." See Romans 7.

The scapegoat system would be introduced to somehow address and attempt to manage the consequences of sin. The typical "eye for an eye, tooth for a tooth" scenario would be substituted with the idea of a scapegoat. And so, every system of sacrifice carried some significance, but only as far as it pointed to its weaknesses in dealing with the root of the problem, and the need for a better solution. We needed more than forgiveness of our sins; we needed a savior who could rescue us from our sinfulness. This was not merely a means whereby we could get rid of the cobwebs; the spider needed to be killed. The "pay now, sin later-system" had a very real sell-by date.

See Hebrews 10:2 & 3, Had it been possible to present the perfect offering that had the power to successfully remove any trace of a sin-consciousness, then the sacrificial system would surely have ceased to be relevant. But in the very repetition of these ritual sacrifices the awareness of guilt is reinforced rather than removed.

God does not demand sacrifice; he provides the sacrifice. The ultimate sacrifice for sins would never be something we did, or brought to God, to appeal to him; but the shocking scandal of the cross, is the fact that mankind is confronted with the extravagant, embarrassing proportions of the love of their Maker; he would go to the most ridiculous extreme to finally convince us of his heart towards us. In order to persuade us of our worth to him, he speaks the most severe scapegoat language: "Behold the Lamb of God, who takes away the sins of the world." This completely disarms religion. Suddenly there is nothing that we can do to persuade God about our sincere intentions; this is God persuading us of his eternal love dream.)

See my notes on "Why the other tree and why the temptation in the Garden?" in 1 John 3:12

See also 1 Peter 1:18,19 It is clear to see that you were ransomed from the futile, fallen mindset that you inherited from your fathers, **not by the currency of your own labor, represented by the fluctuating values of gold and silver, and the economy of your religious efforts; but you were redeemed with the priceless blood of Christ;** he is the ultimate sacrifice; spotless and without blemish. He completes the prophetic picture. (*In him God speaks the most radical scapegoat language of the law of judgment, and brings final closure to a dead and redundant system. In Psalm 40:6,7, it is clearly stated that God does not require sacrifices or offerings. Jesus is the Lamb of God. He collides victoriously with the futile sacrificial system whereby offerings are constantly made to the pseudo, moody, monster gods of our imagination.*)

Notes on An Open Heaven

"Jesus has united heaven and earth, the life of God and human life in himself. Just as it was planned before the time of the ages." Dr Baxter Kruger.

Revelation 3:7 And to the messenger of the ekklesia of ¹Philadelphia write, I am the Holy and True one. I hold the key of David as prophesied in ¹Isaiah 22:22. Yes, I ²unlock the mysteries of the heavenly dimension and no one can shut the door. And I lock the entrance and none (*of the old legalistic mindsets*) **can access it.** (*¹Philadelphos, from philos, fondness; friendship, and adelphos, the same womb; immediate family; kinsfolk; household. ²Isaiah 22:22 And I will place on his shoulder the key of the house of David; he shall open, and none shall shut; and he shall shut, and none shall open. The word ²anoigo from ana upward and agoo, to lead. Also Ezekiel 34: 23 Then I will place one shepherd over them, my servant David, and he will take care of them. He will take care of them and be their shepherd.*)

Revelation 3:21 And everyone's personal triumph will be celebrated together with me, by being jointly seated together in my Kingship. On exactly the same basis of ¹my victory celebration and my joint-seatedness with my Father in his throne. (*Note the words, ¹hōs kagō enikēsa where enikesa is the first Aorist Active Indicative of nikaō, to conquer; looking back on the victory as over in the past. A.T. Roberston compares this to John 16:33 where before the Cross Jesus says egō nenikēka ton kosmon which is in the Perfect Active tense, emphasizing the abiding effect of the victory.*)

Revelation 3:22 Now listen up with your inner ears. Hear with understanding what the Spirit is saying to the ekklesia. (*Paul prays in Ephesians that the eyes of our understanding will be flooded with light so that we may see our co-seatedness.*)

Revelation 4:1 ¹Talking about our co-seatedness, I want you to see something. Oh wow. What I see takes my breath away. A ²wIde-open door in the heavenly realm. The first thing I heard was this voice addressing me. It was distinct and clear, like the sound of a trumpet; it captured my attention, inviting me to enter. "Come up here and I will show you how everything ³coincides with what you have already seen." (*I saw [eidon] second Aorist Active Indicative of horaō. Behold [idou] exclamation of vivid emotion as John looked, "With this I saw."Most translations would translate meta tauta with, "after this" The word ¹meta however refers to, with this; coinciding with this. [Our co-seatedness and enjoying feasting together with him. v 20 and 21 from the previous chapter. Revelation 3:21 And everyone's personal triumph will be celebrated together with me, by being jointly seated together in my Kingship. On exactly the same basis of my victory celebration and my joint-seatedness with my Father in his throne.] Robertson suggests that it is a change in the panorama, not chronology.*

The word ²eneogmene is the Perfect Passive Participle of anoigō to open, from ana, upward and agō, to lead; as in Revelation 3:8 [door of opportunity] and Revelation 3:20 [door of the heart] **A dimension of limitless possibilities open, right in front of my eyes.** *The Passive Participle describes a state that exists at the time coincident with that of the leading verb as a result of action completed prior to the* *time of the main verb, behold. Thus John witnessed the opening of the door. The Perfect tense denotes an action which is completed in the past, but the effects of which are regarded as continuing into the present. The verb **genesthai** is not the future of the verb ¹to be; it is the Aorist Infinitive where the thought is not the prophetic, but the necessity of the inevitable consequence as a result of the crucified and risen Christ. John again, as in verse 1, employs the verb, **ginomai**, to beget, in the Aorist Infinitive tense, **genesthai**, which indicates prior completion of an action in relationship to a point in time. Greek Infinitives could have either a Present or Aorist form. The contrast between the two forms was not necessarily one of time, it is a difference of aspect. The Present Infinitive was used to express progressive or imperfective aspect. It pictures the action expressed by the verb as being in progress. The Aorist Infinitive however does not express progressive aspect. It presents the action expressed by the verb as a completed unit with a beginning and end.)*

Revelation 4:2 So here I am, immersed in this unrestricted space of spirit ecstasy. As the vision opens I immediately notice the throne and One seated upon it. *("Having accomplished purification for sins he sat down." His throne is proof of mankind's redeemed innocence. This unveiling is central to the throne-theme. See Hebrews 1:1-4 in the Mirror.)*

Revelation 4:4 And coiled into a complete circle around the throne were twenty four thrones with twenty four ¹Presbyterians seated upon the thrones. They were enwrapped in white with ²victors' wreaths of gold crowning their heads. Their minds were co-enthroned in the authority of the throne engulfing them in their co-seatedness. *(In the symbolic language of Revelation, we have a circle of people representing the entire human race. ¹Typo drawn again from the Jewish **suneidron** - a co-seatedness around the throne - the 24 **presbuterians** or ¹Elders picture the twelve prophetic Patriarchs and the twelve Apostles, here as two dispensations merged into one, now fully representing the entire ekklesia. The word **kuklothen** is the adverb from **kuklo**; to form a circle, that is, all around; from **kuliō**, rolling together. From the base of **kuma**, from **kuō**, to swell [with young], that is, bend, curve; a billow, as bursting or toppling: - thus, a wave; through the idea of circularity. The word ²**stephanos**, is a victor's wreath.*

Much of what John saw, reflected in the Jewish mind as familiar prophetic pointers and symbols. See the prophetic imagery in Ezekiel 1:1-28. The symbolic pictures John sees of judgment would immediately remind his typical Jewish audience of their prophets imaginary of judgment. This time the slaughtered and risen Lamb brings brand new context. Israel's unfaithfulness is met and eclipsed by God's faithfulness. The Lamb's death and resurrection confronts every idea of judgment that was mankind's due.)

Revelation 13:8 The plan was to engage the entire ¹earthbound population of the planet to worship the Beast [*The counterfeit "slain and risen lamb"*]. **This would endorse the idea** [*of the religious system*], **that there were individuals, since the fall of the ²cosmos, whose names were not included in the slain Lamb's Book of Life.** *(The word ¹**katoikeō** from **kata**, down and **oikeo**, to dwell or set up home - ἐπὶ τῆς γῆς upon the earth - thus, the earthbound population of the planet. Paul invites us to engage our thoughts with resurrection realities and to see ourselves seated together with Christ in heavenly places. Colossians 3:1-3. The word, ²**kosmos** in the NT refers to the entire human family and their social structures.)*

The "earthbound-dilemma" of mankind is addressed in the Incarnate Christ. *(See notes on Armageddon at the end of Chapter 16)*

See **John 1:50 Jesus said, "So you believe because I say I saw you sitting under the fig tree? You haven't seen anything yet.**

John 1:51 Truly I say unto you, Nathaniel *[singular]*, **because of who I am, you** *[plural - You-manity - all the families in heaven and on earth]* **will surely see this communication between the heavenly sphere and earth thrown wide ¹open and the celestial messengers of God ascending and descending upon the Incarnate son of man. Heaven and earth meet in the Incarnate one.** *(In him every definition of separation and distance is canceled. Isaiah 55:10,11 "For as the rain and the snow come down from heaven, and return not there without saturating the earth [all flesh], so shall my word be that goes forth from my mouth; it shall not return to me empty, but it shall accomplish that which I purpose, and prosper in the thing for which I sent it. The prophetic word was destined to become flesh; every nook and cranny of human life is saturated in the incarnation. The word* **aneogota**, *Perfect Active Participle Accusative Masculine Singular, 2nd Conjugation-form; the one who has led us upward- from* **anoigō, ana**, *upward and* **agoo**, *to lead. Jesus reminds Nathaniel of Genesis 28:12-14 And Jacob dreamt that there was a ladder set up on the earth, and the top of it reached to heaven; and behold, the celestial messengers of God were ascending and descending on it. And Jahweh said to him, I am Elohim of Abraham, your seed shall be like the dust of the earth, and you shall spread abroad to the west and to the east and to the north and to the south; and in you and your descendants have all the families of the earth been blessed.)*

Revelation 19:11 Then, in my vision, heaven opened and I saw a white horse appear; and the name of the one seated upon the horse is Faithful and True. Righteousness spans the range of his judgment and warfare.

Ephesians 3:15 Every family in heaven and on earth originates in him; his is mankind's family name and he remains the authentic identity of every nation.

Ephesians 1:3 Let's celebrate God. He lavished every blessing heaven has upon us in Christ.

Ephesians 4:8 Scripture confirms that "he took captivity captive" - *[in dying our death, he arrested captive mankind]* **and in the resurrection, he led us as trophies in his triumphant procession on high. Consider the genius of God, in the incarnate Christ, he repossessed what belonged to us by design, in human form; this is his gift to us.** *(In this verse Paul explains what he just declared in verse 7 - he wants us to know the extravagant extent and dimensions of the measure of the gift of Christ. Remember that he is writing from prison [Ephesians 4:1] He's not asking for prayers to get him out of jail. He is imprisoned in Christ- my complete existence is defined and confined in him. He was once a prisoner of the law of performance, held hostage in his own body, crying in desperation, "Is there anyone who can deliver them from this death trap?" [Romans 7] He now speaks as a prisoner of Christ. He is reminded of and obviously intrigued by the entire context of Psalm 67 which celebrates God rescuing the prisoners from their captivity and even the wayward and stubborn, who already died and are stuck in* *their graves. [mindsets] See Psalm 67:6,7 Also Ephesians 2:6, We are also elevated in his ascension to be equally welcome in the throne room of the heavenly realm where we are now seated together with him in his authority.*

Ephesians 4:9 The fact that he ascended confirms his victorious descent into the deepest pits of human despair. *(See John 3:13, "No one has ascended into heaven but he who descended from heaven, even the son of man." All mankind originates from above; we are **anouthen**, from above. See James 1:17, 18.)*

Ephesians 4:10 He now occupies the ultimate rank of authority, from the lowest regions of our darkness into which he reached in order to rescue us, to the highest authority in the heavens, having executed his mission to the fullest. *(Fallen mankind is fully restored to the authority of the authentic life of their design. [Psalm 139:7,8, Where can I go where your Spirit is absent? Or where shall I flee from your presence? If I ascend to heaven, You. If I make my bed in Sheol, You.])*

From the religious Monster in camouflage, the counterfeit "lamb" who desires to manipulate and control the business of buying and selling with a counterfeit currency of a fear and performance based alliance to its stamped image and inscription on their foreheads and hands, to the true Lamb of God who ransomed the human race with the currency of his self-giving agape and shed blood, revealing their inherent worth, based on Elohim's image and inscription entwined in their inner person.

Colossians 3:1 See yourselves co-raised with Christ. Now ponder with persuasion the consequence of your co-inclusion in him. Relocate yourselves mentally. Engage your thoughts with throne room realities where you are co-seated with Christ in the executive authority of God's right hand.

Colossians 3:2 Becoming affectionately acquainted with throne room thoughts will keep you from being distracted again by the earthly [soul-ruled] **realm.** *("Set your minds upon the things that are above and not upon the things below." RSV. Whatever you face in your daily lives, acquaint yourselves with the greater reality. The things that are above. Do not engage the energy of the things that are below. Also note Romans 1:18, where the word **katecho** is used - to echo downwards is the opposite to **anoche**, to echo upward- Romans 2:4 and Romans 3:26. Also 2 Corinthians 4:18 "We are not keeping any score of what seems so obvious to the senses on the surface; it is fleeting and irrelevant; it is the unseen eternal realm within us which has our full attention and captivates our gaze." A renewed mind conquers the space previously occupied by worthless pursuits and habits.*

The awakening to and engaging in Spirit dimension is not a gradual evolving into spirit awareness – it is not in any way time related – it's as immediate as one's next breath and as refreshing as plunging into a cool pool of mountain water on a hot summers day and as all-consuming as falling head over heels in love. It eclipses night and day; time and season.

Just like the earth is eclipsed by galaxies of planets, moons and stars of innumerable quantities and mind-boggling dimensions, so, the sphere of our visible world is eclipsed in Spirit dimension beyond all comparison. The "heavens" are far more spectacular in every definition, than a mere distant, geographical location, somewhere in outer space. It spans the horizons of Eternity; the ages of the ages are engulfed here and yet closer to us than our breath or thought.

Heavenly places are not located in "Outer Space". It is living from within. Use your GPS. God's Positioning is our Seamless union.

Jesus did not point to the sky when he gave the address of the kingdom of God; he said, "The kingdom of God is within you." Luke 17:21

Also Matthew 13:44 The Kingdom of heaven is the treasure, buried, redeemed and now revealed in the field.)

2 Corinthians 4:6 The light source is founded in the same God who said, "Light, be." And light shone out of darkness. He lit the lamp in our understanding so that we may clearly recognize the features of his likeness in the face of Jesus Christ reflected within us. *(The same God who bade light shine out of darkness has kindled a light in our hearts, whose shining is to make known his glory as he has revealed it in the features of Jesus Christ. — Knox Translation)*

2 Corinthians 4:7 And now, in the glow of this glorious light and with unveiled faces we discover this treasure where it was hidden all along, in these frail skin-suits made of ¹clay. We did not invent ourselves; we are God's idea to begin with and the dynamic of his doing and amazing engineering. *(The word translated earthen vessel or clay jar is the word ¹**ostrakinos** from **ostrakon** "oyster". It is a great visual picture of how we carry a very valuable pearl within us. The cosmetic value of the clay pot can never compete with the treasure it holds. There is so much more to you than what meets the eye. "The kingdom of heaven is like treasure hidden in an agricultural field, which a man found and covered up; then in his joy he goes and sells all that he has and buys the entire field." In order to redeem our minds from the lies that we believed about ourselves, God invested all that he has in the redeeming of our original value. See 1 Peter 1:18,19. He rescued the life of our design. Our inner life hosts this treasure. Jesus said in John 7:37,38, "If you believe that I am what the Scriptures are all about, you will know that you are what I am all about and rivers of living water will gush out of **your innermost being**.")*

2 Corinthians 4:8 We often feel completely hemmed in on every side but our inner space remains unrestricted; when there seems to be no way out, we escape within.

2 Peter 1:3 By his divine engineering he gifted us with all that it takes to live life to the full, where our ordinary day to day lives mirror our devotion and romance with our Maker. His intimate knowledge of us introduces us to ourselves again and elevates us to a position where his original intention is clearly perceived.

2 Peter 1:5... Familiarize yourselves with every ingredient that faith unfolds. See there how elevated you are, and from within this position *[of your co-seatedness in Christ],* **enlightened perspective will dawn within you.**

*See my **notes on Earthbound vs. Heavenly Dimension** at the end of Revelation Chapter 16 [**Armageddon**])*

REVELATION Chapter 14

14:1 Oh wow. You've got to see this. The little Lamb, standing on mount Zion and with him a hundred and forty four thousand(s) with the Lamb's Name and the Name of his Father written on their foreheads. *(Sonship redeemed. Hebrews 1:1-3. Note the 144,000's in plural, representing the symbolic value that includes the entire prophetic significance of the Jews as well as the prophetic context of their representing the entire human race. In you, all the nations of the earth will bless themselves. See Extended Notes, **From Mt Sinai to Mt Zion**.)*

14:2 And I heard a voice emerge from the heavens. It was like the sound of a thunderous torrent of cascading waterfalls. Then arose a choir of voices accompanied by stringed instruments which sounded like harps. *(The word κιθαρῳδός - kitharodos, is from κιθάρα - kithara, a [guitar] harp - a triangular shaped stringed instrument with 7 and later 10 strings traditionally associated with joy and gladness in worship [Psalm 33:2; Psalm 98:5] and ᾠδός - odos, a singer. Revelation 5:8-13*

The feast of Pentecost, also called the feast of harvest and the feast of weeks, Exodus 34:22, was celebrated fifty days after the Passover to commemorate the giving of the law on Mount Sinai, which took place fifty days after, and hence called by the Greeks Pentecost. The new Pentecost has come.)

14:3 There was a strange yet familiar newness to their song; almost as if it was reflected in the face of the throne and echoed in the faces of the living creatures and the elders - a song which could not be taught or learned. It is the song of the redeemed - represented here in the 144,000('s) who were [1]bought from the claim and clutches of the earth. *(The word [1]agoratso, to buy in a typical market context - **apo tes ges**, away from the earth. Just when it seemed that no one could buy or sell any longer unless they were worshipping the Beast, [Revelation 13] a transaction takes place in a superior currency and realm that frees the human race from their slavery. Just like in the prophetic picture of Israel's freedom from Pharaoh. Isaiah 29:13 And the Lord said: "Because these people draw near with their mouth and honor me with their lips, while their hearts are far from me, and their fear of me is a commandment of men learned by repetition.)*

14:4 These boldly exhibit the [3]first fruit of the Lamb's doing. Here we have blameless innocence on display and redefined. What the law of performance failed to do, the Lamb did. They are pure and unblemished in their [1]close association with the Lamb - [2]purchased and rescued out of the grip of an enslaved, fallen humanity; representing the entire human race as first fruits to God and the Lamb. These 'first fruit redeemed ones' have witnessed mankind's joint association in the [4]full range of the Lamb's journey. They are all marriageable maidens with their virginity intact. Their default settings are fully rebooted. *(The word, [1]akolouthentes is the Present Participle in the Nominative case of **akoloutheo**, with a from **hama** as a particle of union and **keleuthos** - a road; thus, travel companions; to be in the same way with, that is, to accompany closely - to be in immediate association with someone. The present Participle describes an action thought of as simultaneous with the action of the main verb, which, in this case is [2]egorasthesan which is the Aorist Passive Indicative of **agorazō**, to go to market, that is to purchase; specifically to redeem: - buy, redeem. Thus in the Aorist Passive it means, having* *been redeemed - redemption is a done deal. The word ³**aparchē** means first fruit. See 1 Corinthians 15:20 However this very moment the risen Christ represents everyone who has ever died; exactly like the first fruit represents the complete harvest. 1 Corinthians 15:21 The same mankind who died in a man was raised again in a man. 1 Corinthians 15:22 In Adam all died; in Christ all are made alive.*

*The words, ⁴**hopou an hupagei** - mean whithersoever he travels - the comprehensive range of his journey. From being the Logos, face to face with God before time was and announced as the slain Lamb and Messiah since the fall of the world; throughout every Messianic, prophetic record of Moses, the Prophets and the Psalm, to the incarnate man Jesus the Christ; in his life, ministry, message and betrayal, his trial, his crucifixion, his burial, his descent into hell, his triumph there and in his taking captivity captive in his resurrection and glorious ascent and leading mankind as his trophies into the throne room where we are now co-seated together with him. See* **Extended Notes on the 144,000 Virgins** *at the end of this chapter.)*

In the imagery that follows, John sees how the triune religious counterfeit system, the Dragon, the Beast and the False Prophet are thoroughly stripped of their influence and dominion and brought to nought.

14:5 This is not make-believe or wishful-thinking. No trace of deceit nor any form of blemish was found in their conversation.

14:6 And I saw another celestial messenger soaring in mid heaven - this messenger was the carrier of the grandest news of the ages. His mission was to announce these glad tidings of everlasting proportion to every single nation, tribe, language and people grouping on the earth. *(Seven times human society is addressed in the most all-inclusive fashion, with a like grouping of words for all mankind of all races and nations; - Revelation 5:9, then also Revelation 7:9, Revelation 10:11, Revelation 11:9 Revelation 13:7; here in Revelation 14:6 and Revelation 17:15.)*

14:7 In a great voice he declared, "Be awestruck with the amazingness of God. Give him glory. The hour of his judgment has come. He is the Maker of the heavenly realm, the earth, the sea and the fountains of the waters." *(See John 12:31-33)*

14:8 And a second celestial messenger followed with more good news. Babylon the great city has crashed. She who sold herself as a prostitute to all the nations and intoxicated them with the wine of her passion will never fly again. *(The language is an echo of Isaiah 21:9, "Babylon has fallen. It has fallen. All the idols they worship lie shattered on the ground." Jeremiah 51:8 Babylon will suddenly fall and be shattered.)*

14:9 Then a third celestial messenger followed and announced with a loud voice that whoever worships the counterfeit lamb and its image and receives its character in their thoughts and deeds,

14:10 will drink the wine of God's passion, undiluted with water but intensified with spices in his cup - they shall be tested as one tests gold or silver with a ¹touchstone; with fire and brimstone in the immediate presence of the Lamb and of ²those who have discovered their wholeness mirrored in him - the dross of their deception will be exposed and cleansed.

*(Note the words, **tou kekerasmenou akratou** - this is a powerful oxymoron, "the mixed unmixed." See Psalm 75:8 For in the hand of the LORD there is a cup, with foaming wine, well mixed; and he will pour a draught from it, and all the wicked of the earth shall drain it down to the dregs.*

*The word ¹**basanizō** means to test (metals) by **the touchstone**, which is a black siliceous stone used to test the purity of gold or silver by the color of the streak produced on it by rubbing it with either metal - a piece of fine-grained dark schist or jasper formerly used for testing alloys of gold by observing the color of the mark which they made on it - thus, a standard or criterion by which something is judged or recognized. The blood of Jesus is the currency. 1 Peter 1:18,19.*

*The fiery brimstone - **theion** - is divine incense, because burning brimstone was regarded as having power to purify, and to ward off disease - the ¹cup he drank on the cross is the touchstone. "What shall I say? Father, remove this cup from me? NO. For this hour I have come." The word, ²**hagios**, saints, refers to wholeness and harmony of spirit, soul and body - see 1 Corinthians 1:30 and Romans 1:7. See my **Extended Notes on the lake of fire** at the end of chapter 19.)*

14:11 Those worshipping the counterfeit Beast and its image, receiving its mark and name as their identity, will have nowhere to hide day or night; the smoke that rises from their ¹testing, will evidence their cleansing for all ages. *(The mindset of a counterfeit religious system has no future. The message of the cross is the ¹touchstone that will forever bear testimony to the triumph of the Lamb. See commentary in the previous verse on the Touchstone.)*

14:12 This calls for the patient steadfastness of ¹those who have discovered their wholeness in Christ - to treasure ²the completeness of God's finished work and the faith of Jesus. *(See 1 John 2:3 Mirror Bible The word, ¹hagios, saints, refers to wholeness and harmony of spirit, soul and body - see 1 Corinthians 1:30. The word ²entole, which is often translated commandment or precept, has two components: **en**, in and **telos**, from **tello**, to set out for a definite point or goal; the point aimed at as a limit, that is, by implication, the conclusion of an act or state, the result; the ultimate or prophetic purpose. Strong's 5056)*

14:13 And I heard a voice from heaven saying, "Write: Blessed are they who, from now on, see their death in union with the Lord - his death is their death. Their wearisome labor follows them into this death bringing closure to their efforts to do what his death alone accomplished.

14:14 And I looked, and behold, I saw a white cloud and One who mirror-reflects the Son of Man with his head crowned in a golden wreath of victory. He was seated upon the cloud and in his hand he held a razor sharp pruning-hook. *(See extended notes on the Son of Man is the Son of God at the end of Chapter 2.)*

14:15 Another celestial messenger appeared out of the most holy place of the temple and with a loud voice addressed the One seated upon the cloud, saying, "Thrust forth your pruning hook, your hour has come - this is your moment to reap for the earth's harvest is ready." *(See John 4:31-36.)*

14:16 And the One seated upon the cloud completed the earth's wheat harvest with a single sweep of his sickle. *(The gathering of the full harvest of both the wheat as well as the wine, endorses the dawn of the New Covenant pictured in his broken body and shed blood.)*

REVELATION Chapter 14

14:17 And another celestial messenger appeared from the most holy place, the Tabernacle located in the heavenly realm; he too had a sharp pruning-hook-type sickle.

14:18 Yet another messenger emerged from the altar of burnt offering - this one was in charge of the fire of the altar. He cried with a loud voice telling the messenger with the sharp pruning hook to thrust forth his sickle and gather the vintage since the earth's grapes were bursting with ripeness.

14:19 And he swung his sickle and gathered the vintage of the earth and cast it into the winepress of God's great ¹passion. *(The word ¹thumos speaks of the passion of Christ as the sacrificed Lamb. See Extended Notes on* **The winepress of the passion of God** *at the end of chapter 19.)*

14:20 And the winepress was trodden outside the city, and the blood that flowed out of the winepress was as deep as a horses' bridle and it flooded a thousand stadia. *(See Hebrews 13:12 According to the prophetic pattern, Jesus, as the final sin sacrifice, was slain outside the city walls. The symbolic depth of a horse's bridle and 1000 Greek stadia speak of the completeness and universality of the world-wide impact of the blood covenant of Jesus. The typical Greek Stadion was 600 Greek feet. [Approx 160 meters.]*

Isaiah 63:2,3 "Why is Your apparel red and your garments like one who treads in the wine press? I have trodden the wine trough alone.

See Colossians 2:14 His body nailed to the cross hung there as the document of mankind's guilt; in dying our death he canceled the detailed hand-written record which testified against us. Every stain on our conscience, reminding of the sense of failure and guilt, was thus fully blotted out. Colossians 2:15 In him dying mankind's death, he defused every possible claim of accusation against the human race and thus made a public spectacle of it in God's brilliant triumph, demonstrated in him. The voice of the cross will never be silenced. (The horror of the Cross is now the eternal trophy of God's triumph over sin. The cross stripped religion of its authority to manipulate mankind with guilt. Every accusation lost its leverage to blackmail the human race with condemnation and shame. The word, **apekduomai**, *is translated from* **apo**, *away from, and* **ekduo**, *to be stripped of clothing; to disarm; the religious facade that disguised the law of works as a means of defining a person's life, was openly defeated. Same word used in Colossians 3:9. The dominance of the tree of the knowledge of good and evil [***poneros**, *hard work and labor] was ended. The word,* **deikmatizo**, *means to exhibit in public. The word,* **parresia**, *comes from* **pas**, *all and* **rheo**, *outspokenness, pouring forth speech. Mirror Bible*

"The slate wiped clean, that old arrest warrant canceled and nailed to Christ's Cross. He stripped all the spiritual tyrants in the universe of their sham authority at the Cross and marched them naked through the streets." — The Message)

Revelation Chapter 14 Extended Notes:

From Mt Sinai to Mt Zion

144,000 Virgins

From Mt Sinai to Mt Zion

The feast of Pentecost, also called the feast of harvest and the feast of weeks, Exodus 34:22, was celebrated fifty days after the Passover to commemorate the giving of the law on Mount Sinai, which took place fifty days after, and hence called by the Greeks Pentecost.

Now, in Mt Zion, a new Pentecost has come.

Revelation 14:1 Oh wow. You've got to see this. The little Lamb, standing on mount Zion and with him a hundred and forty four thousands with the Lamb's Name and the Name of his Father written on their foreheads. *(Sonship redeemed. Hebrews 1:1-3)*

Compare Hebrews 12:18 - 29

Hebrews 12:18 We are not talking of a visible and tangible mountain here, one spectacularly ablaze in a setting of dark blackness and tempestuous winds. *(Witness the vivid contrast between the giving of the law and the unfolding of grace; the exclusiveness of the one and the all inclusive embrace of the other. The dramatic encounter of Moses on the mountain is by far exceeded by the mountaintop experience to which we are now welcomed and co-elevated to through Jesus Christ. Mankind is fully represented and co-seated together with Christ in heavenly places. [Ephesians 2:5, 6, Hosea 6:2])*

Hebrews 12:19 Shrill trumpet sounds and a thunderous voice uttering human language. This filled the people with such terror that they begged for silence.

Hebrews 12:20 Beast and humans alike felt threatened and excluded from that terrible mountain.

Hebrews 12:21 Even Moses, the representative of the people, was extremely terrified. He was shivering and shaking. Who could approach God and live? How impossible it seemed to find favor with such a 'terrifying' God.

Hebrews 12:22 By contrast, we have been welcomed to an invisible mount Zion; the city of peace *(Jerusalem)*, the residence of the living God, the festive assembly of an innumerable celestial host.

Hebrews 12:23 We are participating in a mass joint-celebration of heavenly and earthly beings; the ekklesia-ekklesia of the firstborn mirror-inscribed in the heavenlies. *(Our original identity, ekklesia, from ek, a Preposition that always denotes origin, and kaleo, meaning to identify by name, to surname], is endorsed by Jesus, patterned in him, the first born from the dead.)*

Hebrews 12:24 Jesus is the spokesman and arbitrator of the New Testament order. His blood signature sanctions mankind's innocence. This is a complete new language that communicates better things, in that it is the very substance of what was communicated in the shadow-type message of the blood sacrifice that Abel brought. *(Abel's faith was a prophetic introduction to the sacrificial shadow system of the Old Covenant. Hebrews 11:4 It was faith that made the difference between the sacrifices of Abel and Cain, and* *confirmed Abel's righteousness. God bore witness to righteousness as a gift rather than a reward. Even though he was murdered, his faith still has a most relevant prophetic voice.*

Hebrews 12:25 **If Jesus is the crescendo of God's final message to mankind, you cannot afford to politely excuse yourself from this conversation. Consider the prominent place that Moses plays in the history of Israel: if you think that Moses or any of the Prophets who spoke with authority on earth deserve honor, how much more should this word that God declared from heaven concerning our sonship, and our redeemed innocence revealed in the Messiah himself, deserve our undivided attention.**

Hebrews 12:26 **When he introduced the prophetic shadow of what was to come** *(the Law system),* **his voice visibly shook the earth.** *(Exodus 19:18.) But now the Messiah has come (he is the desire of the nations; he is what heaven and earth were waiting for [Haggai 2:6,7])* **The voice of God** *(articulated in Christ's birth, life, ministry, death, and resurrection)* **has rocked not only the systems on the earth, but also every unseen principality in the heavens, to their very foundations.**

Hebrews 12:27 **In the words of the Prophet, "Yet once more will I shake every unstable system of man's effort to rule himself." God clearly indicates his plan to remove the old and replace it with the new. The second shaking supersedes any significance in the first shaking. Then it was a physical quaking of the earth; now the very foundations of every man-made system was shaken to the core while the heavens were impacted by the announcement of his permanent rule on earth as it is mirrored in heaven.**

Hebrews 12:28 **We are fully associated in this immovable Kingdom; an authority that cannot be challenged or contradicted. Our participation echoes grace** *(and not law-inspired obedience)* **as we accommodate ourselves to God's delight, yielding in awe to his firm embrace.** *(The word, euaresto, means well pleasing, to accommodate yourself to God's delight.)*

Hebrews 12:29 **His zeal for us burns like fire.** *[Deuteronomy 4:24])*

Galatians 4:22 **The law records the fact that Abraham had two sons: one by a slave girl, the other by a free woman.**

Galatians 4:23 **The one is produced by the flesh** *(the DIY-tree),* **the other by faith** *(the promise).*

Galatians 4:24 **There is a parallel meaning in the story of the two sons: they represent two systems, works and grace.**

Galatians 4:25 **Sinai is an Arabian rocky mountain named after Hagar,** *(outside the land of promise).* **Its association with the law of Moses mirrors Jerusalem as the capital of Jewish legalism. Hagar is the mother of the law of works.**

Galatians 4:26 **But the mother from above, the true mother of mankind is grace, the free Jerusalem; she is the mother of the promise.**

Galatians 4:27 For it is written, "Rejoice oh childless one. Erupt in jubilee. For though you have never known travail before, your children will greatly outnumber her who was married." *(Married to the law. Isaiah 54:1)*

Galatians 4:28 We resemble Isaac: we are begotten of faith, the promise is our parent.

Galatians 4:29 Just as when the flesh child persecuted the faith child, so now these Jerusalem Jews in their Christian disguise seek to harass you;

Galatians 4:30 however, Scripture is clear: "Expel the slave mother and her son; the slave son cannot inherit with the free son." *(In exactly the same way, rid your minds radically from the slave mother and child mentality. Light dispels darkness effortlessly.)*A

Galatians 4:31 Realize whose children we are my Family: we are not children of the slave-mother, the law, but children of the free mother; we are begotten of grace.

Psalm 50:2 Out of Zion, the perfection of beauty, God shines forth.

Then in the context of this Psalm Elohim says - do not engage me with blood sacrifices engage me with the fruit of your lips; announcing by Todah the perfection of beauty that shines forth out of Zion - a and I will show you, your salvation - Jeshua.

144,000 Virgins

From the religious Monster in camouflage, the counterfeit "lamb" who desires to manipulate and control the business of buying and selling with a counterfeit currency of a fear and performance based alliance to its stamped image and inscription on their foreheads and hands, [chapter 13] to the true Lamb of God who ransomed the human race with the currency of his self-giving Agape and shed blood, revealing their inherent worth, based on Elohim's image and inscription entwined in their inner person.

Revelation 14:1 Oh wow. You've got to see this. The little Lamb, standing on mount Zion and with him a hundred and forty four thousands with the Lamb's Name and the Name of his Father written on their foreheads. *(Sonship redeemed. Hebrews 1:1-3. Note the 144,000's in plural, representing the symbolic value that includes the entire prophetic significance of the Jews as well as the prophetic context of their representing the entire human race. In you, all the nations of the earth will be blessed. See Extended Notes at the end of this chapter,* **From Mt Sinai to Mt Zion.***)*

Revelation 14:2 And I heard a voice emerge from the heavens. It was like the sound of a thunderous torrent of cascading waterfalls. Then there arose a choir of voices accompanied by stringed instruments which sounded like harps. *(The word κιθαρῳδός - kithardos, is from κιθάρα -* **kithara***, a [guitar] harp - a triangular shaped stringed instrument with 7 and later 10 strings traditionally associated with joy and gladness in worship [Psalm 33:2; Psalm 98:5] and ᾠδός - odos, a singer. Revelation 5:8-13)*

Revelation 14:3 There was a strange yet familiar newness to their song; almost as if it was reflected off the throne and echoed in the faces of the living creatures and the elders - a song which could not be taught or learned. It is the song of the redeemed - represented here in the 144,000('s) who were [1]bought from the claim and clutches of the earth. *(The word* [1]***agoratso***, *to buy in a typical market context -* **apo tes ges**, *away from the earth. Just when it seemed that no one could buy or sell any longer unless they were worshipping the Beast, [Revelation 13] a transaction takes place in a superior currency and realm that frees the human race from their slavery. Just like in the prophetic picture of Israel's freedom from Pharaoh. Isaiah 29:13 And the Lord said: "Because these people draw near with their mouth and honor me with their lips, while their hearts are far from me, and their fear of me is a commandment of men learned by repetition.)*

Revelation 14:4 These boldly exhibit the [3]first fruit of the Lamb's doing. Here we have blameless innocence on display and redefined. What the law of performance failed to do, the Lamb did. They are pure and unblemished in their [1]close association with the Lamb - [2]purchased and rescued out of the grip of an enslaved, fallen mankind; representing the entire human race as first fruits to God and the Lamb. These 'first fruit redeemed ones' have witnessed mankind's joint association in the [4]full range of the Lamb's journey. They are all marriageable maidens with their virginity intact. Their default settings are fully rebooted. *(The word,*

[1]***akolouthentes*** *is the Present Participle in the Nominative case of **akoloutheo**, with a from **hama** as a particle of union and **keleuthos** - a road; thus, travel companions; to be in the same way with, that is, to accompany closely - to be in immediate association with someone. The present Participle describes an action thought of as simultaneous with the action of the main verb, which, in this case is* [2]***egorasthesan*** *which is the Aorist Passive Indicative of **agorazō**, to go to market, that is to purchase; specifically to redeem. Thus in the Aorist Passive it means, having been redeemed - redemption is a done deal. The word* [3]***aparchē*** *means first fruit. See 1 Corinthians 15:20, However this very moment the risen Christ represents everyone who has ever died; exactly like the first fruit represents the complete harvest. 1 Corinthians 15:21 The same mankind who died in a man was raised again in a man. 1 Corinthians 15:22 In Adam all died; in Christ all are made alive.*

The words, [4]***hopou an hupagei*** *- mean whithersoever he travels - the comprehensive range of his journey. From being the Logos, face to face with God before time was and announced as the slain Lamb and Messiah since the fall of the world; throughout every Messianic, prophetic record of Moses, the Prophets and the Psalm, to the incarnate man Jesus the Christ; in his life, ministry, message and betrayal, his trial, his crucifixion, his burial, his descent into hell, his triumph there and in his taking captivity captive in his resurrection and glorious ascent and leading mankind as his trophies into the throne room where we are now co-seated together with him.*

The symbolic "virginity" of the 144,000 ('s), had nothing to do with the law of their performance but their discovery of their inclusion in the Lamb's doing. See Romans 3:9 It is common knowledge that sin holds sway over both Jew and Greek alike. [Just like disease would show the same symptoms regardless of someone's nationality.] Romans 3:10 Scripture records that within the context of the law, no-one succeeds to live a blameless life. [Psalm 14:1-3, They are corrupt and they do abominable deeds, there is none that does good. They have all gone astray, they are all alike corrupt; there is none that does good, no, not one. RSV]." In Genesis 18, Abraham intercedes for Sodom and Gomorrah, "If there perhaps are 50 righteous people, will you save the city on their behalf?" He continues to negotiate with God, until he's down to, "perhaps ten?"..."there was none righteous, no not one ..." This argument is building up to the triumphant conclusion of the fact that there is indeed no distinction; the same people who fell short of the glory of God are now justified through God's work of grace in Christ. If mankind was 100% represented in Adam, then they are equally 100% represented in Christ. [Romans 3:21-24]. Also Romans 9:29, The Lord of the multitudes preserved for us a Seed, to rescue us from the destruction of Sodom and Gomorrah. [From the Hebrew, צבא *tzaba - Strongs H6635, a host/mass of people.] The remnant represents the one Seed that would rescue the mass of mankind. The single grain of wheat did not abide alone. [See John 12:24] Romans 5:18-19 states, "The conclusion is clear: it took just one offense to condemn mankind; one act of righteousness declares the same mankind innocent. The disobedience of the one exhibits mankind as sinners; the obedience of another exhibits mankind as righteous.")*

REVELATION Chapter 15

15:1 The next symbolic picture I saw in the heavens was again a fantastic spectacle. I saw seven celestial messengers representing the completeness and finality of the passion of God in concluding every detail of the final seven symbolic plagues. *(Reminding of some of the same plagues which convinced Pharaoh to free Israel from slavery, which again, prophetically points to the judgment Jesus suffered. Isaiah 53:4 Surely he has borne our sicknesses, and he carried our pain; yet we esteemed him plagued, smitten by God, and afflicted. See **Isaiah 53:10** in the LXX Septuagint. [No, it did not "please the Lord to bruise him!"]*

Isaiah 53:10 The Lord desires to cleanse his wounds of the plague - and in the offering of his life as sacrifice he shall see his seed afar off.

This gives context to verse 11 - *The joy that is set before him, is the offspring; the fruit of the travail of his soul. **Hebrews 12:2**, For the joy that was set before him endured the cross, despising the shame.)*

15:2 Then I saw something that looked like an ocean on fire; its liquid waters became a solid surface like transparent glass ¹molded in its heat. Standing tall in triumph on top of the glassy sea, with their God-harps, were the redeemed ones who ²emerged victorious ³out of the grasp and claim of the false trinity-system of religious indoctrination - the Beast, its image, its character imprint and its password name and number-code. *(The word ²**nikoontas** is the Present Participle of **nikao**, to conquer; the Present Participle describes an action thought of as simultaneous with the action of the main verb, ¹**memigmenen** - a victory having been forged in fire, which is the Perfect Passive Participle of **mignumi**, to mingle, to mix. The Perfect tense denotes an action which is completed in the past, but the effects of which are regarded as continuing into the present.*

A reminder of the prophetic picture of Israel walking as if it were on dry land through the ocean of waters when God led them out of Pharaoh's claim.

*The Preposition **ek** denotes origin - here, clearly pointing to the fact that these have escaped the tyranny of slavery to the corrupt religious system of a false identity.*

*This is the transaction of the ages, where the Lamb that was slain enters the marketplace where slaves are sold and he redeems mankind – purchases us back out of the hands of the claim of accusation – **Satanas** – the Dragon , the Beast of religion, the false Prophet – mankind is redeemed from the idolatry of centuries of devotion to an image of their own making, reflecting a lost identity. The transaction-idea is to persuade our minds of our redeemed value. Jesus didn't buy us back from the Devil. A thief never becomes an owner. Psalm 22:27 and Psalm 24:1 See my Notes on Counterfeit Religion - the Wolf in Sheep's clothing at the end of Revelation 13.)*

15:3 This song of the redeemed echoes the song of Moses, God's servant and the song of the Lamb, singing: "The things you do are spectacular and amazing, Lord God Almighty. Righteousness and truth are your trademarks. You are the King of the ages and of the Nations. *(In the prophetic drama of the first Pascha, celebrating freedom from slavery, the people are suddenly faced with a replay, as it were, of an old enemy that still seems undefeated and unwilling to let them go. Plus the circumstances of a flooded river blocking their way, all seem to play into the hands of the enemy; then Moses is told that, what seems as a setback, God will turn into the final defeat of every threat or claim of*

Pharaoh. "These Egyptians you see today, you will never see again." Exodus 14:13 And Moses said to the people, "Fear not, stand firm, and see the salvation of the LORD, which he will work for you today; for the Egyptians whom you see today, you shall never see again. Exodus 14:14 The LORD will fight for you, and you have only to be still." Exodus 14:15 The LORD said to Moses, "Why do you cry to me? Tell the people of Israel to go forward. Exodus 14:16 Lift up your shepherd staff, and stretch out your hand over the sea and divide it, so that the people of Israel may go on dry ground through the sea." That which could drown and destroy you, becomes your pedestal of triumph; the cross of humiliation becomes the greatest elevation.

Then the triumphant song of Moses is recorded: Exodus 15:1,2 I will sing to the LORD, for he has triumphed gloriously; the horse and its rider he has thrown into the sea. The LORD is my strength and my song, and he has become my salvation; this is my God, and I will praise him; God is my Father and I will exalt him.

Exodus 15:11 Who compares with you, Oh LORD, among the gods? Who is like you, majestic in holiness, awe-inspiring in glorious deeds, working wonders?

Please note, Egypt only serves here as a prophetic picture. They are not "the Enemy." The enemy is whatever mindset enslaves one to an inferior life to the life of our design. Israel and Egypt are all equally included in the Lamb's triumph and Agape of God. Revelation 7:9.

Deuteronomy 32:3,18 I will proclaim the name of the LORD. Ascribe greatness to our God. The Rock, his work is perfect. Even though we have forgotten that we are his workmanship - we have forgotten the Rock that has begotten us...[see Isaiah 51:1, "Look to the Rock from which you were hewn and the quarry from which you were cut."]

David echoes the Lamb's song in conclusion to his graphic, prophetic picture of the cross in Psalm 22 and in verse 27 he sings, "The ends of the earth shall remember and turn to the Lord." And in his shepherd song, David sings in Psalm 23, "By the waters of reflection my soul remembers who I am." And in the next song, Psalm 24:1 he proclaims: "The earth is the Lord's and the fullness thereof, the world and those who dwell in it.")

15:4 Who will not be awestruck by you oh Lord as they recognize their identity in your glorious Name? All your work confirms the truth of who you are. You have no competition. Therefore all the nations will arrive at the same conclusion and they will worship you since your righteousness has been openly shown." *(Sing unto the Lord a new song, for he has done marvelous things. His right hand and his holy arm have gotten him the victory. The Lord has made known his salvation, his righteousness has he openly shown and all the ends of the earth shall see the salvation of our God. Psalm 98:1)*

15:5 And coinciding with this, I saw the inner shrine of the skin-tabernacle of testimony, with the veil wide open in the heavenly dimension. *(The prophetic skin-tabernacle, the Tent of Meeting is now redeemed in the Incarnation - the human body hosts this place of intimate encounter. See Exodus 33:7 the tent of meeting מועד the moyed which is the Niphal [reflexive] of עד - with Ayin as a picture of the eye, in the Ancient Hebrew alphabet, and the Dalet ד is a picture of the door. Combined these mean "see the door". As coming to a tent of meeting and entering in. A place, time or event that is repeated again and again - in the reflexive form; signifying a place of mirror-encounter. In the Septuagint the Greek word **marturion** is used - that which gives evidence - testimony. So the tent of meeting is the tent of testimony. Revelation 11:19.)*

15:6 And the seven celestial messengers - representing the seven wounds - proceeded out of the inner shrine arrayed in spotlessly clean linen, shining with the radiant brightness of a precious stone and with golden girdles wrapped around their chests.

15:7 And one of the four living creatures gave each of the celestial messengers a typical temple golden fire-pan; a broad shallow saucer of pure gold, ¹filled with the coals from the bronze altar where the Lamb was sacrificed - this is the passion of God. These golden fire-pans were loaded with the entire meaning of the sacrifice. *(A golden "fire-pan" was for the purpose of carrying fire, in order to burn incense on the day of Atonement once a year in the ultimate place of worship. Filled, γέμω gémō, to be full, from γόμος gómos, load; cargo. The word **thumos**, passion from **thuo**, to sacrifice, immolate, to slay; the killing of the paschal lamb. The words **phialas chrusas**, refer to a golden fire-pan specifically designed to receive the sweet smelling frankincense which was lighted with coals from the brazen altar, where the sacrifice has just been presented in the outer court and then offered on the golden altar before the veil.*

*The Latin word **fumos** to smoke originates from **thumos**. However, thumos does not mean fumes or smoke. In fact, many of our modern translations give us something totally different. Today, θυμος is translated as "the soul" or something along the lines of the "breath of life". The Greeks believed that their soul was a smoke or a breath that floated within their body. We have images given by ancient philosophers who describe the soul dispersing as a smoke would. By the time of Classical Greece, the word meaning "to sacrifice" was the Greek verb θυω [thuo] from θυμος and is therefore another etymology for Latin's fumus which comes from the Greek words for both soul and sacrifice. θυω is meant to describe any sacrifice that is specifically done by cremation. They were releasing their souls through fire, creating smoke. In the ancient Greek mind, smoke represents the soul of the sacrifice.*

Thus the English word for fumes and the origin of the word to smoke in Romance Languages comes from the ancient Greek words for soul and sacrifice. See these interesting notes on the etymology of the words translated, smoke and sacrifice. https://amarnaletters.wordpress.com/tag/greek/)

15:8 The atmosphere of the inner shrine was saturated with the glorious presence of God's power. The doxa and dunamis of God, manifested in the fire, were carried in these golden fire-pans from the altar and it filled the temple with its smoke. No one was able to enter the inner shrine until the seven wounds of the seven messengers were completed. *(See Exodus 19:18 And Mount Sinai was wrapped in smoke, because the LORD descended upon it in fire; and the smoke of it went up like the smoke of a kiln, and the whole mountain quaked greatly.*

Exodus 19:10 And the LORD said to Moses, "Go to the people and consecrate them today and tomorrow, and let them wash their garments, Exodus 19:11 and be ready by the third day; for on the third day the LORD will come down upon Mount Sinai in the sight of all the people.)

See the Context of Revelation 15 in Hebrews chapter 9. Also my commentary note in Revelation 11:19

REVELATION Chapter 16

16:1 Then I heard the sound of a loud voice coming out of the inner shrine, commanding the seven celestial messengers to pour out upon the earth the weight of the passion of God which had been loaded onto the golden fire-pans they received from the brazen altar of sacrifice. *(A golden "fire-pan" was for the purpose of carrying fire, in order to burn incense on the day of Atonement once a year in the ultimate place of worship. Revelation 8:3 This was a preparation peculiar to the day of expiation. "On other days it was the custom of the priest to take fire from the brazen altar in a silver censer, but on the great Day of Atonement the high priest took the fire from the great altar in a golden censer; and when he was come down from the great altar, he took incense from one of the priests, who brought it to him, and went with it to the golden altar; and while he offered the incense the people prayed without in silence." Sir Isaac Newton.*

The source of every reference to fire in the Book of Revelation would always be from the Brazen Altar of sacrifice, symbolizing the Cross where the Lamb of God died mankind's death.

*See Extended Notes on **the Brazen Altar of Sacrifice** at the end of this chapter.)*

16:2 And the first one departed and poured the contents of his golden fire-pan upon the earth and it broke out in terrible and grievous sores upon all those who worshiped the image and bore its mark. *(Reminding of the sixth Egyptian plague. The broken distorted body - Jesus was wounded by our transgressions.)*

16:3 And the second one poured out his golden fire-pan upon the sea and its waters became like blood which killed every living soul in the sea. *(The death of the old fallen mindset.)*

16:4 And the third did the same to the rivers and fountains which all became like blood. *(Every single water source will give testimony to the covenant sealed in the shed blood of the Lamb.)*

16:5 Then I heard the celestial messenger who interpreted the message in the waters say, "Righteous are you in the conclusion of your judgment. Your I-am-ness defines time - present, past and future." *(There is nothing in prophetic time, past, present or future that distract from God's supreme purpose and ultimate conclusion of redemption - no trace of any definition of Satanas, sin-consciousness or accusation will ever interfere with the sweet bliss of eternal companionship to be celebrated in the romance of the ages.)*

16:6 Since they are the ones who poured out the blood of the saints and the Prophets you gave them blood to drink as their [1]due. *(The word [1]axios - having the weight of another thing of like value - the message of the blood. The blood of Jesus speaks of better things. See Hebrews 12:24 See also my Extended commentary on the Blood at the end of the book.)*

16:7 And I heard the Altar speak again, in the same language of the song of Moses and the Lamb, "Oh Lord God you certainly hold sway over all things. Righteousness and truth are your trademarks in every detail of judgment." *(Oh Lord God, the Almighty - **kurie ho theos ho pantokratōr**. Just as in Revelation 15:3 in the Song of Moses and of the Lamb, See Deuteronomy 32:4*

REVELATION Chapter 16

"Ascribe greatness to our God the Rock, his work is perfect; for all his ways just. A God of faithfulness and without injustice; righteous and truth is he. In God's act of righteousness in which the human race was acquitted and justified, God spoke the language of the highest courts of Justice, having had no-one greater to swear by, he swore by himself, thus, making it impossible for his resolve not to be fulfilled, thereby ending all possible grounds for dispute. See Hebrews 6:13-19.)

16:8 And the fourth celestial messenger poured out his golden fire-pan upon the sun giving it authority to scorch mankind with its heat as in a fiery furnace.

16:9 And mankind's minds were fried in the heat of their own 'natural' light *(the sun, symbolic of how their stubborn mindsets of their own making were placed in the furnace to remove the dross from the gold.)* They, just like in Pharaoh's day, continued to blaspheme the name of God who had the authority over these plagues. They did not show any change of heart towards God to acknowledge his thoughts about them as unveiled in Christ.

16:10 And the fifth celestial messenger poured the content of his golden fire-pan upon the throne of the Beast and it turned the lights off - his entire kingdom was in a black-out and people were gnawing their tongues in anguish and distress.

16:11 They cursed and blasphemed God of heaven out of the agony of their sores and still refused to change their minds about their doings.

16:12 And the 6th celestial messenger poured out the coals from his golden fire-pan upon the great river of Euphrates so that its sweet water dried up, turning the riverbed into a highway of invasion for the kings of the east.

16:13 Then I witnessed three unclean spirits - which had the appearance of frogs - coming out of the mouths of the "triune" Dragon, Beast and False Prophet.

16:14 They are spirits of [1]demons, doing [2]signs - which advertise the great day of conflict to all the kings of the earth, trying to make them gather their combined forces and bring them – and the whole world – to the battle on that great day of God the Almighty. *(The word translated demon, [1]daimōn; from daiō, to distribute fortunes. See extended notes at the end of Revelation 9 on Idols and Demons. The word [2]sēmainō, symbolic imagery; signify; to picture; to portray. There are numeral references to the same "once and for all war" in the heavens. It is however the same hour; the same event. Revelation 12:7; Revelation 17:13,14; Revelation 19:19; Revelation 20:8.)*

16:15 Oh, that you would awaken to my intention. Why must I come to you like a thief who suddenly breaks into your space, unannounced. Guard your apparel lest you feel exposed and embarrassed about your nakedness - just like Adam and Eve when they traded their awareness of their I-am-ness and our sweet communion for the fruit of the alternative tree. *(See Genesis 3:9 And Jahweh God called to the man and said to him, Where are you? Genesis 3:10 And he said, I have heard Your sound in the garden, and I was* *afraid, for I am naked, and I hid myself. Genesis 3:11 And He said, Who told you that you were naked? Have you eaten of the tree of which I commanded you not to eat? Revelation 3:18 I invite you to talk business with me. Come, let us resolve this together. I want to make you really rich. I advise you to buy gold from me. Gold that is thoroughly refined in the fire. Not the flawed currency of your own trade. We're not talking a mixture here. No dross. And from now on, buy your clothing from me; white garments; not the blended brand of your own making. Clothe yourself completely with these and there will not even be a hint of shame. For your eyes, buy eye-salve [kollourion] from me to anoint your eyes so that you may clearly see yourself in Christ. See my note on Why the other Tree in 1 John 3:12)*

16:16 And the frog demons worked as one, gathering the kings of the earth together in a place with a Hebrew name, Armageddon. *(The three unclean spirits working as one -* **sunēgagen** *- second Aorist Active Indicative of* **sunagō***, singular. See Revelation 16:13 - these are the extension of the same counterfeit trinity. See notes at the end of this chapter.)*

16:17 The seventh celestial messenger poured his golden fire-pan into the atmosphere. A loud voice came from the throne in the inner shrine, and said, "It is irreversibly done." *(The verb,* **gegonen***, is a Perfect Active Indicative of ginomai - meaning its effect will never diminish.)*

16:18 This ignited flashes of lightning with the roaring voices of thunder and a massive earthquake such as has never been felt since the beginning of human existence upon the earth. There was never anything remotely like it. The earth rocked, rolled and rumbled.

16:19 And the great city split into three portions and the cities of the nations fell and Babylon the great was remembered in the cup of God's ¹great passion and ²desire to bring everything to conclusion. *(The word* ¹**thumos***, passion and* ²**orge** *from* **oregomai***, to stretch one's self out in order to touch or to grasp something, to reach after with intense desire. The third part is a symbolic expression of a representative portion of the whole. Here, the counterfeit Trinity, represented in the Whore-City Babylon, is divided and conquered.)*

16:20 All islands vanished and not a trace of the mountains could be found. *(There was nowhere to hide on the planet from the far reaching conclusion of God's finished work in Christ; neither a remote island nor even a mountain remained in place. Islands represent the religious, political and social isolation of people groupings; mountains represent the social structures of influence.)*

16:21 The entire economy fell - like massive hailstones the size of talents cast down from the heavens upon the people of the earth and they blasphemed God because of the hail for the plague was most intense. *(The word,* **talantiaios***, talent of gold or silver, from* **talanton***, the scale of balances.)*

At the close of Chapter 16, we reached the end of the three great series of judgments, - the series of the seven Seals, the seven Trumpets, and the seven Vessels. It cannot surprise us, however, that at this point other visions of judgment are to follow. Already we had reached the end at Revelation 6, then again at the end of Revelation 11; yet on both occasions the same

REVELATION Chapter 16

general subject was immediately afterwards renewed, and the same events were again presented to us, though in a different aspect and with heightened coloring. [Expository Bible.]

Extended Notes:
Notes on the Brazen Altar
Armageddon - Earthbound vs. Heavenly Dimension

Notes on the Brazen Altar

Both the brazen altar as well as the altar of incense were made of acacia wood; *[shittim wood]* the brazen altar was overlaid with brass and the incense altar with pure gold. The Acacia tree derives its name from its scourging thorns - שטה shittah, from שוט shôṭêt, to pierce; to flog; a goad: - scourge. The symbolic use of the acacia wood in the building of these altars presents us with powerful imagery of the crucifixion. Exodus 27:1-5; Exodus 30:1.

Revelation 16:1 Then I heard the sound of a loud voice coming out of the inner shrine, commanding the seven celestial messengers to pour out upon the earth the weight of the passion of God which had been loaded onto the golden fire-pans they received from the brazen altar of sacrifice. *(A golden "fire-pan" was for the purpose of carrying fire, in order to burn incense on the day of Atonement once a year in the ultimate place of worship. Revelation 8:3 This was a preparation peculiar to the day of expiation. "On other days it was the custom of the priest to take fire from the brazen altar in a silver censer, but on the great Day of Atonement the high priest took the fire from the great altar in a golden censer; and when he was come down from the great altar, he took incense from one of the priests, who brought it to him, and went with it to the golden altar; and while he offered the incense the people prayed without in silence." Sir Isaac Newton.*

The source of every reference to fire in the Book of Revelation would always be from the Brazen Altar of Sacrifice, symbolizing the Cross where the Lamb of God died mankind's death. See my **Extended notes on the lake of fire** *at the end of chapter 19.*

In each of these plagues we have a graphic symbolic picture of the extent of the Lamb's suffering - wounded by mankind's plagues - see Isaiah 53.

There is a likeness between the seven trumpets and the seven vessels, especially in the first four; as the first four trumpets affect the earth, the sea, the fountains, and rivers of water, and the sun, so the first four vessels are poured out on the same, and that in the same order. Earth and sea represent mankind's natural life and habitat, sustained by water and sunlight.

There is in many of these vessels an allusion to the plagues of Egypt; in the first, Revelation 16:2 to the plague of boils, Exodus 9:8 in the second and third, Revelation 16:3 to that of turning the waters of Egypt into blood, Exodus 7:19 in the fourth, Revelation 16:10 to the darkness that was over all the land of Egypt, Exodus 10:21 and in the fifth there is a manifest reference to the frogs that distressed the Egyptians, Exodus 8:5 and in the seventh, to the plague of hail, Exodus 9:23 and they have much the same effect, even the hardening of those on whom they fall, being far from being brought to a change of heart by them, Revelation 16:9.

Again and again, the obstinate slave-mindsets of the earth-dwellers are addressed in graphic judgmental imagery, in order to overcome and persuade every single individual to awaken them out of slumber to see the triumph of the Lamb on their behalf. The coals from the brazen altar, then the altar of incense and worship at the torn veil, gives new context to everything. The symbolic vessels contain the interpretation and implication of the sacrificed Lamb. As in Isaiah 52:10 "The Lord

NOTES ON THE BRAZEN ALTAR - REV 16

has bared his holy arm before the eyes of all the nations, and all the ends of the earth shall see the salvation of our God." Isaiah 52:14-15 "Just as many were astonished at you—so was he marred in his appearance, more than any human and his form beyond that of human semblance—so will he startle many nations. Kings will shut their mouths because of him; for what had not been told them, they will see and what they had not heard, they will understand."

Yet, initially, we, mankind, esteemed him not. He had no form or comeliness that we should look at him, and no beauty that we should desire him. We thought he was stricken by God. Not realizing that in the drama of the ages, the Son of God presented himself as mankind's scapegoat to be butchered by his own creation. Isaiah 53:3 He was despised and rejected by his own people; a man of sorrows, and acquainted with grief; and as one from whom people hide their faces he was despised, and we esteemed him not.

Isaiah 53:4 Surely he has borne our griefs and carried our sorrows; **yet we esteemed him stricken, smitten by God, and afflicted**. *(See verse 10 in the Septuagint. No. It did not "please the Lord to bruise him.." The Lord desires to cleanse his wounds - and in the offering of his life as sacrifice he shall see his seed afar off. See verse 11 - the joy that is set before him. The offspring is the fruit of the travail of his soul. Hebrews 12:2, for the joy that was set before him endured the cross, despising the shame.)*

Isaiah 53:5 But he was wounded by our transgressions, he was bruised by our iniquities; upon him was the chastisement that made us whole, and by his stripes we are healed.

Isaiah 53:6 All we like sheep have gone astray; we have turned everyone to his own way; and Jahweh gave him for our sins. (The Septuagint renders it. Κύριος παρέδωκεν αὐτὸν ταῖς ἁμαρτίαις ἡμῶν Kurios paredōken auton tais hamartiais hēmōn - 'The Lord gave him for our sins. See Romans 4:25 - He was handed over because of our sins - he was raised because of our redeemed innocence.)

Isaiah 53:7 He was oppressed, and he was afflicted, yet he opened not his mouth; like a lamb that is led to the slaughter, and like a sheep that before its shearers is dumb, so he opened not his mouth.

Isaiah 53:8 By oppression and judgment he was taken away; and as for his generation, who considered that he was cut off out of the land of the living, stricken by the transgression of my people?

He was not bruised by God, but by the very mankind he was about to redeem.

You may ask, "But what about Isaiah 53:10.?" [It pleased the Lord to "crush" him.] Translators of the New Revised Standard Version say in their footnotes to this verse: "Meaning of Hebrew uncertain." The Septuagint [Greek version] of this verse, written 200 years before Jesus, by 70 Hebrew and Greek scholars [with access to much older manuscripts than what we have today;] have rendered the Hebrew text as follows: "The Lord desires to purify him of **the plague**.*" This can also be translated, "The Lord desires to cleanse his wounds." The word, πληγή* **plege** *means a wound. [The Septuagint is 1000 years older than the Masoretic text from which our Old Testament is translated.]*

Armageddon - Earthbound vs. Heavenly Dimension

In the symbolic language of the book of Revelation people's perception of the world is four dimensional: heaven, earth, the ocean and the deep underworld [including under the ocean Ezekiel 28:8; Revelation 5:13. The idea of the earth dwellers of the time was that the planet was flat and square. So the four corners of the earth were not factual but merely to communicate a symbolic picture and principle within their perceptions - as also the idea of an underworld. See these spheres already referenced in Genesis 1:2, the earth being without form and empty, and darkness on the face of the deep, [abussos - LXX] and the Spirit of God moving gently on the face of the waters. Also in Psalm 135:6 Whatever the LORD pleases he does, in heaven and on earth, in the seas and the Abyss. Or in the LXX it is Psalm 134:6.

Armageddon pictures the battle between the lower, earthbound thought patterns and the elevated, heavenly thoughts of God. Colossians 3:1-3; Revelation 17:8.

The "earthbound-dilemma" of mankind is fully addressed in the Incarnate Christ.

Revelation 16:16 And the frog demons worked as one, gathering the kings of the earth together in a place with a Hebrew name, Armageddon. *(The natural topography and history of the land are used symbolically to describe a significant spiritual principle. "Bounded as it is by the hills of Palestine on both north and south, it would naturally become the arena of war between the* **lowlanders** *who trusted in their chariots, and the Israelite* **highlanders** *of the neighboring heights. To this cause mainly it owes its celebrity, as the battle-field of the world, which has, through its adoption into the language of Revelation, passed into an global proverb. If that mysterious book proceeded from the hand of a Galilean fisherman, it is the more easy to understand why, with the scene of those many battles constantly before him, he should have drawn the figurative name of the final conflict between the hosts of good and evil, from the place which is called in the Hebrew tongue,* ארמגדון *Armagedon" [Stanley, "Sinai and Palestine"].*

The scene of a the struggle of good and evil is suggested by that battle plain of Esdraelon, which was famous for two great victories, of Barak over the Canaanites, and of Gideon over the Midianites; and for two great disasters, the deaths of Saul and Josiah. Hence in Revelation a place of great slaughter, the scene of the great triumph of the Lamb over every definition of an enemy in mankind's minds. The RSV translates the name as Har-Magedon, i.e. the hill (as Ar is the city) of Megiddo. Thus Armageddon pictures the battle between the lower earthbound thought patterns and the thoughts of God. Har, mountain or a range of hills and megiddon - a gathering of a crowd - a rendezvous.)

Revelation 17:8 The brutal Beast you saw is a [1]"has been" from the beginning - it indeed has no real existence - yet it seems to make "a come back" as if emerging out of the Abyss only to dissolve again into this state of irrelevance. Meanwhile the minds of those blinded by their [2]earthbound perceptions continue to be mesmerized by its apparent relevance. They are the ones whose identities are not [3]based upon the Lamb's Book of Life. They

ARMAGEDDON - REV 16

do not yet see that their original identity was redeemed in the Lamb." *(The words, ἦν καὶ οὐκ ἔστι [1]en kai ouk esti, meaning, to be and not to be; with the verb en being the Imperfect Indicative of eimi, I am - another meaning of the Imperfect Indicative is to refer to unreal [counterfactual] situations in present or past time.*

This is in total contrast to the One who is I am; who always was and will continually be the accompanying One. An antithesis to "ho ēn kai ho ōn" of Revelation 1:4.)

Revelation 11:16 At that moment, the twenty four elders who were seated on their thrones face to face with God, fell down prostrate before him in adoration

Revelation 11:17 and exclaimed: Our hearts are flooded with gratitude and the affection of your favor. We salute your Lordship oh God. You are the Supreme Authority over all things; your I-am-ness defines time - present, past and future. The [1]due dynamic of your [2]Royal-reign is forever established. *(The word translated due, [1]eilepsas from lambano is in the Perfect Active tense which suggests the continual effect of an action already completed in the past. The word lambano means to take what is one's own, one's due. Then the word esbasileusas from basileuo, to reign, is the Aorist Active tense which speaks of a completed act. Both these tenses emphasize the permanence of God's rule. There was never a time where God's royal rule was in question. Giving himself as scapegoat to be murdered by his own creatures assumes a weakness that does not compromise his authority at all. In the genius of his wisdom he defeats the entire system of judgment under the law of performance, governing the tree of the knowledge of good and evil. The seeming frailty of the slain Lamb never compromised the authority of the Lion of Judah. 1 Corinthians 1:25 It seems so foolish that God should die mankind's death on the cross; it seems so weak of God to suffer such insult; yet mankind's wisest schemes and most powerful display of genius cannot even begin to comprehend or compete with God in his weakest moment on the cross.)*

Revelation 11:18 The culmination of mankind's wrath collided with your passion oh God - this is the critical moment where judgment is met in death. *(Jesus said, "When I am lifted up on the cross, I will draw all judgment unto me.")* **This is the anticipated moment and prize of your bond-friends, the Prophets, the saints and everyone who were awed by your Name - both the insignificant and the prominent - this is the destruction of the corrupting virus in the earth.** *(In the symbolic language of the book of Revelation, the judgment of the Dragon, the Beast and the Whore; the counterfeit Trinity, is not a judgment against an entity, but against a corrupt mindset-system. A virus doesn't have a life of its own - it needs a host.*

Microbiology Professor, Vincent Racaniello writes, "Life is 'an organismic state characterized by capacity for metabolism, growth, reaction to stimuli, and reproduction.' Viruses are not living things. Viruses are complicated assemblies of molecules, including proteins, nucleic acids, lipids, and carbohydrates, but on their own they can do nothing until they enter a living cell. Without cells, viruses would not be able to multiply. Therefore, viruses are not living things."

See also Revelation 18:20)

Ephesians 6:12 People are not the enemy, *[whether they be husbands, wives, children, or parents, slaves, or bosses. They might host hostile, law inspired thought patterns through their unbelief or ignorance but,]* **to target one another is to engage in the wrong combat. We represent the authority of the victory of Christ in the spiritual realm. We are positioned there** *[in Christ]***; we ¹confront the mind games and ²structures of darkness, religious thought patterns, governing and conditioning human behavior.** *(The word, ¹pros, face to face; towards. The word, ²poneros is often translated as evil; this word is described in Thayer's Lexicon as full of annoyances, hardships and labor, which is exactly what the DIY law-system of works produces.)*

1 Corinthians 15:24 The complete conclusion in his work of redemption is celebrated in his yielding the full harvest of his reign to God the Father, having ¹brought to nought the law of works which supported every definition of dominion under the fall, including all ²principalities, all ³authority and every ⁴dynamic influence in society. *(He brought to nought the law of works, ¹katargeo, from kata, meaning intensity, and argos, meaning labor; thus free from all self-effort to attempt to improve what God has already perfected in Christ. All principalities, ²arche, or chief ranks, i.e., kings, governors; this includes any governing system whereby one is ranked above the other on the basis of their performance or preference. All authority, ³exousia, comes from ek, denoting origin and eimi, I am; in this case, because of what I can do I am defined by what I can do better than you; therefore, I have authority over you. Every dynamic influence in society, ⁴dunamis, means power, in this case, willpower. Every government structure in society will be brought under the dominion of grace where the Christ-life rules.*

The kingdom of God is the dominion of the Christ-life in human form, where righteousness is based on who we are and not on what we do; who we are by God's doing and not who we are by our own doing; right being and not merely right acting. Where the law of works was duty and guilt driven; the law of faith is love driven. [Romans 3:27, Galatians 5:6, 2 Corinthians 10:12] when they measure themselves by one another, and compare themselves with one another, they are without understanding.)

John 1:50 Jesus said, "So you believe because I say I saw you sitting under the fig tree? You haven't seen anything yet.

John 1:51 Truly I say unto you, Nathaniel [singular], because of who I am, you [plural - You-manity - all the families in heaven and on earth] will surely see this communication between the heavenly sphere and earth thrown wide ¹open and the celestial messengers of God ascending and descending upon the Incarnate son of man. Heaven and earth meet in the Incarnate one. *(In him every definition of separation and distance is canceled. Isaiah 55:10,11 "For as the rain and the snow come down from heaven, and return not there without saturating the earth [all flesh], so shall my word be that goes forth from my mouth; it shall not return to me empty, but it shall accomplish that which I purpose, and prosper in the thing for which I sent it. The prophetic word was destined to become flesh; every nook and cranny of human life is saturated in the incarnation. The word aneogota, Perfect Active Participle Accusative Masculine Singular, 2nd Conjugation-form; the one who has led us upward- from anoigō, ana, upward and agoo, to lead. Jesus reminds Nathaniel of Genesis 28:12-14 And*

Jacob dreamt that there was a ladder set up on the earth, and the top of it reached to heaven; and behold, the celestial messengers of God were ascending and descending on it. And Jahweh said to him, I am Elohim of Abraham, your seed shall be like the dust of the earth, and you shall spread abroad to the west and to the east and to the north and to the south; and in you and your descendants have all the families of the earth been blessed.

"Jesus has united heaven and earth, the life of God and human life in himself. Just as it was planned before the time of the ages." Dr Baxter Kruger.)

Revelation 19:11 Then, in my vision, heaven opened and I saw a white horse appear; and the name of the one seated upon the horse is Faithful and True. Righteousness spans the range of his judgment and warfare. *(Ephesians 3:15 also Ephesians 1:3 Let's celebrate God. He lavished every blessing heaven has upon us in Christ. Also, Ephesians 4:8-10.)*

Revelation 12:7 Mikael and his celestial colleagues led the war in the heavenly realm against the Dragon and his cohorts. *(Mikael* מיכאל *means, "Who is like God?" The context of the onslaught against the human race has always been identity-related. The fruit of the "I-am-not tree system ." Jesus faced this temptation on mankind's behalf, "If you are the Son of God?" See John 10:30-36)*

Revelation 12:8 The Dragon's influence was totally demolished and rendered powerless - not a trace of its presence was found in the heavens. *(Principalities and powers were completely disarmed on the cross. Colossians 2:14,15 "And their place was not found" see Daniel 2:35 - the little stone against whom the Gates of Hades shall not prevail - the Chip off the old Block demolished the pseudo man-made identity. There are numeral references to the same "once and for all war" in the heavens. It is however the same hour; the same event. Revelation 16:13,14; Revelation 17:13,14; 19:19; Revelation 20:8. Also **John 12:31,32** Now is the judgment of this world; now the ruler of this world shall be cast down. [When I am lifted up on the cross.])*

Revelation 12:9 So the great Dragon, the ¹ancient ²ophis [serpent], also known as the Devil or Satan - whose sole mission was to lead the entire inhabited world astray - was cast down to the earth-dimension, together with all his cohorts. *(The word ¹**archaios**, ancient, of old; from **arche**, from the beginning. As Jesus said that the Devil was a murderer "from the beginning" The Greek word, ²**ophis** is translated serpent and comes from **optomai**, to gaze, in this case, to present a visual idea through illusion. John 8:44. He was stripped of his pseudo rank of authority see Colossians 2:14,15 he was made a public spectacle. Luke 10:18 And Jesus said to them, I saw Satan falling out of heaven like lightning. These all represent mindsets that have blindfolded mankind since the fall of Adam.)*

Revelation 12:12 An ¹eruption of belly-laughter followed in the heavenlies and in all those inhabiting this realm. Woe to the land and sea for the Devil was cast down there in great embarrassment, seeing that his time had run out. *(The word, ¹**euphraino**, jubilant rejoicing, from **eu**, well done; extravagantly good; and **phren**, the midriff or diaphragm, the innermost parts of the heart. This makes Paul's appeal in Colossians 3:1-3 so relevant. Engage your minds with heavenly dimension realities and not with the earthbound soul realm.)*

Revelation 12:13 As soon as the Dragon realized that he had lost his supposed position in the heavenlies and was now confined to the earth realm, he pursued the woman who birthed the male child.

Revelation 12:14 But the woman was given very large eagle wings with which to fly away to her safe place in the wilderness where she would be pampered for a time and times and half a time out of sight of the serpent. *(Beyond the reach of Ophis. 1260 days; 3 and a half years which points to the uninterrupted extent of Jesus' ministry.)*

Revelation 12:15 Then waters flooded out of the mouth of the serpent in an attempt to drown the woman *[the prophetic voice unveiling the Christ]* in his devilish conversation.

Revelation 12:16 But the earth rescued the woman by opening its mouth and gulped down the entire river proceeding from the Dragon's mouth. *(In his death, burial and descent into the lowest parts of the earth. See Ephesians 4:8,9. Note, like in Revelation 12:9, the words for the Serpent-system are interchanged, including the Dragon, Satan, Devil and also in Revelation 12:10, the Accuser,* **kategoros**, *whose business is founded in the industry of accusation.)*

Revelation 12:17 The fact that the woman escaped his pursuit extremely infuriated the Dragon, so he turned his attention to contend with the remnant of her seed who treasured [1]the completeness of God's fulfilled purpose echoing the [2]testimony of Jesus. *(The word* [1]*entole, which is often translated commandment or precept, has two components:* **en**, *in and* **telos**, *from* **tello**, *to set out for a definite point or goal; the point aimed at as a limit, that is, by implication, the conclusion of an act or state, the result; the ultimate or prophetic purpose. Strong's 5056 See 1 John 2:3 Mirror Bible. The* [2]*testimony of Jesus is the spirit of prophecy. Revelation 19:10. See* **Extended Notes on the Word of God and the Testimony of Jesus Christ** *at the end of chapter 20.)*

Revelation 13:6 It hurled its accusations [1]in God's face, while blaspheming his Name and tabernacle and [2]those dwelling in the heavenlies. *(The words,* [1]***pros ton theon*** *positions the Accuser to now face God's image and likeness incarnate in human form, since there was no trace of accusation present in the heavenlies, having been thoroughly expelled from any further presence or relevance in the heavenly sphere. [Revelation 12:8-10] The significance of heaven endorsing the tabernacle of God on earth - in both its prophetic symbolism as well as its tangible unveiling in incarnate human life, is now the target of accusation and every blasphemous utterance of this Beast who takes its authority from Mr. Accusation himself.*

[2]*Those dwelling in the heavenlies;* **kai tous en tō ouranō skenountas** *- in contrast to those whose minds are still trapped in earthbound-mode. See verse 8.)*

Revelation 13:7 And it was given the mission to wage war against those who have discovered their wholeness in Christ in order to conquer them and to dominate the entire spectrum of people-groupings; every tribe, tongue and nation. *(The words remind of Daniel 7:21,22,23. Where there seemed to be no escape from the Beast's rule. However, the fact that the Beast failed in its mission is already celebrated in Revelation 5:13 as well as in Revelation 7:9, At this* *moment I saw a massive throng of people, impossible to count, standing tall and innocent everyone of them dressed in white with palm branches in their hands; they had escaped everything that could possibly define them as a non-Jewish Gentile world. In fact, every sphere of society was there - including the entire spectrum of people-groupings; tribal identities with their unique language-specific dialect preferences; they were all present there facing the throne and the Lamb as the people of the planet.)*

Revelation 13:8 The plan was to engage the entire [1]earthbound population of the planet to worship the Beast [*The counterfeit "slain and risen lamb"*]. **This would endorse the idea** [*of the religious system*], **that there were individuals, since the [3]fall of the [4]cosmos, whose [2]names were not included in the [5]slain Lamb's Book of Life.** *(The word [1]katoikeō from kata, down and oikeo, to dwell or set up home - thus, to be earthbound. Paul invites us to engage our thoughts with resurrection realities and to see ourselves co-raised and seated together with Christ in heavenly places. Colossians 3:1-3. Revelation 17:8 also Revelation 16:16.*

In the context of verse 6, clearly the target of the "blasphemy" was to insult and interrogate the [2]Name. See Ephesians 3:15 Every family in heaven and on earth originates in him; his is mankind's family name and he remains the authentic identity of every nation. The entire industry of accusation is about the blatant blasphemy of the name that reveals and redeems mankind's original identity.

"The Book of Life" - this language is taken from the custom of registering the names of persons in a list, roll, or catalogue. In Jewish tradition there was a prevailing fear that your name might be blotted out of the Book of Life if your behavior did not please God. See Exodus 32:32 Here the suggestion is that some names were not even written in the Lamb's Book of Life to begin with. See also Revelation 17:8, ...the ones whose names have not been written in the Book of Life from the fall of the world." This idea would obviously boost the Calvinistic deception of election, that if you're not "chosen", you're doomed - which is a ridiculous contradiction to the entire context and conclusion of the Gospel. See notes on The Book of Life at the end of chapter 17.

The word [5]esphagmenou is the Perfect Passive Participle of the verb, sphazō, to slay in sacrifice. The Perfect Participle is used to describe a state that exists at the time as a result of action completed prior to the time of the main verb. The basic thought of the Perfect tense is that the progress of an action has been completed and the results of the action are continuing on, in full effect. In other words, the progress of the action has reached its culmination and the finished results are now present.

The word, [4]kosmos in the NT refers to the entire human family and their social structures. The word often translated foundation, kataballo, from kata and ballo, meaning "to fall away, to put in a lower place," instead of themelios, meaning "foundation" [see Ephesians 2:20; also Revelation 21:14,19]; thus, I translated it "the fall of the world," instead of "the foundation of the world." The entire "Fall" was a falling away in our minds from our true identity as image and likeness bearers of Elohim. Just like Eve, were we all deceived to believe a lie about ourselves, which is the fruit of the "I-am-not-tree". We all, like sheep, have gone astray. [Isaiah 53:6]

See 1 Peter 1:20 He was always destined in God's prophetic thought; God knew even before the fall of the world order that his son would be the Lamb, to be made manifest in these last days, because of you. [You are the reason Jesus died and was raised.])

Revelation 13:12 Even though it had the appearance of the lamb, it operated under the same authority as the previous Beast - under the watchful eye of the Dragon. *[Counterfeit-Christianity as a religion is a wolf in sheep's clothing.]* **It's the same old Dragon in a lamb's disguise. Its mission was to engage the ¹earthbound dwellers to worship the counterfeit - the slaughtered animal that was restored to life out of its death.** *(The historic relevance of the death and resurrection of the Lamb is in the revelation of mankind's co-inclusion - Jesus died our death and went into our hell and we were co-quickened in his resurrection and are co-seated together with him in heavenly places.*

*Again John employs the word ¹**katoikeō** from **kata**, down and **oikeo**, to dwell or set up home - thus to be earthbound. Revelation 13:8.*

*Matthew 7:15 "Beware of false Prophets, which come to you in sheep's clothing, but inwardly they are ravening wolves." In his sight - **enōpion autou**. In the eye of the first Beast who gets his authority from the Dragon - Revelation 13:3)*

Revelation 19:19 And I saw the Beast in alliance with the kings of the earth muster their armies to engage a ¹once and for all war against the One seated on the horse and his army. *(The idea of a once and for all war is implied by the Aorist Infinitive tense of the verb, **poiesai**. [Weymouth] This is the Aorist Active Infinitive which indicates prior completion of an action in relationship to a point in time. Greek Infinitives could have either a present or Aorist form. The contrast between the two forms was not necessarily one of time, it is a difference of aspect. The Present Infinitive was used to express progressive or imperfective aspect. It pictures the action expressed by the verb as being in progress. The Aorist Infinitive however does not express progressive aspect. It presents the action expressed by the verb as a completed unit with a beginning and end.*

This is an important fact since there are numeral references to the same "once and for all war" in the heavens. It is however the same hour; the same event. Revelation 12:7; Revelation 16:13,14; Revelation 17:13,14; Revelation 20:8.)

Revelation 20:8 And his obvious strategy would be to deceive the nations on a global scale including the four corners of the earth by assembling Gog and Magog in war; their number is as the sand of the sea. *(Again, every traditional Jewish concept of judgment is addressed. Gog and Magog is now brought into the conversation, since Jewish eschatology viewed Gog and Magog as enemies to be defeated by the Messiah, which will usher in the age of the Messiah. "Then Eldad and Modad [brothers of Moses] both prophesied together, and said, 'In the very end of time Gog and Magog and their army shall come up against Jerusalem, and they shall fall by the hand of the King Messiah; they shall be slain by the flame of fire which shall proceed from under the throne of glory, and afterwards all the dead of Israel shall rise again to life, and shall enjoy the delights prepared for them from the beginning." Quote from the Jewish Targum. See reference in Numbers 11:26 and Ezekiel 38:17.)*

Revelation 20:9 They will spread across the earth and attempt to neutralize the "Queen Bee Bride" of the Lamb by surrounding and besieging God's saints in the beloved city. Then fire will pour out of heaven and consume them. *(Again, the mindsets of satanic accusation are made a meal of - yet another* *reference to the great supper-feast celebrating the new covenant and the conclusion of the old. See the Lake of Fire notes at the end of chapter 19.)*

Ephesians 2:5 This is how grace rescued us: while we were yet in that state of deadness and indifference in our [1]deviations, we were co-quickened together with Christ. We had nothing to do with it. By [2]grace you are - having been saved from the "I am not-lie". Grace defines us and interprets our salvation. *(The word often translated, trespasses, παράπτωμα **paraptoma** from **para** close proximity and **pipto**, to descend from a higher place to a lower; to stop flying, **petomai**, to fly. Losing altitude speaks of mankind's fallen mindset. Colossians 3:1-3. The sentence, [2]χάριτί ἐστε σεσωσμένοι - literally translates, "By grace you are - having been saved." We had no contribution to our salvation. God's masterplan unfolded in the mystery of the gospel declaring our joint inclusion in Christ's death and resurrection. This is the mystery of grace, God reveals us in Christ. Now we may know, even as we have always been known. 1 Corinthians 13:12. Of God's doing are we in Christ. 1 Corinthians 1:30. God saw us in Christ, in his death and resurrection before we saw ourselves there. He declared mankind's co-resurrection with Christ 800 BC. This is the only scripture in the entire Old Testament that specifically mentions the third day resurrection and it includes us. "After two days he will revive us, on the third day, he will raise us up." Hosea 6:2.)*

Ephesians 2:6 We are co-included in his resurrection. We are also co-elevated in his ascension to be equally present in the throne room of the heavenly realm where we are co-seated with him in his executive authority. We are fully represented in Christ Jesus. *(We have wasted so much time trying to get there, when "there" is where we are to begin with. Our joint position in Christ defines us; this can never again be a distant goal to reach through religious devotion or striving, but our immediate location. Colossians 3:1-3.)*

Ephesians 2:7 *[In a single triumphant act of righteousness God saved us from the "guttermost" to the uttermost. Here we are now, revealed in Christ in the highest possible position of bliss. If mankind's sad history could not distract from the extravagant love of God],* **imagine how God is now able for timeless perpetuity, to exhibit the trophy of the wealth of his grace demonstrated in his kindness towards us in Christ Jesus. Grace exhibits excessive evidence of the success of the cross.**

Ephesians 4:8 Scripture confirms that he arrested every possible threat that held mankind hostage. *["he took captivity captive"]* **And in his resurrection, he led us as trophies in his triumphant procession on high. Consider the genius of God, in the incarnate Christ, he repossessed what belonged to us by design, in human form; this is his grace-gift to us.** *(The gifts which Jesus Christ distributes to us he has received in us, in and by virtue of his incarnation. [Adam Clarke.] We were born anew in his resurrection. 1 Peter 1:3, Hosea 6:2, and Ephesians 2:6, We are also elevated in his ascension to be equally welcome in the throne room of the heavenly realm where we are now seated together with him in his authority.)*

Ephesians 4:9 The fact that he ascended confirms his victorious descent into the deepest pits of human despair. *(See John 3:13, "No one has ascended* *into heaven but he who descended from heaven, even the son of man." All mankind originates from above; we are **anouthen**, from above [see James 1:17, 18].)*

Ephesians 4:10 He now occupies the ultimate rank of authority, from the lowest regions of our darkness into which he reached in order to rescue us, to the highest authority in the heavens, having executed his mission to the fullest. *(Fallen mankind is restored to the authority of the authentic life of their design. [Psalm 139:7,8 Wither shall I go from your Spirit? Or wither shall I flee from your presence? If I ascend to heaven, You. If I make my bed in Sheol, You.] Ephesians 1:20,21.)*

See my rendering of Ephesians 6 on Spiritual Warfare. Also 2 Corinthians 10:3-6.

Thoughts on spiritual warfare: Speak tenderly to Jerusalem; and cry to her, that her warfare is accomplished, that her iniquity is pardoned. [Isaiah 40:2]

The Message translation: " ... the slate wiped clean, that old arrest warrant canceled and nailed to Christ's Cross. He stripped all the spiritual tyrants in the universe of their sham authority at the Cross and marched them naked through the streets." [Colossians 2:14, 15]

Spiritual warfare teachings are a popular distraction that many modern-day churches engage in. It preaches a defeated Devil back into business. Pharaoh was taken out of the equation when Israel was delivered out of Egypt. They then became their own worst enemy by continuing to believe a lie about themselves. [See Numbers 13:33 and Joshua 2:11.]

James says that a double-minded person deceives himself.

Neither Jesus or anyone of the Acts ekklesia ever marched around towns to bind so-called "strong men" or poured oil over buildings or places.

Any teaching that distracts from the success of the cross is a waste of time to pursue. The only possible way we can delay the glory that follows the cross is by underestimating what happened there when Jesus died and cried: "It is finished."

Jesus, grilled by the Pharisees on when the kingdom of God would come, answered; "The kingdom of God doesn't come by counting the days on the calendar." [The Message.] - The kingdom of God is within you. Luke 17:20. The kingdom of God is the authority of the Christ-life, the life of our design redeemed to reign in the most attractive practical lifestyle. The world is a ready audience. Your life is the message; Christ is your life.

2 Corinthians 10:4 The dynamic of our strategy is revealed in God's ability to disengage mindsets and perceptions that have held people captive in pseudo fortresses for centuries.

2 Corinthians 10:5 Every lofty idea and argument positioned against the knowledge of God, is cast down and exposed to be a mere invention of our own imagination. We [1]arrest every thought that could possibly trigger an opposing threat to our redeemed identity and innocence at spear point. The caliber of our weapon is empowered by the revelation

of the ultimate consequence of the obedience of Christ. *(The obedience of Christ dwarfs the effect of the disobedience of Adam into insignificance. See Romans 5:12-21. The word aichmalōtizō from aichme, spear and halosis, to capture, thus, to arrest at spear point.)*

2 Corinthians 10:6 Our ears are fine tuned to [1]echo the voice of [3]likeness that resonates within us. We are [2]acquainted with the articulate detail of the [4]authentic language of our origin. *(The word [1]echo, means to hold or embrace; the word [2]hetoimos, is from an old noun heteos [fitness] which means adjusted, ready, prepared. The word [3]ekdikeō from ek, denoting origin + dike, two parties finding likeness in each other. The word [4]parakoē from para, originating from, + akouo, to hear.)*

2 Corinthians 12:7 In sharp contrast to these spiritual revelations, the physical pain that I suffered and my severe discomfort momentarily distracted me. It was as if the old mindset of accusation *[Satan]* persuaded me that this affliction was actually God's way of keeping me humble. *(Note that it was not a messenger from God, but from Satan. The word, satanas means accuser. By these revelations of extreme proportions and consequence Paul understood that we are indeed co-seated together with Christ in heavenly places. In his resurrection he already elevated us beyond any claim of accusation. See Hosea 6:2 and Ephesians 2:5,6. We cannot get any more elevated into the bliss of our redeemed innocence than discovering our joint-seatedness with Christ in the throne room . Colossians 3:1-3.)*

2 Corinthians 12:8 I almost believed this lie and even implored the Lord three times to remove the thorn from my flesh.

2 Corinthians 12:9 Finally it dawned on me that grace is God's language; he doesn't speak "thorn-langauge". He said to me, "My grace [1]elevates you, to be fully content." And now, instead of being overwhelmed with a sense of my own weakness, he overwhelms me with an awareness of his strength. Oh what [2]bliss to rejoice in the fact that in the midst of my frailties I encounter the dynamic of the grace of God to be my [3]habitation. *(The word [1]arkeo, content, stems from the word airo which means to elevate. The word [2]hedista from hedeos, means pleasure. The word [3]episkenoo has two components: epi, continuous influence upon and skenoo, to encamp, to reside in a tent; the noun, skenos reminds of the English word skin. Paul suggests that God's grace fits you like a skin. One feels most at home in the consciousness of his grace.)*

2 Corinthians 12:10 I now enjoy a [1]delightfully different frame of mind when I encounter things that would normally make me feel frail, whether it be from insults or when I am in situations where [2]I'm forced to do things with my arms twisted behind my back; whether I am persecuted or feel squeezed into [3]claustrophobic spaces. Because of Christ, every time that I encounter weakness I escape into the strength of my [4]I am-ness. *(The word, [1]eudokeo is a compound word from, eu, well done, beautiful, and dokeo, to form an opinion. The word [2]anagkē to bend the arm like when your arm is locked behind your back, where your own efforts to clear or save yourself are completely neutralized. The word [3]stenochōria, means a narrowness of place. The word [4]eimi, is the verb, I am.)*

James 3:2 It is a common habit to [1]descend from a higher place *(of faith)* to a lower *(of the senses)*, **especially in conversation. However, if you want to be in perfect charge of your whole person, the best place to begin is to take charge of your tongue.** *(To reflect the word that confirms your true genesis [James 1:18, 19]. The word, [1]peripipto, comes from, peri, meaning surrounded + pipto, from petomai, meaning to fly; thus, to descend from a higher place to a lower, to stop flying.)*

James 3:3 **With bit and bridle we are able to direct the strong body of a horse; it's the little bit in the mouth that makes the difference.**

James 3:4 **Consider the effect of a small rudder on a large ship, when the seasoned captain skillfully steers that vessel on a straight course contrary to fierce winds and weather.**

James 3:5 **As small a member the tongue might be it can make great claims. A little fire can go out of control and consume a large forest.**

James 3:6 **A tongue can strike like lightning and turn the harmony of your world into chaos; one little member can stain the whole body. It can disrupt the pattern of your design, taking its spark from the smoldering garbage heaps of [1]Gehenna.** *(The garbage heap outside Jerusalem, commonly related to hell. **Gehenna**, is the Latin word; **Geenas** is the Greek word used for the Hebrew "**Valley of Hinnom**," גיא בן הינום which is modern day **Wadi er-Rababi**. A fiery place for the disposal of waste matter from the city of Jerusalem. The "Valley of Hinnom" lies outside of ancient Jerusalem. Thus to slander someone is to reduce that person to rubbish.)*

James 3:7 **From tigers to eagles, cobras to dolphins, humans have succeeded in curbing the wild nature of beasts and birds, reptiles and sea creatures.**

James 3:8 **Yet no-one can tame a tongue; no-one can restrain the evil in its fatal venom.** *(The law of works operated by willpower cannot match the effect of the law of perfect liberty. Mirror likeness ignites true freedom to utter that which is precious.)*

James 3:9 **We can say beautiful things about God the Father but with the same mouth curse a fellow human made in his mirror likeness.** *(The point is not what the person did to deserve the insult. The point is that people are image and likeness bearers of God by design. True worship is to touch someone's life with the same devotion and care you would touch Jesus himself; even if the other person seems a most unlikely candidate.)*

James 3:10 **My friends, a blessing and a curse cannot originate from the same source.** *(Discovering our true source brings true freedom. [James 1:17,18])*

James 1:5 **The only thing you could possibly lack is wisdom.** *[One might sometimes feel challenged beyond the point of sanity]* **however, make your request in such a way that you draw directly from the [2]source** *[not filtered through other opinions]*. **God is the origin and author of wisdom; he [1]intertwines your thoughts with good judgment. His gifts are available to all, without regret.** *(The word, [1]haplos, from ha, particle of union; hama,* *together with + **pleko**, meaning to plait, braid, weave together. See Luke 11:34 "The eye is the lamp of the body; if the eye is single the whole body is full of light." Entwining our eyes with Papa's eyes is what enlightens our entire being. Which is exactly what the word,* קוה **Kawa** *in Hebrew means in Isaiah 40:31 they that entwine with the Lord's thoughts mount up with wings like eagles. We are wired by design to entwine. Also Matthew 6:22, "If your eye is entwined with light your whole body will be full of light." See 2 Corinthians 1:12. Wisdom that comes from above remains unaffected by the contradictions of the senses. The word,* ²**didomi**, *to give, to be the author or source of a thing — Wesley J. Perschbacher.)*

See **Notes on An Open Heaven** at the end of Revelation 13.

Also my comment on Revelation 20:3, This is a clear announcement of what happened in Jesus' descent into hell where he defeated the reign and claim of darkness in the HQ of mankind's deepest pits of despair and then, in his resurrection he co-raises the entire human race into a place of joint-reigning with him from the heavenlies. Now here on earth where it all plays out, every enemy is placed under his feet. See Hosea 6:2, Ephesians 2:5,6 and Ephesians 4:8-10, also Colossians 2:14,15. See Extended Notes on the Thousand Years at the end of chapter 20.

Hebrews 2:7 It seems that man briefly descends to a ¹less elevated place than Elohim; yet he is crowned with God's own glory and dignity, and appointed in a position of authority over all the works of his hands." *(The word ἐλαττόω ¹**elattoō** [English, elation] suggests a little less than Elohim.*

Possibly, a copyist felt that the reference to equality with our Maker [Genesis 1:26] was too bold, so the Greek text reads, "he made us a little lower than the celestial messengers." Here is the reference, Psalm 8:4 What is man that you are mindful of him, and the son of man that you care so much for him? Psalm 8:5 Yet you made him little less than God, [Elohim] and crowns him with glory and honor. Psalm 8:6 You have given him dominion over the works of your hands; you have put all things under his feet.)

Hebrews 2:8 God's intention was that human life should rule the planet. He subjected everything without exception to his control. Yet, looking at the human race, it does not seem that way at all.

Hebrews 2:9 But what is apparent, is Jesus. *[Now God spoke to us in a son. Hebrews 1:1-3]* **Let us then consider him in such a way, that we may clearly perceive what God is saying to mankind in him. In the death he suffered, he briefly descended to a seemingly less elevated place than Elohim,** *[Psalm 8:5]* **in order to taste the death of the entire human race, and in doing so, to fulfill the grace of God and be crowned again [as a man, representing all of mankind] with glory and highly esteemed honor.** *(See **Philippians 2:6** His being God's equal in form and likeness was official; his Sonship did not steal the limelight from his Father. Neither did his humanity distract from the deity of God. **Philippians 2:7** His mission however, was not to prove his deity, but to embrace our humanity. Emptied of his reputation as God, he fully embraced our physical human form; born in our resemblance he identified himself as the servant of the human race. His love enslaved him to us. **Philippians 2:8** And so we have* *the drama of the cross in context: the man Jesus Christ who is fully God, becomes fully man to the extent of willingly dying humanity's death at the hands of his own creation. He embraced the curse and shame of the lowest kind in dying a criminal's death. [Thus, through the doorway of death, he descended into our hellish darkness. [In his death, Jesus conquered the underworld and he has the keys; no-one else does.] Revelation 1:18 I am also the Living One; I died and now, see, here I am alive unto the ages of the ages and I have the keys wherewith I have disengaged the gates of Hades and death. Also, Ephesians 4:8-10.]* **Philippians 2:9** *From this place of utter humiliation, God exalted him to the highest rank. God graced Jesus with a Name that is far above every other name.)*

Hebrews 2:10 He towers in conspicuous prominence far above all things. He is both their author and their conclusion. He now summons every son of his, through a perfected salvation, to his own glory. The extent of the suffering he bore is the measure of the perfection of the salvation over which he presides.

Colossians 3:1 See yourselves co-raised with Christ. Now ponder with persuasion the consequence of your co-inclusion in him. Relocate yourselves mentally. Engage your thoughts with throne room realities where you are co-seated with Christ in the executive authority of God's right hand.

Colossians 3:2 Becoming affectionately acquainted with throne room realities, will keep you from being distracted again by the earthly *(soul-ruled)* **realm.**

My friend, Marnitz Smit writes,

"...We were always so focused on the mantle of Elijah that we completely missed his ascension. He did not say if you pick up my mantle, he said if you see me taken up. The mantle was only the outer garment which represented the flesh *(one's own willpower)* that Elijah had to cast off in order to ascend into the heavenly dimension."

Also Acts 1:9 and Luke 10:30

17:1 And one of the seven messengers with the seven golden temple vessels approached me and called me to come and see the judgment of that notorious prostitute who sat enthroned upon the many trade routes of the waters - both the rivers and seas. *(Same language repeated in Revelation 21:9 And one of the seven celestial messengers, having the seven vessels being filled with the seven last wounds, came to me and spoke with me, saying, "Come, I will show you the bride, the Lamb's wife." The Prostitute Society of Babylon [the "Old Jerusalem" is set up against the Bride-society - the New Jerusalem.])*

17:2 She engaged the kings of the earth with her harlotry, intoxicating the earth dwellers with the wine of her passion and fornication.

17:3 The messenger then carried me into a desert place [*in total contrast to the hustle and bustle of the busy trade routes of the oceans and the rivers*] **I was transported there in spirit and saw a woman seated upon a ¹scarlet colored Beast; with ²blasphemous, insulting names written all over them like a label revealing the content of their ³cargo. The Beast had seven heads and ten horns.** *(For reference to the same Beast, Revelation 13:1-10 and its second Partner in verse 11, 12, the Lamb with the Dragon's voice, later called the False Prophet and here, the Harlot. Together in their alliance with the Dragon they form the Counterfeit Trinity. Also Revelation 17:12*

*The word ¹**kokkinos** refers to the crimson or scarlet color which was produced from the berry of the "ilex coccifera"; these "berries" are the clusters of the eggs of a female insect, the "kermes" [resembling the cochineal)] and when collected and pulverized produces a red which was used in dyeing scarlet cloth. The color is so steadfast that it was one of the most difficult dyes to remove from clothing. So when Isaiah compares our sins leaving its stubborn stain upon our consciences, he says in Isaiah 1:18 "Come now, let us reason together, says the LORD: though your sins are like scarlet, they shall be as white as snow; though they are red like crimson, they shall become like wool."*

Again the ²blasphemy and insults against the Name is emphasized. See my comments in Revelation 13:1.

*Revelation 15:7, These golden fire-pans were loaded with the entire meaning of the sacrifice. Filled, γέμω **gémō**, to be full, from γόμος ³**gómos**, load; cargo.)*

17:4 The woman was draped in purple and scarlet fabric, festooned and sprinkled with golden glitter and ornaments. She was elaborately decorated with gold, precious stones and pearls, holding a golden ¹cup in her hand which was brimming with defiling obscenities and the stench of her impurities. *(Again the surface, make-believe beauty and apparent splendor cannot hide her true filthy character - like the white washed tombs Jesus compared the religious system to. "Hypocrites. For you are so careful to clean the outside of the ¹cup [**poterion**] and the dish, but inside you are filthy - full of greed and self-indulgence. You are like beautifully decorated tombs on the outside, desperately trying to hide the stench of decaying corpses within." Matthew 23:25, 27. βδελυγματων ²**bdelugma** derivative of **bdeo** - to stink.*

*The Harlot represents the counterfeit ¹cup [**poterion**] of covenant, to the cup of the Lord.*

1 Corinthians 10:16 The cup [ποτήριον - potērion] of blessing which we bless, is it not the communion of the blood of Christ? The bread which we break, is it not the communion of the body of Christ?

1 Corinthians 10:21 Ye cannot drink the cup [ποτήριον - potērion] of the Lord, and the cup [ποτήριον - potērion] of devils: ye cannot be partakers of the Lord's table, and of the table of devils.

1 Corinthians 11:25 After the same manner also the cup, [ποτήριον - potērion] when he had supped, saying, This cup [ποτήριον - potērion] is the new testament in my blood: this do ye, as oft as ye drink in remembrance of me.

The covenant cup of the Lord communicates the redeemed life of our design incarnate in our person and fellowship and celebrated in our every meal.)

17:5 The words written upon her forehead exposed her mystery identity: 'Babylon the Great, the Mother of the Whores and the filth of the earth.' *(Roman harlots wore a label with their names on their brows - Seneca, Rhet. I. 2. 7; Juvenal VI. 122f.)*

17:6 The woman I saw was intoxicated with the blood of the ¹aints and the blood of ²those who bore the testimony of Jesus. This left me mesmerized, pondering what I saw, desiring to understand the context of it all. *(The cup she drank represented her opposition to everything that the blood of Jesus communicates. She was intoxicated with the thought that accused, sinful mankind could be reckoned blameless saints by the blood of the Lamb. Revelation 7:9,13 &14. Also Revelation 12:11 Mikael and his celestial messengers conquered the Dragon because of the blood of the little Lamb and the word of their testimony. They did not believe that the agape of life discovered in Christ can be threatened or ¹terminated in death. (The blood of the Lamb brought closure to every possible accusation against the human race. This is the testimony of the prophetic word announcing the Good News throughout the ages. The word ¹**achri** - the end; the idea of terminating. Mikael and his messengers represent the entire host of heaven - including all the multitudes previously mentioned. See **Extended Notes on the Word of God and the Testimony of Jesus Christ** at the end of chapter 20.*

*Also Revelation 16:19 And the great city split into three portions and the cities of the nations fell and Babylon the great was remembered in the cup of God's ¹great passion and ²desire to bring everything to conclusion. [The word ¹**thumos**, passion and ²**orge** from **oregomai**, to stretch one's self out in order to touch or to grasp something, to reach after with intense desire.])*

17:7 And the celestial messenger said to me, "Why were you so perplexed? I will explain to you the mystery of the woman and the Beast carrying her; also the meaning of his seven heads and ten horns.

17:8 The brutal Beast you saw is a ¹"has been" from the beginning - it indeed has no real existence - yet it seems to make "a come back", as if emerging out of the Abyss only to dissolve again into perdition. Meanwhile the minds of those blinded by their ²earthbound perceptions continue to be mesmerized

by its apparent relevance. They are the ones whose identities are not [3]based upon the Lamb's Book of Life. They do not yet see that their original identity was redeemed in the Lamb." *(The words, ἦν καὶ οὐκ ἔστι [1]en kai ouk esti, meaning, to be and not to be; with the verb en being the Imperfect Indicative of eimi, I am - another meaning of the Imperfect Indicative is to refer to unreal [counterfactual] situations in present or past time.*

This is in total contrast to the One who is I am; who always was and will continually be the accompanying One. An antithesis to "ho ēn kai ho ōn" of Revelation 1:4.

οἱ κατοικοῦντες ἐπὶ τῆς γῆς *The earthbound ones. The word [2]katoikeō from kata, down and oikeo, to dwell or set up home - thus, to be earthbound. Remember how Paul invites us to engage our thoughts with resurrection realities and to see ourselves seated together with Christ in heavenly places. Ephesians 2:5,6. Also Colossians 3:1-3. Since you are raised together with Christ, engage your thoughts with "throne-room realities" [the things that are above - relevant to your co-setedness] and not with things below - "soul-room realities". As in Revelation 16:16, where Armageddon pictures the battle between the lower earthbound thought patterns and the thoughts of God. Revelation 13:8 The "earthbound" perception is in essence an identity crisis - knowing oneself and one another merely "according to the flesh" as Paul says in 2 Corinthians 5:16.*

Note, the Preposition, [3]epi, upon, as in continuous influence upon. An "earthbound-identity" is based upon the "Fallen Mindset, the fruit of the wrong Tree - the I-am-not Tree. And not [3]upon the Lamb's Book of Life.

The word often translated foundation, kataballo, from kata and ballo, meaning "to fall away, to put in a lower place," instead of themelios, meaning "foundation" [see Ephesians 2:20; also Revelation 21:14,19]; thus, I translated it "the fall of the world," instead of "the foundation of the world." The entire "Fall" was a falling away from our identity as image and likeness bearers of Elohim. Just like Eve, were we all deceived to believe a lie about ourselves, which is the fruit of the "I-am-not-tree ". We all, like sheep, have gone astray. [Isaiah 53:6]

*See extended notes at the end of the chapter on **The Lamb's Book of Life**.*

*Also **notes on Armageddon** at the end of Revelation 16 and Notes on the **lake of fire** at the end of Revelation 19.)*

17:9 Here is understanding for the inquiring mind: the seven heads, or mindsets, upon which the woman was seated represent seven mountains, or typical social structures, found within the city context. *(Many cities besides Rome can boast of their seven hills: also Constantinople, Brussels, and especially Jerusalem. These social structures could typically include the essential building blocks of society, i.e. Family, Education, Religion, Business, Government, Arts/Entertainment and the Media.)*

17:10 These seven social rulers represent five fallen structures, another current *(at the time of writing)* **and another, which is still to come for a very brief spell.** *(The influence of all these typical social spheres under the control of the Harlot, are equally defeated in the Lamb's victory.*

The mindset that the Trinity of Beasts operate in is like a virus hosted by political leaders and their followers - infiltrating societies with its predictable symptoms.

There are also interesting historical parallels - Of the first seven kings, five had come at the time of writing - Julius Caesar, Augustus, Tiberius, Gaius, and Claudius - one was currently in power [Nero, the number values of his name calculated 666] and one had not yet come [Galba], but would only remain a little time [six months.])

17:11 And the "has been" - Beast is the eighth *[the rider on the horse - which is the woman in this symbolic scene];* **she is part and parcel of the seven and dissolves into perdition.**

17:12 The ten horns you saw are ten kings who have not yet received rule until they come to power with the Scarlet Beast for a brief hour to fight against the Lamb. *(The "ten horns" on the seven-headed monster suggests that the horns are closely related and connected to the same head or mindset of the same animal. [Revelation 12:9 The great Dragon, the ancient ophis [serpent] also known as the Devil or Satan, together with all his celestial messengers. Also Revelation 13:11 Then I saw another wild animal; this one emerged out of the earth - it had two horns and resembled a young lamb; yet it had a Dragon's voice. (The counterfeit "trinity" emerges - the one mirroring the other - the Dragon Accuser, the seven-headed sea-monster of religion with its leading role player, the head that was slain but became alive again and now the Dragon clothed in a lamb's-disguise) Revelation 13:12 Even though it had the appearance of the lamb, it operated under the same authority as the previous Beast - under the watchful eye of the Dragon. [Counterfeit-Christianity as a religion is a wolf in sheep's clothing.] It's the same old Dragon in a lamb's disguise. Its mission was to engage the [1]earthbound dwellers to worship the counterfeit - the slaughtered animal that was restored to life out of its death.] Also Revelation 17:3.*

See my extended Commentary at the end of this chapter on **End Times.***)*

17:13 These rulers were in full agreement to hand over their authority to the Beast. *(At the trial and crucifixion of Jesus, former enemies became allies as they banded together against the Lamb see Luke 23:12 That day Herod and Pilate became friends - before this they had been enemies. Psalm 83:5 With one mind they plot together; they form an alliance against you.)*

17:14 These join forces in that hour to wage war against the Lamb, but the Lamb defeats them since he is the Lord of lords and the King of kings. And sharing with him in his victory are his [1]kindred. They recognize their [2]origin in this conversation and are now of the same [3]persuasion. The Lamb led them into freedom from their lost identity, and their doubts. *(The words [1]kletoi from kaleo, to surname; kai [2]eklektoi from ek source and legomai from lego, to speak - the Lamb is the logos, the conversation of God, mankind is his audience; kai [3]pistoi, the persuaded ones. Mankind is joint sharer in the Lamb's triumph and glory. They are the kindred of the Lamb, having their origin in the word that was from the beginning face to face with God [John 1:1,14.] and the recipients of God's faith. There are numeral references to the same "once and for all war" in the heavens. It is however the same hour; the same event. Revelation*

*12:7; Revelation 16:13,14; Revelation 19:19; Revelation 20:8. See extended Notes on **The Triumph of The Lamb** at the end of the chapter.)*

17:15 The same messenger who addressed me earlier to come and see the judgment of that notorious prostitute - the one who sat enthroned upon the many trade routes of the waters, both the rivers and seas - proceeded to explain to me that the waters I saw represent the entire spectrum of people-groupings and tribal identities with their unique language-specific dialect preferences. *(These are the very masses of mankind that were redeemed by the blood of the Lamb as referenced earlier in the book, every sphere of society were there - **laoi kai ochloi eisin kai ethnē kai glōssai** - Revelation 10:11 And he said to me, "Necessity is laid upon you to now disclose with new insight the prophetic word again - this prophecy's time has come and is now relevant and you will declare it before many peoples and different nations and their kings in their specific mother tongue language." - This list of peoples occurs seven times in Revelation with a like grouping of words for all mankind, of all races and nations; - Revelation 5:9, Revelation 7:9, Revelation 10:11, Revelation 11:9 Revelation 13:7; Revelation 14:6 and here in 17:15.*

*See Ezekiel 43:2 And behold, the glory of the God of Israel came from the east; and the sound of his coming was like the sound of many waters; and the earth shone with his glory. Matthew 24:31 and he will send out his celestial messengers with a loud trumpet call, and they will gather his blueprint likeness from the four winds, from one end of heaven to the other. The word, **eklegomai**, traditionally associated with the idea of election, has two components, **ek**, a Preposition that indicates source or origin and **legomai** from **lego**, to speak, meaning to communicate ideas; - the Lamb is the **logos**, the language and conversation of God; mankind is his audience thus, the original blueprint-word, the **logos**; see John 1:1-3 and 12. Matthew 22:14, The many are called, [**kaleo**] but few are "chosen" **eklegomai**, thus, The masses are defined by my name while few yet realize their origin in me.)*

17:16 In realizing their defeat by the Lamb, the ten horns which you saw on the Beast will turn against the prostitute with furious hatred and will strip her of all her decorations, expose her nakedness, consume her flesh and burn her body. *(Again, John sees a counterfeit drama to the slaying of the Lamb of God; here, the figurehead of the religious corrupt system, the great whore, is sacrificed and her flesh is eaten by her previous colleagues, clients and supporters. This reminds of Jesus' conversation about eating his flesh and drinking his blood as remembered in the Last Supper. See Mirror Bible)*

17:17 This happened according to God's strategic plan as he gave them a mind to be united against the woman and to give their kingdom to the Beast until his word would be fulfilled. *(See Colossians 2:15 In him dying mankind's death, he [1]defused every possible claim of accusation against the human race and thus made a public [2]spectacle of every [3]rule and authority in God's brilliant triumph, demonstrated in him. The [4]voice of the cross will never be silenced. (The horror of the Cross is now the eternal trophy of God's triumph over sin. The cross stripped religion of its authority to manipulate mankind with guilt. Every accusation lost its leverage to blackmail the human race with condemnation and shame. The* word, ¹**apekduomai**, *is translated from* **apo**, *away from, and* **ekduo**, *to be stripped of clothing; to disarm; the religious facade that disguised the law of works as a means of defining a person's life, was openly defeated. Same word used in Colossians 3:9. The dominance of the tree of the knowledge of good and evil [***poneros***, *hard work and labor*] *was ended. The word,* ²***deikmatizo***, *means to exhibit in public. See* ³*commentary below of the words* ***arche***, *rule and* ***exousia***, *authority. The word,* ⁴***parresia***, *comes from* ***pas***, *all and* ***rheo***, *outspokenness, pouring forth speech.*

"He stripped all the spiritual tyrants in the universe of their sham authority at the Cross and marched them naked through the streets." — The Message))

17:18 The woman you saw is the great city which dominated the kings of the earth. *(The Prostitute city-society of Babylon stands in contrast to the Bride of Christ as the New Jerusalem.*

Just like Babylon is not a city in the symbolic language of Revelation, it is a "fallen", distorted-mindset-society; so the New Jerusalem is not a city but the redeemed society of mankind. The Bride of Christ.

Babylon has fallen. *See extended notes at the end of this chapter.)*

Revelation Chapter 17 Extended Notes:

The Lamb's Book of Life - Mankind's Redeemed Identity
End Times
The Triumph of the Lamb
Babylon has fallen.

THE LAMB'S BOOK OF LIFE - REV 17

The Lamb's Book of Life - Mankind's Redeemed Identity

The authentic ID of human life is defined in the Book of Life - also called, the Tree of Life, representing the redeemed life of our design, versus the alternative Tree of the knowledge of good and evil, representing mankind's identity under scrutiny and questioning. The "I am not-Tree" heads up the system of a works and performance-based philosophy. To have your name written in the Book of Life simply suggests that you discover your identity there in the Zoe-life, redeemed by the Lamb. You may have only known yourself according to the flesh, as Simon, the son of Jonah, while you really are Petros. Mr. Rock, you are a chip off the old Block. Every evidence of an inferior identity will be cast into the lake of sulphur burning away the dross to reveal the gold. Any idea of an identity outside of the Book of Life, is dissolved. The Lamb's Book of Life and not the law of personal performance, defines us.

Revelation 3:5 Everyone who sees their victory in me, will I clothe in white garments - and they will realize that I am not in the business of fulfilling their law and performance based fears, by blotting out their names from the Book of Life. Instead, I am the one who endorses their identity face to face before my Father and his celestial messengers.

Revelation 20:12 And I saw everyone who ever died, small and great, standing before God. And the books were opened. And another book was opened. The Book of Life. The first volume of books represented mankind's judgment based on their own works, versus the Book of Life which celebrates the triumph of the Lamb.

Revelation 20:15 And [1]everything that was not written in the Book of Life was poured into the lake of fire. *(The Greek, εἴ τις οὐχ εὑρέθη ἐν τῇ βίβλῳ τῆς ζωῆς γεγραμμένος - with, **ei tis**, meaning everything or everyone - but, what is cast into the symbolic lake ablaze with brimstone is not a person but a mindset. A distorted perception of identity. See notes on the Lake of Fire at the end of Chapter 19.)*

Revelation 17:8 ...Meanwhile the minds of those blinded by their earthbound perceptions continue to be mesmerized by its apparent relevance. They are the ones who are convinced that their names were not even included in the Lamb's Book of Life to begin with. *(The idea of a Book of Life is taken from the custom of registering the names of persons in a list, roll, or catalogue. In Jewish tradition there was a prevailing fear that your name might be blotted out of the Book of Life if your behavior did not please God. See Exodus 32:32.*

Here the suggestion is that some names were not even written in the Lamb's Book of Life to begin with. This idea would obviously boost the Calvinistic deception of election, that if you're not "chosen", you're doomed - which is a ridiculous contradiction to the entire context and conclusion of the Gospel.

See Matthew 24:31 And he will send out his celestial messengers with a loud trumpet call, and they will gather his blueprint likeness from the four winds, from one end of heaven to the other. The word, eklegomai, traditionally associated with the idea of election, has two components, ek, a Preposition that indicates source or origin and lego, meaning to communicate ideas; thus, the original blueprint-word, the logos; see John 1:1-3 and 12. The many are called, [kaleo, to surname] but few are "chosen" eklegomai thus, The masses are defined by my name but few yet realize their origin in me. Matthew 22:14

Your in-Christness is not the result of a lucky draw. Calvinism lied to you. Neither is it the result of your "choice" to follow Jesus. Something doesn't become true by popular vote. Or by our beliefs. If it wasn't true to begin with, we are wasting our time trying to "believe" it true. Faith happens to you when you encounter the Good Announcement.

Of God's doing are we IN CHRIST... [1 Corinthians 1:30] For "evangelical theology", to miss the meaning of mankind's inclusion IN CHRIST, before they knew it or believed it, is to completely miss the point of the death, descent into hell, resurrection and ascension of Jesus. This would make Jesus irrelevant and reduce the salvation of the human race to their own fate managed by institutionalized religion, attaching mere sentimental value to an historic Jesus who died and rose again. By dying our death as fully God and fully man, once and for all [not for a "select few."], death became the doorway, whereby Jesus would enter into our hell and deepest darkness and sense of lostness and loneliness as a result of the lies we believed about ourselves - to triumphantly lead us out as his trophies and relocate us face to face with the Father of the universe. Ephesians 4:7,8 and 9 See Mirror Bible. All this happened while we were still dead in our trespasses and sins. Ephesians 2:5,6 Co-quickened, co-raised, co-seated in his Executive authority [his right hand] Now ponder Colossians 3:1-3 and engage your thoughts with throne room realities.)

Revelation 12:7 Mikael and his celestial colleagues led the war in the heavenly realm against the Dragon and his cohorts. *(The Hebrew name* מיכאל *Mikael means, "Who is like God?"* **The context of the onslaught against the human race has always been image and likeness-identity related.** *Mankind's sense of lost identity is the fruit of the "I-am-not tree system ." Jesus faced this temptation on mankind's behalf, where the Devil [Diabolos - through the Fall] tempts Jesus' identity with,"If you are the Son of God..." Jesus rebukes Satan [the Accuser] and sends it off into smithereens. Matthew 4:6,10 The leverage of the Satanas-System is an identity challenge. "Who do people say that I, the son of man, am?" The question Jesus asks in Matthew 16:13 underlines the focus of his mission; "If you discover who I am, you discover who you are." He is about to redeem mankind's lost sense of sonship and identity. Illiterate Simon answers, "Jesus, you, the son of man, are the Messiah, the son of God." Then Jesus immediately endorses him, "Simon, son of Jonah, "Now that you know who I am, allow me to introduce you, to you. You are Peter. [Petros in the Greek means Rock. Actually it means, little rock and Petra, upon which Jesus builds his ekklesia, means Rock. So, son of man, you are Mr. Rock, a Chip off the old Block. We have forgotten the Rock from which we were hewn. Deuteronomy 32:18. "You who seek God and pursue righteousness, here is your clue. "Look to the Rock from which you were hewn." Isaiah 51:1. Then Jesus makes this remarkable statement, that on this Rock [the revelation of mankind's true sonship, redeemed], he would build his* **ekklesia** *[from* **ek**, *origin and* **kaleo**, *to surname; original identity] and the gates of* **Hades** *will not prevail against you. [The word,* **Hades**, *from the negative particle,* **ha**, *and* **eido** *to see] The blindfold mode of the human race will not prevail against the revelation of the son of man as the offspring of God - this is the* *triumph of the ekklesia. Revelation 2:7. [The term, "son of" surnames someone. So the word, ekklesia, translated, ekklesia, literally points to the Source unveiling mankind's true surname.] So, if what we call ekklesia today is not about the unveiling of mankind's true, redeemed Identity, its not the ekklesia that Jesus is building.* **[Revelation 7:9** *where mankind was delivered out of their national, geographical and historical identities.]*

See Extended Notes on **The Son of Man is the Son of God** at the end of chapter 2.

Also in the beautiful encounter of Jesus and the Samaritan woman in John chapter 4, the source-identity of mankind beautifully unfolds. **John 4:6** *The well which Jacob dug was still in operation. Since it was already midday and Jesus felt exhausted and thirsty from their day and a half walk, [40 miles from Aenon] he decided to wait at the well while his disciples would go into the village to buy food. (Having left the Place of Springs, Aenon early the previous morning, one can just imagine how Jesus' mind drifted to the fountain theme.)* **John 4:7** *When a local Samaritan woman finally arrived to draw water, Jesus immediately asked her for a drink.*

John 4:9 *The Samaritan woman obviously anticipated this request and was ready with her response, "You are a Jew, aren't you? So why would you expect to get anything for free from a Samaritan woman?" Within the politics of the day, Jews looked down upon the Samaritans and had no dealings with them. (She knew very well how strategically en-route this precious well was and what political leverage it gave her over weary Jewish travelers.)* **John 4:10** *(Jesus was not at all intimidated or embarrassed by her political stance; he didn't allow his awareness of his weariness and desperate thirst, as well as an obvious opportunity to negotiate for a quick fix-drink, to distract from his Person and mission - instead of associating himself with the Jews as a mere Jew and endorsing the Samaritan's 'inferior' political identity, he immediately engaged her with a far superior conversation. He escaped the temptation to see himself or the lady reduced to a lesser identity. He knew who he was and what his mission was all about, as the Messiah of mankind - by seeing himself he was able to see her in the same light. What he had to offer was not for sale.) He looked her in the eye and said, "If you could see the generosity of God's gift, you would perceive who I am. (I am so much more than a Jewish man and you are so much more than a Samaritan woman.) So here I am asking you for a drink when you should be asking me and I would give you the water of life for free.* **John 4:11** *(Just like Nicodemus in the previous chapter, she struggles to determine which source Jesus was pointing to.) Sir, you have nothing to draw with and the well is deep. How would you reach this living water?)*

Revelation 12:8 The Dragon's influence was totally demolished and rendered powerless - not a trace of its presence was found in the heavens. *(Principalities and powers were completely disarmed on the cross. Colossians 2:14,15 "And their place was not found" see Daniel 2:35 - the little stone against whom the Gates of Hades shall not prevail - the Chip off the old Block demolished the pseudo man-made identity. There are numeral references to the same "once and for all war" in the heavens. It is however the same hour; the same event. Revelation 16:13,14; Revelation 17:13,14; 19:19; Revelation 20:8. Also* **John 12:31,32** *Now is the judgment of this world; now the ruler of this world shall be cast down. [When I am lifted up on the cross.])*

Revelation 12:9 So the great Dragon, the ¹ancient ²ophis [serpent], also known as the Devil or Satan - whose sole mission was to lead the entire inhabited world astray - was cast down to the earth-dimension, together with all his cohorts. *(The word ¹archaios, ancient, of old; from arche, from the beginning. As Jesus said that the Devil was a murderer "from the beginning" The Greek word, ²ophis is translated serpent and comes from **optomai**, to gaze, in this case, to present a visual idea through illusion. John 8:44. He was stripped of his pseudo rank of authority see Colossians 2:14,15 he was made a public spectacle. Luke 10:18 And Jesus said to them, I saw Satan falling out of heaven like lightning. These all represent mindsets that have blindfolded mankind since the fall of Adam.)*

Revelation 12:10 Then I heard a very loud voice in the heavens announcing, This is the moment which the entire prophetic word pointed to and culminates in; it is the realization of mankind's salvation. The power of the kingdom of our God and its authority is endorsed in the I-am-ness of his Christ. The business of accusation is bankrupt. The 24/7 industry of condemning the brotherhood of mankind before the face of God has been annihilated. *(The word ¹**kategoros**, a name given to the Devil by the Rabbis, the one whose business is accusation, from **kata**, downward and **agora**, to trade; a word used for all kinds of business in the public arena.*

Luke 10:18. Also John 12:27 My soul is exceedingly perplexed right now. What shall I say, "Father. Rescue me ¹out of the clutches of this hour." No. This hour is the very culmination of my destiny. [Greek Preposition, ¹ek, out of; source; origin.]

John 12:28 "Father. Glorify your name." And immediately there came a voice out of the heavenly realm saying, "I have glorified it, and I will glorify it again.")

Revelation 13:6 It hurled its accusations ¹in God's face, while blaspheming his Name and tabernacle and ²those dwelling in the heavenlies. *(The words, ¹**pros ton theon** positions the Accuser to now face God's image and likeness incarnate in human form, since there was no trace of accusation present in the heavenlies, having been thoroughly expelled from any further presence or relevance in the heavenly sphere. [Revelation 12:8-10] The significance of heaven endorsing the tabernacle of God on earth - in both its prophetic symbolism as well as its tangible unveiling in incarnate human life, is now the target of accusation and every blasphemous utterance of this Beast who takes its authority from Mr. Accusation himself.*

*²Those dwelling in the heavenlies; **kai tous en tō ouranō skenountas** - in contrast to those whose minds are still trapped in earthbound-mode. See verse 8.*

*See my Extended **Notes on the Battle between the Earthbound and Heavenly perspective** at the end of Revelation 16.*

*Also Extended **Notes From Mt Sinai to Mt Zion** at the end of Revelation 14.)*

Revelation 20:12 And I saw everyone who ever died, small and great, standing before God. And the books were opened. And another book was opened. The Book of Life. The first volume of books represented mankind's judgment based on their own works, versus the Book of Life which celebrates the triumph of the Lamb.

John 5:21 For just as the Father awakens people from their death-sleep and revitalizes them with zoe-life, even so it pleases the Son to awaken people to life.

John 5:22 For the Father judges no-one but has given all judgment to the Son.

John 5:25 Oh how I desire for you to get this. The prophetic hour has come. This is the moment for the dead to hear the voice of the Son of God - C'mon. Hear and live.

John 5:27 The Father has also given the Son of man [1]authentic authority to execute judgment on mankind's behalf. *(The word [1]exousia, often translated as authority has two components, ek, out of, source and eimi, I am.)*

John 5:28 Do not be alarmed by this, but the hour is coming when those in the [1]graves will hear his voice. *(No-one who ever lived will escape the extent of his righteous judgment. Those who have [1]forgotten who they are will hear his incarnate voice. The word for grave, [1]__mnēmeion__, memory, suggests a remembrance - to bring something from memory into the here and now! Like David prophecies in Psalm 22 when he sees the cross-crisis [__krisis__ - judgment, means the 'decisive moment' or, turning point.] a thousand years before it happens. His conclusion in verse 27 sums up the triumph of God's resolve. "All the ends of the earth shall [1]remember and turn to the LORD; and all the families of the nations shall worship before him." See 1 Corinthians 15:21,22 The same mankind who died in a man was raised again in a man. In Adam all died; in Christ all are made alive.)*

1 John 5:17 [1]Disharmony in relationship is [2]unlike the true rhythm of your being. The deception of a distorted image will [3]not face death again. *(The word unrighteousness, [1]__adikia__, from __a__, negative or without and __dikia__, indicating two parties finding likeness in each other; thus relationship in conflict. The root of sin is to believe a lie about yourself. The word sin, is the word [1]__hamartia__, from __ha__, negative or without and __meros__, portion or form, thus to be without your allotted portion or without form, pointing to a disoriented, distorted, bankrupt identity; the word __meros__, is the stem of __morphe__, as in 2 Corinthians 3:18 the word __metamorphe__, with form, which is the opposite of __hamartia__ - without form. Sin is to live out of context with the blueprint of one's design; to behave out of tune with God's original harmony. See Deuteronomy 32:18, "You have forgotten the Rock that begot you and have gotten out of step with the God who danced with you." Hebrew, חול __khul__, also means to dance, as in Judges 21:21. The root of sin is to believe a lie about yourself. Sin is not unto death or, sin will not [3]face [__pros__] death - this is the whole point of the gospel. Jesus as Savior of the world; the Lamb of God took away the sins of the world; he died mankind's death. See Hebrews 9:27,28 The same goes for everyone: a person dies only once, and then faces judgment. Christ died once and faced the judgment of the entire human race. His second appearance has nothing to do with sin, but to reveal salvation for all to [1]fully embrace him. See 2 Corinthians 2:15 We are a sweet savor of Christ unto God evident in everyone we meet. The fragrance of Christ is recognized in all unto salvation. The same gospel that announces the fragrant victory of Christ declares the odor of death; the defeat of destruction in everyone. [This parade of victory is a public announcement of the defeat of the religious systems and* structures based on the law of works. Just like it is in any public game where the victory celebration of the winning team is an embarrassment for the losing team. The death of evil is announced in resurrection life. The word, **apollumi**, is derived from **apo**, away from, and **ollumi**, to destroy, to ruin.] The message we communicate is a fragrance with an immediate association; to darkness, it is the smell of doom [the death of death]; to life it is the familiar fragrance of life itself. We are not competing with those who have added their price tag to the gospel. Our conversation has its source in Christ; we communicate from the transparent innocence of a face to face encounter with God. [The law of personal performance or **kapeleuo**, meaning retail; which is a gospel with a price tag.] Revelation 20:15 also my Extended Notes on the lake of fire and the Second Death at the end of Revelation 19.)

1 John 5:18 What was made absolutely ^{1}**clear** [in the incarnate Christ] **is that whoever is begotten of God cannot be a** ^{2}**distorted image of God. Likeness begets likeness. Jesus did not come to reveal the "otherness" of God, but his likeness in human form. There is nothing wrong with mankind's design, neither with their salvation. To** ^{1}**see one's true revealed and now redeemed genesis in God, is to treasure the person you really are by his divine engineering and to remain** ^{4}**unstained in your thoughts by** ^{3}**the "I am not-Tree system." The** ^{3}**idea that I am not the expression of his image and likeness can no longer** ^{4}**attach itself to my thoughts, neither do I allow it to ignite its destructive cycle of self-righteousness or depression. The system of this world is based on a mentality of separation, which is marked by** ^{3}**hardships annoyances and labors. It becomes an all consuming and most exhausting lifestyle of having to prove oneself in every relationship and a futile striving for recognition; with its inevitable results of disappointment, condemnation, rejection and pretense.** (John begins the 3 sentences in verse 18,19 & 20 with he verb ^{1}**oidamen** which is the Perfect Active tense of ^{1}**eido**, to see, to observe, to pay attention, perceive, to know as an eye-witness. The Perfect Indicative Active tense denotes an action which is perfected or completed in the past, but the effects of which are regarded as continuing into the present. A distorted image is what the word ^{2}**hamartia** suggests; from **ha**, negative and **meros**, portion or form; thus without form. The word ^{3}**poneros,** often translated as evil, refers to the tree of the knowledge of good and evil [**poneros**] which is the fruit of a lost fellowship, identity, value and innocence. Through hardships, labors and annoyances mankind has strived for generations in vain, to redeem themselves from their own judgment and their illusions of separation. This concludes in a judgment based on performance. Which is the opposite to an opinion of approval based on value. The word ^{4}**haptomai** means to fasten itself to, or to cling to something; from **hapto** to kindle a fire; to ignite.

If there is indeed nothing wrong with mankind's design or redemption, there can only be one problem, we are thinking wrong. See Isaiah 55:8,9; "Your thoughts are not my thoughts, therefore your ways are not my ways." Also Jeremiah 29:11 "For I know the thoughts that I think toward you, says the LORD, thoughts of peace and not of evil, to give you a future and a hope." Isaiah 55:9,10 Just like the rain and the snow bridges the distance between heaven and earth and cancels the drought, so shall my word be, it shall cancel distance and drought and saturate the earth (flesh); every nook and cranny of human life shall be filled in the Incarnation. The word *became flesh and indwells us. In the death and resurrection of Jesus Christ, God has brought final closure to the rule of the "I am not Tree-system." The idea of God's absence as well as every definition of distance and separation was canceled. Jesus is God's mind made up about you-manity. He is not more Immanuel to the Jew than what he is to the Gentile. See John 1:14 Suddenly the invisible eternal Word takes on visible form - the Incarnation on display in human life as in a mirror. In him, and now confirmed in us. The most accurate tangible display of God's eternal thought finds expression in human life. The Word became a human being; we are his address; he resides in us. He captivates our gaze. The glory we see there is not a religious replica; he is the authentic begotten Son. The glory [that we lost in Adam] returns in fullness. Only grace can communicate truth in such a complete context.)*

1 John 5:19 We know that we have our origin in God; yet the whole world [1]lies trapped in the blindfold-mode of a lost identity; intoxicated by the poneros system of a futile mentality of hardships labors and annoyances. *(The word **keimai** means to lie prostrate, outstretched; buried.)*

1 John 5:20 This is what has become distinctly clear to us: the [1]coming of the Son of God is God's mission accomplished. He is the incarnate Christ. The moment all of Scripture pointed to has arrived. The Son is [1]present. In him God has given us the greatest gift, [2]a mind whereby we may know him who is true; and in the same knowing, to find ourselves there in him who is true. Mankind is fully included and located in him, in his Son Jesus Christ; this means that whatever Jesus is as Son, we are. This is the true God; this is the life of the ages.

1 John 5:21 This defeats every image of our imagination that could possibly compete with the authentic likeness of our design. Darling children, distance yourselves from every substitute image, which is what idolatry is all about. *(The word [1]**eidolon**, often translated idol, refers to image or likeness. Isaiah 40:18-21 To whom then will you liken God, or what likeness compares with him? The idol? A workman casts it, and a goldsmith overlays it with gold, and casts for it silver chains. He who is impoverished chooses for an offering wood that will not rot; he seeks out a skilful craftsman to set up an image that will not move. Have you not known? Have you not heard? Has it not been told you **from the beginning**? Have you not understood from the foundations of the earth? Remember your beginning. You are God's idea - the Engineer of the Universe imagined you. Genesis 1:26; Colossians 1:15; Colossians 2:9,10.*

Acts 17:28-31 For 'In him we live and move and have our being'; as even some of your poets have said, 'For we are indeed his offspring.' Being then God's offspring, we ought not to think that the Deity is like gold, or silver, or stone, a representation by the art and imagination of human origin. The times of ignorance God overlooked, but now he compels all of mankind everywhere to awaken to their redeemed identity and innocence.

*The word [1]**eikon** means image or likeness - this is the theme of the Bible and redemption; the image and likeness of God revealed and redeemed in human form. Idolatry is a projection of an image of one's own making. Idolatry is the crux of religion - it is an expensive business since your idol is like a slot machine at the casino. It remains hungry and it is wired to bite and bankrupt you.)*

Romans 1:25 Truth suppressed *[Romans 1:18]* became twisted truth. Instead of embracing their Maker as their authentic identity, they preferred the deception of a distorted image of their own making, religiously giving it their affection and worship. The true God is the blessed God of the ages. Hey. He is not defined by our devotion or indifference. *(And all this because they traded the true God for a fake god, and worshiped the god they made instead of the God who made them. Message.)*

Romans 1:26 By being confused about their Maker they became confused about themselves.

In order to now manage the inevitable feelings of failure, guilt, inferiority, condemnation and judgment, the idea of a scapegoat emerged whereby slain animals are sacrificed to appease angry deities of their imagination. This "pay now and sin later" or "sin now and pay later"- idea became the illusion of religion. The sense of relief and self-justification presents a very lucrative and marketable commodity. These ritual sacrifices and the feasts that followed became extravagant indulgences of food, alcohol and licentiousness of every sort.

It is within the background of this pagan mindset that the typical scapegoat-language is adopted in both the Torah and the prophetic writings [including David's Psalm] whereby the promised Messiah is dynamically introduced as the Savior of mankind. Jesus did not come to "conveniently manage" our sins and sense of failure; he came to obliterate our sinfulness and sin-consciousness, bringing closure to a warped identity and mindset that we inherited from our fathers and in his resurrection he re-booted us and raised us into newness of life.

Hebrews 10:2 Had it been possible to present the perfect offering that had the power to successfully remove any trace of a sin-consciousness, then the sacrificial system would surely have ceased to be relevant.

Hebrews 10:3 But in the very repetition of these ritual sacrifices the awareness of guilt is reinforced rather than removed.

Hebrews 10:4 The conclusion is clear: animal sacrifices failed to remove anyone's sinfulness or their sin-consciousness.

Hebrews 10:5 So when Jesus, the Messiah, arrives as the fulfillment of all the types and shadows, he quotes Psalm 40:6-8, and says, "In sacrifices and offerings God takes no pleasure; but you have ordained my incarnation." *(Jesus Christ is revealed as both the Engineer and the Savior of the cosmos. The word, kosmos in the NT refers to the entire human family.)*

John 1:3 The Logos is the source; everything commences in him. He remains the exclusive Parent reference to their existence. There is nothing original, except the Word. The Logic of God defines the only possible place where mankind can trace their origin. *(All things were made by him; and without him was not any thing made that was made. KJV)*

Colossians 1:13 He rescued us from the [1]dominion of darkness *(the sense-ruled world, dominated by the law of performance)* **and relocated us into the**

kingdom where the love of his Son rules. *(Darkness is not a force, it is the absence of light. [See Ephesians 4:18] A darkened understanding veiled the truth of our redeemed design from us. 2 Corinthians 4:4. What "empowered" darkness was the lie that we believed about ourselves. The word, ¹**exousia**, sometimes translated authority, is from **ek**, origin or source, and **eimi**, I am. Thus, I was confused about who I am until the day that I heard and understood the grace of God in truth, as in a mirror. See 2 Corinthians 3:18, John 1:12,13.)*

Colossians 1:15 In him the image and likeness of God is made visible in human form in order that everyone may recognize their true origin in him. He is the firstborn of every creature. *(What darkness veiled from us he unveiled. In him we clearly see the mirror reflection of our original life. The son of his love gives accurate evidence of his image in human form. God can never again be invisible.)*

Colossians 1:16 Everything that is begins in him whether in the heavenly realm or upon the earth, visible or invisible. *(He gives detailed likeness and image to the invisible God, "If you have seen me, you have seen the Father. John 14:9.)*

Colossians 1:19 The full measure of everything God has in mind for mankind indwells him.

1 Peter 1:18 It is clear to see that you were ransomed from the futile, fallen mindset that you inherited from your fathers, not by the currency of your own labor, represented by the fluctuating values of gold and silver, and the economy of your religious efforts;

1 Peter 1:19 but you were redeemed with the priceless blood of Christ; he is the ultimate sacrifice; spotless and without blemish. He completes the prophetic picture. *(Also, please see my commentary on this verse.)*

1 John 3:8 Sin's source is a fallen mindset, from the beginning. For this purpose the Son of God was revealed. His mission was to undo the works of the Devil. *(**diabolos**, a fallen, distorted mindset.)*

1 John 3:9 To discover one's authentic sonship in God, is to discover true freedom from sin. We are born of him and his seed remains in us; this is the only possible reference to sober up the mind from the intoxicating influence of deception.

John 8:31 Jesus then said, "To take my word to its complete conclusion and then to abide in seamless union with its logic is to truly be my disciples.

John 8:32 In this abiding you will fully know the truth about who you are and this knowing will be your freedom.

John 8:33 They answered him, "We are the seed of Abraham; we have never been anybody's slaves. Why do you suggest that we are not free?"

John 8:34 Jesus answered and said, "I say unto you with absolute certainty that everyone engaging in the distorted mindset of sin is a slave to it."

John 8:36 With the freedom found in sonship there is no pretense.

John 8:37 I know you are the seed of Abraham, yet you are seeking opportunity to kill me because my word finds no resonance in you.

John 8:38 I observe my Father's voice with close attention; this inspires my every expression. You hear a different father's voice and behave accordingly.

John 8:39 They immediately responded with, "But Abraham is our father." To which Jesus replied, "If you were conceived by Abraham's faith, you would mirror his persuasion.

John 8:40 But here you are, desiring to destroy me because I declare to you the truth which I heard from a place of intimate acquaintance with God; this certainly does not reflect Abraham's faith.

John 8:41 Your actions clearly show who your father is." They said unto him, "We are not conceived in fornication, God is our only Father."

John 8:42 Jesus said, If you were convinced that God was your Father, you would love me. Look, here I am. I did not arrive here by my own doing; I proceeded from him who sent me.

John 8:43 You do not understand my language because you do not hear my logic.

John 8:44 You are the offspring of a perverse mindset and you prove its diabolical parenthood in your willingness to execute its cravings. The intention was to murder humanity's awareness of their god-identity from the beginning, since it is in violent opposition to the idea of the image and likeness of God in human form. It cannot abide the truth. Lying is the typical language of the distorted desire of the father of deception.

John 8:56 Your father Abraham rejoiced to see my day; he saw it and was glad."

John 8:57 The Jews then said to him, "You are not yet fifty years old, and have you seen Abraham?" John 8:58 Jesus said to them, "Truly, truly, I say to you, before Abraham was, I am."

Two chapters later Jesus addresses the same audience again: **John 10:30 I and the Father are one."**

John 10:31 The Jews took up stones again to stone him.

John 10:32 Jesus answered them, "I have shown you many good works from the Father; for which of these do you stone me?"

John 10:33 The Jews answered him, "It is not for a good work that we stone you but for blasphemy; because you, being a man, make yourself God."

John 10:34 Jesus said, "Is it not written in your law, 'I said you are gods?' *(Genesis 1:26; Psalm 82:6 All of you are like Elohim since you are all sons of the Most High. You are all equal image bearers of the same likeness.) John 10:35 He called them gods, when they encountered the word of God face to face. The prophetic dynamic of Scripture does not dissolve in time. John 10:36 How dare you say of him whom the Father has consecrated and commissioned into the world, "You blaspheme." because I said that I am the Son of God? [Sonship implies union with* *the Father. See Hebrews 1:1-3. Revelation 12:7.] Here Jesus quotes from Psalm 82:6 I say, "You are gods, sons of the Most High, all of you.)*

What does it mean to build your house upon the rock? "Son of man, I say you are Rock; you're a chip off the old block - the son of man is the son of God." Dig deep = Gaze deeply, intently into the mirror likeness of the face of your birth. Luke 6:48; James 1:18,23-25; Isaiah 51:1; Deuteronomy 32:18 Living your life from who you are in Christ [Grace] beats living your life from who you are in Adam [law of works] by far. Plus it is storm-proof.

1 John 3:10 There is a very visible and vast difference between living one's live from your God identity, or from a fallen mindset; the ¹diabolos-fruit has nothing in common with ²righteousness; neither does it know anything about brotherly love. *(The children of the Devil; here translated the ¹diabolos-fruit; the typical fruit that the fallen mindset bears. Righteousness, ²diakaiosune, from dike, two parties finding likeness in each other.)*

1 John 3:11 Our love for one another was the topic of conversation from the start. God had nothing less in mind than a loving family.

1 John 3:12 Cain's ¹killing of his brother Abel, is in such contrast to this. His motivation was clearly ²sourced in the ³poneros tree-system; his idea of Divine ⁴favor was to count on his own works as being superior to his brother's faith righteousness. *(Immediately after the fall, [Genesis 3:20] Adam named the woman Elohim gave him, Eve, [in Hebrew חוה **Chawah**, and in Greek, ζωη **Zoe**.] He thus co-echoes and reinforces the prophetic word that **Elohim** gave him: Life in the face of death. "The seed of the woman, shall crush the deceiver's head." The fallen mindset shall be destroyed. So here, in their two sons, we have the first generation of fallen mankind confronted with their personal pursuit of a lost identity and a lost sense of value and favor. Caleb's motivation was clearly sourced [²ek, out of, origin] in the **diabolos** [cast down], which is so typical of the ³**poneros** tree-system. The tree of the knowledge of good and evil [**ponerus**] represents mankind's lost sense of identity and righteousness, where the global pursuit of mankind would now be their constant effort to achieve righteousness by means of their own works. This inevitably leads to disappointment where shame replaces innocence, and union and fellowship are lost. The word evil, **poneros**, suggests to be full of hardships, labors and annoyances. Genesis 3:19 "In the sweat of your face shall you eat your bread." The sacrifice of Cain is exactly that. It represents his trust in the fruit of his own toil to gain him a ⁴favorable [**charin**] standing with God.*

We have the prophetic picture of a scapegoat repeated here in Genesis 4. Not only in the sacrifice that Abel brought; but also in him being murdered by his brother. Just like we would one day murder our brother Jesus. In Genesis 3, Elohim did not clothe Adam with the skin of an animal because of a divine need to be appeased, but because of their unconditional love for Adam; they spoke the language of Adam's own judgment: Adam, not Elohim, was embarrassed about his nakedness. The clothing was not to make Elohim look at Adam differently, but to make Adam feel better about himself. And ultimately it was to prepare Adam for the unveiling of the mystery of mankind's redemption in the incarnation. Here Deity would clothe themselves in human skin in a Son, and the Lion of Judah, would become the Lamb of God, in order to free our minds to re-discover his image and likeness in our skin. Revelation 5:5,6.)

Romans 1:18 God's ¹passionate persuasion is uncovered from heavens perspective in sharp ²contrast to the foolishness of ³people who ⁴suppress and conceal the truth about their redeemed innocence while they continue to embrace an ⁵inferior reference of themselves. *(The righteousness of God that is endorsed in the heavens is so different to the counterfeit, earthly reference that blindfolds people in their own unrighteousness. The word often translated wrath, ¹orge, means desire - as a reaching forth or excitement of the mind, passion. The Preposition ²epi means over, above, across, against, continuous influence upon; I translated it here as contrast. The word for the ³human species, male or female is* **anthropos**, *from* **ana**, *upward, and* **tropos**, *manner of life; character; in like manner. The word* ⁴**katecho**, *to echo downwards is the opposite of* **anoche**, *to echo upward; see Romans 2:4 and Romans 3:26. In Colossians 3:2 Paul encourages us to engage our thoughts with things above [God's belief], and not below [law of works]. The word* ⁵**adikia**, *unrighteousness, is the opposite of* **dikay**, *two parties finding likeness in each other; thus, without harmony. The law reveals how guilty and sinful mankind is, while the gospel reveals how forgiven and restored to their original blueprint we are. See 2 Corinthians 4:4)*

Romans 1:19 For this reason God is not a stranger to anyone; whatever can be known of God is ¹apparent in human form. God has revealed it in the very core of their design which bears witness within their own conscience.

People are not born Christians, yet every person ever born comes from God. God says in Jeremiah 1:5 "I knew you before I formed you in your mother's womb." We are God's idea: we began in God. We are born into a world where we are bombarded with many diverse cultural and traditional mindsets, most of which directly stems from the Tree of the knowledge of good and evil system, which is the fallen mindset system which says you are not...you have to strive to become. People who do gross things do it from believing a lie about themselves and not knowing the truth of their incredible design as image bearers of God. James says in James 3:9, We can say beautiful things about God the Father but with the same mouth curse a man made in his mirror likeness. The point is not what the man did to deserve the curse. A doctor doesn't slap his patient and command him to stop coughing. You may have the flu but you never become the flu. True worship is to touch someone's life with the same devotion and care you would touch Jesus himself; even if the other person seems a most unlikely candidate. Multitudes of people are living in the darkness of ignorance, not knowing the truth of the integrity of their design and their redeemed value and innocence. The adventure of the Christian life is to declare what we have discovered to be true about every single person. Jesus says that when we discover that the son of man is indeed the son of God then the gates of Hades *(from ha + eido, not to see)* will crumble and the prisoners of darkness will be free to discover themselves in him.

End Times

The Day Of The Lord - The Fullness of Time - The Hour Has Come.

Revelation 1:10 I was in a spiritual trance where I witnessed the ¹Day of the Lord - I heard a loud voice ²behind me, clear and distinct, like the sound of a trumpet. *(The ¹Day of the Lord is the very day to which the prophetic voice of the Spirit of Christ pointed - Jesus the Messiah, is the fulfillment of this Day.*

The word ²opiso points to that which is behind in place and time. The fact that John hears a word behind him is so significant. It means that what he hears already happened within its prophetic context. This reminds of the incident recorded in Genesis 22:7 & 8 where Abraham was asked by Isaac, "We have the fire and the wood; but where is the lamb for a burnt offering?" Abraham answered, "God will provide a lamb for the burnt offering, Son." Then, in Genesis 22:13, we read that Abraham lifted up his eyes and looked, and behold, behind him was a ram, caught in a thicket by its horns. Jesus refers to this in John 8:56-58 when he says, "Abraham saw my day." And, "Before Abraham was, I am.")

Revelation 22:13 I am the Alpha and the Omega - the initiator and the conclusion; the genesis and completeness. *(The union of Alpha and Omega, in Greek, makes the verb αω, I breathe. And in Hebrew the union of the first and last letter in their alphabet, Aleph and Tav makes את et, which the Rabbis interpret of the first matter out of which all things were formed, [see Genesis 1:1] This is untranslatable in English but, says Rabbi Aben Ezra, "it signifies the substance of the thing." In the Ancient Hebrew Alphabet the bull's head is Aleph and the cross is the Tav. †⌒ The revelation of Jesus as the Alpha and Omega is the one in whom we live, and move, and have our being. He is indeed closer to us than the air we breathe. Don't waste a day waiting for another day. I am the initiator and the eschatos. Eschatology is defined in my I-am-ness.)*

The most profound future information pales in significance in the light of what has already happened to mankind in Christ. Religion thrives on two lies, distance and delay; Jesus canceled both. Every possible definition of distance was canceled on the cross. "Every valley shall be lifted up, and every mountain and hill be made low; every crooked place shall be made straight and every rough place smooth. And the glory of the Lord shall be revealed, and all flesh shall see it together." [Isaiah 40:4,5] Every excuse that anyone could have to feel separated from God was deleted in Christ.

A delegation of Greeks arrive in Jerusalem to "see" Jesus:

John 12:23 Jesus, immediately understanding the prophetic significance of the moment, knew that he, the Messiah, was who all the nations were longing for and answered, "The hour is here, for the Son of man to be glorified. *(Jesus studied Scripture as in a mirror - he knew that "in the book, it is written about me." Haggai 2:7 and the desire of the nations shall come...See Colossians 1:27.)*

John 12:24 Most certainly shall the single grain of wheat fall into the earth and die - if it doesn't die it remains alone - but in its death it produces much fruit. *(The hour that has come represents the culmination of all that was prophetically pointed to as recorded in Scripture.)*

John 12:27 My soul is exceedingly perplexed right now. What shall I say, "Father. Rescue me ¹out of the clutches of this hour." No. This hour is the very culmination of my destiny. *(Greek Preposition, ¹ek, out of; source; origin.)*

John 17:1 Having said these things Jesus lifted up his eyes into the ¹heavenly sphere and spoke, "Father, the hour has come; this is the culmination of time. Glorify your Son; endorse your opinion of your Son so that the Son may mirror his opinion of you and cause your dignity and worth to be made renowned and rendered illustrious in order to become manifest and acknowledged throughout. *(The word ¹ouranos, heavenly sphere; from **oros**, mountain, from **airō**, to raise, elevate, to lift up. Here there exists no conflict of interest - only glory repeated in the other. And the glory of the Lord shall be revealed, and all flesh shall see it together. Isaiah 40:5.)*

1 Peter 1:10 This salvation which you now know as your own, is the theme of the prophetic thought; this is what intrigued the Prophets' minds for generations and became the object of their most diligent inquiry and scrutiny. They knew all along that mankind's salvation was a grace revelation, sustained in their prophetic utterance. *(Salvation would never be by personal achievement or a reward to willpower-driven initiative. The law of works would never replace grace.)*

1 Peter 1:11 In all of their conversation there was a ¹constant quest to determine who the Messiah would be, and exactly when this would happen. They knew with certainty that it was the spirit of Christ within them, pointing prophetically and giving testimony to the sufferings of the Christ and the subsequent glory. *(The ¹big question was, Who and When? In Acts 17:31 Paul addresses the Greek Philosophers and reminds them of their own ancient writings and he quotes two of their well-known philosophers: in 600BC Epimenedes wrote a song saying, "We live and move and have our being in God"; and Aratus wrote in 300BC that we are indeed God's offspring. Paul then announces to them that the God whom they worship in ignorance is not far from each one of us. He is not more Immanuel to the Jew than what he is to the Gentile. Now follows the punch line of the gospel: in the context of his Jewish background and personal encounter with Jesus Christ, Paul declares to them the Good News of mankind's redeemed innocence. "God has overlooked the times of ignorance, and is now urging all of mankind, whoever and wherever they are, to a radical mind-shift, since he has prophetically **fixed a day** on which he would judge the world in righteousness **by a man whom he has appointed**, and of this [righteous judgment] he has given proof to all by raising him from the dead." Acts 17:30,31. See also Romans 4:25 where, in Paul's understanding, the resurrection of Jesus from the dead includes mankind's co-resurrection and seals their acquittal and redeemed innocence. This is the predicted subsequent glory that was to follow the cross. Hosea 6:2, After two days he will revive us; on the third day, he will raise us up. Whatever glory was lost in Adam, would be redeemed again in Jesus Christ.)*

1 Peter 1:12 It was revealed to them that this glorious grace message that they were communicating pointed to a specific day and person beyond their own horizon and generation; they saw you in their prophetic view. This ¹heavenly announcement had you in mind all along. They proclaimed glad tidings to you in advance, in the Holy Spirit, commissioned from

END TIMES - REV 17

heaven; the celestial messengers themselves longed to gaze deeply into its complete fulfillment. *(Peter uses the word, [1]anaggello, where the Preposition, ana, points upward to the source of the announcement.)*

1 Peter 1:13 How amazing is that. Jesus is what the Scriptures are all about; and you are what Jesus is all about. Now wrap your minds around that. This unveiling is [1]what tied up all the loose ends that would trip you and frustrate your seamless transition from the old to the new. The revelation of Jesus is no longer a future expectation. Do not allow the old mindset of a future tense glory to intoxicate you and distract you from the relevance of this moment. Stop pointing to a future Messiah. Jesus is who the Prophets pointed to. You are the fruit of his sufferings; you are the glorious resurrection generation. Fully engage your [2]minds with the consequence of this grace in the revelation of Jesus Christ. He [3]completes your every [4]expectation. *(The word [1]anazosamenoi, to gird up, is an Aorist Participle, which translates, "having girded up the loins of your mind, be sober." The word [2]dianoia, suggests deep contemplation, thinking something thoroughly through in order to reach a sober conclusion. Then Peter writes, [3]teleios [4]elpisate, this is the completeness of every expectation. See Colossians 1:27.*

In one act of righteousness, God removed every possible definition of distance and delay. Every excuse that we could have to feel separated from God was canceled. This is what the Prophets saw: "Every valley shall be lifted up, and every mountain and hill be made low; the crooked places shall be made straight, even the rough places shall be made smooth. And the glory of the LORD shall be revealed, and all flesh shall see it together, for the mouth of the LORD has spoken." Isaiah 40:4,5)

1 Peter 1:14 Your [1]accurate hearing is what distinguishes you as the resurrection generation; the days of being driven by every [2]desperate, distorted passion of your former ignorance are over. The [3]fashions and patterns of a redundant system are no longer relevant. *(The word, [1]upoakoo is often translated, obedience, from upo, meaning under, as in under the influence of, and akoo, to hear. In the context of this chapter, Peter urges us to hear accurately what was communicated in the prophetic word concerning the life of our design, now rebooted into newness by our joint resurrection with Jesus Christ. The word, [2]epithumia, translates, desire, craving, longing, desire for what is forbidden, lust. The word, [3]suschēmatizō, from sun, union, and schema, pattern; a typical template.)*

1 Peter 1:15 The one whose [1]idea you are to begin with, designed you to radiate his image and likeness; he is the true pattern of your beingness. So, [2]be who you are in realizing the exact detail of your genesis. You are [3]whole and in perfect harmony; seamlessly one with him. *(The word [1]kaleo, to define by name; to surname. The word [2]genethete, referring to genesis, or birth, is in the Aorist, Passive, imperative case; the distinction between the Aorist Imperative and the Present Imperative is one of aspect, not tense. Thus, to get something over and done with. The word, [3]hagios, holy, separate from common condition and use. See Hebrews 10:14-16)*

1 Peter 1:16 On the very account that what is written in prophetic Scripture, *(and echoed in your innermost being)*, already mirrors the life

of your design, you are free to be who you are. As it is written, "I am, therefore you are. I am wholly separated unto you, and invite you to explore the same completeness of your being in me." *(The word, grapho, to engrave, often refers to the prophetic writings, Old Testament Scripture. The appeal of truth is confirmed in the resonance within us due to the echo of that which is already written in our innermost being by design. "Did not our hearts ignite within us while he opened to us the Scriptures. Luke 24:27,32,44,45. The Textus Receptus uses the word **genesthe**, instead of **esesthe**, from **eimi**, as in the Westtcott & Hort text. This makes a massive difference. So, instead of **ginomai**, to become, the older more authentic manuscripts has the word, **esesthe**, I am. See note in John 1:1 Three times in this sentence John uses the Active Indicative Imperfect form of the verb **eimi**, namely **aen [ἦv]** to continue to be, [in the beginning 'was' the Word etc...] which conveys no idea of origin for God or for the Logos, but simply continuous existence, "I am." Quite a different verb **egeneto**, "became," appears in John 1:14 for the beginning of the Incarnation of the Logos. The Word 'became' flesh. The incarnation is not the origin of Jesus. See the distinction sharply drawn in John 8:58, "before Abraham was [born, **genesthai** from **ginomai**] I am." The word **eimi**, I am; the essence of being, suggesting timeless existence. You did not begin in your mother's womb. You began in God's I-am-ness. You are the most magnificent idea that the Engineer of the Universe has ever had. "I knew you before I formed you in your mother's womb." Jeremiah 1:5. In him we live and move and have our being. Acts 17:28.)*

1 Peter 1:17 Now since you are defined in your Father, who does not judge anyone on face value, but always only according his work; *(his finished work in Christ)* **wherever you find yourself located geographically or emotionally, return to your 'at home-ness' in him; you are not defined by your circumstances.** *(The word **anastrepho**, suggests a radical returning; literally a turning upside down. Actually **ana**, means upward- so, it's actually a turning downside up.)*

1 Peter 1:18 It is clear to see that you were ransomed from the futile, fallen mindset that you inherited from your fathers, not by the currency of your own labor, represented by the fluctuating values of gold and silver, and the economy of your religious efforts;

1 Peter 1:19 but you were redeemed with the priceless blood of Christ; he is the ultimate sacrifice; spotless and without blemish. He completes the prophetic picture. *(In him God speaks the most radical scapegoat language of the law of judgment, and brings final closure to a dead and redundant system. In Psalm 40:6,7, it is clearly stated that God does not require sacrifices or offerings. Jesus is the Lamb of God. He collides victoriously with the futile sacrificial system whereby offerings are constantly made to the pseudo, moody, monster gods of our imagination. This is the scandal of the cross. God does not demand a sacrifice that would change the way he thinks about mankind; he provides the sacrifice of himself in Christ in order to forever eradicate sin-consciousness from our minds and radically change the way we think about our Maker, one another and ourselves. [Sin-consciousness is in essence a works-based consciousness.] God did not clothe Adam with the skin of an* *animal because of a divine need to be appeased, but because of their unconditional love for Adam; they spoke the language of Adam's own judgment: Adam, not God, was embarrassed about his nakedness. The clothing was not to make God look at Adam differently, but to make Adam feel better about himself. And ultimately it was to prophetically prepare Adam for the unveiling of the mystery of mankind's redemption in the incarnation. Here Deity would clothe themselves in human skin, in a son; and the Lion of Judah would become the Lamb of God in order to free our minds to re-discover his image and likeness in our skin. See 1 Peter 1:2.)*

1 Peter 1:20 He was always destined in God's prophetic thought; God knew even before the fall of the world order that his Son would be the Lamb, to be made manifest in these last days, because of you. *(You are the reason Jesus died and was raised. The word, kataballo, meaning "to fall away, to put in a lower place," instead of themelios, meaning "foundation" [see Ephesians 2:20]; thus, translated "the fall of the world," instead of "the foundation of the world." The entire "Fall" was a falling away in our minds from our true identity as image and likeness bearers of Elohim. Just like Eve, were we all deceived to believe a lie about ourselves, which is the fruit of the "I-am-not-tree". We all, like sheep, have gone astray. [Isaiah 53:6] The word **eschatos** means extreme; last in time or in space; the uttermost part, the final conclusion.* **What God said about 'you-manity' in Jesus defines eschatology.**)

1 Peter 1:21 He is the conclusive cause of your belief in God. Seeing then how perfectly you fit into the scheme of things, it is no wonder that your faith in God's act of raising Jesus from the dead becomes the glorious reference to your own new birth. The glory that God gave Jesus by raising him from the dead, is the conclusion of everything that your faith longed for. *(This is the redeemed glory that the Prophets pointed to. Hosea 6:2 "After two days he will revive us; on the third day he will raise us up." Isaiah 40:5 "And the glory of the Lord shall be revealed, and all flesh shall see it together.")*

1 Peter 1:22 As a result of your accurate hearing of the unveiled truth, and through the agency of the Spirit, you have engaged your souls fully with the purifying effect of your inclusion in his glorious work of redemption. *(See commentary note in 1 Peter 1:14. The same Spirit of Christ who spoke from within the Prophets of old, now endorses truth within your spirit.)*

1 Peter 1:23 This co-resurrection-new-birth does not compare to the fading qualities of that which is produced by the perishable seed of the carnal works- and performance-based mindsets. The indestructible living seed of the word of God conceives resurrection life within you; this life is equal to its source. *(The word, meno means, abiding in seamless union, or, to remain the same. You are giving stature to the rise of a new person; a new resurrection generation of a people who are coming out of obscurity into his marvelous light.)*

1 Peter 1:24 "All flesh is grass, and all its glory is like the flower of the field. The grass withers, the flower fades,

1 Peter 1:25 but the word of our God is [1]risen forever. This word is the [2]exact same message of the glad tidings announced by the Prophets and now proclaimed unto you. *(Peter again quotes from Isaiah 40, this time verse 6*

and 8. The Hebrew word, קוּם *Qum, means to ¹rise up; like in Hosea 6:2, "After two days he will revive us, on the third day, he will raise us up." Isaiah 40:6,8; also see note on 1 Peter 1:13. The word ²meno is used in the Septuagint and also here in the Greek text, Peter uses the word, **meno**, to remain the same; to continue to be present.)*

See also **Galatians 4:1 Infant heirs have no more say than a slave, even though they own everything.** *(The best deal the law could possibly broker confirmed mankind's slavery to sin.)*

Galatians 4:2 He would remain under domestic supervision and house rules until the date fixed by his father for his official graduation to the status of sonship.

Galatians 4:3 This is exactly how it was with us; we were kidnapped as it were into infancy and confined to that state through the law. *(An inferior mindset as a result of Adam's fall.)*

Galatians 4:4 But then the day dawned; the most complete culmination of time. *[Everything predicted was concluded in Christ.]* **The son arrived, commissioned by the Father; his legal passport to the planet was his mother's womb. In a human body exactly like ours he lived his life subject to the same scrutiny of the law.**

2 Corinthians 1:14 To some extent you have already understood that our joy is mirrored in one another. The day of the Lord Jesus Christ is no longer a distant promise but a fulfilled reality. *(The word, **kathaper**, often translated, exactly as, comes from **kata**, meaning according to and **per**, which is an enclitic particle significant of abundance and thoroughness which comes from the word, **peiro**, meaning to pierce. The use of the Latin enclitic relates to a word that throws an accent back onto the preceding word, which is here translated as mirrored. The "day of the Lord Jesus Christ," is **hemera**, which is a specific and measured period. Eastern usage of this term differs from our western usage. Any part of a day is counted as a whole day, hence the expression, "three days and three nights," does not mean literally three whole days, but at least one whole day plus part of two other days.*

The day of the Lord Jesus is the theme of Scripture as in 1 Peter 1:10; this was what the Prophets were studying and desiring to know. The content of their message always pointed to the day and the person where the promise of redemption would be realized. The sufferings of the Messiah would redeem and release the glory of God's image and likeness in human life; the glory that Adam lost on behalf of the human race, returns. In Acts 17:31, "In the resurrection, God gave proof to the redeemed innocence of mankind; the "day and the person" prophesied was fulfilled in Jesus." Jesus gives context to this day in John 14:20, ""In that day you will know that we are in seamless union with one another. I am in my Father, you are in me and I am in you.")

Hebrews 11:1 Persuasion confirms confident expectation and proves the unseen world to be more real than the seen. Faith celebrates as certain what hope visualizes as future. *(The shadow no longer substitutes the substance. Jesus is the substance of things hoped for the evidence of everything the prophets foretold. The unveiling of Christ in human life completes mankind's every expectation. Colossians 1:27.)*

Romans 4:17 When God changed Abram's name to Abraham, he made a public statement that he would be the father of all nations. *(Genesis 17:5) Here we see Abraham faced with God's faith; the kind of faith that resurrects the dead and calls things which are not [visible yet] as though they were.)*

Romans 4:18 Faith gave substance to hope when everything seemed hopeless; the words, "so shall your seed be" conceived in him the faith of fatherhood. *(Abraham's case here pictures the hopelessness of fallen mankind, having lost their identity, and faced with the impossibility to redeem themselves.)*

Revelation 14:15 Another celestial messenger appeared out of the most holy place of the temple and with a loud voice addressed the one seated upon the cloud, saying, "Thrust forth your pruning hook, your hour has come - this is your moment to reap for the earth's harvest is ready." *(See John 4:31 In the mean while his disciples were urging him to take some food. John 4:32 But he said, "I am feasting on food you cannot see." John 4:33 His disciples were baffled, "Who brought him anything to eat?" John 4:34 Jesus told them, "My food is to fulfil the desire of him who commissioned me and to leave no detail undone." John 4:35 Would you say that it will take another four months for the seed to ripen in the ear? This is not the food that I am talking about. The fruit of your own toil will never satisfy permanently. I want to show you the real harvest. From now on, look at people differently; see them through your Father's eyes, and you will know that they are ripe and ready to discover how perfectly mirrored they are in me. (Jesus canceled every definition of delay. We've been waiting for the wrong harvest for centuries - the one we've labored for all our lives. A harvest is ripe when the seed in the ear matches the seed that was sown.) John 4:36 This harvest reveals how both he who sows and he who reaps participate in the same joy of the life of the ages.)*

Revelation 14:6 And I saw another celestial messenger soaring in mid heaven - this messenger was the carrier of the grandest news of the ages. His mission was to announce these glad tidings of everlasting proportion to every single nation, tribe, language and people grouping on the earth.

Revelation 14:7 In a great voice he declared, "Be awestruck with the amazingness of God. Give him glory. The hour of his judgment has come. He is the Maker of the heavenly realm, the earth, the sea and the fountains of the waters." *(This announcement echoes in Jesus' declaration in John 12:31 Now is the judgment of this world; this is the moment where the authority of the world-system is cast out. [The serpent's head is about to be crushed. Genesis 3:15; Colossians 2:14,15; Luke 10:18, I saw satan fall like lightning.]*

John 12:32 When I am lifted up from the earth, I will draw all of mankind and every definition of judgment unto me. (He would be lifted up on a cross, descend into the depths of our hell, then, according to the prophetic word in Hosea 6:2, after two days, the entire human race he represents, will be co-quickened and on the third day, be co-raised, out of the lowest parts of the earth and elevated to the highest heavens. Ephesians 4:8,9; see also Ephesians 2:5,6 and Colossians 3:1-3. 'All' includes all of mankind and every definition of judgment. The subject of the sentence, as from the previous verse, is the judgment of the world - thus the primary thought here is that in his death, Jesus would draw all judgment upon himself. John 3:14; John 8:28; Acts 2:33. 1 John 3:5 We have witnessed with our own eyes how, in the unveiling of the *prophetic word, when he was lifted up upon the cross as the Lamb of God, he lifted up our sin and broke its dominion and rule over us. John 1:29 "Behold, the Lamb of God, who takes away [airo] the sin of the world. The word **airo** means to lift up."]*

John 12:33 This he said to point to the way in which he would die. [See John 19:15 - "Lift him up. Lift him up. Crucify him."])

Revelation 14:8 And a second celestial messenger followed with more good news. Babylon the great city has crashed. She who sold herself as a prostitute to all the nations and intoxicated them with the wine of her passion will never fly again. *(The language is an echo of Isaiah 21:9, Jeremiah 51:7 and Jeremiah 51:8. Babylon was used for Rome in late Jewish writings; see also 1 Peter 5:13.*

In the imagery that follows, John sees how the effect of the triune religious counterfeit of the Dragon, the Beast and the fake slain and risen lamb disguised as the great prostitute of Babylon is thoroughly stripped of their influence and dominion and brought to nought.)

Revelation 14:9 Then a third celestial messenger followed and announced with a loud voice that whoever worships the counterfeit lamb and its image and receives its character in their thoughts and deeds,

Revelation 14:10 will drink the wine of God's passion, undiluted with water but intensified with spices in his cup - they shall be tested as one tests gold or silver with a ¹touchstone; with fire and brimstone in the immediate presence of the Lamb and of ²those who have discovered their wholeness mirrored in him - the dross of their deception will be exposed and cleansed. *(Note the words, **tou kekerasmenou akratou** - this is a powerful oxymoron, "the mixed unmixed." See Psalm 75:8 For in the hand of the LORD there is a cup, with foaming wine, well mixed; and he will pour a draught from it, and all the wicked of the earth shall drain it down to the dregs.*

*The word ¹**basanizō** means to test [metls] by the touchstone, which is a black siliceous stone used to test the purity of gold or silver by the color of the streak produced on it by rubbing it with either metal - a piece of fine-grained dark schist or jasper formerly used for testing alloys of gold by observing the color of the mark which they made on it - thus, a standard or criterion by which something is judged or recognized. The blood of Jesus is the currency. 1 Peter 1:18,19.*

*The fiery brimstone - **theion** - is divine incense, because burning brimstone was regarded as having power to purify, and to ward off disease - the ¹cup he drank on the cross is the touchstone. "What shall I say? Father, remove this cup from me? NO. For this hour I have come." The word, ²**hagios**, saints, refers to wholeness and harmony of spirit, soul and body - see 1 Corinthians 1:30 and Romans 1:7.)*

John 5:27 The Father has also given the son of man authentic ¹authority to execute judgment on mankind's behalf. *(The word ¹**exousia**, often translated as authority has two components, **ek**, out of, source and **eimi**, I am.)*

John 5:28 Do not be alarmed by this, but the hour is coming when those in the graves will hear his voice. *(No-one who ever lived will escape the extent of his righteous judgment. Those who have forgotten who they are will hear his* *incarnate voice. The word for grave, mnēmeion, memory, suggests a remembrance - to bring something from memory into the here and now! Like David prophecies in Psalm 22 when he sees the cross-crisis [**krisis** - judgment, means the 'decisive moment' or, turning point.] a thousand years before it happens. His conclusion in verse 27 sums up the triumph of God's resolve. "All the ends of the earth shall remember and turn to the LORD; and all the families of the nations shall worship before him." See 1 Corinthians 15:21,22 The same mankind who died in a man was raised again in a man. In Adam all died; in Christ all are made alive.)*

John 5:29 And they will come forth out of their graves - for those who have engaged themselves with that which is beneficial, it will be a resurrection to life - and for those who have done that which is worthless, it will be a resurrection unto judgment. *(In the context of John chapter 6:28 and 29 the work that is required is not a duty to be performed but a gift to be embraced - If our own good behavior could earn us salvation then there would be no point in Jesus dying our death. - This would be in conflict with the essence and crux of the gospel. It reminds of 2 Corinthians 5:10 "For we must all appear before the judgment seat of Christ, so that each one may receive good or evil, according to what he has done in the body." Now read this verse in the Mirror - 2 Corinthians 5:10 For we have all been thoroughly scrutinized in the judgment of Jesus. We are taken care of and restored to the life of our design, regardless of what happened to us in our individual lives, whatever amazing or meaningless things we encountered in the body. (See 5:14,16. We are mirrored in his life; his life reflects ours, not as an example for us but of us. See 2 Corinthians 3:18. The word,* **phaneroo***, means to render apparent, to openly declare, to manifest. Paul uses the Aorist Passive Infinitive tense* **phanerothenai***, not referring to a future event. The Aorist Infinitive presents the action expressed by the verb as a completed unit with a beginning and end. The word,* **bematos***, comes from* **bayma***, means footprint, also referring to a raised place mounted by steps, or a tribunal, the official seat of a judge The word,* **komitzo***, comes from* **kolumbos***, meaning to tend, to take care of, to provide for, to carry off from harm. Paul's reference was not about how much abuse and affliction he suffered, nor was it the many good times he remembered that defined him; "I am what I am by the grace of God." If we are still to be judged for good or bad deeds that we performed in the body, then the judgment that Jesus faced on mankind's behalf was irrelevant. Galatians 2:21 I do not set aside the grace of God, for if righteousness could be gained through the law, Christ died for nothing. NIV)*

John 6:39 My Sender's desire is for me to rescue every single individual - ¹this is his gift to me - that I will lose ²no detail of mankind's original identity mirrored in me. My rescuing mission will conclude in their joint-resurrection. This is the ³completeness of time. *(This is his gift to me, ¹ho dedoke moi. The phrase, ²hina pan apoleso Exodus auto, meaning, that I should lose nothing out of it. In the eschatology/conclusion/fullness of time - ³te eschate hemera - This phrase occurs only in John - See John 6:39, 6:40, 6:44, 6:54. Also John 4:23 The end of an era has arrived - the future is here. Whatever prophetic values were expressed in external devotional forms and rituals are now eclipsed in true spirit worship from within - face to face with the Father - acknowledging our genesis in him - this is his delight. The Father's desire is the worshipper more than the worship.)*

Ephesians 1:10 In the ¹economy of the fullness of time, everything culminates in Christ. All that is in heaven and all that is on earth is reconciled in him. Jesus is the ²consummation of the ages.

Hebrews 10:37 Time becomes insignificant once the promise is realized. Remember how the promise of his imminent appearance was recorded in Scripture. *(The arrival of Jesus is the fulfillment of the promise and the realizing of righteousness by faith, as Habakkuk prophesied. [Habakkuk 2:2-4.] He is the fullness of time. [Galatians 4:4])*

1 Thessalonians 2:19 We expect nothing less in the context of the gospel than you enjoying a face to face encounter in the ¹immediate presence of our Lord Jesus Christ. This is our delight and wreath of honor. *(The word ¹parousia speaks of the immediate presence of the Lord. From para, a Preposition indicating close proximity, intimate connection; and eimi, I am. There is not even a hint of judgment or punishment in this word. While there are great and accurate definitions in Strongs, please do not believe everything you read there. "G3952 parousia from the Present Participle of G3918 [pareimi]; a being near, that is, advent; often, return; specifically of Christ to punish Jerusalem, or finally the wicked.".? [This is blatant nonsense.] The Greek word parousia, occurs 24 times in the NT, and 22 times it wrongly implies a 2nd coming or coming judgment. Only twice it is translated as presence. 2 Corinthians 10:10, Philippians 2:12. Of all the English translations that I have checked, only the Young's Literal has it correct. What a shame that this word has been so dramatically twisted over the years.)*

*Jurgen Moltmann writes, The **eschaton** is not the temporal end of our historical days. Eschatology is the presence of eternity in every moment of this present history. Anyone who hears the thunderous word of the eternal God in the moment loses interest in the future.*

See *Notes on The Day Of The Lord* in the introduction to Revelation.

Also *Extended Commentary Notes* at the end of the book - **Thoughts on Judgment and Resurrection.**

The Triumph of the Lamb

Revelation 17:13 These rulers were in full agreement to hand over their authority to the Beast. *(At the trial and crucifixion of Jesus, former enemies became allies as the banded together against the Lamb see Luke 23:12 That day Herod and Pilate became friends - before this they had been enemies. Psalm 83:5 With one mind they plot together; they form an alliance against you.)*

Revelation 17:14 These join forces in that hour to wage war against the Lamb but the Lamb defeats them since he is the Lord of lords and the King of kings. And sharing with him in his victory are his kindred, the ones who recognizes their origin in this conversation, they too are now of the same persuasion. *(The Lamb led them into freedom from their lost identity, and their doubts. See Hebrews 1:1 Throughout ancient times God spoke in many fragments and glimpses of prophetic thought to our fathers. Now, this entire conversation has finally dawned in sonship. Suddenly what seemed to be an ancient language falls fresh and new like the dew on the tender grass. He is the sum total of every utterance of God. He is whom the Prophets pointed to and we are his immediate audience. [The word **eschatos** means extreme; last in time or in space; the uttermost part, the final conclusion. What God said about 'you-manity' in Jesus defines eschatology.] Hebrews 1:2 In sonship, God declares the Incarnate Word to be the heir of all things. He is, after all, the author of the ages. We have our beginning and our being in him. [Sonship endorses heirship. See Hebrews 6:16-18.] Hebrews 1:3, Jesus is the crescendo of God's conversation; he gives context and content to the authentic thought. Everything that God had in mind for mankind is voiced in him. Jesus is God's language. He is the radiant and flawless expression of the person and intent of God. He mirrors God's character and exhibits his every attribute in human form. He is the voice of God announcing our redeemed innocence. This voice is the dynamic that sustains the entire cosmos. He is the force of the universe upholding everything that exists as the executive authority of God, enthroned in the boundless measure of his majesty. ["Having accomplished purification of sins, he sat down ..." His throne is proof of mankind's redeemed innocence.])*

Revelation 12:7 Mikael and his celestial messengers led the war in the heavenly realm against the Dragon and his cohorts. *(The Hebrew name* מיכאל *Mikael means, "Who is like God?" The context of the onslaught against the human race has always been their identity-crisis as image and likeness bearers of God. The fruit of the "I-am-not tree system." See John 10:30-36)*

Revelation 1:5 and from Jesus Christ the faithful witness, the first-born of the dead, and the Prince of the kings on earth. To him who loves us and has freed us from our sins by his blood.

Revelation 11:15 When the seventh celestial messenger sounded his trumpet, there was a massive crescendo of voices in the heavenly realm, saying, "The kingdom of the cosmos has become the kingdom of our Lord and of his Christ, and he will reign as king for all the ages of the ages." *(Remember Revelation 10:7 In the days when the sounding of the seventh messenger's trumpet commences, the mystery of God will be fully realized in exact accordance to the Good News he announced to his servants the Prophets -* **euengelisen** *- having announced good news - Aorist tense of* εὐαγγελίζω *with* **eu**, *well done;*

*and **aggelos,** announcement - Good News. The word, **kosmos** in the NT refers to the entire human family and their social structures.)*

Already in chapter 7 we see the eventual outcome of what is portrayed here in Revelation 11:

Revelation 7:9 At this moment I saw a massive throng of people, impossible to count, standing tall and innocent everyone of them dressed in white with palm branches in their hands; they had escaped everything that could possibly define them as a non-Jewish Gentile world. In fact, every sphere of society was there - including the entire spectrum of people-groupings; tribal identities with their unique language-specific dialect preferences; they were all present there facing the throne and the Lamb as the people of the planet. *(Amazing how, in the previous verses the tribes of Israel are associated with a very specific "number" when it comes to the prophetic detail of the entire Jewish nation as a prophetic voice of God's intention in Abraham to release the blessing of the single SEED of God's faith and bless all the nations of the earth. Count the stars, count the sand... The Preposition **ek**, points to source or origin; mankind was delivered out of their national, geographical and historical identities. The palm branches and the white robes are signs of the celebration of victory and joy. The word **stolay**, is the white outer garment worn by kings, priests, and persons of rank.*

I looked again. I saw a huge crowd, too huge to count. Everyone was there—all nations and tribes, all races and languages. And they were standing, dressed in white robes and waving palm branches, standing before the throne and the Lamb. The Msg.)

Revelation 7:10 Then I heard the masses shouting as if with one thundering voice saying, "Our salvation is secure in our God who is seated upon the throne and endorsed in the Lamb's doing."

Colossians 2:14 His body nailed to the cross hung there as the [3]document of mankind's guilt; in dying our death he [1]cancelled the detailed [2]handwritten [3]record which testified against us. Every [1]stain on our conscience, reminding of the sense of failure and guilt, was thus fully blotted out. *(The word, [1]exaleipho, comes from **ek**, out of, and **aleipho**, with **a**, as a particle of union, and **liparos**, to grease, to leave a stain; guilt, as well as all hurtful memories were like grease stains upon the conscience. In N.T. only here and Revelation 3:5; 7:17; 21:4 and in Acts 3:19 "Be awakened in your minds and fully converted to face the fact of your redeemed innocence - your sins have been thoroughly blotted out." Plato used it of blotting out a writing. The word, [2]cheirographon, translates as hand-written. The word, [3]dogma, comes from **dokeo**, a thought pattern; thus thought patterns engraved by human experience of constant failure to do what the law required. In his personal handwriting mankind endorsed their own death sentence. The hands of fallen mankind struck the body of Jesus with the blows of their religious hatred and fury when they nailed his bloodied body to the tree; they did not realize that in the mystery of God's economy, Jesus became the scapegoat of the entire human race. [Isaiah 53:4, 5] See notes on Hebrews 8:12. "The slate wiped clean, that old arrest warrant canceled and nailed to Christ's Cross." —The Message)*

Colossians 2:15 In him dying mankind's death, he [1]defused every possible claim of accusation against the human race and thus made a public [2]spectacle of every [3]rule and authority in God's brilliant triumph, demonstrated in him.

The ⁴voice of the cross will never be silenced. *(The horror of the Cross is now the eternal trophy of God's triumph over sin. The cross stripped religion of its authority to manipulate mankind with guilt. Every accusation lost its leverage to blackmail the human race with condemnation and shame. The word, ¹apekduomai, is translated from apo, away from, and ekduo, to be stripped of clothing; to disarm; the religious facade that disguised the law of works as a means of defining a person's life, was openly defeated. Same word used in Colossians 3:9. The dominance of the tree of the knowledge of good and evil [poneros, hard work and labor] was ended. The word, ²deikmatizo, means to exhibit in public. See ³commentary below of the words **arche**, rule and **exousia**, authority. The word, ⁴parresia, comes from **pas**, all and **rheo**, outspokenness, pouring forth speech.*

"He stripped all the spiritual tyrants in the universe of their sham authority at the Cross and marched them naked through the streets." — The Message.

*Commentary note for 1 Corinthians 15:24, The complete conclusion in his work of redemption is celebrated in his yielding the full harvest of his reign to God the Father, having brought to nought the law of works which supported every definition of dominion under the fall, including all **principalities**, all authority and every dynamic influence in society. [He brought to nought the law of works, **katargeo**, from **kata**, meaning intensity, and **argos**, meaning labor; thus free from all self effort to attempt to improve what God has already perfected in Christ. All principalities, ³**arche**, or chief ranks, i.e., kings, governors; this includes any governing system whereby one is ranked above the other on the basis of their performance or preference. All authority, ³**exousia**, comes from **ek**, denoting origin and **eimi**, I am; in this case, because of what I can do I am defined by what I can do better than you; therefore, I have authority over you. Every dynamic influence in society, **dunamis**, means power, in this case, willpower. Every government structure in society will be brought under the dominion of grace where the Christ-life rules.]*

In 1 Corinthians 2:7-8, We voice words of wisdom that were hidden in silence for timeless ages; a mystery unfolding God's Masterful plan whereby he would redeem his glory in mankind. Neither the politicians nor the theologians of the day had a clue about this mystery [of mankind's association in Christ]; if they did, they would never have crucified the Lord whose death redeemed our glory.

Hebrews 2:8, 1 Corinthians 15:25,27 His dominion is destined to subdue all hostility and contradiction under his feet. ("The Lord said to my Lord, Sit at my right hand until I make your enemies your footstool." [Psalm 110:1] Jesus is Lord of Lords; in his victory mankind is restored to lordship; "I say you are gods, all of you are sons of the Most High." [Psalm 82:6 RSV].)

Revelation 2:25 ¹Lay hold of that which your hearts ²bear witness to ³until you fully grasp the scope and understand the most conclusive significance of ⁴my coming.

Revelation 2:26, Seeing my victory as your victory makes you the overcomer. By embracing the ¹completeness of my works as your ²treasure, you realize my authority in you to possess the nations. *(See verse 23 - the ¹success of my works is to your credit. The words, αχρι τελους achri telous suggest, taking my words to its full conclusion. The word, **tereo** means to treasure, to guard. See Psalm 2:7,8 [also verse 9 as referenced in the next verse, 27] You are my son, today I have begotten you. Ask of me, and I will make the nations your heritage, and the ends of* the earth your possession. Paul quotes Psalm 2 in Acts 13:33 when he preaches the resurrection of Jesus and in Ephesians 2:5,6 and Colossians 3:1-3 he celebrates our co-begotteness. Also Peter announces that we were born anew when Jesus was raised from the dead. 1 Peter 1:3. The word [2]*exousia*, often translated as authority has two components, *ek*, out of, source and *eimi*, I am. The Preposition [3]*epi* suggests continuous influence upon, from a position of authority.)

Revelation 2:27 You will [1]shepherd the nations with a royal scepter and shatter [2]their 'alienated mindsets' like a potter's vessel of clay. *(He quotes Psalm 2:9, "You shall break them with a rod of iron, and dash them in pieces like a potter's vessel." Sadly the Hebrew Masoretic Text uses the word* רעע *RAA - to be bad, be evil; to be displeasing; to be injurious; to be wicked; to do an injury or hurt; to be mischief; instead of the same sounding word,* רעה *RA'AH with a **Hay** at the end and not an **Ayin**, which means **to shepherd**. Also in the Septuagint, the Greek word* ποιμανεῖς [1]*poimaneis is used. You shall feed them as a shepherd nurtures his flock. With reference to the [2]alienated mindsets that ruled the nations see Numbers 24:17, "A scepter shall rise out of Israel; it shall crush the forehead of Moab." [mindset.] The shepherd's staff was never intended to beat up the sheep but to protect and free them from any possible threat.*

*See **Extended Notes on The Rod of Iron** at the end of Chapter 2.)*

Revelation 2:28, In the same way that my shepherding mission is [3]sourced in the Father I have extended it to you. I also give you the [2]Morning Star. *(I've attached part of the previous verse here. The Greek word, [1]para, with the Genitive, indicating source or origin, close and immediate proximity, intimate connection, union. See 2 Peter 1:19, "Take my word as one would take a lamp at night; the day is about to dawn for you in your own understanding. When the [2]Morning Star appears, you no longer need the lamp; this will happen shortly on the horizon of your own hearts." Revelation 22:16 I am Jesus. I sent my celestial messenger to be witness of these things to you before the churches; confirming to them that I am the Root and offspring of David, the radiant Morning Star. See my notes on **The "Fallen Star" is The Bright Morning Star,** at the end of Revelation 9.)*

Revelation 2:29, Now listen up with your inner ears. Hear with understanding what the Spirit is saying to the ekklesia. *(See 1 Corinthians 2:13 The impact of our words are not confined to the familiar wisdom of the world taught by human experience and tradition, but communicated by seamless spirit resonance, combining spirit with spirit.)*

Revelation 5:5, Then one of the elders said unto me, "You need not weep anymore. Look. The Lion has conquered. He who is of the tribe of Judah, the root of David. His victory qualifies him to open the scroll and to break its seven seals." *(Idou enikesen Behold. He has conquered.* **ho leon, ho ek tes phules Jodah, he ritza David***, The Lion who is out of the tribe of Judah, the root of David. Revelation 3:7 I hold the key of David as prophesied in Isaiah 22:22*

See Genesis 49:9 Judah is a lion's whelp; Genesis 49:10 The scepter shall not depart from Judah, nor the ruler's staff from between his feet, until he comes to whom it belongs; and to him shall be the obedience of the peoples. Genesis 49:11 Binding his foal to the vine and his ass's colt to the choice vine, he washes his garments in wine and his vesture in the blood of grapes.)

TRIUMPH OF THE LAMB - REV 17

Revelation 5:6, So I looked to see the Lion, and there, as if fused into one with the throne and in unison with the four Living Beings, taking center stage in the midst of the elders, I saw a little Lamb, alive and standing even though it seemed to have been violently butchered in sacrifice. It had seven horns and seven eyes which are the seven Spirits of God having been sent out to accomplish his bidding in all the earth. *(You cannot see the Lion until you see the Lamb. Mankind's redeemed innocence is the authority of the throne of the Kingdom of God.)*

Revelation 5:11, Then I saw ¹wave upon wave of innumerable celestial messengers ¹engulfing the throne and the elders and the Living Beings and I heard singing. It was a mass choir of ²multi millions. *(The word ¹kuklo, encircle, from kuma, a swelling wave; which also connects with the etymological value of the word muriades, from meu, like in waves of the sea. Countless ²myriads - literally ten thousands times ten thousands and thousands of thousands. The largest number named in Ancient Greek was the myriad, myriad (written MM) or hundred million. In his Sand Reckoner, Archimedes of Syracuse used this quantity as the basis for a numeration system of large powers of ten, which he used to count grains of sand.*

According to PIE, the etymology of the word myriad has been variously connected to meu- "damp" in reference to the waves of the sea and to Greek myrmex [μύρμηξ, "ant"] in reference to their swarms. Proto-Indo-European (PIE) is the linguistic reconstruction of the common ancestor of the Indo-European languages, the most widely spoken language family in the world.)

Revelation 5:12 In their full capacity they exploded in song, proclaiming in unison, "The Lamb's worth is now fully ¹realized. ²Having been slain in sacrifice, the power, wealth, wisdom, strength, honor, glory, and blessing belong to him." *(The word ¹labein, to have taken/realized, from lambano, to take, to grasp, to receive; here in the Aorist Infinitive tense, which indicates prior completion of an action in relationship to a point in time. The word ²esphagmenon is the Perfect Passive Participle of the verb, sphazō, to slay in sacrifice. It is used to describe a state that exists at the time coincident with that of the leading verb as a result of action completed prior to the time of the main verb. The basic thought of the Perfect tense is that the progress of an action has been completed and the results of the action are continuing on, in full effect. In other words, the progress of the action has reached its culmination and the finished results are now in existence.)*

Revelation 5:13, At that point the entire universe burst out in praise. I heard every created being in the heavenly realm and upon the earth and under the earth, and upon the ocean and everything within all these spheres, declaring to the One seated upon the throne and to the Lamb: "The most ¹articulate language, the admiration, the supreme magnificence, the might until the ages of the ages." *(The word ¹eulogia, from eu, good, well done, and logos; thus, polished language; such language which is artfully adapted to captivate the hearer: fair speaking, fine speeches.)*

It is almost unspeakable that of all the themes God could choose from to celebrate the central authority of the throne Room, he chose the Lamb. The jubilant commemoration of mankind's redeemed innocence is the theme of the throne of heaven.

Babylon has fallen.

Revelation 17:18 The woman you saw is the great city which dominated the kings of the earth. *(The Prostitute city-society of Babylon stands in contrast to the Bride of Christ as the New Jerusalem.)*

The repeat of the same scene recorded in **Revelation 14:6 And I saw another celestial messenger soaring in mid heaven - he was the carrier of good news and his mission was to announce these glad tidings of everlasting proportions to every single nation, tribe, language and people grouping of the earth.**

Revelation 14:7 In a great voice he declared, "Be awestruck with the amazingness of God. Give him glory. The hour of his judgment has come. He is the Maker of the heavenly realm, the earth, the sea and the fountains of the waters." *(This announcement echoes in Jesus' declaration in John 12:31 Now is the judgment of this world; this is the moment where the authority of the world-system is cast out. [The serpent's head is about to be crushed. Genesis 3:15; Colossians 2:14,15; Luke 10:18.] John 12:32 When I am lifted up from the earth, I will draw all of mankind and every definition of judgment unto me. (He would be lifted up on a cross, descend into the depths of our hell, then, according to the prophetic word in Hosea 6:2, after two days, the entire human race he represents, will be co-quickened and on the third day, be co-raised, out of the lowest parts of the earth and elevated to the highest heavens. Ephesians 4:8,9; see also Ephesians 2:5,6 and Colossians 3:1-3. 'All' includes all of mankind and every definition of judgment. The subject of the sentence, as from the previous verse, is the judgment of the world - thus the primary thought here is that in his death, Jesus would draw all judgment upon himself. John 3:14; John 8:28; Acts 2:33. 1 John 3:5 We have witnessed with our own eyes how, in the unveiling of the prophetic word, when he was lifted up upon the cross as the Lamb of God, he lifted up our sin and broke its dominion and rule over us. John 1:29 "Behold, the Lamb of God, who takes away [**airo**] the sin of the world. The word **airo** means to lift up.")*

Revelation 14:8 And a second celestial messenger followed with more good news. Babylon the great city crashed and will never fly again. She who sold herself as a prostitute to all the nations and intoxicated them with the wine of her passion. *(The language is an echo of Isaiah 21:9, "Babylon has fallen. It has fallen. All the idols they worship lie shattered on the ground." Jeremiah 51:8 "Babylon will suddenly fall and be shattered." Babylon was used for Rome in late Jewish writings; see also 1 Peter 5:13. In the imagery that follows, [in Revelation 15-17] John sees how the effect of the triune religious counterfeit of the Dragon, the Beast and the fake slain and risen lamb disguised as the great prostitute of Babylon is thoroughly stripped of their influence and dominion and brought to nought.*

The same announcement of the utter defeat of Babylon continues in Chapter 18...

Revelation 18:2 He announced in a thunderous voice, The great Babylon is utterly crushed.)

REVELATION Chapter 18

18:1 With this I saw another celestial messenger descending out of the heavenly sphere with blazing light beaming out of him. The light lit up the earth with the brightness of his glorious presence.

18:2 He announced in a thunderous voice, The great Babylon is utterly crushed - it has become a ghost town of demons, haunted by every unclean spirit, held in it like in a cage for eerie, spooky birds.

18:3 The masses of mankind became intoxicated with the wine of her passion and adultery while their kings flirted with her and the travelling traders of the world made their wealth with the powerful lure of her attractions.

18:4 And I heard another voice saying out of the heavens, Come on out of the grasp of her deception. You are my people; you have nothing in common with her distortions and need not participate in her plagues.

18:5 Her perverted twistedness of God's image in you, has piled up and polluted every square inch of earth and sky. In the death and resurrection of the slain Lamb, God confronted every [1]remembrance of the unrighteousness she represents. *(Aorist Active Indicative of **mnēmoneuō**, remembered; here with the Accusative case [**adikēmata**, unrighteousness] - the sum-total of unrighteousness that she represents. The prophetic Aorist is used to describe a future event, to show that it is so certain that you can view it as already completed. There was no time in history where God was not already persuaded of what he always knew to be true of mankind's deliverance from deception. He called things that were not as though they were. Romans 4:17. See also Hebrews 8:12. Then John 5:28.)*

18:6 The Lamb's suffering dealt a double blow to the whore and Beast-system. The counterfeit cup she had mixed turned on her and proved to be her defeat. *(Give back to her as also she gave back to you, and double to her double, according to her works. In the cup which she mixed, mix to her double. LITV. Their apparent initial victory in the brutal unjust trial and crucifixion of the Lamb turned against their tyranny in double measure - not only were they outwitted in his death, when the document of mankind's guilt in the scarred body of Jesus was nailed to the cross, whereby every possible claim against the human race was nullified, but in his resurrection God presented the receipt, documenting the justification and redeemed innocence and righteousness of the entire human race. This reminds of what the Prophet Isaiah saw, Isaiah 40:2 Speak tenderly to Jerusalem, and cry to her that her warfare is ended, that her iniquity is pardoned, that she has received from the LORD's hand double for all her sins. The judgment that sin has brought in its hellish torment as an inevitable consequence upon mankind is now atoned for in double proportions in the Lamb's suffering and in the reversal of the lamb's judgment brought upon all principalities and powers.)*

18:7 This is a complete reversal of her self-inflated glory and luxurious lifestyle to the exposure of her falsehood - like when metal is [1]tested with a touchstone and proves to be fool's gold - and gladness is turned into sorrow. You said in your heart, I am established as a queen and not a widow - I will not know grief. *(The word [1]torment **basanismos** from **basanizō**, to test metals by the touchstone, which is a black siliceous stone used to test the purity of gold or silver by the color of the streak produced on it by rubbing it with either* *metal - a piece of fine-grained dark schist or jasper formerly used for testing alloys of gold by observing the color of the mark which they made on it - thus, a standard or criterion by which something is judged or recognized. The cup Jesus drank on the cross is the touchstone. "What shall I say? Father, remove this cup from me? NO. For this hour I have come.")*

18:8 Her calamity strikes in one day - death, sorrow and starvation - her entire dynasty is burnt to ashes in the fire of the passionate judgment of the Lord God. *(See Isaiah 47:8 Now therefore hear this, you lover of pleasures, who sit securely, who say in your heart, "I am, and there is no one besides me; I shall not sit as a widow or know the loss of children":*

Isaiah 47:9 These two things shall come to you in a moment, in one day; the loss of children and widowhood shall come upon you in full measure, in spite of your many sorceries and the great power of your enchantments.

All of her "offspring" are rescued out of her sway.)

18:9 And the kings of the earth, the executives of the mindsets of the Beastly system, her faithful fornicating friends and clients, are weeping and wailing bitterly while the smoke of her burning rises.

18:10 They stand completely detached from her, embarrassed by their association with her in her ¹exposed, pretentious identity, crying, Alas. Alas. The mighty city of Babylon is doomed in one hour. *(Repeat note of verse 7; The word ¹torment **basanismos** from **basanizō**, to test metals by the touchstone.)*

18:11 Also the money-power emperors of the world who control the global trade-routes, the merchants and economists were wailing and mourning because the judgement on her caused the loss of all their clients - no one buys their cargo anymore. The touchstone currency of God has exposed the fake currency system of the world economy. *(Revelation 17:15)*

18:12 Suddenly no one shows any interest in their most precious cargo of gold, silver, rare gems, pearls, fine linen fabrics, purple, silk, scarlet, all kinds of scented wood, ivory carvings and articles, expensive hard woods, bronze, iron and marble.

18:13 The list goes on and on. Cinnamon, spices, incense, perfume, frankincense, wine, olive oil, flour, wheat, cattle, sheep, horses, wagons and slaves. No buyers.

18:14 The entire economy crashed. None of the sought after seasonal fruits or any delicacy associated with their luxurious living were available any longer. Not even a trace of these could be found.

18:15 The once mighty merchants and money brokers who gleaned their wealth from her, were standing afar off, afraid and disoriented. They weep and wail bitterly since the touchstone currency of their economy has been exposed as fake.

18:16 Alas the great model city of the world is doomed. Dressed to perfection in the most expensive and elegant fashion. Draped in purple and scarlet fabric, festooned and sprinkled with golden glitter and

ornaments; she was elaborately decorated with gold, precious stones and pearls.

18:17 In a brief moment all this pomp has come to nothing. The great shipping tycoons of the world, their workforce and clients all stood in bewilderment, witnessing from afar the ruin of their entire enterprise as it went up in smoke.

18:18 They wept bitterly in lament, "Who would have thought that this great city of unequalled   prominence could come to nothing."

18:19 In their sense of hopelessness and bafflement they cast dust upon their heads as if to wrap their minds around the ultimate reduction of their vibrant life to lifeless dust. They are weeping and wailing in shock for the great city which has fallen. "Oh what a shame that the famous icon of prosperity who made every ship owner rich is now [1]left utterly desolate in just one hour." *(The word [1]eremos, desolate; also used of a woman neglected by her husband, from whom the husband withholds himself. The whore-city is now bereft of all her lovers.)*

18:20 A [1]deep sense of relief is felt in the heavens as all the saints, the Apostles and the Prophets celebrate how God caused the whore's judgment of others to be her own judgment. *(The word [1]euphrainō, to be delighted, eu plus **phren** - innermost being; - ἔκρινεν τὸ κρίμα ὑμῶν ἐξ αὐτῆς literally, has judged your judgment out of her - what she has judged concerning you.)*

18:21 And a huge celestial messenger lifted what seemed like a massive millstone and cast it into the sea, saying, so shall Babylon the great Prostitute-City, be hurled into the ocean and not a single trace of her existence shall ever be found again. *(Matthew 18:6 but whoever causes one of these little ones who believe in me to sin, it would be better for him to have a great millstone fastened round his neck and to be drowned in the depth of the sea. See my commentary note in Luke 12:5. See my commentary note in Luke 12:5. Also my notes on Lake of Fire chapter 19.)*

18:22 Never again will the festive sound of harpists, singers, flautists and trumpeters be heard in you. Not even a trace of any art or creative skills and crafts will remind of days gone by. The familiar grinding sound of the millstone will be silent forever.

18:23 Not even a hint of a candlelight or any lamp will ever bear testimony to your forgotten night-life again. The voice of the bridegroom and bride will forever be silent in you. Her merchants were the great untouchable tycoons of the world who seduced all the nations with her pharmaceutical potions and spells.

18:24 The blood of the Prophets and the saints and every one [1]slaughtered in the scapegoat-sacrificial system of the world order were evidenced in her. *(The word, [1]sphazō is the verb used for the slain Lamb.)*

REVELATION Chapter 19

19:1 With this I heard a great multitude singing as with one voice in the heavens, saying Hallelujah. Salvation, glory and power belongs to our God. *(The Great Hallel [a title for Psalm 113-118] is sung chiefly at the feasts of the Passover and Tabernacles. In this context, John reminds his Israeli audience of triumphant praise as the voice celebrating the great Salvation wrought at the Passover of the Lamb of God who has become our permanent Tabernacle and habitation. Pesach, פסח protecting and rescuing. From an Arabic root which means to expand; to save. See my comment in John 11:56. The days of wandering around in a wilderness, outside of the Promise, are forever over. Also, in leading up to* **the great wedding feast of the Lamb***, this introduction of the praises sung during Passover and the Feast of Tabernacles, are most significant. See commentary notes on* **the City-Bride** *at the end of chapter 3. See my commentary note on John 5:1.)*

19:2 For everyone of his ¹judgments are established in righteousness and truth. He has sentenced the great Harlot-system who has caused the world to ²shrivel up and pine away with the poison of her prostitution and vindicated the blood of his servants out of her hand. The spell of her judgment upon the earth was broken. *(¹John's Jewish audience here are familiar with the fact, and are reminded, that Psalm 89:14 as well as Psalm 97:2 speak of righteousness and truth being the foundation/habitation of his throne. Revelation 15:3 Righteousness and truth are your trademarks.*

*The word, ²****phteiro***, means to pine or waste away, to wither. Any idea of separation causes one to wither away in loneliness. Prostitution can never substitute true marriage. See 2 Corinthians 11:2 I feel a divine jealousy for you; like a grooms-man who wooed you to belong solely to your one husband and presented you as a pure bride to Christ. 2 Corinthians 11:3 I am concerned for you that you might pine away through the illusion of separation from Christ and that, just like Eve, you might become blurry-eyed and deceived into believing a lie about yourselves. The temptation was to exchange the truth about our completeness [I am] with the idea of incompleteness [I am not] and shame; thinking that perfection required your toil and all manner of wearisome labor. [Again the word,* **phteiro***, is used, meaning to pine or waste away, to wither. Any idea of separation causes one to wither away in loneliness. The word* **haplotes** *from* **hama***, a particle of union, and* **pleko***, to braid or plait together; sometimes translated, simplicity or unmixed. The Greek word,* **ophis** *is translated serpent and comes from optomai, to gaze, in this case, to present a visual idea through illusion. The word* **exapataō** *from* **ek,** *source +* **apateo***, apathy is the source of deception, to be without faith, believing a lie about yourself. Hebrews 4:6 Israel died in the wilderness because of their unbelief. [Both Adam and Israel believed a lie about themselves. Numbers 13:33, Joshua 2:11, 2 Corinthians 4:4.] The word* **panourgia***, from the words,* **pas***, all, and* **ergon***, work or toil, where your entire existence is reduced to wearisome labor. This word is often translated, cunning or craftiness. See also 2 Corinthians 4:2 "We have renounced hidden agendas [employing a little bit of the law in an attempt to "balance" out grace]; we have distanced ourselves from any obscure craftiness to manipulate God's word to make it mean what it does not say."])*

19:3 Yet again they would say, Hallelujah. For the smoke of her destruction rises up as a trophy-testimony for all times and ages.

REVELATION Chapter 19

19:4 And the twenty four elders and the four living creatures fell on their faces in worship to God upon the throne, saying, Amen; Hallelujah.

19:5 And a voice proceeded from the environment of the throne saying, ¹recount the amazing stories of God's praise to all his bond-servants small and great, everyone who is awed by him. *(The verb, ¹aineō from ainos, story; thus, tell the story. See Philippians 4:8 Study stories that celebrate life - epainos, commendable, praise worthy, from epi, indicating continuous influence upon, and ainos, story.)*

19:6 Then I heard the voice of an innumerable mass of people exploding like a thunderous torrent of mighty cascading waterfalls, bellowing, Hallelujah. The Lord our God has claimed his kingdom and established his sovereign rule over everything.

19:7 This is the climax of the ages. Celebrate his glory with ecstatic joy and extreme delight, for the wedding feast of the Lamb has come. The day didn't catch her by surprise. His bride has prepared herself appropriately. She is ready and fully ¹fit for the occasion. *(The word, ¹hetoimasen, is in the Aorist Active Indicative tense pointing to what has already happened. This word derives from an old word, heteos, fitness. She has gotten herself ready. Verse 8 tells us how she did it. See my extended notes on **the City-Bride** at the end of this chapter.)*

19:8 She ¹was given the finest linen to clothe herself; there she stands, wrapped in radiant white - dressed in ²spotless, saintly innocence. *(The verb, edothe from didomi, was given, Aorist Passive Indicative. The word innocence, ²dikaiōma stems from the word dike, two parties finding likeness in each other. Dike is also the root for the word dikaiosune, righteousness. Sadly, many translations have it completely wrong here. This is not the righteous "deeds" of the saints. Our redeemed innocence gives testimony to the merits of the Redeemer. Paul says in Philippians 3:9, "And be found in him, not having my own righteousness, which is of the law, but what is through the faith of Christ, the righteousness which is of God by faith." Zechariah 3:4 And the celestial messenger said to those who were standing before him, "Remove the filthy garments from him." And to him he said, "Behold, I have taken your iniquity away from you, and I will clothe you with righteousness." Aramaic Targum. See my extended notes on **the City-Bride** at the end of Revelation 3.)*

19:9 And he instructed me to record this in writing: Oh the ¹blessedness of this bliss which is the supreme celebration of the union of the ages. You have individually been ²identified by name and invited to the Lamb's supper, concluding in the ultimate wedding feast. This is the Grand Finale in the ³unveiling of God's word. *(This is not a wedding where you are invited simply because you're a friend of a friend of the Groom or the Bride - or a distant second cousin to a relative of a relative on someone's mother's side. No. You're the Bride.*

The word, ¹makarios, usually translated, blessed, suggests a special intensity of delight. It is another beatitude [makarioi] like that in Revelation 14:13 [fourth of the seven in the book]

*The verb, κεκλημενοι ²**kekelemenoi** is a Perfect Passive Participle of **kaleo**, to identify by name, to surname. The Passive Participle describes a state that exists at the time coincident with that of the leading verb as a result of action completed prior to the time of the main verb, [in previous verse] **edothe** from didomi, was given [v8] which is in the Aorist Passive Indicative. The Perfect Participle endorses the fact that this is a standing invitation. See the extended notes on **ekklesia** at the end of chapter 1. The word, ³**alethinos**, from **alethes**; from the negative particle, **a** and **lanthanō**, to lie hidden; thus, that which is unveiled truth.*

*Just like Babylon is not a city in the symbolic language of Revelation, it is a "fallen", distorted-mindset-society; so the New Jerusalem is not a city but the redeemed society of mankind. The Bride of Christ. Revelation 17:18. See my extended notes on **the City-Bride** at the end of this chapter.)*

19:10 I was so overwhelmed that I fell down at his feet to worship him; he immediately asked me to see him as a fellow bond-servant and a fellow brother, jointly echoing the testimony of Jesus. Worship God, he said, the testimony of Jesus is the spirit of prophecy. This wedding is the entire culmination of the prophetic word.

19:11 Then, in my vision, heaven opened and I saw a white horse appear; the Name of the one seated upon the horse is Faithful and True. Righteousness spans the range of his judgment and warfare. *(See notes on the **Open heaven** at the end of chapter 13.)*

19:12 And his eyes were like flashing flames of fire. His head was adorned with many royal diadems. He has a Name written upon him which he alone understands; no one recognizes him by that name. *(The Jews knew God as the "unpronounceable Name, and therefore called him, **HaShem** - השם The Name. See my commentary on Revelation 1:4*

They could not connect this most sacred Name to the Messiah-Christ, JESUS, born in Bethlehem, condemned and crucified by them."

John 1:11 It was not as though he arrived on a foreign planet; he came to his own, yet his own did not recognize him. (The Jews should have been the first to recognize him.)

Isaiah 7:14 Therefore the Lord himself will give you a sign. Behold, a virgin shall conceive and bear a son, and shall call his name Immanuel. See Luke 1:28,31.

*"...and you shall call his Name Jesus, for he will save his people from their sins." See Jeremiah 23:6 "In his days Judah will be saved, [**yâsha`**, a primitive root; properly to be open, wide or free, that is, [by implication] to be safe; causatively to free or succor, defend, deliver [-er], help, preserve, rescue, be safe, bring [having] **salvation**, get victory.] And Israel will dwell securely. And **this is his Name** by which he will be called:* יהוה צדקנו *- Jahweh Tzadeknu - **Jahweh our righteousness.**"*

The One with eyes ablaze as in Revelation 1:14 and Revelation 2:17,18, also Revelation 3:12...And I will engrave upon them the name of my God, also the name of the city [the bride.] of my God, the new Jerusalem that descends from heaven; as well as my own new Name.

*See extended **notes on the hidden Name at the end of the chapter**.)*

REVELATION Chapter 19

19:13 The robes he wore were dipped in blood and his ¹Name has always been the Word of God. *(He is the Logos that was before time was; the completeness of prophecy, the Incarnate One. See John 1:1-3,14. See **Notes on the Hidden Name** at the end of this chapter.)*

19:14 And heaven's armies followed him, on white horses; they were dressed in the finest, dazzling white linen.

19:15 And from his mouth proceeds a sharp sword - the words of his utterance cut to the core of the heart of the nations and he shall shepherd them with an iron scepter. And on his own he will tread out the winepress of the ¹intensity of the passion of the sovereign God of the universe. *(See my comments in Revelation 2:16 on the imagery of the Sword.*

*The words, **tou thumou tes orges tou theo**, speaks of the intensity of the passion of God, with the word thumos, passion, and the word often translated wrath, **orge**, meaning strong desire - as a reaching forth or excitement of the mind, from the word, **oregomai**, meaning to stretch one's self out in order to touch or to grasp something.*

*See my commentary notes in Revelation 2:26,27 **at the end of Revelation chapter 2** with reference to Psalm 2:7,8,9 on **the Rod of Iron**.*

*See my notes at the end of this chapter, on **The shepherd-King of the Nations**.*

*Also on, **The Winepress of the Passion of God & The Great Supper**)*

19:16 And a Name is written on his robe and thigh: King of kings and Lord of lords. *(Psalm 45:3 Gird your sword upon your thigh, Oh, mighty one, in your glory and majesty.*

Revelation Revelation 3:11 Do not let tough times make me seem distant from you. I am at hand - see my nearness, not my absence. And don't let temporal setbacks diminish your own authority either. Remember that you call the shots; you wear the crown. My crown endorses your crown. Revelation 3:12, And I will engrave upon the individual the name of my God, also the name of the city [the bride.] of my God, the new Jerusalem that descends from heaven; as well as my own new Name. ²My Father's Name, John 5:43, I have come in my Father's Name. John 12:28 Father, glorify your Name. Abba Father.

See Psalm 103:4 He redeems his life from the Pit and weaves a crown for him out of loving-kindness and tender mercies.

Revelation 21:2 And I saw the holy city, new Jerusalem, coming down out of heaven from God, prepared as a bride adorned for her husband;

Psalm 87:3 Glorious things are spoken of you, Oh city of God - "This one and that one were born in her" Psalm 87:7 Singers and dancers together say, "All my springs of joy are in you.")

19:17 Then I saw another celestial herald standing in the luminous light of the sun. With a loud voice he invited all the birds of the sky to flock together for the great supper of God. *(Another symbolic reference to the Last [Final] Supper - the Lamb's flesh and blood introduce the New Covenant where every judgment is concluded and the Incarnate Word is now our feast - his* *flesh is bread indeed and becomes our flesh his blood is drink indeed and becomes our blood - celebrated in every meal me have. His broken body pictures the broken body of the human race - one died for all, therefore, all have died. 2 Corinthians 5:14.)*

19:18 Come feast on the flesh of all mankind. The flesh of kings and the flesh of the high ranking captains, the flesh of the mighty men, the flesh of the horses and their riders; all flesh, slave and free, both the prominent and the least. *(This reflects on Ezekiel 39:17 As for you, son of man, thus says the Lord GOD: Speak to the birds of every sort and to all beasts of the field, 'Assemble and come, gather from all sides to the sacrificial feast which I am preparing for you, a great sacrificial feast upon the mountains of Israel, and you shall eat flesh and drink blood. Ezekiel 39:20 And you shall be filled at my table with horses and riders, with mighty men and all kinds of warriors,' says the Lord GOD. Ezekiel 39:21 "And I will set my glory among the nations; and all the nations shall see my judgment which I have executed, and my hand which I have laid on them.*

*See extended notes on **The Winepress of the Passion of God & The Great Supper** at the end of the chapter.)*

19:19 And I saw the Beast in alliance with the kings of the earth muster their armies to engage in a ¹once-and-for-all war against the One seated on the horse and his army. *(The idea of a once-and-for-all war is implied by the Aorist Infinitive tense of the verb, **poiesai**. [Weymouth] This is the Aorist Active Infinitive which indicates prior completion of an action in relationship to a point in time. Greek Infinitives could have either a present or Aorist form. The contrast between the two forms was not necessarily one of time, it is a difference of aspect. The Present Infinitive was used to express progressive or imperfective aspect. It pictures the action expressed by the verb as being in progress. The Aorist Infinitive however does not express progressive aspect. It presents the action expressed by the verb as a completed unit with a beginning and end.*

This is an important fact since there are numeral references to the same "once and for all war" in the heavens. It is however the same hour; the same event. Revelation 12:7; Revelation 16:13,14; Revelation 17:13,14; Revelation 20:8.)

19:20 And the Beast and the miracle working Puppet Partner, the False Prophet were arrested and cast into the lake ablaze with sulphur. These two were the ones who were empowered by the Dragon to amaze and deceive those who were tattooed in their heads and hands with the character of the Beast and make them pay religious homage to its image. *(The word ¹**theion**, sulphur, from **theios**, godlike [neuter as noun, divinity]: - divine, godhead. Sulphur is a yellow inflammable mineral substance found in quantities on the shores of the Dead Sea. This was also known as divine incense, because burning brimstone was regarded as having power to purify, and to ward off disease. Its medicinal values are well known even today.*

Revelation 14:8-20 In the imagery here, John sees how the triune religious counterfeit system, the Dragon, the Beast and the False Prophet are thoroughly stripped of their influence and dominion and brought to nought. The False Prophet is mentioned in Revelation 16:13 (KJV) "And I saw three unclean spirits like frogs come out of the mouth of the Dragon, and out of the mouth of the

*Beast, and out of the mouth of the False Prophet." Here in Revelation 19:20 and also in Revelation 20:10 the Devil, who led them astray will be hurled into the lake of fire and brimstone where his puppet partners, the Beast and the False Prophet have already been confined to. Day and Night they will be the subject of God's touchstone for the ages of the ages - the very atmosphere of the entire universe will be thoroughly fumigated from any evidence of Satanas. [See my notes on the Touchstone in Revelation 14:10] Revelation 13:11 Then I saw another wild animal; this one emerged out of the earth - it had two horns and resembled a young lamb; yet it had a Dragon's voice. [The counterfeit "trinity" emerges - the one mirroring the other - 1/ the Dragon-Accuser; 2/ the seven headed sea-monster of religion with its leading role player, the head that was slain but became alive again; 3/ and now, here, the Dragon clothed in a lamb's-disguise; later called, the false Prophet.] See extended **Notes on The Lake of Fire** at the end of this chapter.)*

19:21 The One seated upon the horse, with the sword that proceeded from his mouth, has slain the allies of the Beast and its puppet False Prophet, the kings and their hosts, while all the fowls of the air feasted on their flesh. *(The word, **rhomphaia** a large, long sword; used in Luke 2:35, where Simon prophecies over Mary: "and a sword will pierce through your own soul also, then the thought processes, reasonings and dialogues of many hearts will be uncovered." This word is used 6 times in Revelation, Revelation 1:16, Revelation 2:12, Revelation 2:16, Revelation 6:8, Revelation 19:15, Revelation 19:21 - in the LXX [Greek Septuagint] it is used for the sword of the Lord. It is an exaggerated size to emphasize its symbolic use. See also my notes on **the Sword of the Lord**, Revelation 2:16 and Revelation 1:16 The Sword would always point back to mankind's original identity. The Hebrew word in Genesis 3:24, [where the cherub with the flaming sword was positioned at the Eastern Gate of Eden] הפך **hâpak** is a primitive root; meaning to turn about; by implication to change, to return, to be converted, turn back. Also in the Septuagint the same thought is communicated in the Greek word, **strephō**, which is the strengthened from the base of **tropay**; to turn around or reverse: - convert, turn again, back again, to turn self about. In Luke 15 the prodigal son returns to himself - Plato is quoted by Ackerman [Christian Element in Plato] as thinking of redemption as coming to oneself.*

See also Hebrews 4:12 The message God spoke to us in Christ, is the most life giving and dynamic influence in us, cutting like a surgeon's scalpel, sharper than a soldier's sword, piercing to the deepest core of human conscience, to the dividing of soul and spirit; ending the dominance of the sense realm and its neutralizing effect upon the human spirit. In this way a person's spirit is freed to become the ruling influence again in the thoughts and intentions of their heart. The scrutiny of this word detects every possible disease, discerning the body's deepest secrets where joint and bone-marrow meet.)

Revelation Chapter 19 Extended Notes:

The Hidden Name
The Shepherd-King of the Nations
The Winepress of the Passion of God & The Great Supper
The Lake of Fire and the Second Death

The Hidden Name

Revelation 19:11 Then, in my vision, heaven opened and I saw a white horse appear; and the Name of the one seated upon the horse is Faithful and True. Righteousness spans the range of his judgment and warfare.

Revelation 19:12 And his eyes were like flashing flames of fire. His head was adorned with many royal diadems. He has a Name written upon him which he alone understands, no one recognizes him by that name. *(The Jews knew God as the "unpronounceable Name, and therefore called him, HaShem - השם The Name. See my commentary on Revelation 1:4, ... him who ²is I am; he always ³was and ⁴will continually be the accompanying one...This phraseology is purely Jewish, and taken from the Tetragrammaton. The Four Letters referring to the unpronounceable Name of God -* **YHVH** *- יהוה - Jahweh "Existing" יהוה includes in itself all time, past, present, and future. Hidden in this word are three words, היה hajah, was, הוה havah, is, and יהיה jahjah, shall be. The Word* **Adonai** *means Lord - so the vowels of* **Adonai** *-a- o- e-are used to fit in between the four consonants of the name YHWH to make it Jeho͟va͟h so that the unpronounceable* **YHVH** *- יהוה - Jahweh is then translated* **Jehovah** *and often translated LORD in the Bible.*

They could not connect this most sacred Name to the Messiah-Christ, JESUS, born in Bethlehem, condemned and crucified by them.

John 1:11 It was not as though he arrived on a foreign planet; he came to his own, yet his own did not recognize him. (The Jews should have been the first to recognize him.)

Isaiah 7:14 Therefore the Lord himself will give you a sign. Behold, a virgin shall conceive and bear a son, and shall call his name Immanuel. See Luke 1:28,31.

"...and you shall call his Name Jesus, for he will save his people from their sins." See Jeremiah 23:6 "In his days Judah will be saved, [yâsha`, a primitive root; properly to be open, wide or free, that is, [by implication] to be safe; causatively to free or succor, defend, deliver [-er], help, preserve, rescue, be safe, bring [having] **salvation***, get victory.] And Israel will dwell securely. And* **this is his Name** *by which he will be called:* יהוה צדקנו *- Jahweh Tzadeknu -* **Jahweh our righteousness.***"*

The One with eyes ablaze as in Revelation 1:14 and Revelation 2:17,18, also Revelation 3:12...And I will engrave upon them the name of my God, also the name of the city [the bride.] of my God, the new Jerusalem that descends from heaven; as well as my own new Name.)

John 1:11 It was not as though he arrived on a foreign planet; he came to his own, yet his own did not recognize him. *(The Jews should have been the first to recognize him.)*

Isaiah 7:14 Therefore the Lord himself will give you a sign. Behold, a virgin shall conceive and bear a son, and shall call his name Immanuel.

John 1:45 Philip immediately went looking for Nathaniel and told him the news. We have found the one Moses wrote about in the Torah and he whom the Prophets announced when they spoke about Jesus, *[the Savior]* **the son of Joseph from Nazareth.** *(See Deuteronomy 18:15, "The LORD your God will raise up for you a Prophet like me from among you, from your brethren-*

him you shall heed. Deuteronomy 18:18 I will raise up for them a Prophet like you from among their brethren; and I will put my words in his mouth, and he shall speak to them all that I command him. Genesis 49:10, The scepter shall not depart from Judah, nor the ruler's staff from between his feet, until he comes to whom it belongs; and to him shall be the obedience of the peoples. Isaiah 7:14 Therefore the Lord himself will give you a sign. Behold, a virgin shall conceive and bear a son, and you shall call his name Immanuel. Also Isaiah 53:1-12; Isaiah 9:6,7 For unto us a child is born, unto us a son is given: and the government shall be upon his shoulder: and his name shall be called Wonderful, Counselor, The mighty God, The everlasting Father, The Prince of Peace. Of the increase of his government and peace there shall be no end, upon the throne of David, and upon his kingdom, to order it, and to establish it with judgment and with justice from henceforth even forever. The zeal of the LORD of hosts will perform this. Daniel 9:24-27; Jeremiah 23:5-6. See also John 5:39,40 You search the Scriptures, because you think that in them you have eternal life; and it is they that bear witness to me; yet you refuse to come to me that you may have life. John 5:46, 47 If you believed Moses, you would believe me, for he wrote of me. But if you do not believe his writings, how will you believe my words?")

John 1:46 To which Nathaniel answered, "How does ¹Nazareth fit into the picture of God's promised goodness? Philip said to him, "Come and see for yourself." *(Another etymological link to the prophetic picture of Nazareth, from the Hebrew word,* נצר *natsar a shoot, or branch Isaiah 11:1.*

τι αγαθον, 'what good thing?' Nathaniel refers to Scriptures like Jeremiah 33:14 & 15 Behold, the days come, says the LORD, that I will perform that good thing which I have promised. In those days and at that time I will cause a righteous Branch to spring forth for David; and he shall execute justice and righteousness in the land. Also Micah 5:2 But you, Oh Bethlehem Ephrathah, who are the least among the clans of Judah, from you shall come forth for me one who is to be ruler in Israel, whose origin is from old, from ancient days. Nathanael's question seems to imply that not Nazareth, but Bethlehem, was to be the birth-place of the Messiah.) John 1:47 When Jesus saw Nathaniel approach him, he made the following observation, "Now here is a man of Israel, in whom there is no guile." (Note the wisdom of Jesus, instead of engaging Nathaniel in a doctrinal debate around the Scriptures, he endorses him.) John 1:48 Nathaniel was surprised. How can you possibly know me if we have never met? Jesus answered him, "Long before Philip spoke to you, I saw you under the fig tree."

Matthew 1:18 This is how the birth of Jesus Christ unfolded, Mary was betrothed to Joseph, yet before they came together, she was found to be pregnant by Holy Spirit.

Matthew 1:19 But her man Joseph, was perplexed about this and determined to secretly break the engagement in order to avoid a public scandal.

Matthew 1:20 And as he pondered these things, the celestial messenger of the Lord appeared to him in a dream, saying, Joseph, son of David, do not be afraid to marry Mary. For the child within her is conceived by Holy Spirit.

THE HIDDEN NAME - REV 19

Matthew 1:21 And she shall bear a son, and you shall name him JESUS: for he shall save his people from their distortedness. *(Iēsoús is the Greek translation of the Hebrew word,* עישׁוהי *Yehoshia, Jahweh rescued. This verb is the Hif'il 3rd person Past tense. Moses changed Joshua's name from* עשוה *Hoshea, meaning "he rescued" - to* עשוהי *Yehoshua - Jahweh rescued. In prophetic commemoration of God's salvation unveiled in Jesus. Numbers 13:16. These are the names of the men whom Moses sent to spy the land; and Moses called Hoshea [he saved] son of Nun, Yehoshua -* Ἰησοῦς *- Iēsous in the LXX Septuagint [H3091] See John 12:13.)*

Matthew 1:22 Now all this happened, fulfilling that which was spoken of the LORD by the prophet, saying,

Matthew 1:23 Behold, a ¹virgin shall conceive and will bear a son. And they will call his name ²Immanuel, which means, God with us. *([1] The word* ¹***parthenos***, *literally, "from Athens" - an epithet meaning "Virgin", applied by the Greeks to several goddesses, especially Athena. Always associated with a virgin girl - as in LXX* **Isaiah 7:14.** *[The LXX was the Jewish Scriptures of the time. The discovery of the Qumran scrolls reveal that the LXX represents much older manuscripts than our OT, which used the 1000 years later Masoretic text.] In the Masoretic text the word virgin was changed to, a young woman. See Luke 1:27*

²***Immanuel*** *- The entire salvation conclusion is unveiled in his name - every idea of separation from God is taken out of the equation! See Isaiah 40:3-5 & 2 Corinthians 3:18; also Colossians 1:27 The mystery that was hidden for ages and generations is now revealed! It is Christ in us!* τίς ὁ πλοῦτος τῆς δόξης τοῦ μυστηρίου τούτου ἐν τοῖς ἔθνεσιν, ὅς ἐστι **Χριστὸς ἐν ὑμῖν**, ἡ ἐλπὶς τῆς δόξης·*)*

Jeremiah 23:4 I will put shepherds over them. Those shepherds will take care of them. My sheep will no longer be afraid or terrified, and not one of them will be missing, declares Jahweh. *[Luke 15]* **Jeremiah 23:5 Behold, the days come, declares Jahweh, that I will raise unto David a righteous Branch, and a King shall reign and prosper, and shall execute the verdict of righteousness in the earth.**

Jeremiah 23:6 In his days Judah shall be saved, and Israel shall dwell safely: and this is the Name that he will be given: Jahweh, Our Righteousness. *("In his days Judah will be saved, [yâsha`, Ya[weh is Savior] And Israel will dwell securely. And this is his name by which he will be called:* יהוה צדקנו *Jahweh our righteousness.")*

The One with eyes ablaze as in Revelation 1:14 and Revelation 2:17,18, also **Revelation 3:12...And I will engrave upon them the name of my God, also the name of the city** *[the bride.]* **of my God, the new Jerusalem that descends from heaven; as well as my own new Name.**

Revelation 2:17 Your victory is secure in your hearing the word of the Spirit addressing the ekklesia - feast on the revelation of the hidden manna in the Ark *[which prophetically pointed to the Messiah - the mystery that was hidden for ages and generations is Christ in you.]* **I also give you a little white pebble used in the courts of justice, signifying your acquittal - take it as your secret source of strength in the midst of accusation - it has your**

THE HIDDEN NAME - REV 19

new name on it. No one knows you by this name, until you ¹realize your own identity reflected in it. *(This beautifully reminds of Simon's encounter in Matthew 16 - "Blessed are you Simon, son of Jonah for flesh and blood has not known that the son of man is indeed the son of God. Now that you know who I am, allow me to introduce you to you. Your real name, as son of God, is **Petros** - little stone - son of **Petra** [the Rock] - yes. You're a chip off the old block. See notes at the end of this chapter on **The Son of Man is the Son of God.** Also my notes on John 1:12 - Our grasping [¹**lambano**] is simply the awakening to the fact that our genesis is already completed in the **Logos**. [See John 1:3] The **Logos** is the source; everything commences in him. He remains the exclusive Parent reference to their Genesis. There is nothing original, except the Word. We are his offspring. [See Acts 17:28]. "He has come to give us understanding to know him who is true and to realize that we are in him who is true." [1 John 5:20].)*

The royal diadems on his head and the Name written upon him, are in such contrast to **Revelation 13:1 As I stood upon the sand of the sea shore I saw a ferocious Beast emerging out of the waters. It had ten horns and seven heads and every horn was wrapped in royal diadems. And written upon its heads were slanderous, blasphemous names.** *(Have you ever wondered why the name Jesus, not Buddha, Mohammed or Elvis Presley or any other influential name in history or modern times, is the name that is most commonly used as a swear word?)*

Ephesians 3:15 Every family in heaven and on earth originates in him; his is mankind's family name and he remains the authentic identity of every nation.

Ephesians 1:20 Do you want to measure the mind and muscle of God? Consider the force which he unleashed in Jesus Christ when he raised him from the dead and forever seated him enthroned as his executive authority in the realm of the heavens. Jesus is God's right hand of power. He was raised up from the deepest dungeons of human despair to the highest region of heavenly bliss. *[See Ephesians 2:5,6 & 4:8,9]*

Ephesians 1:21 Infinitely above all the combined forces of rule, authority, dominion or governments; he is ranked superior to any name that could ever be given to anyone of this age or any age still to come in the eternal future.

Ephesians 1:22 I want you to see this: he subjected all these powers under his feet. He towers head and shoulders above everything. He is the head;

Ephesians 1:23 the ¹Ekklesia is his body. The completeness of his being that fills all in all resides in us. God cannot make himself more visible or exhibit himself more accurately. *(The word, ¹**Ekklesia**, comes from **ek**, a Preposition always denoting origin, and **klesia** from **kaleo**, to identify by name, to surname; thus the "ekklesia" is his redeemed image and likeness in human form.)*

The salvation that he accomplished is the greatest source of frustration and embarrassment to the religious systems of this world. What the Name of Jesus represents puts religion out of business.

Revelation 19:13 The robes he wore were dipped in blood and his ¹Name has always been the Word of God. *(He is the Logos that was before time was; the completeness of prophecy, the Incarnate One. See John 1:1-3,14.*

His blood stained garments have always borne his Name in the prophetic conversation of God. Psalm 22:16..."they have pierced my hands and feet— Psalm 22:17 I can count all my bones—they stare and gloat over me; Psalm 22:18 they divide my garments among them, and for my raiment they cast lots. κέκληται τὸ ὄνομα αὐτοῦ, ὁ λόγος τοῦ Θεοῦ. The word, ¹kekletai from kaleo, to surname, is in the perfect Passive tense which denotes an action which is completed in the past, but the effects of which are regarded as continuing into the present without end. Nothing that happens in time could possibly intercept this act of God's redemptive genius.

See Isaiah 63:1 Who is this that comes from Edom, in crimsoned garments from Bozrah, he that is glorious in his apparel, marching in the greatness of his strength? "It is I, announcing vindication, mighty to save." Isaiah 63:2 Why is thy apparel red, and thy garments like his that treads in the wine press? Isaiah 63:3 "I have trodden the wine press alone, and from the peoples no one was with me; I trod them in my ¹face [anger] and trampled them in my ²passion; their lifeblood is sprinkled upon my garments, and I have stained all my raiment. (In my face ¹aph אף *- Brown-Driver-Briggs Hebrew dictionary [BDB] Definition: nostril, nose, face. The word, ²chêmâ'* חמא *- BDB Definition, heat; from yâcham* יחם *- BDB Definition: to be hot, conceive. Isaiah 63:4 For the year of my redemption has come. The word,* גאל *gâ'al, BDB Definition: to redeem, act as kinsman-redeemer, avenge, revenge, ransom, do the part of a kinsman; by marrying brother's widow to beget a child for him, to redeem from slavery, to redeem land. In Leviticus 25 the word "redeem" is used over a dozen times in connection with the Jubilee year. The Jubilee was a special year-long Sabbath that occurred once every forty-nine years. Prophetically pointed to the Sabbath substance in the "tetelestai" finished work of Jesus on the cross.)*

Revelation 19:16 And a Name is written on his robe and thigh, King of kings and Lord of lords. *(According to Vincent, The writing across the breast from shoulder to shoulder reminds of the cross where the Lamb's victory was secured. The historian, Herodotus [440BC] describes a figure of a Pharaoh, Sesostris, bearing across the breast from shoulder to shoulder the inscription written in the sacred character of Egypt: "With my own shoulders I conquered this land" [ii., 106])*

Revelation 3:11 Do not let tough times make me seem distant from you. I am at hand - see my nearness, not my absence. And don't let temporal setbacks diminish your own authority either. Remember that you call the shots; you wear the crown. My crown endorses your crown. *[Revelation 1:5.]*

Revelation 3:12, And I will engrave upon the individual the name of my God, also the name of the city *[the bride.]* **of my God, the new Jerusalem that descends from heaven; as well as my own new Name.** *(My Father's Name, John 5:43, I have come in my Father's Name. John 12:28 Father, glorify your Name. Abba Father.)*

Philippians 2:8 And so we have the drama of the cross in context: the man Jesus Christ who is fully God, becomes fully man to the extent of willingly dying mankind's death at the hands of his own creation. He embraced the curse and shame of the lowest kind in dying a criminal's death. *(Thus, through the doorway of mankind's death, he descended into our hellish darkness. Revelation 9:1 and Ephesians 4:8-10.)*

Philippians 2:9 From this place of utter humiliation, God exalted him to the highest rank. God graced Jesus with a Name that is far above every other name.

Philippians 2:10 What his name unveils will persuade every creature of their redemption. Every knee in heaven and upon the earth and under the earth shall bow in spontaneous worship. *(See Isaiah 45:23 "My own life is the guarantee of my conviction, says the Lord, every knee shall freely bow to me in worship, and every tongue shall spontaneously speak from the same God-inspired source.")*

Philippians 2:11 Also every tongue will voice and resonate the same devotion to his unquestionable Lordship as the Redeemer of life. Jesus Christ has glorified God as the Father of creation. This is the ultimate conclusion of the Father's [1]intent. *(The word [1]doxa, intent, opinion, often translated, glory. Revelation 5:13 And I heard every creature in heaven and on earth and under the earth and in the sea, and all therein, saying, "To him who sits upon the throne and to the Lamb be blessing and honor and glory and might forever and ever." Also my commentary note on Romans 14:11. Paul, here quotes Isaiah 45:23 See verse 20,22,& 23 "Face me and **be** saved all the ends of the earth. [Note, '**Be saved**.' Not 'become saved.'] I am God; your idols are figments of your invention and imagination." Isaiah 45:23 "I have sworn by myself; the word of my mouth has begotten righteousness; this cannot be reversed." (The Hebrew word, יצא **Yatsa** can be translated, begotten like in Judges 8:30) "Every knee shall bow to me and every tongue shall echo my oath." (Thus, speak with the same certainty sourced in me. The Hebrew word, שבע **Shaba** means to seven oneself, that is, swear - thus in the Hebrew mind, by repeating a declaration seven times one brings an end to all dispute. See Hebrews 6:13.16,17.)*

THE SHEPHERD KING - REV 19

The Shepherd-King of the Nations

Revelation 19:15 And from his mouth proceeds a sharp sword - the words of his utterance cut to the core of the heart of the nations and he shall shepherd them with an iron scepter. And on his own he will tread out the winepress of the intensity of the passion of the sovereign God of the universe. *(See my commentary notes at the end of Revelation 2 with reference to Psalm 2:7,8,9 on the **Rod of Iron**.)*

Revelation 2:27 You will ¹shepherd the nations with a royal scepter and shatter ²their 'alienated mindsets' like a potter's vessel of clay. *(He quotes Psalm 2:9, "You shall break them with a rod of iron, and dash them in pieces like a potter's vessel." Sadly the Hebrew Masoretic Text uses the word* רעע *RAA - to be bad, be evil; to be displeasing; to be injurious; to be wicked; to do an injury or hurt; to be mischief; instead of the same sounding word,* רעה *RA'AH with a **Hay** at the end and not an **Ayin**, which means **to shepherd**. Also in the Septuagint, the Greek word* ποιμανεῖς ¹*poimaneis is used. You shall feed them as a shepherd nurtures his flock. With reference to the ²alienated mindsets that ruled the nations see Numbers 24:17, "A scepter shall rise out of Israel; it shall crush the forehead of Moab." (mindset.) The shepherd's staff was never intended to beat up the sheep but to protect and free them from any possible threat.)*

Revelation 11:15, When the seventh celestial messenger sounded his trumpet, there was a massive crescendo of voices in the heavenly realm, saying, "The kingdom of the ¹cosmos has become the kingdom of our Lord and of his Christ, and he will reign as king for all the ages of the ages." *(Remember Revelation 10:7 In the days when the sounding of the seventh messenger's trumpet commences, the mystery of God will be fully realized in exact accordance to the Good News he announced to his servants the Prophets. Already in Revelation 7 we see the eventual outcome of what is portrayed here in Revelation 11 etc) Revelation 7:9 At this moment I saw a massive throng of people, impossible to count, standing tall and innocent everyone of them dressed in white with palm branches in their hands; they had escaped everything that could possibly define them as a non-Jewish Gentile world. In fact, every sphere of society was there - including the entire spectrum of people-groupings; tribal identities with their unique language-specific dialect preferences; they were all present there facing the throne and the Lamb as the people of the planet. (Amazing how, in the previous verses the tribes of Israel are associated with a very specific "number" when it comes to the prophetic detail of the entire Jewish nation as a prophetic voice of God's intention in Abraham to release the blessing of the single SEED of God's faith and bless all the nations of the earth. Count the stars, count the sand... The Preposition **ek**, points to source or origin; mankind was delivered out of their national, geographical and historical identities. The palm branches and the white robes are signs of the celebration of victory and joy. The word **stolay**, is the white outer garment worn by kings, priests, and persons of rank.*

I looked again. I saw a huge crowd, too huge to count. Everyone was there—all nations and tribes, all races and languages. And they were standing, dressed in white robes and waving palm branches, standing before the throne and the Lamb. [The Message]

*Revelation 7:10 Then I heard the masses shouting as if with one thundering voice saying, "Our salvation is secure in our God who is seated upon the throne and endorsed in the Lamb's doing." The word, ¹**kosmos** in the NT refers to the entire human family and their social structures.)*

Revelation 11:16 At that moment, the twenty four elders who were seated on their thrones face to face with God, fell down prostrate before him in adoration

Revelation 11:17 and exclaimed: Our hearts are flooded with gratitude and the affection of your favor. We salute your Lordship oh God. You are the Supreme Authority over all things; your I-am-ness defines time - present, past and future. The ¹due dynamic of your ²Royal-reign is forever established. *(The word translated due, ¹**eilepsas** from **lambano** is in the Perfect Active tense which suggests the continual effect of an action already completed in the past. The word **lambano** means to take what is one's own, one's due. Then the word **esbasileusas** from **basileuo**, to reign, is the Aorist Active tense which speaks of a completed act. Both these tenses emphasize the permanence of God's rule. There was never a time where God's royal rule was in question. Giving himself as scapegoat to be murdered by his own creatures assumes a weakness that does not compromise his authority at all. In the genius of his wisdom he defeats the entire system of judgment under the law of performance, governing the tree of the knowledge of good and evil. The seeming frailty of the slain Lamb never compromised the authority of the Lion of Judah. 1 Corinthians 1:25 It seems so foolish that God should die mankind's death on the cross; it seems so weak of God to suffer such insult; yet mankind's wisest schemes and most powerful display of genius cannot even begin to comprehend or compete with God in his weakest moment on the cross.)*

Revelation 11:18 The culmination of mankind's wrath collided with your passion oh God - this is the critical moment where judgment is met in death. *(Jesus said, "When I am lifted up on the cross, I will draw all judgment unto me.")* **This is the anticipated moment and prize of your bond-friends, the Prophets, the saints and everyone who were awed by your Name - both the insignificant and the prominent - this is the destruction of the corrupting virus in the earth.** *(In the symbolic language of the book of Revelation, the judgment of the Dragon, the Beast and the Whore; the counterfeit Trinity, is not a judgment against an entity, but against a corrupt mindset-system. A virus doesn't have a life of its own - it needs a host.*

Microbiology Professor, Vincent Racaniello writes, "Life is 'an organismic state characterized by capacity for metabolism, growth, reaction to stimuli, and reproduction.' Viruses are not living things. Viruses are complicated assemblies of molecules, including proteins, nucleic acids, lipids, and carbohydrates, but on their own they can do nothing until they enter a living cell. Without cells, viruses would not be able to multiply. Therefore, viruses are not living things."

*See my **notes on Armageddon** at the end of chapter 16.)*

THE WINE-PRESS OF THE PASSION OF GOD - REV 19

The Winepress of the Passion of God & The Great Supper

Revelation 19:15 And from his mouth proceeds a sharp sword - the words of his utterance cut to the core of the heart of the nations and he shall shepherd them with an iron scepter. And on his own he will tread out the winepress of the ¹intensity of the passion of the sovereign God of the universe. *(The words, **tou thumou tes orges tou theo**, speaks of the intensity of the passion of God, with the word **thumos**, passion, and the word often translated wrath, **orge**, meaning strong desire - as a reaching forth or excitement of the mind, from the word, **oregomai**, meaning to stretch one's self out in order to touch or to grasp something. See Hebrews 4:3 Hear the echo of God's cry through the ages, "Oh. If only they would enter into my rest." [Sadly most translations read, "I have sworn in my wrath that they will never enter into my rest." The word, wrath is derived from **orge**, meaning passionate desire, any strong outburst of emotion. The text doesn't say "they will never enter my rest." Both the Septuagint and the Hebrew text quoted here from Psalm 94:11 in the Septuagint, which is Psalm 95:11 in the Hebrew, read, "Oh that they would enter into my rest." Greek **ei** and Hebrew, אם im.])*

Revelation 2:16 I urge you to come to your senses immediately. The sword of my mouth will swiftly wage war against this type of conversation. *(Cutting to the division of soul and spirit - see Hebrews 4:12 The message God spoke to us in Christ, is the most life giving and dynamic influence in us, cutting like a surgeon's scalpel, sharper than a soldier's sword, piercing to the deepest core of human conscience, to the dividing of soul and spirit; ending the dominance of the sense realm and its neutralizing effect upon the human spirit. In this way a person's spirit is freed to become the ruling influence again in the thoughts and intentions of their heart. The scrutiny of this word detects every possible disease, discerning the body's deepest secrets where joint and bone-marrow meet. [The moment we cease from our own efforts to justify ourselves, by yielding to the integrity of the message that announces the success of the Cross, God's word is triggered into action. What God spoke to us in sonship (the incarnation), radiates his image and likeness in our redeemed innocence. [Hebrews 1:1-3] This word powerfully penetrates and impacts our whole being; body, soul and spirit.)*

Compare Revelation 14:10 - 20

Revelation 14:10 will drink the wine of God's passion, undiluted with water but intensified with spices in his cup - they shall be tested as one tests gold or silver with a ¹touchstone; with fire and brimstone in the immediate presence of the Lamb and of ²those who have discovered their wholeness mirrored in him - the dross of their deception will be exposed and cleansed. *(Note the words, **tou kekerasmenou akratou** - this is a powerful oxymoron, "the mixed unmixed." See Psalm 75:8 For in the hand of the LORD there is a cup, with foaming wine, well mixed; and he will pour a draught from it, and all the wicked of the earth shall drain it down to the dregs.*

*The word ¹**basanizō** means to test (metals) by the touchstone, which is a black siliceous stone used to test the purity of gold or silver by the color of the streak produced on it by rubbing it with either metal - a piece of fine-grained dark schist or jasper formerly used for testing alloys of gold by observing the color of the mark*

THE WINE-PRESS OF THE PASSION OF GOD - REV 19

which they made on it - thus, a standard or criterion by which something is judged or recognized. The blood of Jesus is the currency. 1 Peter 1:18,19.

The fiery brimstone - **theion** *- is divine incense, because burning brimstone was regarded as having power to purify, and to ward off disease - the ¹cup he drank on the cross is the touchstone. "What shall I say? Father, remove this cup from me? NO. For this hour I have come." The word, ²***hagios***, saints, refers to wholeness and harmony of spirit, soul and body - see 1 Corinthians 1:30 and Romans 1:7. See my* **Extended Notes on the Lake of Fire** *at the end of chapter 19.)*

Revelation 14:13 And I heard a voice from heaven saying, "Write, Blessed are they who from now on see their death in union with the Lord - his death is their death and their wearisome labor follows them into this death bringing closure to their efforts to do what his death alone accomplished.

Revelation 14:14 And I looked, and behold, I saw a white cloud and one who mirror-reflects the Son of Man with his head crowned in a golden wreath of victory, seated upon the cloud and in his hand he held a razor sharp pruning-hook.

Revelation 14:15 Another celestial messenger appeared out of the most holy place of the temple and with a loud voice addressed the one seated upon the cloud, saying, "Thrust forth your pruning hook, your hour has come - this is your moment to reap for the earth's harvest is ready." *(See John 4:31 Meanwhile his disciples were urging him to take some food. John 4:32 But he said, "I am feasting on food you cannot see." John 4:33 His disciples were baffled, "Who brought him anything to eat?" John 4:34 Jesus told them, "My food is to fulfil the desire of him who commissioned me and to leave no detail undone." John 4:35 The bread you labor for takes four months from the day you sow the seed until it ripens in the ear, doesn't it? This is not the food that I am talking about. The fruit of your own toil and performance will never satisfy permanently; from now on, look at yourselves and everyone else differently; see them through your Father's eyes and you will know that they too are ripe and ready to discover how fully included they are in my finished work. They are perfectly mirrored in me. (A harvest is ripe when the seed in the ear matches the seed that was sown. My mission is to reveal and redeem the image and likeness of God in human form.) John 4:36 This harvest reveals how both he who sows and he who reaps participate in the same joy of the life of the ages.)*

Revelation 14:16 And the one seated upon the cloud completed the earth's wheat harvest with a single sweep of his sickle. *(The gathering of the full harvest of both the wheat as well as the wine pictures the new covenant of his broken body and shed blood.)*

Revelation 14:17 And another celestial messenger appeared from the most holy place, the Tabernacle located in the heavenly realm; he too had a sharp pruning-hook-type sickle.

Revelation 14:18 Yet another messenger emerged from the altar of burnt offering this one was in charge of the fire of the altar and cried with a loud voice telling the messenger with the sharp pruning hook to thrust forth

his sickle and gather the vintage since the earth's grapes were bursting with ripeness.

Revelation 14:19 And he swung his sickle and gathered the vintage of the earth and cast it into the winepress of God's great passion. *(The word* ***thumos*** *speaks of the passion of Christ as the sacrificed Lamb.)*

Revelation 14:20 And the winepress was trodden outside the city, and the blood that flowed out of the winepress was as deep as a horses' bridle and it flooded a thousand stadia. *(See Hebrews 13:12 According to the prophetic pattern, Jesus, as the final sin sacrifice, was slain outside the city walls. The symbolic depth of a horse's bridle and 1000 Greek stadia speak of the completeness and universality of the world-wide impact of the blood covenant of Jesus. The typical Greek stadion was 600 Greek feet. [Approx 160 meters.]*

Isaiah 63:2,3 "Why is Your apparel red and your garments like one who treads in the wine press? I have trodden the wine trough alone.)

See Colossians 2:14 His body nailed to the cross hung there as the document of mankind's guilt; in dying our death he canceled the detailed handwritten record which testified against us. Every stain on our conscience, reminding of the sense of failure and guilt, was thus fully blotted out.

Colossians 2:15 In him dying mankind's death, he defused every possible claim of accusation against the human race and thus made a public spectacle of every rule and authority in God's brilliant triumph, demonstrated in him. The voice of the cross will never be silenced. *(The horror of the Cross is now the eternal trophy of God's triumph over sin. The cross stripped religion of its authority to manipulate mankind with guilt. Every accusation lost its leverage to blackmail the human race with condemnation and shame.*

"He stripped all the spiritual tyrants in the universe of their sham authority at the Cross and marched them naked through the streets." — The Message

Revelation 8:3 ...The following words are all connected to the idea of sacrifice - thusiastērion - the place of sacrifice - altar - from thusia, sacrifice, from thuo, to slay and burn the sacrifice; thumiama, the smoke or in the Greek mind, the soul of the sacrifice; thumos passion. All the Romansch languages derive their word for smoke, or smoking, fumar from thumos. Also the word perfume originates from the same idea. Much perfume was given him, thumiamata, again the sweet smelling, favorable fumes from the sacrifice is implied.

Isaiah 25:6 The LORD of hosts will prepare a lavish banquet for all peoples on this mountain; A banquet of aged wine, choice pieces with marrow, And refined, aged wine. Isaiah 25:7 And on this mountain He will swallow up the covering which is over all peoples, Even the veil which is stretched over all nations. Isaiah 25:8 He will swallow up death for all time, And the Lord GOD will wipe tears away from all faces, And He will remove the reproach of His people from all the earth; For the LORD has spoken....Holman Christian Standard Bible

THE WINE-PRESS OF THE PASSION OF GOD - REV 19

On this mountain He will destroy the burial shroud, the shroud over all the peoples, the sheet covering all the nations; International Standard Version)

Revelation 16:19 And the great city split into three portions and the cities of the nations fell and Babylon the great was remembered in the cup of God's ¹great passion and ²desire to bring everything to conclusion. *(The word ¹**thumos**, passion and ²**orge** from **oregomai**, to stretch one's self out in order to touch or to grasp something, to reach after with intense desire. The third part is a symbolic expression of a representative portion of the whole. Here, the counterfeit Trinity, represented in the Whore-City Babylon, is divided and conquered.)*

Revelation 17:4 The woman was draped in purple and scarlet fabric, festooned and sprinkled with golden glitter and ornaments; she was elaborately decorated with gold, precious stones and pearls. Holding a golden ¹cup in her hand, brimming with defiling obscenities, and the stench of her impurities. *(Again the surface, make-believe beauty and apparent splendor cannot hide her true filthy character - like the white washed tombs Jesus compared the religious system to. "Hypocrites. For you are so careful to clean the outside of the ¹cup [**poterion**] and the dish, but inside you are filthy - full of greed and self-indulgence. You are like beautifully decorated tombs on the outside, desperately trying to hide the stench of decaying corpses within." Matthew 23:25, 27. βδελυγματων ²**bdelugma** derivative of **bdeo** - to stink.*

*The Harlot represents the counterfeit ¹cup [**poterion**] of covenant to the cup of the Lord.*

1 Corinthians 10:16 The cup [ποτήριον - potērion] of blessing which we bless, is it not the communion of the blood of Christ? The bread which we break, is it not the communion of the body of Christ?

1 Corinthians 10:21 Ye cannot drink the cup [ποτήριον - potērion] of the Lord, and the cup [ποτήριον - potērion] of devils: ye cannot be partakers of the Lord's table, and of the table of devils.

1 Corinthians 11:25 After the same manner also the cup, [ποτήριον - potērion] when he had supped, saying, This cup [ποτήριον - potērion] is the new testament in my blood: this do ye, as oft as ye drink in remembrance of me.

The covenant cup of the Lord communicates the redeemed life of our design incarnate in our person and fellowship and celebrated in our every meal.)

Revelation 17:5 The words written upon her forehead, exposed her mystery identity: 'Babylon the Great, the Mother of the Whores, and the filth of the earth.' *(Roman harlots wore a label with their names on their brows - Seneca, Rhet. I. 2. 7; Juvenal VI. 122f.)*

Revelation 17:6 The woman I saw was intoxicated with the blood of the ¹saints and the blood of ²those who bore the testimony of Jesus - *[the cup she drank represented her opposition to everything that the blood of Jesus communicates.]* **This left me mesmerized, pondering what I saw, desiring to understand the context of it all.** *(She was intoxicated with the thought* that accused, sinful mankind could be reckoned blameless saints by the blood of the Lamb. Revelation 7:9,13 &14. Also Revelation 12:11 Mikael and his celestial messengers [representing the entire host of heaven - including all the multitudes previously mentioned in revelation] conquered the Dragon because of the blood of the little Lamb and the word of their testimony.)

Revelation 18:6 The Lamb's suffering dealt a double blow to the whore and Beast-system. The counterfeit cup she had mixed turned on her and proved to be her defeat. *(Give back to her as also she gave back to you, and double to her double, according to her works. In the cup which she mixed, mix to her double. LITV*

Their apparent initial victory in the brutal unjust trial and crucifixion of the Lamb turned against their tyranny in double measure - not only were they outwitted in his death, when the document of mankind's guilt in the scarred body of Jesus was nailed to the cross, whereby every possible claim against the human race was nullified, but in his resurrection God presented the receipt, documenting the justification and redeemed righteousness of the entire human race.

This reminds of what the Prophet Isaiah saw, Isaiah 40:2 Speak tenderly to Jerusalem, and cry to her that her warfare is ended, that her iniquity is pardoned, that she has received from the LORD's hand double for all her sins.

The judgment that sin has brought in its hellish torment as an inevitable consequence upon mankind is now atoned for in double proportions in the Lamb's suffering and in the reversal of the lamb's judgment brought upon all principalities and powers.)

Revelation 18:7 This is a complete reversal of her self-inflated glory and luxurious lifestyle to the exposure of her falsehood - like when metal is [1]tested with a touchstone and proves to be fool's gold - and gladness is turned into sorrow. You said in your heart, I am established as a queen and not a widow - I will not know grief. *(The word [1]torment basanismos from basanizō, to test metals by the touchstone, which is a black siliceous stone used to test the purity of gold or silver by the color of the streak produced on it by rubbing it with either metal - a piece of fine-grained dark schist or jasper formerly used for testing alloys of gold by observing the color of the mark which they made on it - thus, a standard or criterion by which something is judged or recognized. The cup Jesus drank on the cross is the touchstone. "What shall I say? Father, remove this cup from me? NO. For this hour I have come.")*

Revelation 18:8 Her calamity strikes in one day - death, sorrow and starvation - her entire dynasty is burnt to ashes in the fire of the passionate judgment of the Lord God. *(See Isaiah 47:8 Now therefore hear this, you lover of pleasures, who sit securely, who say in your heart, "I am, and there is no one besides me; I shall not sit as a widow or know the loss of children":*

Isaiah 47:9 These two things shall come to you in a moment, in one day; the loss of children and widowhood shall come upon you in full measure, in spite of your many sorceries and the great power of your enchantments. All of her "offspring" are rescued out of her sway.)

THE WINE-PRESS OF THE PASSION OF GOD - REV 19

Revelation 18:9 And the kings of the earth, the executives of the mindsets of the Beastly system, her faithful fornicating friends and clients, are weeping and wailing bitterly while the smoke of her burning rises.

Revelation 18:10 They stand completely detached from her, embarrassed by their association with her in her [1]exposed, pretentious identity, crying, Alas. Alas. The mighty city of Babylon is doomed in one hour. *(Repeat note of verse 7; The word [1]torment basanismos from basanizō, to test metals by the touchstone.)*

Revelation 18:11 Also the money-power emperors of the world who control the global trade-routes, the merchants and economists were wailing and mourning because the judgement on her caused the loss of all their clients - no one buys their cargo anymore. The touchstone currency of God has exposed the fake currency system of the world economy. [Revelation 17:15]

Revelation 18:18 They wept bitterly in lament, "Who would have thought that this great city of unequalled prominence could come to nothing."

Revelation 18:19 In their sense of hopelessness and bafflement they cast dust upon their heads as if to wrap their minds around the ultimate reduction of vibrant life to lifeless dust. Weeping and wailing in shock for the great city which has fallen. "Oh what a shame that the famous icon of prosperity who made every ship owner rich is now [1]left utterly desolate in just one hour." *(The word [1]eremos, desolate; also used of a woman neglected by her husband, from whom the husband withholds himself. The whore-city is now bereft of all her lovers.)*

Revelation 18:20 A [1]deep sense of relief in the heavens as all the saints and the Apostles and the Prophets celebrate how God caused the whore's judgment of others to be her own judgment. *(The word [1]euphrainō, to be delighted, eu plus phren - innermost being; - ἔκρινεν τὸ κρίμα ὑμῶν ἐξ αὐτῆς literally, has judged your judgment out of her - what she has judged concerning you.)*

Revelation 18:21 And a huge celestial messenger lifted a stone like a massive millstone and cast it into the sea, saying, so shall Babylon the great city be hurled into the ocean and not a single trace of her existence shall ever be found again. *(Matthew 18:6 but whoever causes one of these little ones who believe in me to sin, it would be better for him to have a great millstone fastened round his neck and to be drowned in the depth of the sea.)*

Revelation 18:24 The blood of the Prophets and the saints and every one [1]slaughtered in the scapegoat-sacrificial system of the world order were [2]vindicated in her destruction. *(The word, [1]sphazō is the verb used for the slain Lamb. The word, [2]eurisko, to find conclusive evidence by scrutiny.)*

Notes on The Great Supper of God

Revelation 19:9 And he instructed me to record this in writing: Oh the [1]blessedness of this bliss which is the supreme celebration of the union of the ages. You have individually been [2]identified by name and invited to the Lamb's supper concluding in the ultimate wedding feast. This is the Grand Finale in the ³unveiling of God's word. *(The word, ¹makarios, usually translated, blessed, suggests a special intensity of delight. It is another beatitude (**makarioi**) like that in Revelation 14:13 [fourth of the seven in the book]*

*The verb, κεκλημενοι ²**kekelemenoi** is a Perfect Passive Participle of **kaleo**, to identify by name, to surname. The Passive Participle describes a state that exists at the time coincident with that of the leading verb as a result of action completed prior to the time of the main verb, [in previous verse] **edothe** from didomi, was given [v8] which is in the Aorist Passive Indicative. The Perfect Participle endorses the fact that this is a standing invitation. See the extended notes on **ekklesia** at the end of chapter 1. The word, ³**alethinos**, from **alethes**; from the negative particle, **a** and **lanthanō**, to lie hidden; thus, that which is unveiled truth.*

This is not a wedding where you are invited simply because you're a friend of a friend of the Groom or the Bride - or a distant second cousin to a relative of a relative on someone's mother's side. No. You're the Bride.....

Matthew 26:26-29 While they were eating, Jesus took bread, and when he had given thanks, he broke it and gave it to his disciples, saying, "Take and eat; this is my body." Then he took a cup, and when he had given thanks, he gave it to them, saying, "Drink from it, all of you. This is my blood of the covenant, which is poured out for the many for the forgiveness of sins. I tell you, I will not drink from this fruit of the vine from now on until that day when I drink it new with you in my Father's kingdom."

Hosea 2:19, And I will betroth you to me forever; I will betroth you to me in righteousness and in justice, in steadfast love, and in mercy. Isaiah 54:5 For your Maker is your husband, the LORD of hosts is his name; and the Holy One of Israel is your Redeemer, the God of the whole earth he is called.

The Prostitute becomes the Bride. See Hosea 1:2, "The LORD said to Hosea, 'Go, take to yourself a wife of whoredom and have children of whoredom.'" In Hosea 3:1, after Gomer had left Hosea and was living in immorality, the Lord commanded Hosea to find her and buy her back.)

Revelation 19:17 Then I saw another celestial messenger standing in the luminous light of the sun; with a loud voice he invited all the birds of the sky to flock together for the great supper of God. *(Another symbolic reference to the Last [Final] Supper - the Lamb's flesh and blood introduce the New Covenant where every judgment is concluded and the Incarnate Word is now our feast - his flesh is bread indeed and becomes our flesh his blood is drink indeed and becomes our blood - celebrated in every meal me have. His broken body pictures the broken body of the human race - one died for all, therefore, all have died. 2 Corinthians 5:14.)*

Revelation 19:18 Come feast on the flesh of all mankind. The flesh of kings and the flesh of the high ranking captains, the flesh of the mighty men, the flesh of the horses and their riders; all flesh, slave and free, both the prominent and the least. *(This reflects on Ezekiel 39:17 As for you, son of man, thus says the Lord GOD: Speak to the birds of every sort and to all beasts of the field, 'Assemble and come, gather from all sides to the sacrificial feast which I am*

THE WINE-PRESS OF THE PASSION OF GOD - REV 19

preparing for you, a great sacrificial feast upon the mountains of Israel, and you shall eat flesh and drink blood. Ezekiel 39:20 And you shall be filled at my table with horses and riders, with mighty men and all kinds of warriors,' says the Lord GOD. Ezekiel 39:21 "And I will set my glory among the nations; and all the nations shall see my judgment which I have executed, and my hand which I have laid on them.)

Revelation 6:15 And the kingdoms of the earth and their great and most influential people in high standing in society, also the highest ranked military commanders, along with the wealthiest business personalities, the high and mighty, everyone from the lowest ranked slave to the freeborn were suddenly on equal terms and facing the same predicament. They all ran for cover into the dens and caves,

Revelation 6:16 pleading with the mountains and the hills to cover and protect them. "Hide us from the face of the One seated upon the throne and from the ¹reach of the Lamb." *(The word, ¹orge, means excitement of mind, from the word, orgeomai, meaning to stretch one's self out in order to touch or to grasp something, to reach after or desire something. See Hebrews 4:3, Hear the echo of God's cry through the ages, "Oh. If only they would enter into my rest." (Some translations read, "As I have sworn in my wrath" derived from orge, meaning passionate desire, any strong outburst of emotion. "Oh. If only they would enter into my rest.") Just like Adam and Eve who went into hiding to escape their perceptions of Papa's judgment.*

Psalm 139:7 Where shall I go from Your Spirit? Or where shall I flee from Your face? Psalm 139:8 If I go up to heaven, You; if I make my bed Sheol, behold, You.

Hosea 10:8 Also, the high places of Aven, the sin of Israel, shall be destroyed. The thorn and the thistle shall come up on their altars. [Their sacrificial system has failed them.] And they shall say to the mountains, Cover us. And to the hills, Fall on us.)

Revelation 6:17 For the great day of his ¹passion ²has already arrived and who would have imagined it would be possible for anyone ³to have been restored and positioned in a place of innocence? *(The word orgay to desire [as a reaching forth or excitement of the mind], that is, [by analogy] passion and only by implication often translated punishment: - anger, indignation, vengeance, wrath. The word ²elthen, Aorist Active Indicative of erchomai, to come. The word ³stathenai is the Aorist Passive Infinitive tense of histēmi, [this tense, is not not referring to a future event; it presents the action expressed by the verb as a completed unit with a beginning and end], to stand, also to be placed in a balance, to weigh; in the presence of others, in the midst, before judges, before members of the Sanhedrin, to cause a person or a thing to keep his or its place, be kept intact [of family, a kingdom], to escape in safety, to establish a thing, cause it to stand, to uphold or sustain the authority or force of anything, to set or place in a balance, to weigh: money to one [because in very early times before the introduction of coinage, the metals used to be weighed] continue safe and sound, stand unharmed, of quality, one who does not hesitate, does not waiver.)*

John 2:3 When Mary learned that they had run out of wine, she informed Jesus.

John 2:4 He responded with, "Well Ma'am, that's their problem - or do you want me to steal the show here at somebody else's wedding, when my hour of fulfilling my mission has not yet come? *(Religion has run out of wine – Jesus lived aware of his mission which was to redeem and restore the joyous celebration of the union and Romance of the ages – marrying mankind and divinity. While he is the true joy and wine of the party, he fully understood what it would cost him to drink the cup of mankind's injustice and violence on the cross. See John 12:27 "Now my soul is troubled. And what shall I say? 'Father, save me from this hour'? No, for this purpose I have come to this hour.)*

1 Corinthians 11:23 The night in which the Lord Jesus was betrayed, he took bread

1 Corinthians 11:24 and gave thanks; breaking the bread into portions, he said, "[1]Realize your association with my death, every time you eat, remember my body that was broken for you." *(Meaning [1]take, grasp, **lambamo**, to take what is one's own, to associate with one's self.)*

1 Corinthians 11:25 He did exactly the same with the cup after supper and said, "This cup holds the wine of the New Covenant in my blood; you celebrate me every time you drink [1]with this understanding." *(From now on our meals are meaningful. We celebrate the fact that the incarnation reveals our redemption; the promise became a person. The word, [1]αναμνησιν **ana**, upwards, and **mnesin**, remembrance - to bring something from memory into the here and now!*

He redeemed our original value, identity, and innocence; he died our death and defines the life we now live. He fulfills the theme of Scripture: the sufferings of the Messiah and the subsequent glory. [1 Peter 1:10, 11])

1 Corinthians 11:26 Your every meal makes the [1]mandate of his [2]coming relevant and communicates the meaning of the New Covenant. *(Whether you eat or drink, you are declaring your joint inclusion in his death and resurrection, confirming your redeemed innocence. Some translations read, "until I come..." The word translated until is, [1]**achri**, from **akmen**, which means extremity, conclusion, the present time; Jesus is the conclusion of prophetic time. The word [2]**erchomai**, to come is in the Aorist Subjunctive Mood, **elthe,** which is similar to the Optative expressing a wish. The Mood of the Greek verb expresses the mode in which the idea of the verb is employed. Thus, we are communicating the desire to have all people realize the meaning of the New Covenant. See 2 Peter 1:19 "For us the appearing of the Messiah is no longer a future promise but a fulfilled reality. Now it is your turn to have more than a second-hand, hearsay testimony. Take my word as one would take a lamp at night; the day is about to dawn for you in your own understanding. When the Morning Star appears, you no longer need the lamp; this will happen shortly on the horizon of your own hearts.")*

THE LAKE OF FIRE AND THE 2ND DEATH - REV 19

The Lake of Fire and the Second Death

When the imagery of the Lake of Fire is introduced, it suggests a judgment, whereby every possible trace of both the source [the counterfeit Trinity system], as well as the effect within the recipients [their distorted perceptions and mindsets], are forever consumed.

Every single person who ever dies in ignorance, indifference or unbelief, is immediately confronted with, and mirrored in the once and for all death and resurrection of Jesus. This is pictured here in the lake of burning sulphur, cleansing and purifying like in a furnace; separating the gold from the dross in the mindsets of the masses.

The Greek word for sulphur is **theion**, *from* **theios**, *godlike [neuter as noun, divinity]: - divine, godhead. Sulphur is a yellow inflammable mineral substance found in quantities on the shores of the Dead Sea. This was also known as divine incense, because burning brimstone was regarded as having power to purify, and to ward off disease. Its medicinal values are well known even today.*

All the symbolic pictures of fire, referenced in the book of Revelation, come from the same source, the brazen altar, the prophetic picture of the cross.

THE SECOND DEATH

Revelation 2:11 Now, listen up with your inner ears. Hear with understanding what the Spirit is saying to the ekklesia: the individual who [1]continues to see their triumph mirrored in mine [*their co-seatedness with me in the throne room*]**, is [2]most certainly not threatened by any [3]contradiction to their true likeness; there is nothing to fear [4]in the second death.** (*The word* [1]***nikoon****, is the Present Active Participle Nominative, form of the verb* ***nikao****, to emphasize a continual or habitual victory. Then the double negative,* οὐ μὴ ἀδικηθῃ [2]***ou mey****, plus the verb,* [3]***adikeō****, meaning unrighteous; out of sync with likeness - with* **a**, *negative and* **dikeo**, *two parties sharing likeness -* **adikeythey** *is the Aorist Subjunctive form, meaning a definite outcome that will happen as a result of another stated action. The Preposition,* ἐκ [[4]***ek***, *mostly pointing to source, but here used for the agent or instrument*] τοῦ θανάτου τοῦ δευτέρου *the second death.*

So, in context of the previous verse [Revelation 2:10], "You have no need to fear anything you might suffer at any time", the Second Death is not to distract from the once and for all death that Jesus died, but to endorse it. In the lake of fire, Death and Hades are eradicated from memory.

The **First Death** *is the once and for all death that Jesus died, representing the global death of humankind. Jesus' death took mankind's death in Adam, out of the equation.*

The idea of the **Second Death** *has to do with the fact that the revelation of the full extent of everyone's inclusion in the death of Jesus, has not yet dawned on some - so it will take a crisis, even their own death, to immediately engage them with the symbolic cleansing [from their doubts, ignorance and unbelief] represented by the lake of burning sulphur, purifying like in a furnace, separating the gold from the dross-mindsets.*

This is the ultimate awakening to the success of the cross - the realizing that even Death and Hades itself died in Jesus' death. It is indeed the death of Death.

Revelation 20:14. But here, specifically in Smyrna's case, the intensity of their persecution is neutralized by their realizing that gold is never threatened by fire.

Remember the One talking is he who said, I am the Living One; I died and now, see, here I am alive unto the ages of the ages and I have the keys wherewith I have disengaged the gates of Hades and death. Revelation 1:18. Also Hebrews 9:25-28.

As representative of the human race, Jesus Christ fulfilled mankind's destiny with death and judgment. *[1 Corinthians 15:3-5, Romans 4:25, Acts 17:30, 31.] Note: Jesus did not come to condemn the world. The Father judges no one for he has handed over all judgment to the Son, who judged the world in righteousness.)*

John 12:31 Now is the judgment of this world; this is the moment where the ruler of the world-system is conclusively cast out.

John 12:32 When I am lifted up from the earth, I will draw all of mankind and every definition of judgment unto me. *(He would be lifted up on a cross, descend into the depths of our hell, then, according to the prophetic word in Hosea 6:2, after two days, the entire human race he represents, will be co-quickened and on the third day, be co-raised, out of the lowest parts of the earth and elevated to the highest heavens. Ephesians 4:8,9; see also Ephesians 2:5,6 and Colossians 3:1-3. 'All' includes all of mankind and every definition of judgment. The subject of the sentence, as from the previous verse, is the judgment of the world - thus the primary thought here is that in his death, Jesus would draw all judgment upon himself. John 3:14; John 8:28; Acts 2:33. 1 John 3:5 We have witnessed with our own eyes how, in the unveiling of the prophetic word, when he was lifted up upon the cross as the Lamb of God, he lifted up our sin and broke its dominion and rule over us. John 1:29 "Behold, the Lamb of God, who takes away [**airo**] the sin of the world. The word **airo** means to lift up.")*

John 12:33 This he said to point to the way in which he would die.

Revelation 20:14 Then Death and Hades were cast into the lake of fire. This is the second death.

He thus broke the spell of the supposed claim of judgment and death over the Adamic race. The significance of the implications of Jesus' death cannot be exaggerated. It reaches into the entire past, present and future of human history.

Hebrews 2:15 As a fellow human, he re-defined death and delivered them from the lifelong dread of death. *(He brought final closure to the idea of judgment, which is what the system of works is all about. Hebrews 9:27,28. Evil is not immortal, love is.)*

1 John 4:17 So now, with us awakening to [1]our full inclusion in this love union, everything is perfect. Its completeness is not compromised in contradiction. Our [2]confident conversation [3]echoes this fellowship even in the face of [4]crisis; because, as he is, so are we in this world - our lives are mirrored in him. We are as blameless in this life as Jesus is. This perfect love union is the source of our confidence whenever we [5]face the scrutiny of contradiction. *(This place of seamless union is the perfection of Agape - **en toutoo teteleotai he agape meth'hemoon**; notice, the word [1]**meth'hemoon**, together with us; from **meta**, together with and **hemoon**, us; to be included in the same togetherness. The word [2]**parresia**, from **para**, a Preposition indicating close proximity, and **rheo**, to pour forth; to flow freely, suggesting unreservedness*

THE LAKE OF FIRE AND THE 2ND DEATH - REV 19

in speech; bold utterance, confidence. The word, ³echo, to hold, like sound is held in an echo; to resonate. The word ⁴krisis is often translated, judgment. So, the ⁵day of judgment, "in the face of crisis", can be translated, "facing the scrutiny of contradiction in our daily lives.")

1 John 4:18 Fear cannot co-exist in this love realm. The perfect love union that we are talking about expels fear. Fear holds on to an expectation of crisis and judgment *[which brings separation]* **and interprets it as due punishment** *[a form of karma.]* **It echoes torment and only registers in someone who does not yet realize the completeness of their love union** *[with the Father, Son and Spirit and with one another.]*

1 John 4:19 We love because he loved us first. *(We did not invent this fellowship; we are invited into the fellowship of the Father and the Son.)*

1 Corinthians 15:54 What was spoken in Isaiah 25:8 is finally realized even in our physical death: "Death is swallowed up in victory."

1 Corinthians 15:55 Oh death where is your sting? Oh grave, where is your victory?

1 Corinthians 15:56 The sting of death is sin; the strength of sin is the law. *(It was sin that made death so frightening and law-code guilt that gave sin its leverage. Msg)*

1 Corinthians 15:57 Your victory is not a maybe; because of the magnanimous doing of Jesus Christ, it is a given. *(But now in a single victorious stroke of Life, all three—sin, guilt, death—are gone, the gift of our Master, Jesus Christ. Thank God. — The Message)*

A PURIFYING CONVERSATION

The picture of a lake ablaze with sulphur, portrays a persuasion in **conversation** where the success of the cross in disarming principalities and powers, is endorsed. "Was our hearts not set ablaze while he spoke to us?"

This sulphur lake represents the environment of a faith fellowship in the authority of light, where the reign of Agape dissolves the dominion of darkness in people's minds. This is the picture Jesus painted in Matthew 16 when he spoke about his ekklesia, founded in the discovery that the son of man is indeed the Son of God and in this understanding of mankind's sonship, the Gates of Hades would be disengaged and imprisoned mankind be set free. Jesus builds his *ekklesia [from ek, origin and kaleo, to surname; original identity]* and the gates of **Hades** will not prevail against you. *[The word, **Hades**, from the negative particle, **ha**, and **eido** to see]* The blindfold mode of the human race will not prevail against the revelation of the Son of man as the offspring of God - this is the triumph of the ekklesia. "Did not our hearts burn within us while he talked to us on the road, while he opened to us the Scriptures?" Luke 24:32.

1 Thessalonians 4:18 The fact that we are all deeply connected in the same source of our 'beingness' causes us to be constantly engaged in this conversation with one another. *(Within this conversation, every possible* *definition of Sin, Judgment, Death, Hades, Satan, Devil, Demon, Dragon, Beast and False Prophet-Prostitute is addressed and dissolved and thus rendered irrelevant.)*

Revelation 17:14 These join forces in that hour to wage war against the Lamb, but the Lamb defeats them since he is the Lord of lords and the King of kings. And, sharing with him in his victory, are his kindred, recognizing their origin in this conversation; they too are now of the same persuasion.

The Lamb led them into freedom from their lost identity, and their doubts.

Colossians 1:13 He rescued us from the dominion of darkness *(the sense-ruled world, dominated by the law of performance)* **and relocated us into the kingdom where the love of his Son rules.**

John 3:22 From there Jesus and his followers went to the region of Judea and spent some ¹bonding-time together - ²immersed in conversation. *(The word ¹**diatribo** carries the idea of a road well traveled; tarrying together - the text says and there he baptized - yet in chapter 4:2 John comments that Jesus himself did not baptize anyone. The word ²**baptitso** means to immerse; for what it is worth, I thought to reflect on the bonding and cleansing that takes place in conversation, "You are already made clean by the word which I have spoken to you." John 15:3. I'm not disputing the fact that water baptism as a cleansing ritual is the context here; but Jesus' baptism shifts the emphasis from the prophetic water symbol to a baptism into words and spirit thoughts. He knows and communicates that his baptism into mankind's death, as the Lamb of God, is what John's prophetic baptism pointed to in the first place.)*

John 3:25 Some of the disciples of John were arguing with a Jew, who was probably baptized by the disciples of Jesus. They debated about the meaning of these purifying rituals - comparing notes as to which baptism would be the most significant between Jesus and John's. *(See Hebrews 6:2*

All the Jewish teachings about ceremonial washings *[baptisms]*, the laying on of hands *(in order to identify with the slain animal as sacrifice)*, and all teachings pertaining to a sin consciousness, including the final resurrection of the dead in order to face judgment, are no longer relevant. *(All of these types and shadows were concluded and fulfilled in Christ, their living substance. His resurrection bears testimony to the judgment that he faced on mankind's behalf and the freedom from an obstructive consciousness of sin that he now proclaims. [Romans 4:25; Acts 17:31; John 12:31-33] Jesus said, "and when I am lifted up on the cross, I will draw all judgment unto me." [Hebrews 9:28])*

John 3:26 They anxiously informed John that the one who was with him beyond the Jordan, whose life and mission he endorsed and bore witness to, is now attracting everyone to him - his baptism could put them out of business.

John 3:27 To which John responded, well, he obviously has heaven's backing, so let's not be jealous; everything we have is a gift.

Ephesians 5:26 Christ is the voice of God's language, immersed in this conversation, his love words bathe us and remove from us every stain of sin.

Ephesians 5:27 This intimate language presents the ekklesia *(his restored image and likeness)* **to himself, to his delightful approval without any distraction or**

reminder of a blemished past; no wrinkle or scar of sin's abuse remains; she stands before him in immaculate innocence. *(1 Kings 6:7)*

Remember that all the symbolic pictures of fire, referenced in the book of Revelation, come from the same source, the brazen altar, the prophetic picture of the cross - each one of the elders also had a ***phialas chrusas***, a golden fire-pan specifically designed to receive the sweet smelling frankincense which was lighted with coals from the brazen altar, where the sacrifice has just been presented in the outer court and then the sweet smelling frankincense was offered on the golden altar before the veil. Both the brazen altar as well as the altar of incense were made of acacia wood; *[shittim wood]* the brazen altar was overlaid with brass and the incense altar with pure gold. The Acacia tree derives its name from its scourging thorns - שטה *shittah*, from שטט *shôṭêṭ*, to pierce; to flog; a goad: - scourge. The symbolic use of the acacia wood in the building of these altars presents us with powerful imagery of the crucifixion. Exodus 27:1-5; Exodus 30:1.

Revelation 8:5 Then the celestial messenger took the golden censer for frankincense and filled it with burning coals from the altar and cast it upon the earth. And the burning coals became thunder and voices and lightning shaking the earth like an earthquake. *(The altar is central in the vision of the Lamb that was slain - the triumph of the cross is unveiled, in redeeming mankind's innocence. "Having accomplished purification of sins, he sat down ..." His throne is proof of mankind's redeemed innocence. Hebrews 1:3.*

This reminds of Isaiah 6:6 Then flew one of the Seraphim to me, having in his hand a burning coal which he had taken with tongs from the altar. Isaiah 6:7 And he touched my mouth, and said: "Behold, this has touched your lips; **your guilt is taken away, and your sin forgiven."** *Zechariah 3:9 For behold, upon the stone which I have set before Joshua, upon a single stone with seven facets [eyes], I will engrave its inscription, says the LORD of hosts, I will remove the guilt of the earth in a single day. Isaiah 66:8 Who has heard such a thing? Who has seen such things? Shall a land be born in one day? Shall a nation be brought forth in one moment? Hosea 6:2 After two days he will revive us; on the third day he will raise us up, that we may live before him. Acts 17:31, Romans 4:25, 1 Peter 1:3, Ephesians 2:5,6.*

In Zechariah chapter 3 Jesus/Joshua is vividly portrayed as the High Priest on trial and condemned by the Accuser. Representing Jerusalem, the Bride, he is plucked out of the fire and every Satanic accusation is silenced. The guilt of the earth is removed in a single day. The filthy garments are stripped off him and he is clothed from head to toe in Royal robes. Revelation 5:5,6 I saw a little Lamb, alive and standing even though it seemed to have been violently butchered in sacrifice. It had seven horns and seven eyes, which are the seven Spirits of God, sent out to accomplish his bidding in all the earth.

In the following scenes where the seven trumpets are sounded, every known sphere of the universe is pictured: The **earth** *with its green trees and fields of grass; then the* **ocean,** *both with its hidden life within, as well as the trade ships upon the seas. Then the burning star descending from* **heaven** *upon the rivers and their sources - from where their waters gush forth - [waters gushing from innermost being.] Then the sun moon and stars in the heavenly sphere are struck and darkness ensues upon the*

THE LAKE OF FIRE AND THE 2ND DEATH - REV 19

*earth. Every external source of light is taken away in order to usher in the new day dawning within. Revelation 21:23 "The city doesn't need any sun or moon to give it light because the glory of God gave it light. The Lamb was its lamp." Even the smoke rising from the **bottomless pit** [the symbolic "under-world"] clearly reveals that the fire from the altar had its effect there. The Lamb descended into the lowest parts of the earth when he set the captives free and led them as his trophies in his triumphant procession on high. Ephesians 4:8-10. The entire known world is addressed in the slain and risen Lamb. The old things have passed away, behold **everything** has become new. An earthquake takes place because of fault lines - a great shifting is taking place along the fault-lines of people's thinking. Isaiah 55:9,10,11)*

In the imagery that follows, John sees how the Triune religious counterfeit system, the Dragon, the Beast and the False Prophet are thoroughly stripped of their influence and dominion and brought to nought.

Revelation 18:21 And a huge celestial messenger lifted what seemed like a massive millstone and cast it into the sea, saying, so shall Babylon the great Prostitute-City, be hurled into the ocean and not a single trace of her existence shall ever be found again. *(See Matthew 18:6-9, But whoever causes one of these little ones who believe in me to stumble, it would be better for him to have a great millstone fastened round his neck and to be drowned in the depth of the sea. The context is clearly about the offense and judgment that the legalistic mindset brings - if your hand, foot or eye offends you [causes you to stumble], cut it off and pluck it out in order to escape **burning in Gehenna**. This was obviously a familiar comparison to judgment. Jesus graphically and almost sarcastically points to the inability of the law of works to save us from judgment. The hand, foot or eye are not the culprits; the mindset is. Note also that here, the depths of the sea is used on par with the fires of Gehenna - the idea was to emphasize a judgment that will ultimately, in the full comprehension of the human race, of the death and resurrection of Jesus Christ and their co-inclusion in it, as well as their awakening to their joint-seatedness in the throne of God, bring a final end to the threat and existence of evil.*

*The garbage heap outside Jerusalem, commonly related to hell. **Gehenna**, is the Latin word; **Geenas** is the Greek word used for the Hebrew "**Valley of Hinnom**," גיא בן הינום which is modern day **Wadi er-Rababi**. A fiery place for the disposal of waste matter from the city of Jerusalem. The "Valley of Hinnom" lies outside of ancient Jerusalem.)*

Revelation 19:20 And the Beast and the miracle working Puppet Partner, the False Prophet were arrested and cast into the lake ablaze with ¹sulphur. These two were the ones, empowered by the Dragon to amaze and deceive those who were tattooed in their heads and hands with the character of the Beast and paying religious homage to its image. *(The word ¹theion, sulphur, from **theios**, godlike (neuter as noun, divinity): - divine, godhead. sulphur is a yellow inflammable mineral substance found in quantities on the shores of the Dead Sea. This was also known as divine incense, because burning brimstone was regarded as having power to purify, and to ward off disease. Its medicinal values are well known even today.)*

Revelation 13:11 Then I saw another wild animal; this one emerged out of the earth - it had two horns and resembled a young lamb; yet it had a Dragon's voice. *(The counterfeit "Trinity" emerges - the one mirroring the other -*

THE LAKE OF FIRE AND THE 2ND DEATH - REV 19

1/ the Dragon-Accuser; 2/ the seven-headed sea-monster of religion with its leading role player, the head that was slain but became alive again; 3/ and now, here, the Dragon clothed in a lamb's-disguise; later called, the False Prophet.)

Revelation 14:8 And a second celestial messenger followed with more good news. Babylon the great city has crashed. She who sold herself as a prostitute to all the nations and intoxicated them with the wine of her passion will never fly again. *(The language is an echo of Isaiah 21:9, "Babylon has fallen. It has fallen. All the idols they worship lie shattered on the ground." Jeremiah 51:8 Babylon will suddenly fall and be shattered. See Notes on Babylon at the end of chapter 17.)*

Revelation 14:9 Then a third celestial messenger followed and announced with a loud voice saying that whoever worships the counterfeit lamb and its image and receives its character in their thoughts and deeds,

Revelation 14:10 will drink the wine of God's passion, undiluted with water but intensified with spices in his cup - they shall be tested as one tests gold or silver with a ¹touchstone; with fire and brimstone in the immediate presence of the Lamb and of ²those who have discovered their wholeness mirrored in him - the dross of their deception will be exposed and cleansed. *(Note the words, **tou kekerasmenou akratou** - this is a powerful oxymoron, "the mixed unmixed." See Psalm 75:8 For in the hand of the LORD there is a cup, with foaming wine, well mixed; and he will pour a draught from it, and all the wicked of the earth shall drain it down to the dregs.*

*The word ¹**basanizō** means to test (metals) by the touchstone, which is a black siliceous stone used to test the purity of gold or silver by the color of the streak produced on it by rubbing it with either metal - a piece of fine-grained dark schist or jasper formerly used for testing alloys of gold by observing the color of the mark which they made on it - thus, a standard or criterion by which something is judged or recognized. The blood of Jesus is the currency. 1 Peter 1:18,19.*

*The fiery brimstone - **theion** - is divine incense, because burning brimstone was regarded as having power to purify, and to ward off disease - the ¹cup he drank on the cross is the touchstone. "What shall I say? Father, remove this cup from me? NO. For this hour I have come." The word, ²**hagios**, saints, refers to wholeness and harmony of spirit, soul and body - see 1 Corinthians 1:30 and Romans 1:7.)*

Revelation 14:11 Those worshipping the counterfeit Beast and its image, receiving its mark and name as their identity, will have nowhere to hide day or night; the smoke that rises from their ¹testing, will evidence their cleansing for all ages. *(The mindset of a counterfeit religious system has no future. The message of the cross is the ¹touchstone that will forever bear testimony to the triumph of the Lamb.)*

Revelation 20:8 And his obvious strategy would be to deceive the nations on a global scale including the four corners of the earth by assembling Gog and Magog in war; their number is as the sand of the sea. *(Again, every traditional Jewish concept of judgment is addressed. Gog and Magog is now brought into the conversation, since Jewish eschatology viewed Gog and Magog as enemies to be defeated by the Messiah, which will usher in the age of the Messiah. "Then Eldad and Modad [brothers of Moses] both prophesied together, and said, 'In the very end of time Gog and*

THE LAKE OF FIRE AND THE 2ND DEATH - REV 19

Magog and their army shall come up against Jerusalem, and they shall fall by the hand of the King Messiah; they shall be slain by the flame of fire which shall proceed from under the throne of glory, and afterwards all the dead of Israel shall rise again to life, and shall enjoy the delights prepared for them from the beginning." Quote from the Jewish Targum. See reference in Numbers 11:26 and Ezekiel 38:17.There are numeral references to the same "once and for all war" in the heavens. It is however the same hour; the same event. Revelation 12:7; Revelation 16:13,14; Revelation 17:13,14; Revelation 19:19.

See Extended Notes on Israel at the end of Revelation 20.)

Revelation 20:9 They will spread across the earth and attempt to neutralize the "Queen Bee Bride" of the Lamb by surrounding and besieging God's saints in the beloved city. Then fire will pour out of heaven and consume them. *(Again, the mindsets of Satanic accusation and judgments are made a meal of - yet another reference to the great supper-feast celebrating the new covenant and the conclusion of the old. The fire from the altar of the slain Lamb of God consumes every definition of Israel's and indeed, mankind's perceived enemies.)*

Revelation 20:10 The Devil, who led them astray will be hurled into the lake of fire and brimstone where his puppet partners, the Beast and the False Prophet have already been confined to. Day and Night they will be the subject of God's touchstone for the ages of the ages - the very atmosphere of the entire universe will be thoroughly fumigated from any evidence of Satanas.

Revelation 20:11 And I saw a huge white throne and it was as if heaven and earth fled away from the presence of the One seated upon the throne and its place was never found again. *(This means that there is no accusation in the heavens or upon the earth that could possibly stand in the presence of the Lamb, the One seated upon the throne of the judgment of righteousness – his throne gives testimony to mankind's redeemed acquittal. See Hebrews 1:3 "Having made purification for sins he sat down." There exists no evidence that could be brought from any sphere or dimension that could possibly testify against the human race - Acts 17 The God of creation has overlooked the times of ignorance and now urgently persuades all of mankind everywhere to awaken in their understanding to the fact of their innocence – he appointed a day and a person and on that day and in that person God would judge he world in righteousness and of this he has given proof by raising Jesus from the dead. The resurrected Jesus is the official receipt and verdict confirming mankind's redeemed innocence. Romans 4:25. Revelation 20:4; also Matthew 19:28 Jesus said to them, "Truly, I say to you, in the [1]rebooting of mankind, when the Son of man shall sit on his glorious throne, you who have followed me will also sit on twelve thrones, judging the twelve tribes of Israel. See the word, [1]paliggenesia, suggests a complete restoration to the original, in modern terms, rebooted. From palin, again by repetition and genesis, source. Only used here and in Titus 3:5 Salvation is not a reward for good behavior. It has absolutely nothing to do with anything that we have done. God's mercy saved us. The Holy Spirit endorses in us what happened to us when Jesus Christ died and was raised. When we heard the glad announcement of salvation it was like taking a deep warm bath. Our minds were [1]thoroughly cleansed and re-booted into [2]newness of life. (The word [1]paliggenesia suggests a complete restoration to the original, in modern terms, rebooted. The word [2]anakainosis, from ana, upward, and kainosis, newness,*

THE LAKE OF FIRE AND THE 2ND DEATH - REV 19

speaks of a fresh upward focus; a re-engaging with heavenly thoughts. See Colossians 3:1-3; also 1 Thessalonians 1:5. We realized that we were indeed co-included, co-crucified, and co-raised and are now co-seated together with Christ in heavenly places. [See 2 Corinthians 5:14-21; Hosea 6:2; Ephesians 2:5, 6; and 1 Peter 1:3])

Revelation 20:12 And I saw everyone who ever died, small and great, standing before God. And the books were opened. And another book was opened. The Book of Life. The first volume of books represented mankind's judgment based on their own works, versus the Book of Life which celebrates the triumph of the Lamb. *(Revelation 3:5 Everyone who sees their victory in me will I clothe in white garments - and they will realize that I am not in the business of fulfilling their law and performance based fears by blotting out their names from the Book of Life. Instead I am the one who endorses their identity face to face before my Father and his celestial messengers. [This language is taken from the custom of registering the names of persons in a list, roll, or catalogue. In Jewish tradition there was a prevailing fear that your name might be blotted out of the Book of Life if your behavior did not please God. See **Extended Notes on the Lamb's Book of Life** at the end of Chapter 17.)*

Revelation 20:13 Every domain where the dead was held, yielded them up to be judged according to his work. Everyone was there; the sea yielded up its dead and Death and Hades yielded up their dead.

Revelation 20:14 Then Death and Hades were cast into the lake of fire. This is the second death.

Revelation 20:15 And [1]everything that was not written in the Book of Life was poured into the lake of fire. *(The Greek, εἴ τις οὐχ εὑρέθη ἐν τῇ βίβλῳ τῆς ζωῆς γεγραμμένος - with, **ei tis**, meaning everything or everyone - but, what is cast into the symbolic lake ablaze with brimstone is not a person but a mindset. A distorted perception of identity.*

The authentic ID of human life is defined in the Book of Life - or the Tree of Life, representing the redeemed life of our design, versus the alternative Tree of the knowledge of good and evil, representing mankind's identity under scrutiny and questioning. The "I am not-Tree" heads up the System of a Works and Performance Based Philosophy. To have your name written in the Book of Life simply suggests that you discover your identity there in the Zoe-life redeemed by the Lamb. You may have only known yourself according to the flesh, as Simon, the son of Jonah, while you really are Petros. Mr. Rock, you are a chip off the old Block. Every evidence of an inferior identity will be cast into the lake of sulphur burning away the dross to reveal the gold. Any idea of an identity outside of the Book of Life, is dissolved. The Lamb's Book of Life and not the law of personal performance, defines us.

*See **Extended Notes on the Lamb's Book of Life** at the end of Chapter 17.*

Also my Extended Commentary Notes at the end of the Mirror- Thoughts on Judgment and Resurrection.)

It is almost unspeakable that of all the themes God could choose from to celebrate the central authority of the throne Room, he chose the Lamb. Our redeemed innocence is the theme of the throne of heaven, forever.

THE LAKE OF FIRE AND THE 2ND DEATH - REV 19

Revelation 2:23 The offspring of these 'mindsets', conceived in your licentious idolatry has no future. I will cause it ¹to utterly perish. And every ekklesia shall ²know that I scrutinize the hidden thoughts of the heart. And I will expose every single work of your own doing as judged in my work. *(See verse 26 - my works vs your works. To ¹kill in death is a very strong expression,* **apokteuno en thanato***. The symbolic significance of killing the children of the ekklesia's idolatrous adultery in death can only be understood in the context of the unveiling of Jesus the Christ who already died mankind's death and in that death brought final closure to the offspring of mankind's guilt-ridden mindsets that we have inherited from our world systems which were founded in the fruit of the "I-am-not tree system". He thus broke the spell of the claim of judgment and death over the Adamic race. This signifies the death of death. The significance of the implications of Jesus' death cannot be exaggerated. It reaches into the entire past, present and future of human history. The word ²***ginosontai*** *is the future ingressive punctiliar middle of* **ginosko***, 'we shall certainly come to know', this confirms the theme of the book of Revelation. The unveiling of Jesus Christ and his finished work will most definitely complete God's purpose of redeeming mankind's lost sense of sonship, value, innocence, identity and royalty in the earth.)*

Revelation 21:8 The fear-driven and unbelieving, those having become rotten to the core; sex peddlers and sorcerers, idolaters and deceivers, their measure is the lake burning with brimstone; this is the second death.

Romans 6:11 This reasoning is equally relevant to you. ¹Calculate the cross; there can only be one logical conclusion: he died your death; that means you died to sin, and are now alive to God. Sin-consciousness can never again feature in your future. You are in Christ Jesus; his Lordship is the authority of this union. *(We are not being presumptuous to reason that we are in Christ. "¹Reckon yourselves therefore dead to sin" The word,* ¹***logitsomai***, *means to make a calculation to which there can only be one logical conclusion. [See Ephesians 1:4 1 Corinthians 1:30].*

Philippians 2:8 And so we have the drama of the cross in context: the man Jesus Christ who is fully God, becomes fully man to the extent of willingly dying mankind's death at the hands of his own creation. He embraced the curse and shame of the lowest kind in dying a criminal's death. *(Thus, through the doorway of mankind's death, he descended into our hellish darkness. Revelation 9:1 and Ephesians 4:8-10.)*

Philippians 2:9 From this place of utter humiliation, God exalted him to the highest rank. God graced Jesus with a Name that is far above every other name. *(Ephesians 1:20 Do you want to measure the mind and muscle of God? Consider the force which he unleashed in Jesus Christ when he raised him from the dead and forever seated him enthroned as his executive authority in the realm of the heavens. Jesus is God's right hand of power. He was raised up from the deepest dungeons of human despair to the highest region of heavenly bliss. [See Ephesians 2:5,6 & 4:8,9] Ephesians 1:21 Infinitely above all the combined forces of rule, authority, dominion or governments; he is ranked superior to any name that could ever be given to anyone of this age or any age still to come in the eternal future. The name of Jesus endorses his mission as fully accomplished. He is the Savior of the world. Titus 2:11 The grace of God shines as bright as day making the salvation*

THE LAKE OF FIRE AND THE 2ND DEATH - REV 19

of mankind undeniably visible. See also Ephesians 3:15, Every family in heaven and on earth originates in him; his is mankind's family name and he remains the authentic identity of every nation.)

Philippians 2:10 What his name unveils will persuade every creature of their redemption. Every knee in heaven and upon the earth and under the earth shall bow in spontaneous worship. *(See Isaiah 45:23 "My own life is the guarantee of my conviction, says the Lord, every knee shall freely bow to me in worship, and every tongue shall spontaneously speak from the same God-inspired source.")*

Philippians 2:11 Also every tongue will voice and resonate the same devotion to his unquestionable Lordship as the Redeemer of life. Jesus Christ has glorified God as the Father of creation. This is the ultimate conclusion of the Father's [1]intent. *(The word [1]doxa, intent, opinion, often translated, glory. Revelation 5:13 And I heard every creature in heaven and on earth and under the earth and in the sea, and all therein, saying, "To him who sits upon the throne and to the Lamb be blessing and honor and glory and might forever and ever." Also my commentary note on Romans 14:11. Paul, here quotes Isaiah 45:23 See verse 20,22,& 23 "Face me and be saved all the ends of the earth. [Note, 'Be saved.' Not 'become saved.'] I am God; your idols are figments of your invention and imagination." Isaiah 45:23 "I have sworn by myself; the word of my mouth has begotten righteousness; this cannot be reversed." (The Hebrew word, יצא Yatsa can be translated, begotten like in Judges 8:30) "Every knee shall bow to me and every tongue shall echo my oath." (Thus, speak with the same certainty sourced in me. The Hebrew word, שבע Shaba means to seven oneself, that is, swear - thus in the Hebrew mind, by repeating a declaration seven times one brings an end to all dispute. See Hebrews 6:13.16,17.)*

Revelation 17:8 The brutal Beast you saw is a [1]"has been" from the beginning - it indeed has no real existence - yet it seems to make "a come back" as if emerging out of the Abyss only to dissolve again into perdition. Meanwhile the minds of those blinded by their [2]earthbound perceptions continue to be mesmerized by its apparent relevance. They are the ones whose identities are not [3]based upon the Lamb's Book of Life. They do not yet see that their original identity was redeemed in the Lamb." *(The words, ἦν καὶ οὐκ ἔστι [1]en kai ouk esti, meaning, to be and not to be; with the verb en being the Imperfect Indicative of eimi, I am - another meaning of the Imperfect Indicative is to refer to unreal (counterfactual) situations in present or past time.*

This is in total contrast to the One who is I am; who always was and will continually be the accompanying One. An antithesis to "ho ēn kai ho ōn" of Revelation 1:4.)

In the symbolic language of the book of Revelation, the judgment of the Dragon, the Beast and the Whore; the counterfeit Trinity, is not a judgment against an entity, but against a corrupt mindset-system. A virus doesn't have a life of its own - it needs a host.

Microbiology Professor, Vincent Racaniello writes, "Life is 'an organismic state characterized by capacity for metabolism, growth, reaction to stimuli, and reproduction.' Viruses are not living things. Viruses are complicated assemblies of molecules, including proteins, nucleic acids, lipids, and carbohydrates, but on their own they can do nothing until they enter a living cell. Without cells, viruses would not be able to multiply. Therefore, viruses are not living things.")

See **Ephesians 6:12 People are not the enemy,** *[whether they be husbands, wives, children, or parents, slaves, or bosses. They might host hostile, law inspired thought patterns through their unbelief or ignorance but,]* **to target one another is to engage in the wrong combat. We represent the authority of the victory of Christ in the spiritual realm. We are positioned there** *[in Christ]***; we ¹confront the mind games and ²structures of darkness, religious thought patterns, governing and conditioning human behavior.** *(The word, ¹**pros**, face to face; towards. The word, ²**poneros** is often translated as evil; this word is described in Thayer's Lexicon as full of annoyances, hardships and labor, which is exactly what the DIY law-system of works produces.)*

1 Corinthians 15:24 The complete conclusion in his work of redemption is celebrated in his yielding the full harvest of his reign to God the Father, having ¹brought to nought the law of works which supported every definition of dominion under the fall, including all ²principalities, all ³authority and every ⁴dynamic influence in society. *(He brought to nought the law of works, ¹**katargeo**, from **kata**, meaning intensity, and **argos**, meaning labor; thus free from all self-effort to attempt to improve what God has already perfected in Christ. All principalities, ²**arche**, or chief ranks, i.e., kings, governors; this includes any governing system whereby one is ranked above the other on the basis of their performance or preference. All authority, ³**exousia**, comes from **ek**, denoting origin and **eimi**, I am; in this case, because of what I can do I am defined by what I can do better than you; therefore, I have authority over you. Every dynamic influence in society, ⁴**dunamis**, means power, in this case, willpower. Every government structure in society will be brought under the dominion of grace where the Christ-life rules.*

The kingdom of God is the authority of the Christ-life in ordinary, day to day life, where righteousness is based on who we are and not on who we are trying to impress. The law of works is duty and guilt driven, whereas the law of faith is love driven. [Romans 3:27, Galatians 5:6. Also 2 Corinthians 10:12 When they measure themselves by one another, competing and comparing, they are without understanding.)

It is most significant to consider Paul's reasoning when he declares, I have determined to know nothing within you, except Jesus Christ, and him crucified. **1 Corinthians 2:2 My ¹mind is fully made up about you. The only possible way in which I can truly ²know you, is in the light of God's mystery, which is ³Christ in you. Jesus died mankind's death on the cross and thus brought final closure to any other basis of ¹judgment.** *(The word, ¹**krino**, to judge, to determine, to deem in a forensic sense, here, in the Aorist tense, **ekrina**, which suggests a once and for all completed act. The Aorist tense presents an occurrence in summary, viewed as a whole from the outside, almost like a snapshot of the action.*

*Paul makes a very bold and radical statement, confining his ministry focus to "know" the full scope and consequence of the revelation of mankind's redeemed innocence as communicated in the cross of Jesus Christ. This is the essence of the mystery of God. "For I am determined to ²know [- ²**eido**, to see, to perceive] nothing in you except Jesus Christ and him crucified." Paul continues to unfold the mystery of our redeemed oneness. In the previous chapter, he concludes that we are in Christ by God's doing; here he clearly points to ³Christ in us. [As Jesus declared in John 14:20])*

2 Corinthians 3:4 Christ is proof of our persuasion about you before God.

2 Corinthians 1:18 God's certainty is our persuasion; there is no maybe in him.

2 Corinthians 1:19 The son of God, Jesus Christ, whom I, Paul, Sylvanus and Timothy boldly announced in you, is God's ultimate yes to mankind. Jesus is God's yes to You. Human life is associated in all that he is. In God's mind, there exists not even a hint of hesitation about this.

See also **2 Corinthians 5:14,16 I am convinced that if one died for all, then all have died. Therefore, from now on, I no longer know anyone from a human point of view.** *Also Galatians 1:16 and Colossians 1:27.)*

John 14:20 In that day you will know that we are in seamless union with one another. I am in my Father, you are in me and I am in you. *(The incarnation does not divide the Trinity; the incarnation celebrates the redeemed inclusion of humanity. Picture 4 circles with the one fitting into the other - The outer circle is the Father, then Jesus in the Father, then us in Jesus and the Holy Spirit in us. This spells inseparable, intimate oneness. Note that it is not our knowing that positions Jesus in the Father or us in them or the Spirit of Christ in us. Our knowing simply awakens us to the reality of our redeemed oneness. Gold does not become gold when it is discovered but it certainly becomes currency.)*

Galatians 1:16 This is the heart of the gospel that I proclaim; it began with an unveiling of his Son ¹in me, freeing me to announce the same sonship ²in the masses of non-Jewish people. I felt no immediate urgency to compare notes with those who were familiar with Christ from a mere historic point of view. *(The Greek text is quite clear: "It pleased the Father to reveal his Son in me in order that I may proclaim him in the nations." The words,* **en emoi***, translate as "in me," and* **en ethnos** *translate as in the Gentile nations, or the masses of non Jewish people. Not "among" the Gentiles as most translations have it. Later, when Barnabas is sent to investigate the conversion of the Greeks in Acts 11, instead of reporting his findings to HQ in Jerusalem, he immediately finds Paul, knowing that Paul's gospel is the revelation of the mystery of Christ in the nations [see Colossians 1:27]. No wonder then that those believers were the first to be called Christians, or Christ-like Anointed ones.)*

Jesus Christ confirms that the son of man is the son of God. "Call no man your father on earth, for you have one Father who is in heaven." [Matthew 23:9] Paul reminds the Greek philosophers in Acts 17 that we live and move and have our being in God; mankind is indeed the offspring of God. He is quoting from their own writings, Epimenedes 600 BC and Aratus, 300 BC. The incorruptible seed of sonship is as much present in every person as the seed is already in all soil, even in the desert, waiting for the rain to awaken and ignite its life.

"For as the rain and the snow come down from heaven and water the earth, making it bring forth and sprout, so shall my word be that proceeds from my mouth, it shall not disappoint my purpose, it shall saturate the soil and cause it to bring forth and sprout. Instead of the thorn the cyprus and instead of the brier the myrtle." [Isaiah 55:8-11, 13]

In Matthew 13:44, Jesus says that the kingdom of heaven is like a treasure hidden in an agricultural field. There is much more to the field than what meets the eye.

In 2 Corinthians 4:4, 7 Paul says that we have this treasure in earthen vessels. But the god of this world has blindfolded our minds through unbelief [believing a lie about ourselves, Numbers 13:33] to keep us from seeing the light of the gospel revealing the glory of God in the face of Christ who is the image of God, as in a mirror.

When Jesus speaks of the sinner he speaks of him as the lost sheep, coin, or son. [Luke 15] You cannot be lost unless you belong. The inscription and image did not disappear from the coin when it was lost. How can we praise God and with the same mouth curse a person made in his image? [James 3:9 and Luke 20:20-26] Mankind has forgotten what manner of people they are by design; we are the image and likeness bearer of our Maker; this is exactly what Jesus came to reveal and redeem.

We may now behold him with unveiled faces as in a mirror and be immediately transformed [in our understanding] into his likeness. From the glory [opinion] of the flesh to the glory [opinion] of God. Legalistic religion kept the veil in place; the proclaiming of the liberating truth of the Good News, removes the veil. The "ugly duckling" didn't need a face-lift or lessons on how to fake the swan life. It only needed to know the truth about itself to be free indeed.)

See also **2 Corinthians 13:5 I implore you to ¹examine faith for yourselves in order to test what it is that you really believe. Faith is so much more than the mere veneer of a superstitious belief in a historic Christ; faith is about realizing Jesus Christ in you, in the midst of contradiction. Just ²as ore is placed into a crucible, where the dross is separated from the gold in a furnace, come to the conclusion for yourselves of his indwelling. Should it appear to you that Christ is absent in your life, look again, you have obviously done the test wrong.** *(You cannot measure temperature with a ruler. Paul uses the word, ¹**peiratzo**, to examine closely, from **peira**, to pierce; a test to determine the hidden value of something; also from the word **peras**, which speaks of extremity or the furthest boundary. Faith is not a veneer to cover up potential depression or disappointment when faced with trying times. Note that Paul is not speaking about you putting your beliefs to the test; but you testing **the** faith for yourself. There is only one valid faith, not what we believe about God or about ourselves, but what God believes about us. Paul wants you to discover for yourselves what God believes about you. God is persuaded about Christ indwelling you, now he wants you to be equally persuaded. Then he uses the word, ²**dokimatzo**, as in the testing of metals. Self-examination has nothing to do with finding hidden sins and flaws in you; it is all about realizing Christ in you.* **The object of the furnace is not to reveal the dross, but the gold.** *Christ himself is the proof of faith, he is the substance of things hoped for, the evidence of things not seen. Hebrews 11:1. The test of truth is foolproof. See verse 8. Truth is not threatened by our scrutiny.*

See also **2 Corinthians 4:18 We are not keeping any score of what seems so obvious to the senses on the surface, it is fleeting and irrelevant; it is the unseen eternal realm within us that has our full attention and captivates our gaze. 2 Corinthians 4:7 We have discovered this treasure where it was hidden all along, in these frail skin-suits made of clay.**

1 Corinthians 1:6 You certainly have the testimony of Christ evidenced in you. *[You possess full knowledge and give full expression because in you the evidence for the truth of Christ has found confirmation. — NEB]*

THE LAKE OF FIRE AND THE 2ND DEATH - REV 19

See **1 Peter 1:7** *This will help you in those difficult times: think of your belief as something much more precious than any possible evaluation of gold; remember that fire does not destroy the metal, it reveals it. Now even gold is an inferior comparison to faith. Gold as a currency has only temporal and unpredictable value; it fluctuates as the market changes. Now, in the same way that fire reveals gold, your faith in the midst of contradiction, makes Jesus Christ visible and gives much reason to testimony ^{1}stories worth telling. This is what has permanent ^{2}value, and the price is fixed.)*

See **John 5:27 The Father has also given the son of man ^{1}authentic authority to execute judgment on mankind's behalf.** *(The word ^{1}exousia, often translated as authority has two components, ek, out of, source and eimi, I am.)*

John 5:28 Do not be alarmed by this, but the hour is coming when those in the ^{1}graves will hear his voice. *(No-one who ever lived will escape the extent of his righteous judgment. Those who have ^{1}forgotten who they are will hear his incarnate voice. The word for grave, ^{1}mnēmeion, memory, suggests a remembrance - to bring something from memory into the here and now! Like David prophecies in Psalm 22 when he sees the cross-crisis [**krisis** - judgment, means the 'decisive moment' or, turning point.] a thousand years before it happens. His conclusion in verse 27 sums up the triumph of God's resolve. "All the ends of the earth shall ^{1}remember and turn to the LORD; and all the families of the nations shall worship before him." See 1 Corinthians 15:21,22 The same mankind who died in a man was raised again in a man. In Adam all died; in Christ all are made alive.)*

John 5:29 And they will come forth out of their graves - for those who have engaged themselves with that which is beneficial, it will be a resurrection to life - and for those who have done that which is worthless, it will be a resurrection unto judgment. *(In the context of John chapter 6:28 and 29 the work that is required is not a duty to be performed but a gift to be embraced - John 6:28 They immediately wanted the recipe. Tell us then what we must do in order to accomplish God's work? John 6:29 This is the work of God; your belief in the One whom he has sent. (Even your ability to believe is God's work. Realizing your authentic sonship on exhibit in Jesus is God's gift to you and cannot be earned. How can your labor compete with what God's rest celebrates as complete.)*

*If our own good behavior could earn us salvation then there would be no point in Jesus dying our death. - This would be in conflict with the essence and crux of the gospel. It reminds of 2 Corinthians 5:10 which reads in the RSV as follows, "For we must all appear before the judgment seat of Christ, so that each one may receive good or evil, according to what he has done in the body." Now read this verse in the Mirror Bible - 2 Corinthians 5:10 For we have all been thoroughly scrutinized in the judgment of Jesus. We are taken care of and restored to the life of our design, regardless of what happened to us in our individual lives, whatever amazing or meaningless things we encountered in the body. The word, ^{1}**phaneroo**, means to render apparent, to openly declare, to manifest. Paul uses the Aorist Passive Infinitive tense **phanerothenai**, not referring to a future event. The Aorist Infinitive presents the action expressed by the verb as a completed unit with a beginning and end. The word,* **bematos***, comes from* **bayma***, means footprint, also referring to a raised place mounted by steps, or a tribunal, the official seat of a judge The word,*

THE LAKE OF FIRE AND THE 2ND DEATH - REV 19

*komitzo, comes from **kolumbos**, meaning to tend, to take care of, to provide for, to carry off from harm. Paul's reference was not about how much abuse and affliction he suffered, nor was it the many good times he remembered that defined him; "I am what I am by the grace of God." If we are still to be judged for good or bad deeds that we performed in the body, then the judgment that Jesus faced on mankind's behalf was irrelevant. Galatians 2:21 I do not set aside the grace of God, for if righteousness could be gained through the law, Christ died for nothing. NIV [See also 2 Corinthians 5:14,16. We are mirrored in his life; his life reflects ours, not as an example for us but of us. As well as 2 Corinthians 3:18 The days of window-shopping are over. Now, with unveiled faces we are gazing at the glory of the Lord as in a mirror and metaporhe happens - image and likeness awakens within us.])*

In their encounter of the risen Jesus, hidden from them at first, on their way from Jerusalem to Emmaus, their response revealed the impact of the conversation Jesus had when he pointed to himself in Scripture - in the writings of Moses and the prophets - suddenly, familiar text lit up in their hearts. "Did not our hearts ignite within us." When the "Stranger" joined them that evening around the dinner table, he took the bread and broke it, and their eyes were opened and they recognized him. Every meal celebrates the Incarnation.

In John 6:32 Jesus reminds the Jews that it wasn't Moses who gave them the bread from heaven - My Father is the one who gives the real bread from heaven. *(The manna was a prophetic pointer to the Messiah.)*

John 6:33 For the bread from God that comes down from heaven is that which gives life to the entire world. *(Mankind is designed, not to define life by the bread-harvest of their own labor, but by daily feasting on **every Word** that proceeds from God's mouth, mirrored in its most complete language, the Incarnation. The Hebrew word translated, **every**, is the word, בל **Kohl** from בלל **Kalal** which means complete - thus, the word in its most complete context, which is the Incarnation, the Word that is face to face before God from before time was, is now made flesh, radiating the invisible Father's character and image in human form, as in a mirror. The incarnation is the global language of the Planet. Paul says in 2 Corinthians 3:2,3, The living Epistle is known and read by all mankind in their mother-tongue language.)*

John 6:34 They said, Oh Lord, this is the bread we crave. Give us this bread. *See notes on John 12, verses 19-25 "Look. The entire world is running after him." He is indeed the desire of the Nations.*

John 6:35 Jesus said, I am the bread of life. He that comes face to face with me shall never hunger and he who finds his faith resting in me shall never thirst.

John 6:36 But even though you have seen me, you are not persuaded. *(You might be happy with the healings and be entertained by the signs, but still you fail to understand who I am. I'm not here to impress you with me. I'm here to persuade you about you. Your sonship is what I am all about. And the only way that I can persuade you about you is to take you with me into your death and darkness and overcome your fear and hell and birth you again into newness of life in my resurrection.)*

John 6:37 Everyone whom the Father has given me will come [1]face to face with me. And here, mirrored in me they will see that I am not the Judge. I will not cast anyone out. *(The Preposition pros is used here again as in John 1:1.)*

THE LAKE OF FIRE AND THE 2ND DEATH - REV 19

John 6:38 For I have stepped down out of heaven, not to make a name for myself. I did not come to become a mere historic hero. I have come to communicate the resolve of him who sent me. *(I am here to demonstrate to you how persuaded my Father is about you.)*

John 6:39 My Sender's desire is for me to rescue every single individual - ¹this is his gift to me - that I will lose ²no detail of mankind's original identity mirrored in me. My rescuing mission will conclude in their joint-resurrection. This is the ³completeness of time. *(This is his gift to me, ¹ho dedoke moi. The phrase, ²hina pan apoleso Exodus auto, meaning, that I should lose nothing out of it. In the eschatology/conclusion/fullness of time - ³te eschate hemera - This phrase occurs only in John - John 6:39, 6:40, 6:44, 6:54. Also John 4:23 The end of an era has arrived - the future is here. Whatever prophetic values were expressed in external devotional forms and rituals are now eclipsed in true spirit worship from within - face to face with the Father - acknowledging our genesis in him - this is his delight. The Father's desire is the worshipper more than the worship.)*

John 6:40 And this is the desire of my Father, that everyone who ¹sees the Son, through his eyes, and finds the conclusion of *(eis)* their persuasion in him, will resonate *(echo)* the life of the ages. And I will ²raise him up in the ³final day. *(Jesus speaks here of mankind's joint resurrection in his resurrection as the final day. The word ¹theōreo means to gaze attentively. See Hosea 6:2 After two days he will revive us; ²on the third day he will raise us up, that we may live before him. The word ³eschatos means extreme; last in time or in space; the uttermost part, the final conclusion. What God said about 'you-manity' in their co-resurrection in Jesus, defines eschatology. Hebrews 1:1-3; Ephesians 2:5,6. See Revelation 20:5 on **the First Resurrection**.)*

John 6:41 The religious Jews were no longer paying any attention - they were shocked and offended at the idea that he said he was the bread from heaven.

John 6:42 They reasoned that since they knew his parents to be Joseph and Mary, he had no valid claim to any heavenly Source.

John 6:43 Then Jesus addressed them saying, Your murmuring and reasoning amongst yourselves will continue to veil me from you. *(Knowing me from a human point of view will not satisfy your quest.)*

John 6:44 No one is forcing you to believe - it is the Father who sent me who draws you to see me ¹face to face - only once you've seen how in the mystery of God I mirror you, will you understand that I will co-raise you in the grand-finale of my mission. *(The word ¹pros is used again, face to face. This happened exactly as Hosea prophesied 800 BC, "After two days he would revive us. On the third day, he would raise us up.")*

John 6:45 It is written in the Prophets that every single individual will be taught of God. To hear the Father's instruction concerning me, is to come ¹face to face with me. *(The word ¹pros is used again. See Isaiah 54:13; Jeremiah 31:34 And no longer shall each man teach his neighbor and each his brother, saying, 'Know the LORD,' for they shall all know me, from the least of them to the greatest, says the LORD; for I will forgive their iniquity, and I will remember their sin no more." Micah 4:1-4)*

John 12:19 The Pharisees were perplexed about this and said, "Look, we are gaining no ground against him. The entire world is running after him."

John 12:20 There were also a number of Greeks who came to worship at the feast because of the rumors they have heard.

John 12:21 They approached Philip who was from Bethsaida in Galilee and asked him, "Sir, we would be delighted to see Jesus. Is there perhaps any chance that you could introduce us to him?" *(He had a Greek name and the Greeks may have seen Philip in Galilee where there were many Greeks)*

John 12:22 Philip went and told Andrew and the two of them told Jesus.

John 12:23 Jesus, immediately understanding the prophetic significance of the moment, knew that he, the Messiah, was who all the nations were longing for and answered, "The hour is here for the Son of man to be glorified." *[Jesus studied Scripture as in a mirror - he knew that "in the book, it is written about me." Haggai 2:7 and the desire of the nations shall come…See Colossians 1:27.]*

John 12:24 Most certainly shall the single grain of wheat fall into the earth and die - if it doesn't die it remains alone - but in its death it produces much fruit.

John 12:25 To hold on desperately to a mere life defined by the soul realm is to lose it; but to abandon the soul substitute for the real deal is to observe your spiritual life which is the life of the ages.

1 Thessalonians 2:19 We expect nothing less in the context of the gospel than you enjoying a face to face encounter in the [1]immediate presence of our Lord Jesus Christ. This is our delight and wreath of honor. *(The word [1]parousia speaks of the immediate presence of the Lord. From para, a Preposition indicating close proximity, intimate connection; and eimi, I am. There is not even a hint of judgment or punishment in this word. While there are great and accurate definitions in Strongs, please do not believe everything you read there. "G3952 parousia from the Present Participle of G3918 [pareimi]; a being near, that is, advent; often, return; specifically of Christ to punish Jerusalem, or finally the wicked.".? [This is blatant nonsense.] The Greek word parousia, occurs 24 times in the NT, and 22 times it wrongly implies a 2nd coming or coming judgment. Only twice it is translated as presence. 2 Corinthians 10:10, Philippians 2:12. Of all the English translations that I have checked, only the Young's Literal has it correct. What a shame that this word has been so dramatically twisted over the years.)*

1 Thessalonians 4:13 I do not want you to be ignorant concerning those who seem to be fast asleep in their indifference and unbelief. There is no need for you to grieve as if they are beyond hope. *(See 1 Corinthians 15:51 [1]Ponder this mystery, I want to show you something that you have never seen before: [2]everyone will awaken out of sleep; we will [3]all experience exactly the same change. (In other words, [1]idou musterion, Look. A Mystery. And [2]pantes ou koimethesometha, means no one will sleep; and [3]pantes de allangesometha; everyone will be changed.)*

1 Thessalonians 4:14 We believe that Jesus died and rose again, and that he fully represents and includes even those who have not awoken unto

him yet. God will ¹lead them to realize that they are in Jesus. *(The word ¹ago means to lead as a shepherd leads his sheep. See 1 Corinthians 1:30, Ephesians 1:4.)*

1 Thessalonians 4:15 We give voice to the word of the Lord; we are God's wake-up call to them that are asleep. We are exhibiting the ¹immediate tangible presence of the Lord and shall not ²exclude them. *(The word ¹**parousia** means immediate presence. See my comment in 1 Thessalonians 2:19. See the use of the word ²**phthanō**, to prevent, to hinder or exclude, also in 2 Corinthians 10:14, Our ministry to you is proof that there are no geographic limitations which could possibly exclude you from the gospel of Jesus Christ. See also 1 Thessalonians 3:12, "We can already see how the Lord causes the love we have for you to dynamically impact each of you and burst its banks to flood the entire world." The people who dwelt in darkness have seen a great light. The true light that enlightens everyone has come. And the glory of the Lord shall be revealed and all flesh shall see it together.)*

1 Thessalonians 4:16 The Lord will personally step out of the invisible heavenly realm into our immediate visible horizon with an inciting shout, announcing his triumphant reign in the trumpet-like billowing voice of God; and even the dead will rise from their sleep, since they too are included in Christ.

1 Thessalonians 4:17 In the wake of their arising we will all be gathered into a large dense multitude of an innumerable throng of people, united as one, like the particles of water in a cloud, and we will encounter the Lord in the very air we breathe and so shall we continually celebrate our I-am-ness in our union with him. *(This is the moment which redemption declares, where Deity and humanity are married. The Bride and her Groom are united.)*

1 Thessalonians 4:18 The fact that we are all deeply connected in the same source of our 'beingness' causes us to be constantly engaged in this conversation with one another.

When Mother Teresa was asked what motivates her to go out into the streets of Calcutta in the odd hours of the night, her reply revealed her mission, "I go to minister to my Lord in his most disturbing disguises."

In Romans 12, Paul gives significant context to the idea of heaping coals of fire on your enemy's head to confirm the principle under discussion in this commentary on the lake of fire.

Romans 12:20 "If your enemy is hungry, feed him; if he is thirsty, give him something to drink." These acts of kindness will be like heaping coals of fire on his head and certainly rid him of the dross in his mind and win him as a friend. *(A refiner would melt metal in a crucible and intensify the process by heaping coals of fire on it [Proverbs 25:21,22]. This is good strategy; be sensitive to the needs of your enemies. God sees gold in every person. Hostility cannot hide our true value. He won us while we were hostile towards him [see also Romans 5:8, 10]. His kindness led us to the radical awakening of our minds. [Romans 2:4].)*

Romans 12:21 Do not let evil be an excuse for you to feel defeated, rather seize the opportunity to turn the situation into a victory for good.

Paul continues in 1 Corinthians 3:12 Imagine the contrast in building materials, one builds with gold, silver and precious stones, while another uses wood, hay and stubble. *(By comparison, the teaching of the cross and its glorious effect in human life is like building with gold, silver, and precious stones, whereas the wisdom of this world system based upon religious good works and not faith is like building with wood, hay, and stubble which is fuel for fire.)*

1 Corinthians 3:13 Everyone's work shall be tested in the scrutiny of real life; it shall be made apparent as in broad daylight just as gold is tested in fire: what you live will either burn like stubble or shine like gold. *(The revelation of mankind's co-crucifixion and co-resurrection with Christ is the gold of the gospel.)*

1 Corinthians 3:14 If what you teach is based on the revelation of the success of the cross it will certainly be confirmed in the heat of contradiction.

1 Corinthians 3:15 Obviously to witness the fruit of one's labor go up in smoke would be devastating, even though you escape with your own life.

1 Corinthians 3:16 Realize that your life is God's building; his sanctuary, designed for his permanent abode. His Spirit inhabits you. *(He designed every cell in your body to accommodate and express him.)*

1 Corinthians 3:17 Just like fire would burn away the dross, any defilement of God's temple would be destroyed in order to preserve human life as his permanent sanctuary.

REVELATION Chapter 20

20:1 And I witnessed a celestial messenger descending out of the heavenly sphere and he had the key of the bottomless Abyss and a great chain over his hand. *(Ephesians 4:8,9 He who ascended is also he who descended into the lowest parts of the earth. Ephesians 4:9 The fact that he ascended confirms his victorious descent into the deepest pits of human despair. Revelation 9:1 When the fifth celestial messenger blew his trumpet, I saw a star that had fallen to earth from the sky. The star was given the key to the shaft into the fathomless depths of the Abyss. [Jesus is the bright Morning Star Revelation 2:28 and 22:16 I am the bright Morning Star. Also 2 Peter 1:1:19.] See my Extended Notes on **the Bottomless Pit** at the end of chapter 9.)*

20:2 And he overpowered the Dragon, in its every disguise as the old Serpent in the garden in Genesis, also called the Devil, or going under the name, Satan, and chained him up for a thousand years. *(From David to Jesus is a thousand years. Revelation 3:7 I hold the key of David as prophesied in Isaiah 22:22. Yes, I unlock the mysteries of the heavenly dimension and no one can shut the door. And I lock the entrance and none [of the old mindsets] can access it. **The links in the chain**, are the prophetic words in the mouth of David and the Prophets till John the Baptist. These words already chained Satanas to the irreversible intention of God. Matthew 12:29 Or how can one enter a strong man's house and plunder his goods, unless he first binds the strong man? Then indeed he may plunder his house. See Extended Notes on **The Thousand Years** at the end of this chapter. Also **Notes on Ophis, the old Serpent** at the end of chapter 12.)*

20:3 He then hurled him into the bottomless Abyss, shut him up and set a seal upon him, and thus made it impossible for him to continue to deceive the nations for the complete duration of the symbolic thousand years; he would then be let loose on the earth for a very brief moment. *(Not to deceive the nations, μη πλανηση* **me planesey** *in the Aorist Active subjunctive which is based on the function of the mood; the subjunctive mood suggests probability. The time of the action of the subjunctive mood is relative to the time of the main verb[s], which in this case are εβαλεν* **ebalen** *[cast down] and εκλεισεν* **ekleisen** *[shut up] as well as εσφραγισεν* **esphragisen** *[sealed], all three in the Aorist Active Indicative. These are completed acts accomplished in the **tetelestai** of Jesus on the cross. The defeat of the diabolos-system is a sealed deal - its deception of the nations is only possible with their consent - Paul announces in Acts 17 that God has overlooked the times of ignorance and now implores all mankind wherever they are in space or time, to awaken to their redeemed innocence. [The word **metanoia,** does not mean "repentance" it suggests an awakening to the awareness of God's thoughts; from* **meta**, *together with and* **noieō**, *to perceive with the mind. It describes the awakening of the mind to that which is true; it is a gathering of one's thoughts, a co-knowing. Faith is not a decision; it is a discovery. It has nothing in common with the Latin word* **paenitentia** *- where the idea of penance and repentance stems from.]*

The complete contrast of Jesus' resurrection is pictured here, Jesus tomb was secured with a large rock, then sealed and guarded by Roman soldiers; yet Jesus rose and came back with the keys of Death and Hades, the stone was rolled away and he stepped out Victor, leading mankind out as his trophies. What happened in the brief moment of Jesus' descent into the Abyss is paralleled against its enduring effect of chaining up the Devil for a symbolic thousand years.

REVELATION Chapter 20

*This is a clear announcement of what happened in Jesus' descent into hell where he defeated the reign and claim of darkness in the HQ of mankind's deepest pits of despair and then, in his resurrection he co-raised the entire human race into a place of joint-reigning with him from the heavenlies. Now here on earth where it all plays out, every enemy is placed under his feet. See Hosea 6:2, Ephesians 2:5,6 and Ephesians 4:8-10, also Colossians 2:14,15. See Extended **Notes on the Thousand Years** at the end of this chapter. Also my **notes on Armageddon** at the end of chapter 16.)*

20:4 And I saw thrones and those seated upon the thrones have been given judgment. They are the souls who didn't worship the Beast or its image, and did not take his mark in their foreheads or on their hands. The system of the Beast ¹discarded them because of the testimony of Jesus and because of the Word of God, since they didn't fit into their religious mold. They are the living beings, joined together in the Christ-life, reigning from their joint-seatedness in the throne of the Lamb for a thousand years. *(Revelation 1:2 John gave accurate evidence to **the word of God and the testimony of Jesus Christ**, exactly as he saw it. [The Word of God, is the testimony of Jesus. The testimony of Jesus Christ is the context of the prophetic word.] The word, ¹**pelekizō**, axe, to cut off, from **plassō**, to form, mold something from clay, wax, etc. - used of a potter - they would not be molded into a distorted image-mindset. Revelation 21:1, also Matthew 19:28 Jesus said to them, "Truly, I say to you, in the rebooting of mankind, when the Son of man shall sit on his glorious throne, you who have followed me will also sit on twelve thrones, judging the twelve tribes of Israel. See the word, **paliggenesia**, suggests a complete restoration to the original, in modern terms, rebooted. From **palin**, again by repetition and **genesis**, source. Only used here and in Titus 3:5 See **Extended Notes on the Word of God and the Testimony of Jesus Christ** at the end of this chapter.)*

20:5 This is the first resurrection. *(The words, "But the rest of the dead lived not again until the thousand years were finished" were added at a time when the ekklesia claimed to be fulfilling the thousand-year reign of Christ. The Sinaitic MS., remarkable as being the oldest as well as for its completeness and accuracy, is the only Greek authority on Revelation ante-dating the fifth century: and it does not contain the clause.*

John 6:40 And this is the desire of my Father, that everyone who sees the Son, through his eyes, and finds the conclusion of [eis] their persuasion in him, will resonate [echo] the life of the ages. And I will raise him up in the final day. **[Jesus speaks here of mankind's joint resurrection in his resurrection as the final day.** *The word **theōreo** means to gaze attentively. See Hosea 6:2 After two days he will revive us; on the third day he will raise us up, that we may live before him. The word **eschatos** means extreme; last in time or in space; the uttermost part, the final conclusion. What God said about 'you-manity' in their co-resurrection in Jesus, defines eschatology. Hebrews 1:1-3; Ephesians 2:5,6.]*

See 1 Corinthians 15:13 If our co-resurrection is not proclaimed then the resurrection of Jesus from the dead is no longer relevant. 1 Corinthians 15:20 However this very moment the risen Christ represents everyone who has ever died; exactly like the first fruit represents the complete harvest. 1 Corinthians 15:21 The same mankind who died in a man was raised again in a man. 1 Corinthians 15:22 In Adam all

REVELATION Chapter 20

*died; in Christ all are made alive. The first [most significant] revelation of Jesus' resurrection is the fact that his resurrection is mankind's resurrection. See Hosea 6:2, "After two days he will revive us; on the third day he will raise us up, that we may live before him." Paul reveals in Ephesians 2:5,6 that, while we were dead in our sins and trespasses, God co-quickened us and co-raised us and co-seated us in heavenly places. In Colossians 3:1-3 Paul urges us to engage our thoughts with throne room realities, since we are raised together with Christ. See **Extended Notes on the Word of God and the Testimony of Jesus Christ** at the end of this chapter.)*

20:6 Oh the ¹blessedness of this bliss, celebrated in the redeemed innocence of every single individual, discovering their inclusion in this first resurrection as their own - realizing that the second death has no bearing on them whatsoever - they will continue in their priesthood unto God and Christ and they will co-reign with him for a thousand years. *(The word, ¹**makarios**, usually translated, blessed, suggests a special intensity of delight. This is the fifth beatitude; Revelation 1:3; Revelation 14:13; Revelation 16:15; Revelation 19:9 and two more to come; Revelation 22:7, Revelation 22:14, seven in all. See **Extended notes on the thousand years** at the end of this chapter.)*

20:7 Their reign and priesthood will be fully established within the context of the vastness of this symbolic thousand year period. In sharp contrast then, only to emphasize the complete and utter defeat of the Satanas-system, he will be let loose very briefly, out of his prison. *(From the Abyss, the "Bottomless Pit-Underworld", where he was imprisoned when Jesus went there to free mankind. Jesus came back with the keys, remember. Revelation 20:3.)*

20:8 And his obvious strategy would be to deceive the nations on a global scale including the four corners of the earth by assembling Gog and Magog in war; their number is as the sand of the sea. *(Again, every traditional Jewish concept of judgment is addressed. Gog and Magog is now brought into the conversation, since Jewish eschatology viewed Gog and Magog as enemies to be defeated by the Messiah, which will usher in the age of the Messiah. "Then Eldad and Modad [brothers of Moses] both prophesied together, and said, 'In the very end of time Gog and Magog and their army shall come up against Jerusalem, and they shall fall by the hand of the King Messiah; they shall be slain by the flame of fire which shall proceed from under the throne of glory, and afterwards all the dead of Israel shall rise again to life, and shall enjoy the delights prepared for them from the beginning." Quote from the Jewish Targum. See reference in Numbers 11:26 and Ezekiel 38:17.*

There are numeral references to the same "once and for all war" in the heavens. It is however the same hour; the same event. Revelation 12:7; Revelation 16:13,14; Revelation 17:13,14; Revelation 19:19. See Extended Notes on Israel at the end of this chapter.)

20:9 They will spread across the earth and attempt to neutralize the "Queen Bee Bride" of the Lamb by surrounding and besieging God's saints in the beloved city. Then fire will pour out of heaven and consume them. *(Again, the mindsets of satanic accusation and judgments are made a meal of - yet another reference to the great supper-feast celebrating the new covenant and* *the conclusion of the old. The fire from the altar of the slain Lamb of God consumes every definition of Israel's and indeed, mankind's perceived enemies. See extended notes on the lake of fire, at the end of chapter 19.)*

20:10 The Devil, who led them astray will be hurled into the lake of fire and brimstone where his puppet partners, the Beast and the False Prophet have already been confined to. Day and Night they will be the subject of God's touchstone for the ages of the ages - the very atmosphere of the entire universe will be thoroughly fumigated from any evidence of Satanas. *(See my notes on the Touchstone in Revelation 14:10; also on the lake of fire and brimstone at the end of chapter 19.)*

20:11 And I saw a huge white throne and it was as if heaven and earth fled away from the presence of the One seated upon the throne and its place was never found again. *(This means that there is no accusation in the heavens or upon the earth that could possibly stand in the presence of the Lamb, the One seated upon the throne of the judgment of righteousness – his throne gives testimony to mankind's redeemed acquittal. See Hebrews 1:3 "Having made purification for sins he sat down." There exists no evidence that could be brought from any sphere or dimension that could possibly testify against the human race - Acts 17:30,31, - The God of creation has overlooked the times of ignorance and now urgently persuades all of mankind everywhere to awaken in their understanding to the fact of their innocence – he appointed a day and a person and on that day and in that person God would judge he world in righteousness and of this he has given proof by raising Jesus from the dead. The resurrected Jesus is the official receipt and verdict confirming mankind's redeemed innocence. Romans 4:25. Revelation 20:4; also Matthew 19:28 Jesus said to them, "Truly, I say to you, in the ¹rebooting of mankind, when the Son of man shall sit on his glorious throne, you who have followed me will also sit on twelve thrones, judging the twelve tribes of Israel. The word, ¹**paliggenesia**, suggests a complete restoration to the original, in modern terms, rebooted. From **palin**, again by repetition and **genesis**, source. Only used here in Matthew 19:28 and in Titus 3:5.)*

20:12 And I saw everyone who ever died, small and great, standing before God. And the books were opened. And another book was opened. The Book of Life. The first volume of books represented mankind's judgment based on their own works, versus the Book of Life which celebrates the triumph of the Lamb. *(Revelation 3:5 Everyone who sees their victory in me will I clothe in white garments - and they will realize that I am not in the business of fulfilling their law and performance based fears by blotting out their names from the Book of Life. Instead I am the one who endorses their identity face to face before my Father and his celestial messengers. [This language is taken from the custom of registering the names of persons in a list, roll, or catalogue. In Jewish tradition there was a prevailing fear that your name might be blotted out of the Book of Life if your behavior did not please God.] See **Extended Notes on the Lamb's Book of Life** at the end of Chapter 17.)*

20:13 Every domain where the dead was held, yielded them up to be judged according to his work *[The work of Jesus]*. **Everyone was there; the sea yielded up its dead and Death and Hades yielded up their dead.** *(The* *singular, ὁ ἔργον αὐτός, his work, rather than, plural, their works, is the text by Tischendorf. [See my notes on TEXT at the introduction to Revelation] Also note Revelation 22:12 Behold. [again Aorist Imperative.] Now get the message, once and for all. I am come. There are no further delays. This is the hour the Prophets pointed to. And my reward is with Me, to give to each as his [the Lamb's] work is.)*

20:14 Then Death and Hades were cast into the lake of fire. This is the second death. *(The Second Death is not to distract from the once and for all death that Jesus died, but to endorse it. In the lake of fire, Death and Hades are eradicated from memory. The first death is the once and for all death that Jesus died, representing the global death of humankind. Jesus' death took mankind's death in Adam, out of the equation. [Hebrews 9:27,28; 2 Corinthians 5:14-17] The idea of the Second Death has to do with the fact that the revelation of everyone's inclusion in the death of Jesus, has not yet dawned on some - so it will take a crisis, often, their own death, to immediately engage them with the symbolic cleansing [from their unbelief] represented by the lake of burning sulphur, purifying like in a furnace, separating the gold from the dross-mindsets. Revelation 2:11 and Revelation 20:6. See* **Extended notes on the lake of fire** *at the end of Chapter 19)*

20:15 And ¹everything that was not written in the Book of Life was poured into the lake of fire. *(The Greek, εἴ τις οὐχ εὑρέθη ἐν τῇ βίβλῳ τῆς ζωῆς γεγραμμένος - with,* **ei tis***, meaning everything or everyone - but, what is cast into the symbolic lake ablaze with brimstone is not a person but a mindset. A distorted perception of identity.*

The authentic ID of human life is defined in the Book of Life - or the Tree of Life, representing the redeemed life of our design, versus the alternative Tree of the knowledge of good and evil, representing mankind's identity under scrutiny and questioning. The "I am not-Tree" heads up the System of a Works and Performance Based Philosophy. To have your name written in the Book of Life simply suggests that you discover your identity there in the Zoe-life redeemed by the Lamb. You may have only known yourself according to the flesh, as Simon, the son of Jonah, while you really are Petros. Mr. Rock, you are a chip off the old Block. Every evidence of an inferior identity will be cast into the lake of sulphur burning away the dross to reveal the gold. Any idea of an identity outside of the Book of Life, is dissolved. The Lamb's Book of Life and not the law of personal performance, defines us.

See **Extended Notes on the Lamb's Book of Life** *at the end of Chapter 17.)*

Revelation Chapter 20 Extended Notes:

The Thousand Years

The Word of God and the Testimony of Jesus Christ

Extended Notes on Israel

NOTES ON THE THOUSAND YEARS - REV 20

The Thousand Years

The Satanas-system was cast into the Abyss, bound and sealed for a thousand years, then loosed for a very brief time.

Revelation 20:2 And he overpowered the Dragon, in its every disguise as the old Serpent in the garden in Genesis, also called the Devil, or going under the name, Satan, and chained him up for a thousand years. *(From David to Jesus is a thousand years. While many of the Psalm are powerful and significant prophetic pointers to he Messiah, David's 22nd Psalm is a most stark and graphic prophetic picture of the crucifixion. The Psalm was written 1000 years BC and 700 years before crucifixion was even a known practice. Revelation 3:7 I hold the key of David as prophesied in Isaiah 22:22. Yes, I unlock the mysteries of the heavenly dimension and no one can shut the door. And I lock the entrance and none [of the old mindsets] can access it.* **The links in the chain, are the prophetic words** *in the mouth of David and the Prophets till John the Baptist.* **These words already chained Satanas to the irreversible intention of God.** *Matthew 12:29 Or how can one enter a strong man's house and plunder his goods, unless he first binds the strong man? Then indeed he may plunder his house. See John 5:28 Do not be alarmed by this, but the hour is coming when those in the graves will hear his voice. [No-one who ever lived will escape the extent of his righteous judgment. Those who have forgotten who they are will hear his incarnate voice. The word for grave,* **mnēmeion**, *memory, suggests a remembrance - to bring something from memory into the here and now! Like David prophecies in Psalm 22 when he sees the cross-crisis [krisis - judgment] a thousand years before it happens. His conclusion in verse 27 sums up the triumph of God's resolve. "All the ends of the earth shall remember and turn to the LORD; and all the families of the nations shall worship before him." See 1 Corinthians 15:21,22 The same mankind who died in a man was raised again in a man. In Adam all died; in Christ all are made alive.]*

Thus, in **prophetic language**, *every definition of the Satanas-system is already chained by the prophetic significance in Scripture recorded in the Psalm and the Prophets. The Spirit of Christ within them pointed to and concluded in the cross and resurrection of Jesus Christ. His death was the doorway into the very domain wherein mankind was held captive, to be freed and led out triumphantly as the Lamb's trophies. In* **symbolic language**, *the effect of Jesus' victory is compared to a thousand years. Against the very brief 3 days of his cross, descent into hell and resurrection, on the one hand as well as the very "brief" time of the Devil's apparent release on the planet.)*

Revelation 20:3 He then hurled him into the bottomless Abyss, shut him up and set a seal upon him, and thus made it impossible for him to continue to deceive the nations for the complete duration of the symbolic thousand years; he would then be let loose on the earth for a very brief moment. *(Not to deceive the nations, μη πλανηση* **me planesey** *in the Aorist Active subjunctive which is based on the function of the mood; the subjunctive mood suggests probability. The time of the action of the subjunctive mood is relative to the time of the main verb[s], which in this case are εβαλεν* **ebalen** *[cast down] and εκλεισεν* **ekleisen** *[shut up] as well as εσφραγισεν* **esphragisen** *[sealed],* *all three in the Aorist Active Indicative. These are completed acts accomplished in the **tetelestai** of Jesus on the cross. The defeat of the diabolos-system is a sealed deal - its deception of the nations is only possible with their consent - Paul announces in Acts 17 that God has overlooked the times of ignorance and now implores all mankind wherever they are in space or time, to awaken to their redeemed innocence. [The word **metanoia**, does not mean "repentance" it suggests an awakening to the awareness of God's thoughts; Like most Greek words, μετάνοια metanoia is a compound word, from **meta**, together with and νοιέω **noieō**, to perceive with the mind. It describes the awakening of the mind to that which is true; a re-alignment of one's reasoning; it is a gathering of one's thoughts, a co-knowing. Faith is not a decision; it is a discovery. It has nothing in common with the Latin word **paenitentia** - where the idea of penance and repentance stems from. Sadly the word repentance became the popular English translation of **metanoia**.]*

The complete contrast of Jesus' resurrection is pictured here, Jesus tomb was secured with a large rock, then sealed and guarded by Roman soldiers; yet Jesus rose and came back with the keys of Death and Hades, the stone was rolled away and he stepped out Victor, leading mankind out as his trophies. What happened in the brief moment of Jesus' descent into the Abyss is paralleled against its enduring effect of chaining up the Devil for a symbolic thousand years.

This is a clear announcement of what happened in Jesus' descent into hell where he defeated the reign and claim of darkness in the HQ of mankind's deepest pits of despair and then, in his resurrection, he co-raises the entire human race into a place of joint-reigning with him from the heavenlies. Now here on earth where it all plays out, every enemy is placed under his feet. See Hosea 6:2, Ephesians 2:5,6 and Ephesians 4:8-10, also Colossians 2:14,15.)

Ephesians 1:20 Do you want to measure the mind and muscle of God? Consider the force which he unleashed in Jesus Christ when he raised him from the dead and forever seated him enthroned as his executive authority in the realm of the heavens. Jesus is God's right hand of power. He was raised up from the deepest dungeons of human despair into the highest region of heavenly bliss.

Ephesians 1:21 Infinitely above all the combined forces of rule, authority, dominion or governments; he is ranked superior to any name that could ever be given to anyone of this age or any age still to come in the eternal future.

Ephesians 1:22 I want you to see this: he subjected all these powers under his feet. He towers head and shoulders above everything. He is the head;

Ephesians 1:23 the ekklesia is his body. The completeness of his being that fills all in all resides in us. God cannot make himself more visible or exhibit himself more accurately. *(The word, ekklesia, comes from ek, a Preposition always denoting origin, and klesia from kaleo, to identify by name, to surname; thus the "ekklesia" is his redeemed image and likeness in human form.)*

Colossians 2:14 His body nailed to the cross hung there as the document of mankind's guilt; in dying our death he canceled the detailed hand-written record which testified against us. Every stain on our conscience,

reminding of the sense of failure and guilt, was thus fully blotted out. *(The word, **exaleipho**, comes from **ek**, out of, and **aleipho**, with **a**, as a particle of union, and **liparos**, to grease, to leave a stain; guilt, as well as all hurtful memories were like grease stains upon the conscience. In N.T. only here and Revelation 3:5; 7:17; 21:4, then also in **Acts 3:19** "Be awakened in your minds and fully converted to face the fact of your redeemed innocence - your sins have been thoroughly blotted out." Plato used it of blotting out a writing. The word, **cheirographon**, translates as hand-written. The word, **dogma**, comes from **dokeo**, a thought pattern; thus thought patterns engraved by human experience of constant failure to do what the law required. In his personal handwriting mankind endorsed their own death sentence. The hands of fallen mankind struck the body of Jesus with the blows of their religious hatred and fury when they nailed his bloodied body to the tree; they did not realize that in the mystery of God's economy, Jesus became the scapegoat of the entire human race. [Isaiah 53:4, 5] See notes on Hebrews 8:12. "The slate wiped clean, that old arrest warrant canceled and nailed to Christ's Cross." —The Message)*

Colossians 2:15 In him dying mankind's death, he defused every possible claim of accusation against the human race and thus made a public spectacle of every rule and authority in God's brilliant triumph, demonstrated in him. The voice of the cross will never be silenced. *(The horror of the Cross is now the eternal trophy of God's triumph over sin. The cross stripped religion of its authority to manipulate mankind with guilt. Every accusation lost its leverage to blackmail the human race with condemnation and shame. The word, **apekduomai**, is translated from **apo**, away from, and **ekduo**, to be stripped of clothing; to disarm; the religious facade that disguised the law of works as a means of defining a person's life, was openly defeated. Same word used in Colossians 3:9. The dominance of the tree of the knowledge of good and evil [**poneros**, hard work and labor] was ended. The word, **deikmatizo**, means to exhibit in public. See commentary below of the words **arche**, rule and **exousia**, authority. The word, **parresia**, comes from **pas**, all and **rheo**, outspokenness, pouring forth speech.*

"He stripped all the spiritual tyrants in the universe of their sham authority at the Cross and marched them naked through the streets." — The Message)

We are living in "the very brief moment" of a defeated Devil let loose on the planet. *Paul calls it "a slight, momentarily affliction" compared to the eternal weight of glory.*

2 Corinthians 4:17 We are fully engaged in an exceedingly superior reality; the extent and [1]weight of this glory makes any degree of suffering vanish into insignificance. The suffering is fleeting and ever so slight by comparison to the weight and enduring effect of this glory we participate in for all eternity. *(In Hebrew the word* כבוד *Kabod, means weight - this is also the word for glory - Paul reflects on this weight as the standard measure of everything that defines the glory of God. According to 2 Corinthians 3:18 mankind is his glory. This glory is the true currency of life. Paul reasons that by comparison, any size contradiction is dwarfed into insignificance and appears ever so slight when positioned against the enormity of the weight of glory that dwells within us.)*

NOTES ON THE THOUSAND YEARS - REV 20

2 Corinthians 4:18 We are not keeping any score of what seems so obvious to the senses on the surface; it is fleeting and irrelevant; it is the unseen eternal realm within us which has our full attention and captivates our gaze.

Hebrews 2:7 It seems that man briefly descends to a [1]less elevated place than Elohim; yet he is crowned with God's own glory and dignity, and appointed in a position of authority over all the works of his hands." *(The word ἐλαττόω [1]elattoō [English, elation] suggests a little less than Elohim. Possibly, a copyist felt that the reference to equality with our Maker [Genesis 1:26] was too bold, so the Greek text reads, "he made us a little lower than the celestial messengers." Here is the reference, Psalm 8:4 What is man that you are mindful of him, and the son of man that you care so much for him? Psalm 8:5 Yet you made him little less than God, [Elohim] and crowns him with glory and honor. Psalm 8:6 You have given him dominion over the works of your hands; you have put all things under his feet.)*

Hebrews 2:8 God's intention was that human life should rule the planet. He subjected everything without exception to his control. Yet, looking at the human race, it does not seem that way at all.

Hebrews 2:9 But what is apparent, is Jesus. *[Now God spoke to us in a son. Hebrews 1:1-3]* Let us then consider him in such a way, that we may clearly perceive what God is saying to mankind in him. In the death he suffered, he briefly descended to a seemingly less elevated place than Elohim, *[Psalm 8:5]* in order to taste the death of the entire human race, and in doing so, to fulfill the grace of God and be crowned again *[as a man, representing all of mankind]* with glory and highly esteemed honor. *(See Philippians 2:6 His being God's equal in form and likeness was official; his Sonship did not steal the limelight from his Father. Neither did his humanity distract from the deity of God. Philippians 2:7 His mission however, was not to prove his deity, but to embrace our humanity. Emptied of his reputation as God, he fully embraced our physical human form; born in our resemblance he identified himself as the servant of the human race. His love enslaved him to us. Philippians 2:8 And so we have the drama of the cross in context: the man Jesus Christ who is fully God, becomes fully man to the extent of willingly dying humanity's death at the hands of his own creation. He embraced the curse and shame of the lowest kind in dying a criminal's death. [Thus, through the doorway of death, he descended into our hellish darkness. [In his death, Jesus conquered the underworld and he has the keys; no-one else does.] Revelation 1:18 I am also the Living One; I died and now, see, here I am alive unto the ages of the ages and I have the keys wherewith I have disengaged the gates of Hades and death. Also, Ephesians 4:8-10.] Philippians 2:9 From this place of utter humiliation, God exalted him to the highest rank. God graced Jesus with a Name that is far above every other name.)*

Revelation 9:1 When the fifth celestial messenger blew his trumpet, I saw a star that had fallen to earth from the sky. The star was given the key to the shaft into the fathomless depths of the Abyss.

Revelation 9:2 He opened the shaft of the bottomless pit, and smoke came out of the shaft like the smoke from a large [1]furnace. The smoke darkened the sun and the atmosphere. *(The smoke is evidence of the fire from* *the altar of worship which was lit by the coals from the brazen altar - the prophetic picture of the cross where the Lamb of God was slaughtered - Revelation 8:5. The word **kaminos** is an old word for a smelting-furnace; Revelation 1:15, "His feet were like a brilliant bronze fashioned in a furnace." How lovely and powerfully equipped are the feet of them who proclaim Good News from the mountains. In contrast to the feet of mingled iron and clay of the image Daniel saw in Daniel 2:38. The army of God is set to swallow up the consciousness of good and evil, the fruit of the "I-am-not-tree , in people's minds. The natural light was veiled and even the atmosphere was filled with smoke for the moment while the effect of Jesus' presence in our hell was released. See notes on **The bottomless pit** at the end of chapter 9.)*

Revelation 9:11 Their reigning king was the celestial messenger of the bottomless pit; his name in Hebrew was Abaddon and in Greek, Apollyon the One who breaks the bonds. *(Abaddon* אבדון *from **abad**, to wander away, - we all like sheep have gone astray. He did not leave a stone unturned in seeking and finding every single lost sheep. He went into the most extreme depths of our lostness and hell. He is called the Searcher of those who have wandered away. See 2 Corinthians 2:15 [This parade of victory is a public announcement of the defeat of the religious systems and structures based on the law of works. Just like it is in any public game where the victory celebration of the winning team is an embarrassment for the losing team. The death of evil is announced in resurrection life. The word, **apollumi**, is derived from **apo**, away from, and **luo**, to loosen, to undo, to dissolve.] The message we communicate is a fragrance with an immediate association; to darkness, it is the smell of doom [the death of Death] See also my comment on John 3:16. 1 John 3:8 Sin's source is a fallen mindset, from the beginning. For this purpose the son of God was revealed. His mission was to undo the works of the Devil. (The word, **diabolos**, from **dia**, because of and **ballo**, to cast down. Isaiah 54:16)*

John 3:16 The entire cosmos is the object of God's affection. And he is not about to ¹abandon his creation - the gift of his Son is for mankind to realize their origin in him who mirrors their authentic birth - begotten not of flesh but of the Father. *[See John 1:13]* **In this persuasion the life of the ages echoes within the individual and announces that the days of regret and sense of lost-ness are over.** *(The KJV reads, Whoever ⁴believes in him shall not ¹perish but have eternal life. The same word translated in the KJV to perish is translated in Luke 15 to be lost. In order to underline the value of the individual, Jesus tells the famous three parables in Luke 15 of the lost sheep, coin and son; now all found, safe and sound. In everyone he repeats the word ¹lost, **apollumi**, to lose, to emphasize the fact that you cannot be lost unless you belong - to begin with. The word ¹**apollumi**, also suggests a sense of uselessness; that which comes to ruin and amounts to nothing. In him we recognize our true beginning - as in the authentic original mold. See my commentary note to John 1:12. The word ⁴**echo**, to hold, or embrace, as in echo. The word, ⁵**kosmos** in the NT refers to the entire human family.)*

John 3:17 God has no intention to condemn anyone - he sent his Son, not to be the Judge but the Savior of the world.

("It is important to note that parallels, patterns, symmetry and symbolism should never be used to form doctrine; they merely support the revelation of the Good News." [Scripture Reveal]

NOTES ON THE THOUSAND YEARS - REV 20

In this context it is compared to "the brief time" of the apparent resurgence of a defeated Devil's presence on the planet.

The word "thousand" appears 521 times in the King James Version Bible.

The number one thousand (1,000) symbolizes "immensity," "fullness of quantity" or "multitude." The number evokes a very long time according to most Bible passages. The number sometimes is used in a reference to paradise and everlasting happiness.

1 Chronicles 16:15 (KJV) – "Be ye mindful always of his covenant; the word which he commanded to a thousand generations;"

Psalm 84:10 (KJV) – "For a day in thy courts is better than a thousand."

Psalm 90:4 (KJV) – "For a thousand years in thy sight are but as yesterday when it is past,"

Psalm 105:8 (KJV) – "He hath remembered his covenant forever, the word which he commanded to a thousand generations."

In Isaiah 60:22 during the prophesied Messianic time there will be an increase from 1 to 1000. "A little one shall become one thousand".

Psalm 50:10 we read – "For every Beast of the forest is mine, and the cattle upon a thousand hills.")

THE TESTIMONY OF JESUS - REV 20

The Word of God and the Testimony of Jesus Christ

Revelation 1:2 John gave accurate evidence to the word of God and the Testimony of Jesus Christ, exactly as he saw it. *(The Testimony of Jesus Christ is the context of the prophetic word. Colossians 3:4 The unveiling of Christ, as defining our lives, [1]immediately implies that, what is evident in him, is equally mirrored in you. The exact life on exhibit in Christ is now repeated in us. We are included in the same bliss and joined-oneness with him; just as his life reveals you, your life reveals him. The testimony of Jesus is what gives relevance and context to the Word of God. Jesus is what the Scriptures are all about and you are what Jesus is all about.)*

Revelation 19:10 For the testimony of Jesus is the Spirit of prophecy.

1 Peter 1:11 The prophets knew with certainty that it was the Spirit of Christ within them pointing prophetically and giving testimony to the sufferings of the Christ and the subsequent glory.

Just like the ore that carries the gold, the Bible contains the Word - the ore is not the gold, neither is the Bible the Word. Jesus is The Word. John 1:1-3,14; John 5:39.

John 1:1 To go back to the very beginning, is to find the Word already present there; face to face with God. The Word is I am; God's eloquence echoes and concludes in him. The Word equals God.

John 1:2 The beginning mirrors the Word face to face with God. *(Nothing that is witnessed in the Word distracts from who God is. "If you have seen me, you have seen the Father." [John 14:9] The Word that was from the beginning was not yet written or spoken; it was simply face to face with God. The beginning declares the destiny of the Word, it would always only be who God is and conclude in God.)*

John 1:3 The Logos is the Source; everything commences in him. He remains the exclusive Parent reference to their existence. There is nothing original, except the Word. The Logic of God defines the only possible place where mankind can trace their genesis. *(All things were made by him; and without him was not any thing made that was made. KJV See Colossians 1:16.)*

John 1:4 His life is the light that defines our lives. *(In his life mankind discovers the light of life.)*

John 1:5 The darkness was pierced and could not comprehend or diminish this light. *(Darkness represents mankind's ignorance of his redeemed identity and innocence [Isaiah 9:2-4, Isaiah 60:1-3, Ephesians 4:18, Colossians 1:13-15].)*

John 1:14 Suddenly the invisible, eternal Word takes on visible form - the Incarnation, on display in a flesh and blood Person, as in a mirror.

John 5:31 If this was just about me trying to make a name for myself then you can certainly reject my testimony as phony.

John 5:32 Yet there is someone else who endorses who I am and I recognize his testimony of me as absolutely true.

John 5:33 You cross examined John and he too gave testimony to the truth of who I am.

THE TESTIMONY OF JESUS - REV 20

John 5:34 I do not draw my inspiration from your applause; I'm not here to win a few votes for a noble cause - I am on a rescue mission.

John 5:35 John was a man on fire, a bright beaming light and for a brief moment you were jumping with joy in his radiance.

John 5:36 My testimony exceeds John's, since the work which my Father has ordained me to finish, gives ultimate context to my mission.

John 5:37 The Father himself who has sent me continues to bear witness to me; yet you are not familiar with his voice and did not discern his prophetic utterance throughout ancient times and therefore you could not recognize his image nor do you realize his appearance at this present time. *(In the incarnate Word.)*

John 5:38 Your doubting him whom the Father has sent shows that you have not taken his word to its full conclusion.

John 5:39 You scrutinize the Scriptures tirelessly, assuming that in them you embrace the life of the ages - yet I am what the Scriptures are all about. *(Echo, to hold, embrace, resonate.)*

John 5:40 Still you refuse to resort to me as the very Source of the life you seek. *(I echo the life of the ages within you.)*

John 8:13 The Pharisees took offense at this and responded with, "You assume things about yourself; how can you expect us to believe your record to be true?"

John 8:14 Jesus answered, "Whatever I declare concerning myself is absolutely true because I know where I am from and where I am going. You have no clue where I come from and therefore cannot discern my destiny.

John 8:15 You form your own judgment according to the flesh; I judge no-one.

John 8:16 And even if I do make a judgment, it is true since I am not making it up in my imagination or on my own accord, my reference reflects the testimony of the Father who sent me.

John 8:17 That should settle it for you since it is written in your law that the testimony of two is true. *(This combined witness of two is not true just because they agree, unless true in fact separately. But if they disagree, the testimony falls to the ground. Deuteronomy 17:6; and Deuteronomy 19:15. - Robertson's Word Pictures.)*

John 8:18 I am witness to who I am and my Father himself also bears witness to me.

Hebrews 6:13 Since God had no one greater by whom to swear, he swore by himself. He could give Abraham no greater guarantee but the integrity of his own Being; this makes the promise as sure as God is.

Hebrews 6:16 It is common practice in human affairs to evoke a higher authority under oath in order to add weight to any agreement between parties, thereby silencing any possibility of quibbling. *(The word* **peras**, *means the end of all dispute; the point beyond which one cannot go.)*

Hebrews 6:17 In the same context we are confronted with God's eagerness to go to the last extreme in his dealing with us as heirs of his promise, and to cancel out all possible grounds for doubt or dispute. In order to persuade us of the unalterable character and finality of his resolve, he confined himself to an oath. The promise which already belongs to us by heritage is now also ¹**confirmed under oath.** *(The word* ¹***mesiteo*** *is used, interposed or mediated. Compare* **mesites**, *mediator, from* **mesos**, *midst. In the incarnation, God has positioned himself in the midst, of his creation. See Galatians 3:20 With Abraham there was no middleman; it was just God. [The Mosaic law required mediators [the Levitical priesthood] because it was an arrangement whereby mankind had a part and God had a part. Mankind's part was to obey the commandments and God's part was to bless. God's covenant with Abraham was a grace covenant pointing to the man Jesus Christ, in whom God himself would fulfil mankind's part and therefore needed no mediator apart from himself.*

The Word is the promise; the Incarnate, crucified and risen Christ is the proof. He desires to show more convincingly to the heirs of the promise the unchangeable character of his purpose. RSV

Mankind was not redeemed from the Devil; a thief never becomes an owner; neither did Jesus do what he did to change his Father's mind about us. It was our minds that needed persuasion. God was not to be reconciled to his creation; God was in Christ when he reconciled the world to himself. 2 Corinthians 5:18-20.)

Hebrews 6:18 So that we are now dealing with two irreversible facts which make it impossible for anyone to prove God wrong; thus our persuasion as to our redeemed identity is powerfully reinforced. We have already escaped into that destiny; our expectation has come within our immediate grasp. *(The promise of redemption sustained throughout Scripture and the fulfillment of that promise in Jesus. See John 8:13-18* **John 8:17** *That should settle it for you since it is written in your law that the testimony of two, is true. (This combined witness of two is not true just because they agree, unless true in fact separately. But if they disagree, the testimony falls to the ground. Deuteronomy 17:6; and Deuteronomy 19:15. - Robertson. Also Revelation 10:6 See notes on the Oath at the end of Revelation 10.)*

Hebrews 6:19 Our hearts and minds are certain; anchored securely within the innermost courts of God's immediate Presence; beyond the *[prophetic]* **veil.**

Hebrews 6:20 By going there on our behalf, Jesus pioneered a place for us and removed every type of obstruction that could possibly distance us from the promise. In him we are represented for all time; he became our High Priest after the order of Melchizedek. We now enjoy the same privileged access he has. *(He said, "I go to prepare a place for you so that you* *may be where I am. On that day you will no longer doubt that I and the Father are one; you will know that I am in the Father and you in me and I in you."[John 10:30, 14:3, 20])*

Revelation 20:4 And I saw thrones and those seated upon the thrones have been given judgment. They are the souls who didn't worship the Beast or its image, and did not take his mark in their foreheads or on their hands. The system of the Beast ¹axed them because of the testimony of Jesus and because of the Word of God, since they didn't fit into their religious mold. They are the living beings, joined together in the Christ-life, reigning from their joint-seatedness in the throne of the Lamb for a thousand years. *(Revelation 1:2 John gave accurate evidence to **the word of God and the testimony of Jesus Christ**, exactly as he saw it. [The Word of God, is the testimony of Jesus. The testimony of Jesus Christ is the context of the prophetic word.] The word, ¹**pelekizō**, axe, to cut off, from **plassō**, to form, mold something from clay, wax, etc. - used of a potter - they would not be molded into a distorted image-mindset. Revelation 21:1, also Matthew 19:28 Jesus said to them, "Truly, I say to you, in the rebooting of mankind, when the Son of man shall sit on his glorious throne, you who have followed me will also sit on twelve thrones, judging the twelve tribes of Israel. See the word, **paliggenesia**, suggests a complete restoration to the original, in modern terms, rebooted. From **palin**, again by repetition and **genesis**, source. Only used here and in Titus 3:5 See Notes on the thousand years.)*

Revelation 3:11 Do not let tough times make me seem distant from you. I am at hand - see my nearness, not my absence. And don't let temporal setbacks diminish your own authority either. Remember that you call the shots; you wear the crown. My crown endorses your crown. *(Lit. Let nothing take your crown. Revelation 1:5)*

Revelation 6:9 And when he opened the fifth seal I saw underneath the altar the souls of those slain in sacrifice because of the word of God and their testimony. *(Addressing the murdered prophets. Matthew 23:37 "Jerusalem, Jerusalem, who kills the prophets and stones those who are sent to her. How often I wanted to gather your children together, the way a hen gathers her chicks under her wings, and you were unwilling.")*

Revelation 6:10 Their voice was loud and urgent. How long, our holy and true ¹Husband, will you not judge and balance the scales of justice in the shedding of innocent blood? Are we mere scapegoats in the futile sacrificial system of the rest of the earth-dwellers.? *(The word **despotes** from **deo**, binding as in wedlock and **posis**, husband. The word **ekdikea** from **ek**, source and **dikay**, two parties finding likeness in each other - the stem for righteousness, **dikaiosune** - where **dikay** reminds of the Greek goddess of Justice typically portrayed holding a scale of balances in her hand.)*

Revelation 6:11 Then white robes were given to each and everyone of them. Mankind's redeemed innocence is about to be announced. While you briefly rest with your ¹faces turned upward, and be rejuvenated; until your prophetic word be ²fulfilled. And your fellows, co-included in the sufferings of the Christ *[even his murderers]* are about to be revealed as your friends who are themselves co-slain in the Lamb of God. *("And there was given to each one white robes, and it was said to them that they may rest themselves yet a little time, till may be fulfilled also their fellow-servants and their brethren, who are about to be killed—even as they. Young's Literal Translation." One has died for all, therefore all have died. 2 Corinthians 5:14. "While you briefly rest with your faces turned upward" [¹anapauō, ana, upward and pauo, rest; also refresh, far more than mere rest, rejuvenation. The English expression "rest up" is close to the idea of the Greek compound **anapauō**.] This suggests a resting in the awareness of the significance of their lives and death in prophetic context; the word of your testimony pointing to my day. The word, ²pleroo is in the Aorist Passive Subjunctive, suggesting the inevitable fulfillment of that which the prophetic word pointed to. In the slaughtered Lamb's death, God dramatically brings closure to every definition of sacrifice -* **he takes mankind's appointment with death and judgment out of the equation and introduces resurrection life to be our true portion.** *See 1 Peter 1:10,11 In all of their conversation there was a constant quest to determine who the Messiah would be, and exactly when this would happen. They knew with certainty that it was the spirit of Christ within them pointing prophetically and giving testimony to the sufferings of the Christ and the subsequent glory. Revelation 7:9)*

See 1 Corinthians 15. **The first [most significant] revelation of Jesus' resurrection is the fact that his resurrection is mankind's resurrection.** *(Hosea 6:2, "After two days he will revive us; on the third day he will raise us up, that we may live before him." Paul reveals in Ephesians 2:5,6 that, while we were dead in our sins and trespasses, God co-quickened us and co-raised us and co-seated us in heavenly places. In Colossians 3:1-3 Paul urges us to engage our thoughts with throne room realities, since we are raised together with Christ.)*

Revelation 1:5 May this grace and peace of Jesus Christ overwhelm you. He is the first born from the dead and embodies the evidence and testimony of everything that God believes about you. He heads up the authority in which we reign as kings on the earth. His crown endorses our crown. He always loves us and loosed us once and for all from the dominion of sin in the shedding of his blood. *(We are crowned with the triumph of Jesus' resurrection. See 1 Peter 1:3. Also, Psalm 103:4,* **He redeems your life from the Pit and weaves a crown for you** *out of loving-kindness and tender mercies. Psalm 103:5 He satisfies you with good as long as you live so that your youth is renewed like the eagle's.)*

Revelation 1:6 He fashioned us a kingdom of priests unto his God and Father. The glory and the ruling authority of the ages belong to him through all time. Amen

Revelation 1:7 Behold he comes with a ¹large dense multitude; an innumerable throng of people, united as one, like the particles of water in a cloud. Every eye will see him, not merely as observers, but they will perceive him for who he really is - even those who participated in his murder, when they pierced his hands and his side. Every single tribe of

the earth will see him and weep greatly at the thought of their foolish rejection of him. This will surely be. *(The word ¹nephos is a cloud, a large dense multitude, a throng. 1 Thessalonians 4:16, The Lord will personally step out of the invisible heavenly realm into our immediate visible horizon with an inciting shout, announcing his triumphant reign in the trumpet-like billowing voice of God. Even the dead will rise from their sleep, since they too are included in Christ. 1 Thessalonians 4:17, In the wake of their arising we will all be gathered into a large dense multitude; an innumerable throng of people, united as one, like the particles of water in a cloud, and we will encounter the Lord in the very air we breathe and so shall we continually celebrate our I-am-ness in our union with him. (This is the moment which redemption declares, where Deity and humanity are married. The Bride and her Groom are united.) 1 Thessalonians 4:18, The fact that we are all deeply connected in the same source of our 'beingness' causes us to be constantly engaged in this conversation with one another.)*

Revelation 1:8 The God who is Lord over all things says: I am the Alpha and the Omega - my I-am-ness defines time - I am present, past and future. *(The union of **Alpha** and **Omega**, in Greek, makes the verb αω, I breathe. And in Hebrew the union of the first and last letter in their alphabet, **Aleph** and **Tav** makes את **et**, which the Rabbis interpret as the first matter out of which all things were formed, [see Genesis 1:1]. The particle **et**, is untranslatable in English but, says Rabbi Aben Ezra, "it signifies the substance of the thing." In the Ancient Hebrew Alphabet the bull's head is Aleph and the cross is the Tav. †ע)*

Revelation 1:9 I John am your brother and companion in tribulation - in the midst of which we are equally participating in the authority of the kingdom and steadfastness of Jesus Christ - I was on the Isle of Patmos because of the Word of God and because of the Testimony of Jesus Christ.

1 John 5:9 Now if it is reasonable for us to be readily persuaded by the evidence that people may lay out before us, how much more certainty is there in the evidence that God has so compellingly borne witness to concerning his Son.

1 John 5:10 Whoever shares in the same persuasion concerning the Son of God, has God's testimony confirmed within themselves.

1 Corinthians 1:6 You certainly have the testimony of Christ evidenced in you. *(You possess full knowledge and give full expression because in you the evidence for the truth of Christ has found confirmation. — NEB)*

Revelation 12:11 Mikael and his celestial messengers conquered the Dragon because of the blood of the little Lamb and the word of their testimony. They did not believe that the agape of life discovered in Christ can be threatened or ¹terminated in death. *(The blood of the Lamb brought closure to every possible accusation against the human race. This is the testimony of the prophetic word announcing the Good News throughout the ages. The word ¹achri - the end; the idea of terminating. Mikael and his messengers represent the entire host of heaven - including all the multitudes previously mentioned.)*

Extended Notes on Israel

Revelation 20:7 Their reign and priesthood will be fully established within the context of the vastness of this symbolic thousand year period. In sharp contrast then, only to emphasize the complete and utter defeat of the Satanas-system, he will be let loose very briefly, out of his prison. *(From the Abyss, the symbolic "Bottomless Pit-Underworld", where he was imprisoned when Jesus went there to free mankind. Jesus came back with the keys, remember.)*

Revelation 20:8 And his obvious strategy would be to deceive the nations on a global scale including the four corners of the earth by assembling Gog and Magog in war; their number is as the sand of the sea. *(Again, every traditional Jewish concept of judgment is addressed. Gog and Magog is now brought into the conversation, since Jewish eschatology viewed Gog and Magog as enemies to be defeated by the Messiah, which will usher in the age of the Messiah. "Then Eldad and Modad [brothers of Moses] both prophesied together, and said, 'In the very end of time Gog and Magog and their army shall come up against Jerusalem, and they shall fall by the hand of the King Messiah; they shall be slain by the flame of fire which shall proceed from under the throne of glory, and afterwards all the dead of Israel shall rise again to life, and shall enjoy the delights prepared for them from the beginning." Quote from the Jewish Targum. See reference in Numbers 11:26 and Ezekiel 38:17.)*

Hosea 1:10 Yet the Israelites will be like the sand on the seashore, which cannot be measured or counted. In the place where it was said to them, 'You are not my people,' they will be called 'children of the living God.'

Genesis 22:17 indeed I will greatly bless you, and I will greatly multiply your seed as the stars of the heavens and as the sand which is on the seashore; and your seed shall possess the gate of their enemies.

Genesis 32:12 "For You said, 'I will surely prosper you and make your descendants as the sand of the sea, which is too great to be numbered.'"

Romans 9:10 Rebecca and Isaac also conceived, consistent with the promise, to further prove the point of faith versus performance.

Romans 9:11 God spoke to Rebecca while the twins were still in the womb. Nothing distinguished them in terms of good looks or performance. *[Except the fact that the one would be born minutes before the other, which would give him 1st born preference, according to human tradition.]* **It was recorded to emphasize the principle of ¹faith-identity as the ultimate value above any preference according to the flesh.** *(The word often translated as "election" is the word ¹ekloge, from ek, origin, source and lego from logos, the word, see John 1:1,14. Faith nullifies any ground the flesh has to boast in. Romans 3:27)*

Romans 9:12 She was told, "the elder shall serve the younger."

Romans 9:13 We would say that Esau had the raw deal; he was disliked while Jacob was favored. *(And the Lord said to her, "Two nations are in your womb, and two peoples, born of you, shall be divided; the one shall be stronger than the other; the elder shall serve the younger." [Genesis 25:23].*

The two come out of the same mold; yet they represent two types of people: one who understands his true identity by faith and one who seeks to identify himself after *the flesh. Again, the law of performance versus the law of faith is emphasized in order to prepare the ground for the promise-principle. Mankind's salvation would be by promise and not by performance; i.e. it would not be a reward for good behavior. No one will be justified by the tree of the knowledge of good and evil; **poneros**, "evil," full of hardships, annoyances and labor.)*

Romans 9:14 To say that God is unfair, is to miss the point.

Romans 9:24 Being Jewish or Gentile no longer defines us; God's faith defines us. *(He "called" us; kaleo, to identify by name, to surname.)*

Romans 9:25 Hosea voiced the heart of God when he said, "I will call a people without identity, my people, and her who was unloved, my Darling." *(Even Esau whom you said that I hated. [See v 13]. It was common among the Hebrews to use the terms "love" and "hatred" in this comparative sense, where the former implied strong positive attachment, and the latter, not positive hatred, but merely a less love, or the withholding of the expressions of affection [compare Genesis 29:30-31; Luke 14:26].)*

Romans 9:26 He prophecies that the very same people who were told that they are not God's people, will be told that they are indeed the children of the living God.

Romans 9:27 Isaiah weeps for Israel: "You might feel lost in the crowd, because your numbers equal the grains of the sand of the sea, but God does not abandon the individual." Numbers do not distract God's attention from the value of the one. *("Isaiah maintained this same emphasis: If each grain of sand on the seashore were numbered and the sum labelled 'chosen of God,' They'd be numbers still, not names; salvation comes by individual realization. God doesn't just count us; he calls us by name. Arithmetic is not his focus." — The Message)*

Romans 9:28 For his word will perfect his righteousness without delay; his word is poetry upon the earth. *(John 1:1,14; Romans 1:16,17.)*

Romans 9:29 The Lord of the ¹multitudes preserved for us a Seed, to rescue us from the destruction of Sodom and Gomorrah. *(From Hebrew, צבא tzaba [Strongs H6635], a host/mass of people. [See note on Romans 3:10] In Genesis 18, Abraham intercedes for Sodom and Gomorrah, "If there perhaps are 50 righteous people, will you save the city on their behalf?" He continues to negotiate with God, until he's down to "perhaps ten?" " ... there was none righteous, no not one ... ." The remnant represents the one Seed that would rescue the mass of mankind. In Romans 5:17, "one man's obedience and act of righteousness, surpasses the effect of a multitude of sins." If [spiritua] death saw the gap in one sin, and grabbed the opportunity to dominate mankind in Adam, how much more may we now seize the advantage to reign in righteousness in this life through that one act of Christ, who declared us innocent by his grace. Grace is superior in authority to the transgression. The single grain of wheat did not abide alone. [See John 12:24] Romans 5:18-19 states, "The conclusion is clear: it took just one offense to condemn mankind; one act of righteousness declares the same mankind innocent. The disobedience of the one exhibits mankind as sinners; the obedience of another exhibits mankind as righteous.")*

Romans 9:30 This means that the nations that stood outside and excluded, the very Gentiles who did not pursue righteousness through religious discipline of any kind, have stumbled upon this treasure of faith.

Romans 9:31 Yet Israel who sought to achieve righteousness through keeping the law, based upon their own discipline and willpower, have failed to do so.

Romans 9:32 How did they fail? Faith seemed just too good to be true. They were more familiar and felt more comfortable with their own futile efforts than what they did with faith. Their faith identity *[reflected in Christ]* was a stone of offense.

Romans 9:33 The conclusion of the prophetic reference pointed towards the rock as the spirit identity of human life. In Messiah, God has placed his testimony of mankind's identity in front of their eyes, in Zion, the center of their religious focus, yet, blinded by their own efforts to justify themselves, they tripped over him. But those who recognized him by faith, as the Rock from which they were hewn, are freed from the shame of their sense of failure and inferiority. *(See Deuteronomy 32:18, "you have forgotten the Rock that birthed you…", and in Isaiah 51:1, "Look to the Rock from which you were hewn." It is only in him that mankind will discover what they are looking for. "Who is the son of man?" Mankind's physical identity is defined by their spiritual origin, the image and likeness of God, "I say you are Petros, you are Mr. Rock, a chip off the old block. [See Matthew 16:13-19]. Mankind's origin and true identity is preserved and revealed again in the Rock of ages. The term "rock" in those days represented what we call the "hard drive" in computer language; the place where data is securely preserved for a long time. Rock fossils carry the oldest data and evidence of life.)*

Romans 11:1 I want to make it clear that I am not saying that God rejected Israel, my own life bears witness to that, and I am as Jewish as you can get; you can trace me back to Benjamin and Abraham.

Romans 11:2 God did not push his people aside; his reference is his [1]knowledge of them before they rejected him. Scripture accounts occasions where God had abundant reason to abandon Israel. Elijah hits out against them and lists their sins to persuade God to utterly cast them off. *([1]proginosko - to know in advance.)*

Romans 11:3 "Lord, they butchered your Prophets, and undermined your provision through the sacrificial altar; I am the only one left and scared to death." *(1 Kings 19:14.)*

Romans 11:4 Yet God answers him in a completely different tone, "You are counting wrong, you are not alone; I have seven times a thousand on reserve who have not bowed the knee to Baal. They have not exchanged me for a foreign owner." *(Seven times a thousand refers to an innumerable amount and not to an exact 7000 people. The Hebrew word בעל "Baal" means owner, husband or master [1 Kings 19:18].)*

Romans 11:9 David sees how the very table of blessing has become a stumbling block to them through their ignorance. The table of the Lord is the prophetic celebration of the sacrificed Lamb, where God himself provides redemption according to the promise; yet therein they were trapped and snared and they stumbled by their own unbelief. Now their only reward is the table they set for themselves. *(Commentary by John Gill: "... the table may be called an altar." 'You put unclean bread on my altar. And you say, 'How have we made it unclean?' By your saying, the table of the Lord is of no value [Mal 1:7].*

The sacrifices offered up upon "the table;" their meat offerings and drink offerings, and all others, likewise the laws concerning the differences of meats and indeed the whole ceremonial law which lay in meats and drinks and such like things; now the Jews are placing their justifying righteousness before God, in the observance of these rites and ceremonies, and imagining that by these sacrifices their sins are really expiated and atoned for; they neglected and submitted not to the righteousness of Christ, but went about to establish their own so that which should have led them to Christ became a handwriting of ordinances against them, and rendered Christ of no effect to them. Moreover, the sacred writings, which are full of spiritual food and divine refreshment, the prophecies of the Old Testament which clearly pointed out Christ, are not understood but misapplied by them, and proved a trap, a snare, and a stumbling block to them.)

Romans 11:10 This is the penalty of their disbelief; eyes that constantly fail to focus on the fact that Christ took their burdens and now their backs are still bending to the point of breaking under the strain of their own burdens.

Romans 11:11 Does this mean that the Jews are beyond redemption? Is their stumbling permanent? No, not at all! Their failure emphasized the inclusion of the Gentile nations. May it only prove to be their wake-up call.

Romans 11:12 If their stumbling enriched the rest of the world and their lack empowered the Gentiles, how much more significant will their realizing their completeness be?

Romans 11:24 You were cut out of the unfruitful olive tree and were grafted into the stock of the original tree. How much more will these natural branches be grafted again into their original identity.

Romans 11:25 Do not be ignorant then of the mystery of their temporal exclusion; their blindness opened your eyes to the fullness of God's plan for the whole world.

Romans 11:26 Once the nations realize the full extent of their inclusion, then all Israel shall also be saved. Just as it is written prophetically, "There shall come a Deliverer out of Zion; he shall turn ungodliness away from Jacob.

Romans 11:27 For this is my covenant with them that I shall take away their sins." *("And as a Savior he will come to Zion, turning away sin from Jacob, says the Lord." [Isaiah 59:20] "And as for me, this is my agreement with them, says the Lord: my spirit which is on you, and my words which I have put in your mouth will not depart from your mouth, or from the mouth of your children, or from the mouth of your children's children, says the Lord, from now and for the ages to come." [Isaiah 59:21])*

Romans 11:28 In your estimation they appear to be enemies of the gospel, but their Father's love for them has not changed. He knows their original worth.

Romans 11:29 For God's grace gifts and his persuasion of mankind's original identity are irrevocable. *(kaleo - to surname, to identify by name.)*

Romans 11:30 In days gone by, you did not believe God; yet in a sense Israel's unbelief opened the door for you to realize God's mercy.

Romans 11:31 Now you are returning the favor as it were; your testimony of his mercy extends an opportunity to them to turn from their unbelief and embrace mercy.

Romans 11:32 In God's calculation the mass of mankind is trapped in unbelief. This qualifies all mankind for his mercy.

Romans 11:33 Oh, how amazing is the depth of the wealth of God's wisdom and knowledge. The understanding of his judgements can only be sourced in a conversation that originates from above; also his ways are only accessible in the footprints of his thoughts. *(The word ἀνεξερεύνητος **anexereunētos** from **ana**, upward and **exereunaō**, to search out [1 Peter 1:10] from **ek**, source, and **ereo**, to utter to speak - [only here and in Ephesians 3:8] Again the next word begins with the Preposition **ana** - ἀνεξιχνίαστος **anexichniastos** from **ana**, upward and **ek**, source and **ichnos**, a footprint. Sadly, both these words have been wrongly translated to suggest that it is impossible to explain God's decisions or to understand his ways. Sounds like Isaiah 55:8,9 until verse 10 comes to the rescue. "BUT. Just as the rain and the snow come down from heaven [from above] and saturate the soil, SO shall my Word be. The Incarnation is the key to understanding God's thoughts and his ways.)*

REVELATION Chapter 21

21:1 Then I saw a new heaven and a new earth, for the age of the previous heaven and earth has passed away. Also the sea was no longer present. *(Isaiah 65:17 For behold, I create new heavens and a new earth; and the former things shall not be remembered or come into mind. See **Notes on the New heaven and Earth** at the end of this chapter.)*

21:2 And I saw her, in spotless magnificence, the Holy City, the New Jerusalem, descending out of the heavens; having been fully prepared as a bride and beautifully adorned for her husband. *(In total contrast to the symbolic religious Prostitute city of Babylon. In John 7:37,38 when Jesus speaks of waters gushing forth out of your innermost being, he says that you are the city. You are the bride. God's redeemed society. See notes on **The City-Bride** at the end of Chapter 3.)*

21:3 And a glorious announcement was heralded out of the throne, "Behold, God's tabernacle is with humanity." He has taken up permanent residence in human ¹skin to be with them in the closest possible association of oneness. They are his own possession; his tribe and he is their God inseparably entwined with them. *(The word for tabernacle is σκηνή skene - skin. Revelation 7:15 Standing free and forgiven in their redeemed innocence and union, face to face before the throne of God, they are fully engaged, day and night in their priestly service of worship in the inner sanctuary. **The one seated upon the throne is their tabernacle - he shelters them with his presence.**)*

21:4 He wipes every tear from their eyes and ¹blots out every hurtful memory. And death shall be no more. Nor any association with it; no more mourning and bitter weeping nor any reference to pain. For the former things have passed away. *(The word, ¹**exaleipho**, comes from **ek**, out of, and **aleipho**, with **a**, as a particle of union, and **liparos**, to grease, to leave a stain; scars of hurtful experiences were like grease stains stored in memory. Revelation 7:16,17)*

21:5 And the one seated upon the throne said, Behold, I make all things new. And he instructed me to write, because these words are true and to be relied on. *(Isaiah 43:18 Do not remember former things, nor consider the things of old.)*

21:6 And he said to me, everything is now ¹fully accomplished. I am the Alpha and the Omega, the sum total of the entire prophetic conversation concerning mankind's redemption. I am both the origin and the conclusion of all things. Anyone thirsty can come and drink freely from the gift of the waters of life direct from its source. *(The word ¹**gegonan** from **ginomai**, to make or give birth is in the Perfect Active Indicative tense denoting an action which is completed in the past, but the effects of which are regarded as continuing into the present. Isaiah 55:1 "Ho, everyone who thirsts, come to the waters; and he who has no money, come, buy and eat. Come, buy wine and the finest wheat without money and without price. Isaiah 55:2 Why do you spend your money for that which is not bread, and your labor for that which does not satisfy? Hearken diligently to me, and eat what is good, and delight yourselves in fatness. Isaiah 55:3 Incline your ear, and come to me; hear, that your soul may live; and I will make with you an everlasting covenant, my steadfast, sure love for David.)*

REVELATION Chapter 21

21:7 The conquering one inherits all things and I will be God to him and he will be my son. *(This was said of Solomon - 2 Samuel 7:13 He shall build a house for my name, and I will establish the throne of his kingdom forever. 7:14 I will be his father, and he shall be my son. And applied to David later in Psalm 89:26 He shall cry to me, 'Thou art my Father, my God, and the Rock of my salvation.' 89:27 And I will make him, the first-born [Jesus], the highest of the kings of the earth.)*

21:8 The ¹fear-driven and unbelieving, those having become ²rotten to the core; sex peddlers and sorcerers, idolaters and deceivers, their measure is the ³lake burning with brimstone; this is the Second Death. *(¹deilos, timid, from doeis, dread; an adjective derived from deidō, "fear-driven"*

The word ²bdelussō, to become rotten, abhorred, foul; from bdelugma derivative of bdeo - to stink.

Revelation 17:4 The woman was draped in purple and scarlet fabric, festooned and sprinkled with golden glitter and ornaments; she was elaborately decorated with gold, precious stones and pearls. Holding a golden chalice in her hand, brimming with defiling obscenities, and the stench of her impurities. [βδελυγματων bdelugma derivative of bdeo - to stink. Again the surface, make-believe beauty and apparent splendor cannot hide her true filthy character - like the white washed tombs Jesus compared the religious system to. "Hypocrites. For you are so careful to clean the outside of the cup and the dish, but inside you are filthy - full of greed and self-indulgence. You are like whitewashed tombs, which outwardly appear beautiful, but within are full of dead people's bones and all uncleanness." Matthew 23:25, 27.]

See Extended notes on the lake of fire & the Second Death at the end of chapter 19.)

21:9 And one of the seven celestial messengers, having the seven vessels being filled with the seven last wounds, came to me and spoke with me, saying, "Come, I will show you the bride, the Lamb's wife." *(The numphē, Bride, is placed in sharp contrast with the pornē, Harlot. See same setting in Revelation 17:1; Also Revelation 15:6 And the seven celestial messengers representing the seven wounds proceeded out of the inner shrine being arrayed in spotlessly clean linen shining with the radiant brightness of a precious stone and with golden girdles wrapped around their chests. Revelation 15:7 And one of the four living creatures gave each of the celestial messengers a typical temple vessel; a broad shallow saucer of pure gold, filled with the coals from the bronze altar where the Lamb was sacrificed - this is the passion of God. These golden fire-pans were loaded with the entire meaning of the sacrifice. This golden saucer was for the purpose of carrying fire, in order to burn incense on the day of Atonement once a year in the ultimate place of worship.)*

21:10 He carried me away in spirit onto a great and high mountain, and pointed out to me the holy city, Jerusalem, descending out of heaven from God. *(See Ezekiel 40:2. See same language in Revelation 17:7)*

21:11 Possessing the glory of God her radiance resembled a very precious and flawless jasper stone, transparent like crystal.

21:12 She had an impressive high wall with twelve gates and the names of the twelve tribes of the sons of Israel inscribed in them. *(See Ezekiel 48:31 - 34 the gates of the city being named after the tribes of Israel.)*

21:13 From the east, three gates; from the north, three gates; from the south, three gates; and from the west, three gates.

21:14 And the wall of the city had twelve foundations or thresholds to the gates, and in them the names of the twelve Apostles of the Lamb. *(See Ephesians 2:17 On that basis he made his public appearance, proclaiming the Good News of peace to the entire human race; both those who felt left out in the cold [as far as the promises and covenants were concerned], as well as to those who were near all along [because of their Jewish identity]. Ephesians 2:18 Because of Christ both Jew and Gentile now enjoy equal access to the Father in one Spirit. Ephesians 2:19 The conclusion is clear; you are no longer frowned upon as a foreigner; you are where you belong and part of an intimate family. Ephesians 2:20 Your lives now give tangible definition to the spiritual structure, having been built into it by God upon the foundation that the Prophets and Apostles proclaimed. The first evidence of this building was Jesus Christ himself being the chief cornerstone. (He is the visible testimony to the restored image and likeness of God in human form.) Ephesians 2:21 In him everyone of us are like ¹living Lego blocks fitted together of the same fabric (¹conversation), giving ever ²increasing articulation to a global mobile ³sanctuary intertwined in the Lord. (The word, ¹**sunarmologeo**, has 3 components, **sun**, meaning union, **harmo** meaning harmony, and **logeo** meaning conversation. The word, ²**auxano**, means expanding with growth. The word, ³**naos**, is translated as the most sacred dwelling space.) Ephesians 2:22 In him you are co-constructed together as God's permanent spiritual residence. You are God's address.)*

21:15 And the one speaking with me had a golden reed wherewith to measure the city, its gates, and its wall.

21:16 And the city was structured in a perfect quadrangular cube. And he measured the city with the reed at twelve thousand stadia; its length and width and height are equal. *(As eight furlongs make a mile, the extent of the walls, therefore, must have been three hundred and seventy-five miles each. [1500 miles divided by 4] The symbolic picture emphasizes that its height, three hundred and seventy-five miles, suggests a fusion with the heavens, and is equal to its width and length. [Earth's atmosphere is about 300 miles.] The vertical dimensions equal the horizontal dimensions - the Bride-city's relationship with he Bridegroom in her fusion with heaven equally translates to her horizontal relationships on earth. A perfect cube like the Holy of Holies in Solomon's temple. 1Ki 6:19,20*

Adam Clarke suggests that the quadrangular form intimates its perfection and stability, for the square figure was a figure of perfection among the Greeks; αντρ τετραγωνος, the square or cubical man, was, with them, a man of unsullied integrity, perfect in all things.)

21:17 And he also measured its wall, a hundred and forty four cubits; his measure was the stature of a man which is the measure of the celestial messenger. *[The Incarnate Messiah]. (Ephesians 4:13, ...to bring everyone into the realization of the fullness of the measure of Christ in them. The word, **xristos**, the Anointed one, from χρίω **chriō**, to smear or rub with oil, to anoint; to draw the hand over, to measure; from χείρ **cheir**, hand. [We still measure the height of horses*

REVELATION Chapter 21

by hand - ie. "A seventeen hand horse."] See also the Hebrew/Aramaic for Messiah, משיח from משח mashach, to draw the hand over, to anoint; to measure. [Analytical Hebrew and Chaldee Lexicon, B Davidson.] In Jesus Christ, God has measured mankind innocent, he is the blueprint of our design. Christ in us defines us. He measures our identity, our sonship, our belonging, our value, our innocence and our royalty.

*See Isaiah 60:18 "You shall call your walls Salvation, ישועה yeshû`âh and your gates Praise." See Notes on **The Measure of the temple** at the end of Chapter 11.)*

21:18 And the structure of its wall was jasper; and the city was pure gold, like pure glass.

21:19 And the thresholds of every gate in the wall of the city was beautifully adorned with every precious stone: The first threshold, jasper; the second, sapphire; the third, chalcedony; the fourth, emerald;

21:20 the fifth, sardonyx; the sixth, sardius; the seventh, chrysolite; the eighth, beryl; the ninth, topaz; the tenth, chrysoprasus; the eleventh, ¹hyacinth; the twelfth, amethyst. *(The twelve gems correspond closely with the twelve stones on the high priest's breastplate. Exodus 28:17-20; Exodus 39:10. The Hebrew term for the breastplate, חשן ḥōšen, describes its appearance, probably derived from the same source as Arabic, ḥasuna, meaning "to be beautiful" See Ezekiel 28:12,13.*

*See Notes on **The splendor of the Gates - the redeemed beauty of the Bride** at the end of this chapter.)*

21:21 And each one of the twelve gates were an individual giant pearl. And the street of the city was pure gold like transparent glass.

21:22 And I saw no temple in it, for the Lord God, the supreme power vested in the Lamb, is its temple. *(The entire city is now one holy temple of God. We are made kings and priests. Revelation 1:6. Revelation 21:3 And a glorious announcement was heralded out of the throne, "Behold, God's tabernacle is with the human race." He has taken up permanent residence in human skin to be with them in the closest possible association of oneness. Also Revelation 7:15 The one seated upon the throne is their tabernacle - he shelters them with his presence. It is almost unspeakable that of all the themes God could choose from to celebrate the central authority of the throne Room, he chose the Lamb. Mankind's redeemed innocence is the theme of the throne of heaven, forever. "Having accomplished purification of sins, he sat down ..." His throne is proof of mankind's redeemed innocence. Hebrews 1:3.)*

21:23 And the city had no need of the sun, nor of the moon, that they might shine in it, for the glory of God illuminated it; the Lamb is its lamp. *(The natural light is eclipsed by the true light of the Lamb.)*

21:24 And the nations will conduct their lives in the Lamb's light; and the kings of the earth bring their glory [their people] **into her.** *(Erasmus added τῶν σωζομένων, "of the ones saved" and so did innumerable editors, evidently following his authority without any further examination. Codex 1 dates from the 11th or 12th century, which Erasmus used in making his Greek text. The words, "of* *the ones saved" eventually became part of the Textus Receptus and were translated into the KJV and the NKJV. These words were not in the older manuscripts. Again a manipulation of the text in order to exclude the majority of the masses who didn't know or responded to the Good News. This reminds of a similar miss-translation of Isaiah 35:8 The highway in the wilderness will be called the Highway of holiness. It will be so obvious that no "unclean person" will miss it. Not even fools will get lost. This is their way of escape. This is their salvation from the wilderness of their lostness. [Sadly the KJV says the opposite. "...the unclean shall not pass over it.] Isaiah 35:10 And the ransomed of the LORD shall return, and come to Zion with singing; everlasting joy shall be upon their heads; they shall obtain joy and gladness, and sorrow and sighing shall flee away. See the beautiful context. Isaiah 35:1 The wilderness and the dry land shall be glad, the desert shall rejoice and blossom; like the crocus Isaiah 35:2 it shall blossom abundantly, and rejoice with joy and singing. The glory of Lebanon shall be given to it, the majesty of Carmel and Sharon. They shall see the glory of the LORD, the majesty of our God. Isaiah 35:3 Strengthen the weak hands, and make firm the feeble knees. Isaiah 35:4 Say to those who are of a fearful heart, "Be strong, fear not. Behold, your God will come and save you." Isaiah 35:5 Then the eyes of the blind shall be opened, and the ears of the deaf unstopped; Isaiah 35:6 then shall the lame man leap like a hart, and the tongue of the dumb sing for joy. For waters shall break forth in the wilderness, and streams in the desert.)*

21:25 And your gates will be open continually. Day or night they'll never be shut. *(See Isaiah 60:11.)*

21:26 And they will bring the glory and the honor of the nations into her. The nations will discover their redeemed, authentic doxa-identity and priceless value in the light of the Lamb. *(See commentary in the next verse.)*

21:27 And no-one classified as ¹common will enter into her, nor anyone making an abomination or a lie; but only the ones whose lives are defined in the Lamb's Book of Life. That which were common, abominable and the fruit of deception were all dealt with in the Lamb's doing. Now, the Lamb's Book of Life defines us and never again our own doing. *(The word **koinos**, to have all things in common; [Acts 2:44, Acts 4:32] reminds one of the word, **koinonia**. But **koinos,** in this context, means common - non Jewish - often referring to the nations - See Acts 10:14 But Peter said, "No, Lord; for I have never eaten anything that is **common** or unclean." Acts 10:15 And the voice came to him again a second time, "What God has cleansed, you must not call common." Also Acts 10:28, and he said to them, "You yourselves know how unlawful it is for a Jew to associate with or to visit any one of another nation; but God has shown me that I should not call anyone **common** or unclean."*

Behold the Lamb of God who takes away the sin of the world.

Here John clearly records that the nations and their kings have been equally cleansed and embraced in innocence and are equally part of the Bride. Their old Jewish fears, perceptions and definitions have all been conclusively addressed.

Also Ephesians 3:14 Overwhelmed by what grace communicates, I bow my knees in awe before the Father.

Ephesians 3:15 Every family in heaven and on earth originates in him; his is mankind's family name and he remains the authentic identity of every nation.)

Isaiah saw the new Jerusalem-Bride in the context of the powerful prophetic salvation poetry recorded in Isaiah chapters 52,53 and 54.

Isaiah 52:1 Awake, awake; put on thy strength, O Zion; put on your beautiful garments, O Jerusalem, the holy city. *(Addressing the city of Jerusalem in the feminine singular in Hebrew. Through the feminine form of the command 'awake.'* **uri. uri.** עורי *and* **livshi.** לבשי *'put on', as well as the feminine singular possessive and objective pronoun endings on the words,* **izech**, עזך *'your strength',* **tifartek**, תפארתך *'your beauty' and* בך **bak**, *'in you'.)*

The Jewish narrative explains the entire context of the Gospel.

Revelation Chapter 21 Extended Notes:
The New Heaven and Earth
The Splendor of the Gates - Celebrating the Redeemed Beauty of the Bride.

NEW HEAVEN & EARTH - REV 21

The New Heaven and Earth

Revelation 20:10 The Devil, who led them astray will be hurled into the lake of fire and brimstone where his puppet partners the Beast and the False Prophet have already been confined to. Day and Night they will be the subject of God's [1]touchstone for the ages of the ages - the very atmosphere of the entire universe will be thoroughly fumigated from any evidence of Satanas. *(See my notes on the [1]Touchstone in Revelation 14:10)*

Revelation 20:11 And I saw a huge white throne and it was as if heaven and earth fled away from the presence of the one seated upon the throne and its place was never found again. *(This means that there is no accusation in the heavens or upon the earth that could possibly stand in the presence of the Lamb, the One seated upon the throne of the judgment of righteousness – his throne gives testimony to mankind's redeemed acquittal. See Hebrews 1:3 "Having made purification for sins he sat down." There exists no evidence that could be brought from any sphere or dimension that could possibly testify against the human race - Acts 17 The God of creation has overlooked the times of ignorance and now urgently persuades all of mankind everywhere to awaken in their understanding to the fact of their innocence - he appointed a day and a person and on that day and in that person God would judge he world in righteousness and of this he has given proof by raising Jesus from the dead. The resurrected Jesus is the official receipt and verdict confirming mankind's redeemed innocence. Romans 4:25.* **The entire universe now bears witness to mankind's redeemed innocence.***)*

Revelation 20:4 And I saw thrones and those seated upon the thrones have been given judgment. They are the souls who didn't worship the Beast or its image, and did not take his mark in their foreheads or on their hands. The system of the Beast [1]axed them because of the Testimony of Jesus and because of the Word of God, since they didn't fit into their religious mold. They are the living beings, joined together in the Christ-life, reigning from their joint-seatedness in the throne of the Lamb for a thousand years. *(See **notes on the thousand years** at the end of Chapter 20. Revelation 1:2 John gave accurate evidence to* **the Word of God and the Testimony of Jesus Christ***, exactly as he saw it. [The Testimony of Jesus Christ is the context of the prophetic word.] The word, [1]**pelekizō**, axe, to cut off, from* **plassō***, to form, mold something from clay, wax, etc. - used of a potter - they would not be molded into a distorted image-mindset. Revelation 21:1, also Matthew 19:28 Jesus said to them, "Truly, I say to you, in the rebooting of mankind, when the Son of man shall sit on his glorious throne, you who have followed me will also sit on twelve thrones, judging the twelve tribes of Israel. See the word,* **paliggenesia***, [Matthew 19:28 & Titus 3:5] suggests a complete restoration to the original, in modern terms,* **rebooted***. From* **palin***, again by repetition and* **genesis***, source.)*

Hebrews 12:22 By contrast, we have been welcomed to an invisible mount Zion; the city of peace [Jerusalem], the residence of the living God, the festive assembly of an innumerable celestial host.

Hebrews 12:23 We are participating in a mass joint-celebration of heavenly and earthly beings; the [1]Ekklesia-ekklesia of the firstborn mirror-inscribed in the heavenlies. *(Our original identity, [1]Ekklesia, from* *ek, a Preposition that always denotes origin, and **kaleo**, meaning to identify by name, to surname], is endorsed by Jesus, patterned in him, the first born from the dead.)*

Hebrews 12:24 Jesus is the spokesman and arbitrator of the New Testament order. His blood signature sanctions mankind's innocence. This is a complete new language that communicates better things, in that it is the very substance of what was spoken in the shadow-type message of the blood sacrifice that Abel brought. *(Abel's faith was a prophetic introduction to the sacrificial shadow system of the Old Covenant. Jesus is the substance of things hoped for. Hebrews 11:4 It was faith that made the difference between the sacrifices of Abel and Cain, and confirmed Abel's righteousness. God bore witness to righteousness as a gift rather than a reward. Even though he was murdered, his faith still has a most relevant, prophetic voice.)*

Hebrews 12:25 If Jesus is the crescendo of God's final message to mankind, you cannot afford to politely excuse yourself from this conversation. Consider the prominent place that Moses plays in the history of Israel: if you think that Moses or any of the Prophets who spoke with authority on earth deserve honor, how much more should this word that God declared from heaven concerning our sonship, and our redeemed innocence revealed in the Messiah himself, deserve our undivided attention.

Hebrews 12:26 When he introduced the prophetic shadow of what was to come *(the Law system),* **his voice visibly shook the earth.** *(Exodus 19:18.)* **But now the Messiah has come** *(he is the desire of the nations; he is what heaven and earth were waiting for [Haggai 2:6,7])* **The voice of God** *(articulated in Christ's birth, life, ministry, death, and resurrection)* **has rocked not only the systems on the earth, but also every unseen principality in the heavens, to their very foundations.**

Hebrews 12:27 In the words of the Prophet, "Yet once more will I shake every unstable system of man's effort to rule himself." God clearly indicates his plan to remove the old and replace it with the new. The second shaking supersedes any significance in the first shaking. Then it was a physical quaking of the earth; now the very foundations of every man-made system was shaken to the core while the heavens were impacted by the announcement of his permanent rule on earth as it is mirrored in heaven.

Hebrews 12:28 We are fully associated in this immovable Kingdom; an authority that cannot be challenged or contradicted. Our participation echoes grace *(and not law-inspired obedience)* **as we ¹accommodate ourselves to God's delight, yielding in awe to his firm embrace.** *(The word, ¹euaresto, means well pleasing, to accommodate yourself to God's delight.)*

Hebrews 12:29 His zeal for us burns like fire. *[Deuteronomy 4:24.]*

Isaiah 9:6 For to us a child is born, to us a son is given; and the government will be upon his shoulder, and his name will be called "Wonderful Counselor, Mighty God, Everlasting Father, Prince of Peace."

NEW HEAVEN & EARTH - REV 21

Isaiah 9:7 Of the increase of his government and of peace there will be no end, upon the throne of David, and over his kingdom, to establish it, and to uphold it with justice and with righteousness from this time forth and for evermore. The zeal of the LORD of hosts will do this.

2 Corinthians 5:17 The old things have passed away, behold, everything has become new.

Revelation 21:3 And a glorious announcement was heralded out of the throne, "Behold, God's tabernacle is with the human race." He has taken up permanent residence in human skin to be with them in the closest possible association of oneness. They are his own possession; his tribe and he is their God inseparably entwined with them. *(Revelation 7:15 Standing free and forgiven in their redeemed innocence and union, face to face before the throne of God, they are fully engaged, day and night in their priestly service of worship in the inner sanctuary. **The one seated upon the throne is their tabernacle - he shelters them with his presence.**)*

Revelation 21:4 He wipes every tear from their eyes and ¹blots out every hurtful memory. And death shall be no more. Nor any association with it; no more mourning and bitter weeping nor any reference to pain. For the former things have passed away. *(The word, ¹**exaleipho**, comes from **ek**, out of, and **aleipho**, with **a**, as a particle of union, and **liparos**, to grease, to leave a stain; scars of hurtful experiences were like grease stains stored in memory. Revelation 7:16 & 17.*

Isaiah 25:6 The LORD of hosts will prepare a lavish banquet for all peoples on this mountain; a banquet of aged wine, choice pieces with marrow, and refined, aged wine. Isaiah 25:7 and on this mountain He will swallow up the covering which is over all peoples, even the veil which is stretched over all nations. Isaiah 25:8 He will swallow up death for all time, And the Lord GOD will wipe tears away from all faces, And he will remove the reproach of his people from all the earth; For the LORD has spoken....Holman Christian Standard Bible

And on this mountain, he will swallow up the burial shroud that enfolds all peoples, the veil that is spread over all nations—

Isaiah 51:11 And the redeemed of the LORD shall return, and come to Zion with singing; everlasting joy shall be upon their heads; they shall obtain joy and gladness, and sorrow and sighing shall flee away.

Socrates observes, "How thrice happy those of mortals, who, having had these ends in view, depart to Hades; for to them alone is it given there to live; but to others, all things there are evil" ["Fragment"]. And Euripides: "The dead, tearless, forgets his pains.")

Revelation 7:16 Here there is no memory of hunger or thirst or a scorching sun to plague them. (Isaiah 49 is fulfilled. See Isaiah 49:6 "I will give you as a light to the nations, that my salvation may reach to the end of the earth." The tribes of Judah as prophetic pointer to the entire population of the planet are gathered as one in worship." Isaiah 49:10 "They shall not hunger or thirst, neither scorching wind nor sun shall smite them, for he who has pity on them will lead them, and by springs of water will guide them.")

Revelation 7:17 For the little Lamb who occupies the center stage of the throne will shepherd them and lead them beside living springs of water and God shall blot out every hurtful memory of the tears they have cried.

A similar scene is set here to mirror the historic deliverance of Israel out of slavery in the build-up to the first prophetic Passover - this time the dramatic symbolic pictures reflect on the final Passover and the slain Lamb on the throne addressing and bringing closure and conclusion to the many ideas of judgment so deeply entrenched in Jewish consciousness. Pesach, פסח protecting and rescuing. From an Arabic root which means to expand; to save. See John 11:56. **Their stories and symbolic prophetic pictures are repeated again and again, waging war against their perceived reasonings and philosophies portrayed in their own historic priesthood and altar services.**

The number seven brings out the varied forms as well as their essential oneness; whether the "seven Spirits of God"; the "seven churches," the "seven horns" and "seven eyes" of the Lamb, the "seven seals," the "seven trumpets", and the "seven bowls.")

Revelation 21:5 And the one seated upon the throne said, Behold, I make all things new. And he instructed me to write, because these words are true and to be relied on. *(See Isaiah 43:18 Do not remember former things, nor consider the things of old.)*

Revelation 21:6 And he said to me, everything is now [1]fully accomplished. I am the Alpha and the Omega, the sum total of the entire prophetic conversation concerning mankind's redemption. I am both the origin and the conclusion of all things. Anyone thirsty can come and drink freely from the gift of the waters of life direct from its source. *(The word [1]gegonan from **ginomai**, to make or give birth is in the Perfect Active Indicative tense denoting an action which is completed in the past, but the effects of which are regarded as continuing into the present. Isaiah 55:1 "Ho, everyone who thirsts, come to the waters; and he who has no money, come, buy and eat. Come, buy wine and the finest wheat without money and without price. Isaiah 55:2 Why do you spend your money for that which is not bread, and your labor for that which does not satisfy? Hearken diligently to me, and eat what is good, and delight yourselves in fatness. Isaiah 55:3 Incline your ear, and come to me; hear, that your soul may live; and I will make with you an everlasting covenant, my steadfast, sure love for David.)*

THE SPLENDOR OF THE GATES - REV 21

The Splendor of the Gates - Celebrating the Redeemed Beauty of the Bride.

Revelation 21:18 And the structure of its wall was jasper; and the city was pure gold, like pure glass.

Revelation 21:19 And the thresholds of every gate in the wall of the city was beautifully adorned with every precious stone: The first threshold, jasper; the second, sapphire; the third, chalcedony; the fourth, emerald;

Revelation 21:20 the fifth, sardonyx; the sixth, sardius; the seventh, chrysolite; the eighth, beryl; the ninth, topaz; the tenth, chrysoprasus; the eleventh, ¹hyacinth; the twelfth, amethyst. *(See commentary note on ¹Hyacinth in Revelation 9:17.)*

Revelation 21:21 And each one of the twelve gates were an individual giant pearl. And the street of the city was pure gold like transparent glass.

Revelation 21:22 And I saw no temple in it, for the Lord God, the supreme power vested in the Lamb, is its temple. *(The twelve gems correspond closely with the twelve stones on the high priest's breastplate. Exodus 28:17-20; Exodus 39:10.*

*The Hebrew term for the breastplate, חשן hosen, describes its appearance, probably derived from the same source as Arabic, hasuna, meaning "to be beautiful" See Ezekiel 28:12,13.See Exodus 24:10 and they saw the God of Israel; and there was under his feet as it were a pavement of **sapphire** stone, like the very heaven for its transparency.*

Isaiah 54:10 For the mountains may depart and the hills be removed, but my steadfast love shall not depart from you, and my covenant of peace shall not be removed, says the LORD, who has compassion on you.

*Isaiah 54:11 "O afflicted one, storm-tossed, and not comforted, behold, I will set your stones in beautiful colors, and **lay your foundations with sapphires**.*

Isaiah 54:12 I will make your pinnacles of rubies, and your gates of sparkling jewels, and all your walls of precious stones.

Isaiah 54:13 All your sons shall be taught by the LORD, and great shall be the prosperity of your sons.

Isaiah 54:14 In righteousness you shall be established; you shall be far from oppression, for you shall not fear; and from terror, for it shall not come near you.

Everything mankind lost in Adam and Eve is now fully redeemed in the Bride.

A graphic narrative is recorded on the perfect beauty of mankind in the Garden of Eden and their fall from glory into the Prostitute-mindset-system of the DIY-Tree. See Ezekiel 28:12 "You were the signet of perfection, full of wisdom and perfect in beauty. Ezekiel 28:13 You were in Eden, the garden of God; every precious stone was your covering, carnelian, topaz, and jasper, chrysolite, beryl, and onyx, sapphire, carbuncle, and emerald; and wrought in gold were your settings and your engravings. On the day that you were created they were prepared. Ezekiel

*28:14 With an anointed guardian cherub I placed you; you were on the holy mountain of God; in the midst of the stones of fire you walked. Ezekiel 28:15 You were blameless in your ways from the day you were created, till iniquity was found in you. Ezekiel 28:16 In the abundance of your **trade** [See notes on the currency of sin-consciousness at the end of Revelation 13] you were filled with violence, and you sinned; so I cast you as a profane thing from the mountain of God, and the guardian cherub drove you out from the midst of the stones of fire. Ezekiel 28:17 Your heart was proud because of your beauty; you corrupted your wisdom for the sake of your splendor. I cast you to the ground; I exposed you before kings, to feast their eyes on you. Ezekiel 28:18 By the multitude of your iniquities, in the unrighteousness of your trade you profaned your sanctuaries; so I brought forth fire from the midst of you; it consumed you, and I turned you to ashes upon the earth in the sight of all who saw you. Ezekiel 28:19 All who know you among the peoples are appalled at you; you have come to a dreadful end and shall be no more forever." See Notes on the **lake of fire** at the end of Revelation 19. Also my notes on **the Sword of the Lord**, Revelation 2:16 and Revelation 1:16 The Sword would always point back to mankind's original identity. The Hebrew word in Genesis 3:24, [where the cherub with the flaming sword was positioned at the Eastern Gate of Eden] הפך **hâpak** is a primitive root; meaning to turn about; by implication to change, to return, to be converted, turn back. Also in the Septuagint the same thought is communicated in the Greek word, **strephō**, which is the strengthened from the base of **tropay**; to turn around or reverse: - convert, turn again, back again, to turn self about. In Luke 15 the prodigal son returns to himself - Plato is quoted by Ackerman [Christian Element in Plato] as thinking of redemption as coming to oneself.*

In symbolic language the judgment of the Dragon, the Beast and the Whore; the counterfeit Trinity, is not a judgment against an entity, but against a corrupt mindset-system. A virus doesn't have a life of its own - it needs a host.)

REVELATION Chapter 22

22:1 And he pointed me to a river with crystal clear, living waters, flowing out of God's throne, endorsing the reign of the Lamb. *(See Further Notes at the end of the chapter.)*

22:2 The Tree of Life is the central theme throughout the City - right down the middle of the street, as well as on each side of the River, producing twelve varieties of ripe fruit, all year round. The [1]leaves of the Tree are for the healing of the nations. *(See Further Notes at the end of the chapter.)*

22:3 There will be no memory of any [1]curse. God's throne, endorsing the reign of the Lamb will be the presence in her. Mankind's redeemed innocence is the central theme of the city. And they, his [2]bond-bride, will [3]worship him for all eternity. *(See Further Notes at the end of the chapter.)*

22:4 And you will gaze upon him, face to face; recognizing every distinct detail of his divine features mirrored in you. His Name is tattooed in your innermost thoughts. *(See Further Notes at the end of the chapter.)*

22:5 No more night. No lamps; not even sunlight required. The Lord God engulfs them with light. And in this light will they reign supreme forever and ever. *("And the nations shall come to your light and their kings to the brightness of your rising." Isaiah 60:3 "In your light do we see the light." Psalm 36:9. Also 2 Corinthians 4:6.*

See also Revelation 21:23 And the city had no need of the sun, nor of the moon, that they might shine in it, for the glory of God illuminated it; the Lamb is its lamp.)

22:6 And he said to me, "These words are certain and true; the Lord God of the spirits of the Prophets, has commissioned his celestial messenger to point his [1]bond-servants, to that, which according to all the prophetic pointers, was to inevitably have happened in a brief moment of time. *(See Further Notes at the end of the chapter.)*

22:7 Behold, I am not distant from you. I am at hand - see my closeness, not my absence. Blessed is the one who treasures the prophetic values of the Scriptures.*(Revelation 1:2,3 John gave accurate evidence to the word of God and the testimony of Jesus Christ, exactly as he saw it. Blessed is the one who reads and those who hear with understanding the words of this prophetic enlightenment and treasure what is recorded in this writing; its time has come.)*

22:8 I, John am the one hearing and perceiving these things. I have indeed heard and seen. I fell prostrate in worship at the feet of the celestial messenger who showed me these things.

22:9 He immediately stopped me and said, "I want you to see something else. As a celestial messenger I am a joint bond-servant and brother of your family, the Prophets. We are all one family." *(See also Revelation 19:10, I was so overwhelmed that I fell down at his feet to worship him; he immediately asked me to see him as a fellow bond-servant and a fellow brother, jointly echoing the testimony of Jesus. Worship God, he said, the testimony of Jesus is the spirit of prophecy. This wedding is the entire culmination of the prophetic word.)*

22:10 He told me not to seal this conversation in futuristic, prophetic language since its time has come.

REVELATION Chapter 22

22:11 *[This is the final conclusion where mankind's self-help programs are brought to nought.]* **This is not about how ¹out of sync or righteous you are; neither about how soiled your garments or how squeaky clean and holy you are by your own efforts and standards. Those who are out of ¹sync, ²so be it. Those whose garments are soiled ²so be it. Those who are righteous and holy ²so be it.** *(See my explanatory notes at the end of the chapter.)*

22:12 Behold. *[Again the Aorist Imperative.]* **Now get the message, once and for all. I ¹am come. There are no further delays. This is the hour the Prophets pointed to. And my reward is with Me, to give to each as his** *[the Lamb's]* **work is.** *(See Further Notes at the end of the chapter.)*

22:13 I am the ¹Alpha and the Omega - the initiator and the ²conclusion; the genesis and completeness. *(See Further Notes at the end of the chapter.)*

22:14 Oh the ¹bliss and intense delight of those clothed in ²washed garments - having realized the ³authority of their redeemed innocence and identity; they have sourced their I-am-ness in the Tree of Life. This is their access through the gates into the city. *(The word, ¹makarios, blessed, suggests a special intensity of delight. The ²Textus Receptus again has a **wrong** reading here: "those who DO his commandments! [See my notes on this verse at the end of the chapter.] The word translated authority, ³exousia, from ek, source and eimi, I am.)*

22:15 *[In total contrast to this bliss, are the thirsty ones.]* **Those who love and live lies are outside the city gates like stray dogs. The sorcerers and their witchcraft, selling their bodies in prostitution; murderers, consumed by the business of idolatry.** *(To them the Spirit and the Bride say, COME... Revelation 22:17)*

22:16 I am Jesus. I sent my celestial messenger to be witness of these things to you before the churches; confirming to them that I am the Root and offspring of David, the radiant Morning Star. *(See Further Notes on verse 16 at the end of this chapter.)*

22:17 The Spirit and the Bride beckons, "Come." And let everyone in whom this bold bidding resonates, extend the same urgent invitation, "Oh yes, come." This is for the thirsty to come and quench their deepest longings by freely drinking from the water of life. *(See notes at the end of the chapter.)*

22:18-19 *(See my explanatory notes at the end of the chapter.)*

22:20 The One, responding to the bidding of the Bride on a disillusioned mankind's behalf, says yes. I am the evidence of your return. Without any delay. *[Just like the prodigal returning home in the resurrection-return of Jesus from our lostness and darkness.]* **"Oh, you're so welcome Lord Jesus.", says the Bride. I can't wait to embrace you home, my Lord and my God.**

22:21 The grace of the Lord Jesus is with everyone. *(Revelation ends with one final surprise, in the form of a textual variant in verse 21. Is grace declared to 'all the saints' [NRSV text], or 'to all' [NRSV footnote]? The shorter reading is the more original. The words μετὰ πάντων, **meta pantoon**, with everyone is the original ending - some copyist felt more comfortable sneaking in another "conditional clause." μετὰ τῶν ἁγίων, **meta toon hagion**, with "the saints.")*

Revelation Chapter 22 Extended Notes

NOTES ON REVELATION Chapter 22

Revelation Chapter 22 Extended Notes

Notes on Revelation 22:1

And he pointed me to a river with crystal clear, living waters, flowing out of God's throne, endorsing the reign of the Lamb. *(Again this picture is taken from familiar Jewish prophetic narrative. Zechariah 14:7 And there shall be continuous day, no night; every evening will be a new morning. Zechariah 14:8 On that day living waters shall flow out from Jerusalem, it shall continue in summer as in winter. Zechariah 14:10 The land will stretch out spaciously around Jerusalem—to Geba in the north and Rimmon in the south, with Jerusalem towering at the center, and the commanding city gates—Gate of Benjamin to First Gate to Corner Gate to Hananel Tower to the Royal Winery—encircling the city. Zechariah 14:11 And they shall live in it. And there shall not again be a shutting in, but Jerusalem shall dwell safely. Zechariah 14:16 Then all the nations shall go up year after year to worship the King, the LORD of hosts, and to keep **the Feast of Tabernacles**. And the LORD will be king over all the earth; on that day the LORD will be One and his Name One. See John 7:37 On **the last day of the feast [of Tabernacles]**, the great day, Jesus stood up and proclaimed, "If any one thirst, let him come to me and drink. John 7:38 He who believes in me, as the Scripture has said, 'Out of his heart shall flow rivers of living water.'" Just like Babylon is not a city in the symbolic language of Revelation, it is a fallen-mindset society; so the New Jerusalem is not a city but the redeemed society of mankind. The Bride of Christ. In John 7:37,38 when Jesus speaks of waters gushing forth out of your innermost being, he says that you are the city. You are the bride. God's redeemed society.)*

Notes on Revelation 22:2

The Tree of Life is the central theme throughout the City - right down the middle of the street, as well as on each side of the River, producing twelve varieties of ripe fruit, all year round. The [1]leaves of the Tree are for the healing of the nations. *(The leaves of the tree define the tree. This is also where the remarkable process of photosynthesis takes place. With sunlight, the leaves convert carbon dioxide into oxygen.*

Again these beautiful pictures are reflections of Jewish prophetic writings... See Ezekiel 47:12 "But the river itself, on both banks, will grow fruit trees of all kinds. Their leaves won't wither, the fruit won't fail. Every month they'll bear fresh fruit because the river from the Sanctuary flows to them. Their fruit will be for food and their leaves for healing."

*See Genesis 3:22 on the Tree of Life, "Behold, The man, who **was already created** like one of us, now also partook of the knowledge of the evil; [the idea of, "I am not who God says I am and created me to be;"] and now, lest he puts forth his hand, and take also of the tree of life, only to continue to live in this "lost identity" state..." The text does not say, "he has now become like one of us." The original Hebrew and the most authentic versions use the Perfect tense, היה **hayah**, which is the **Qal** Stem, masculine, third person, Active, and in the Perfect form, and signifies was, not is. The Perfect tense denotes an action which is completed in the past, but the effects of which are regarded as continuing into the present. The Samaritan text, the Syriac, and the Septuagint, have the same tense. The Greek verb, γέγονεν, is the*

NOTES ON REVELATION Chapter 22

Perfect Active Indicative tense of **ginomai**. See my commentary notes on 1 John 3:12 Thoughts on, "Why the other tree and why the temptation in the Garden?")

Notes on Revelation 22:3

There will be no memory of any [1]curse. God's throne, endorsing the reign of the Lamb will be the presence in her. Mankind's redeemed innocence is the central theme of the city. And they, his [2]bond-bride, will [3]worship him for all eternity. (See Galatians 3:11 Habakkuk confirms conclusively that righteousness by God's faith is the only basis to life; this terminates any possible justification before God based on behavior. [Habakkuk 2:4, Habakkuk 3:17-19.] Galatians 3:12 Law and faith have nothing in common. Law measures a person's doing and experience as defining their life. (Faith measures God's doing in redeeming his design in us, as defining our lives.) Galatians 3:13 Christ redeemed us from the [1]**curse** as consequence of our failure to keep the law. In his cross he concentrated the total curse of the human race upon himself. In his abandoning himself to death, he absorbed and dissolved the horror of the curse in his own person. Scripture declares that anyone hanging on a tree embodies the curse. [Deuteronomy 21:23] Galatians 3:14 This act of Christ released the blessing of Abraham upon the Gentiles. Now we are free to receive the blessing of the Spirit. (The blessing of the Spirit is righteousness by God's faith in the achievement of Christ, and not as a reward for our behavior. In the obedience of Christ Deuteronomy 28 is out-dated. [Romans 5:19, Ephesians 1:3] The mass of non-Jewish nations are equally included.)

Again quoting from Jewish Scripture, Zechariah 14:11 And the city shall be inhabited, for there shall be no more [1]curse; Jerusalem shall dwell in security. RSV.

*The word, [2]**doulos**, slave from **deo**, to bind; also, to be bound together in wedlock.*

*Here John intentionally employs the Jewish word for worship, [3]**latreuō**; to serve [in some contexts, for a wage; for hire,] but in the Jewish context describing their sacrificial service to God; See Paul's use in Acts 26:6 "And now for the hope of the promise having been made by God to the fathers; Acts 26:7 to which our twelve tribes hope to arrive, worshipping [latreuo] in earnestness night and day."*

A Jew would be offended by the application of this term to Christian worship. In Philippians 3:3 Paul, however, takes this word and converts it to spirit worship, "We give "circumcision" its true spiritual meaning. Our worship [latreuo] is not defined by anything external that would even remotely resemble the law of works and religious rituals. We worship God in the certainty of our redeemed innocence and rejoice in the finished work of Jesus Christ. Faith-righteousness gives substance to spiritual worship; the flesh occupies the religious mind with its own futile efforts to attain to righteousness." Philippians 3:3)

Notes on Revelation 22:4

*And you will gaze upon him, face to face; recognizing every distinct detail of his divine features mirrored in you. His Name is [1]tattooed in your innermost thoughts. (The word [1]**metopon**, from **meta**, together with, and ὤψ - **ops**, countenance; face; the space between the eyes, the forehead; focus. Also Revelation 3:12. See Psalm 17:15, As for me, I shall behold your face in righteousness; when I awake, I shall be satisfied, beholding your form. Beholding God's face in Jesus (our righteousness) as in a*

NOTES ON REVELATION Chapter 22

mirror, awakens me to my true likeness. Psalm 34:5 Look him in the face - you'll glisten with God. You'll gleam, your face'll scream, "GOD." 2 Corinthians 3:18, "We've got our masks off; God's brilliance is bouncing off our faces. We're glowing from knowing." Rob Lacey. "The whole earth is full of his glory." Isaiah 6:3.)

Notes on Revelation 22:6

And he said to me, "These words are certain and true; the Lord God of the spirits of the Prophets, has commissioned his celestial messenger to point his ¹bond-servants, to that, which according to all the prophetic pointers, was to inevitably have happened in a brief moment of time. *(A ¹bond servant is one who cleaves to his master out of no other obligation but total loving devotion.*

*This is a repeat of Revelation 1:1 Jesus Christ ¹unveiled. This is the revelation of God's ²gift which was wrapped up ³in him, in order to clearly illustrate to his bond-servants that, which according to prophetic pointers, ⁴inevitably ⁵was to have happened in a brief moment of time; this message was ⁶vividly portrayed in symbolic pictures by his celestial messenger, commissioned to communicate its mystery to his bond-servant John. (The word, ¹**apokalupsis** means an uncovering. The word ²**didōmi** means to give; to furnish; to extend; to present. The word ³**autoo** is the Personal Pronoun in the Dative Case, indicating location in. The word ⁴**dei** is from **deoo**, to bind; thus predictably, necessarily, inevitably. John employs the verb, ⁵**ginomai**, to beget, in the Aorist Infinitive tense, **genesthai**, which indicates prior completion of an action in relationship to a point in time. Greek Infinitives could have either a Present or Aorist form. The contrast between the two forms was not necessarily one of time, it is a difference of aspect. The Present Infinitive was used to express progressive or imperfective aspect. It pictures the action expressed by the verb as being in progress. The Aorist Infinitive however does not express progressive aspect. It presents the action expressed by the verb as a completed unit with a beginning and end. The word ⁶**sēmainō**, to give a symbolic sign; signify; to picture; to portray. Symbolism and imagery play a significant role throughout the book. John would employ pictures that his mostly Jewish audience was already familiar with in their own prophetic writings.)*

Notes on Revelation 22:11

[This is the final conclusion where mankind's self-help programs are brought to nought.] **This is not about how ¹out of sync or righteous you are; neither about how soiled your garments or how squeaky clean and holy you are by your own efforts and standards. Those who are out of ¹sync, ²so be it. Those whose garments are soiled ²so be it. Those who are righteous and holy ²so be it.** *(The word often translated, unrighteous, ¹**adike**, from **a**, negative and **dikay**, two parties in sync with one another; shared likeness - thus, **adike** means to be out of sync. Your own doing does not define you. It is the Lamb's doing that defines you. From beginning to end. He is your Alpha and Omega.*

*The ²Aorist Imperative is employed here again and again, Let them be. ²So be it. - and thus, very intentionally, emphasizes the fact that whatever it was that people based their moral condition on, was just that - now leave it there; don't try and change yourself - realize **once and for all** that it's not your efforts that's gonna get it right. The distinction between the Aorist Imperative and the Present Imperative is one of aspect, not tense. It's important to distinguish between tense [eg past, present,* *future] and aspect [eg completed, repeated, one-time, ongoing]. The Aorist Imperative points to a once and for all completed action, "Get it over and done with.")*

Notes on Revelation 22:12

Behold. *[again Aorist Imperative.]* **Now get the message, once and for all. I ¹am come. There are no further delays. This is the hour the Prophets pointed to. And my reward is with Me, to give to each as his** *[the Lamb's]* **work is.** *(The verb, ¹ερχομαι erchomai, is in the Present Indicative tense, I am come. Here John again repeats what the Prophets spoke concerning this time. [Isaiah 62:11] Behold, the LORD has made it to be heard to the end of the earth. Tell the daughter of Zion, Behold.* **Your salvation comes.** *Behold. His reward is ²with himself, and* **his work** *³before him. The ²Hebrew,* את *are the first and last letters of their Alphabet just as* **Alpha** *and* **Omega** *are the first and last letters of the Greek Alphabet. My work is ³before me, Hebrew,* פנים *pawneem face to face. Same word in Psalm 16:11 In your "presence"* פנים *pawneem is fullness of joy. There is definitely no reference here of man's work - the entire prophetic context of salvation points to the work of the Messiah. Note,* **Your salvation is his work.** *Isaiah 62:11. See 1 Peter 1:17 Now since you are defined in your Father, who does not judge anyone on face value, but always only according his work; [his finished work in Christ] wherever you find yourself located geographically or emotionally, return to your 'at-homeness' in him; you are not defined by your circumstances. [The word* **anastrepho**, *suggests a radical returning; literally a turning upside down. Actually* **ana**, *means upward- so its a turning downside up.] And to further emphasize the strong influence of the Hebrew text quoted here, the next verse continues with the same theme and further conclusion of the* את **Aleph Tav** *and* Αλφα Ωμέγα **Alpha Omega**.*)*

Notes on Revelation 22:13

I am the ¹Alpha and the Omega - the initiator and the ²conclusion; the genesis and completeness. *(I am the entire Alphabet of God's conversation.* **Ego to A kai to Ω, ho protos kai ho eschatos; arche kai telos.** *The union of* **Alpha** *and* **Omega**, *in Greek, makes the verb* αω, *I breathe. And in Hebrew the union of the first and last letter in their alphabet,* **Aleph** *and* **Tav** *makes* את, **et**, *which the Rabbis interpret of the first matter out of which all things were formed, [see Genesis 1:1] This is untranslatable in English but, says Rabbi Aben Ezra, "it signifies the substance of the thing." In the Ancient Hebrew Alphabet the bull's head is Aleph and the cross is the Tav.* ✝🐂 *The revelation of Jesus as the Alpha and Omega is the one in whom we live, and move, and have our being. He is indeed closer to us than the air we breathe. Don't waste a day waiting for another day. I am the initiator and the* **eschatos**. *Eschatology is defined in my I-am-ness.)*

Notes on Revelation 22:14

Oh the ¹bliss and intense delight of those clothed in ²washed garments - having realized the ³authority of their redeemed innocence and identity; they have sourced their I-am-ness in the Tree of Life. This is their access thru the gates into the city. *(The word, ¹makarios, blessed, suggests a special intensity of delight. Sadly, again, the King James Bible, using the Textus Receptus, reads, Blessed are they that do his commandments, that they may have right to the tree of life, and may enter in* *through the gates into the city -* ποιουντες *[do]* τας εντολας *[the commandments]; instead of the much older manuscripts which read* πλυνοντες *washed* τας στολας *garments. The variation here is clearly a deliberate change. The observation of the commandments elsewhere uses* τηρειν *terein, treasure not poiountes, do. The word translated authority, ³***exousia***, from **ek**, source and **eimi**, I am. Also note that The oldest Greek manuscripts were all written in uncials - all upper case letters.* ΠΛΥΝΟΝΤΕΣ ΤΑΣ ΣΤΟΛΑΣ ΑΥΤΩΝ *– wash their robes vs Textus Receptus* ποιοῦντες τὰς ἐντολὰς αὐτοῦ *- do his commandments. See Also Revelation 7:14.)*

Notes on Revelation 22:16

I am Jesus. I sent my celestial messenger to be the witness of these things to you before the churches; confirming to them that I am the Root and offspring of David, the radiant Morning Star. *(In Jesus, the prophetic word, which shone all along like a lamp in the night; now also compared to the radiant Morning Star, rising in our hearts, announcing the full unveiling of the day. Also Revelation 9:1 When the fifth celestial messenger blew his trumpet, I saw a star that had fallen to earth from the sky. The star was given the key to the shaft into the fathomless depths of the Abyss. [The symbolic value of the number five is divine grace.] Jesus is the bright Morning Star Revelation 2:28 and 22:16 I am the bright Morning Star. Also 2 Peter 1:19 We have the prophetic word made more sure. RSV For us the appearing of the Messiah is no longer a future promise but a fulfilled reality. Now it is your turn to have more than a second-hand, hearsay testimony. Take my word as one would take a lamp at night; the day is about to dawn for you in your own understanding. When the Morning Star [**phōsphoros**] appears, you no longer need the lamp; this will happen shortly on the horizon of your own hearts. In his death Jesus conquered the underworld and he has the keys; no-one else does. Revelation 1:17 Observing all this I fell at his feet like a dead man; then he laid his right hand on me and said, "Do not be afraid. I am the origin and conclusion of all things. Revelation 1:18 And the Living One; I died and now, see, here I am alive unto the ages of the ages and I have the keys wherewith I have disengaged the gates of Hades and Death. See Isaiah 14:12,* הילל *heilel, means "shining one" In the Greek,* **phōsphoros** *- bearer of light - LXX Septuagint. Which translates, Lucifer in Latin. Here, in Isaiah 14, Babylon's rule is compared to the bright morning star - ushering in the rule of its day - which is the counterfeit image - Isaiah 14:14 "I will make myself like the Most High." The fallen mindset-system is based on the idea that we are not image bearers of God - the Ophis lie in Genesis 5 - we have to eat the fruit of the tree of the knowledge of good and evil [**poneros** - hardships labor and annoyances] in order to become like God.* **Genesis 3:22** *does not say, "he has now become like one of us." It says, "Behold, the man, who was already created like one of us, now also partook of the knowledge of evil; [the Greek word 'evil' is* **poneros** *- full of labors, hardships and annoyances - which describes the system which tries to manage the fruit of the "I am not-Tree" - I am not good enough, I am not this- or that-enough, etc etc.] and now, lest he puts forth his hand, and take also of the tree of life, and eat only to continue to live in this "lost identity" state..." [See note on Genesis 3:24 at the end of Revelation 3 on* **Our God-identity**.*] The incarnate Jesus, the only true Morning Star descended into the deepest pits of mankind's hellish darkness and despair in their lost identity on his rescue mission to lead us out as God's trophies in his triumphant procession on high. Ephesians 4:8 also Ephesians 2:5,6.*

NOTES ON REVELATION Chapter 22

*See notes on **The "Fallen Star" is The bright Morning Star,** at the end of Revelation 9.*

*Revelation 5:5 Then one of the elders said unto me, "You need not weep anymore. Look. The Lion has conquered. He who is of the tribe of Judah, **the root of David.** His triumph qualifies him to open the scroll and its seven seals." Revelation 5:6 So I looked to see the Lion, and there, as if fused into one with the throne and in unison with the four living beings, taking center stage in the midst of the elders, I saw a little Lamb, alive and standing even though it seemed to have been violently butchered in sacrifice. It had seven horns and seven eyes which are the seven Spirits of God having been sent out to accomplish his bidding in all the earth.*

Further notes on the root of Jesse.

Eve was not an afterthought! Adam was put into a deep sleep; then God took her out of the word that was already made flesh! Mankind redeemed, the Bride, began the same way! Co-quickened, co-raised we are! When Adam awoke from his sleep, Eve was there! Behold, Bone of my bone, flesh of my flesh! She shall be called woman...

*Hidden in the name Jesse is the prophetic picture of the incarnation - Jahweh embracing man. The word for man, איש ish and woman, adding the ה breath-sound, hey, **ishah** אשה - Thus, Jesse also includes the jod connecting Jahweh with **ish**, man - Jahweh, the incarnate man.*

*Isaiah 11:1 Then a shoot will come out from the stump of Jesse, and a branch from its roots will bear fruit. See notes on Jesse in Luke 3:32 Son of **Jesse** ישי Jahweh is my husband - from יאיש from יֵשׁ yêsh/yaysh. From an unused root meaning to stand out, or exist; entity; used adverbially or as a copula for the substantive verb היה hâyâh H1961 to breathe; to be; to exist; from the core of the name of Jahweh, יהוה "existing". Thus, the root word for Jesse, היה **hajah,** in the Ancient Hebrew is, - the pictograph represents one who is looking at a great sight with his hands raised. In David's father, Jesse, it is the one looking at the other in mirror likeness. See Acts 13:22, Romans 15:12, And further Isaiah says, "The root of Jesse shall come, he who rises to rule the Gentiles; in him shall the Gentiles hope." And further Isaiah says, "The root of Jesse shall come, he who rises to rule the Gentiles; in him shall the Gentiles hope."*

Isaiah 11:2 The Spirit of the LORD will rest on him- the Spirit of wisdom and understanding, the Spirit of counsel and power, the Spirit of knowledge and godliness shall fill him;.

Isaiah 11:3 He will bear witness to the awe of the LORD with joy. He will not judge acording to humqn standards by what his eyes see or decide by what his ears hear.

Isaiah 11:4 He will judge the poor justly. He will make fair decisions for the humble people on earth. He will touch the earth with a rod from his mouth. He will lift up ungodliness with the breath from his lips. [ana + aireo to lift up; John 1:29; 12:32.]

Isaiah 11:5 Justice will be the belt around his waist. Faithfulness and truth will be the belt around his hips.

Isaiah 11:6 Wolves will live with lambs. Leopards will lie down with goats. Calves, young lions, and year-old lambs will be together, and a little child shall lead them.

Isaiah 11:7 Cows and bears will eat together. Their young will lie down together. Lions will eat straw like oxen. [Symbolic language - all your enemies shall be reconciled.]

Isaiah 11:8 Infants will play near cobras' holes. Toddlers will put their hands into vipers' nests. [The triumph of the Lamb. Ephesians 2:11-22 See Luke 1:17 Mirror Bible]

Isaiah 11:9 They will not hurt or destroy anyone anywhere on my holy mountain. All the world will be filled with the knowledge of the LORD like water covering the sea.

Isaiah 10:10 And in that day there shall be a root of Jesse, and he shall arise to rule over the Gentiles; in him shall the Gentiles trust, and his rest shall be glorious. LXX)

Notes on Revelation 22:17

The Spirit and the Bride beckons, "Come." And let everyone in whom this bold bidding resonates, extend the same urgent invitation, "Oh yes, come." This is for the thirsty to come and quench their deepest longings by freely drinking from the water of life. (Hear the prophetic echo in Isaiah's pleading in chapter 55:1 Ho, everyone who thirsts, come to the waters; and he who has no money, come, buy and eat. Come, buy wine and the finest wheat without money and without price.

Isaiah 55:2 Why do you spend your money for that which is not bread, and your labor for that which does not satisfy? Hearken diligently to me, and eat what is good, and delight yourselves in fatness.

Isaiah 55:3 Incline your ear, and come to me; hear, that your soul may live; and I will make with you an everlasting covenant, my steadfast, sure love for David.

Isaiah 55:4 Behold, I made him a witness to the peoples, a leader and commander for the peoples.

Isaiah 55:5 Behold, you shall call nations that you know not, and nations that knew you not shall run to you, because of the LORD your God, and of the Holy One of Israel, for he has glorified you.

Isaiah 55:6 "Seek the LORD while he may be found, call upon him while he is near;

Isaiah 55:7 let the wicked forsake his way, and the unrighteous man his thoughts; let him return to the LORD, that he may have mercy on him, and to our God, for he will abundantly pardon.

Isaiah 55:8 For my thoughts are not your thoughts, neither are your ways my ways, says the LORD.

Isaiah 55:9 For as the heavens are higher than the earth, so are my ways higher than your ways and my thoughts than your thoughts.

Isaiah 55:10 "For as the rain and the snow come down from heaven, and return not thither but water the earth, making it bring forth and sprout, giving seed to the sower and bread to the eater,

Isaiah 55:11 so shall my word be that goes forth from my mouth; it shall not return to me empty, but it shall accomplish that which I purpose, and prosper in the thing for which I sent it.

Isaiah 55:12 "For you shall go out in joy, and be led forth in peace; the mountains and the hills before you shall break forth into singing, and all the trees of the field shall clap their hands.

Isaiah 55:13 Instead of the thorn shall come up the cypress; instead of the brier shall come up the myrtle; and it shall be to the LORD for a memorial, for an everlasting sign which shall not be cut off.")

Notes on Revelation 22:18,19

I wrote the following on my introduction page of the Mirror Bible, never realizing that this specific quote from Revelation 22:18,19 carried so much controversy.] "Jesus is God's language and message to mankind. He is the context of Scripture. To add anything to his completed work in revealing and redeeming the image of God in human form, or taking anything away from what God spoke to us in him, is to depart from the essence of the Gospel. Revelation 22:18, 19."

It is a typical threat to copyist of the book, that they are not to add to or remove any of its words. Similar imprecations can be found scattered throughout the range of early Christian writings. Commentators disagree keenly about the words in Revelation 22:18, Revelation 22:19. Robert Charles rejects them as an interpolation and out of harmony with the rest of the book. [A critical and exegetical commentary on the Revelation of St. John by Charles, R. H. (Robert Henry), 1855-1931]

Revelation 22:18-19 assumes a settled text. You cannot disobey a prohibition against adding or taking away words when those words are uncertain to begin with.

There are more than 500,000 variants in the 5300 surviving manuscripts. These are not necessarily "errors", but variant readings, the vast majority of which are strictly grammatical; but according to the warning you dare not add or take away any. Any of which manuscripts are we talking about?

The first edition of the New Testament with a Greek text was prepared by Erasmus and published in 1516. For Revelation, he based his Greek text on a single manuscript, minuscule 1r, which is now, numbered 2814 according to the new Gregory-Aland number. This minuscule 1r however, lacks the final verses of the book of Revelation, and in order to have a complete text, Erasmus retranslated these verses into Greek from Latin. Elements of his re-translation survive in every edition of the so-called, Textus Receptus, the standard text of the printed Greek New Testament until the nineteenth century.

Deliberate changes to the wording of the Book of Revelation itself were made to improve and clarify the force of its message. Here's one of many examples, see note on Revelation 20:5 The words, "But the rest of the dead lived not again until the thousand years were finished" were added at a time when the ekklesia claimed to be fulfilling the thousand-year reign of Christ. The Sinaitic MS., remarkable as being the oldest as well as for its completeness and accuracy, is the only Greek authority on Revelation ante-dating the fifth century: and it does not contain the clause.

Someone remarked, "If you're going to be cutting verses from the Bible, you should probably start with the one that's usually taken to threaten dire consequences for anyone who, er, cuts verses from the Bible.")

Extended **Notes on Judgment and Resurrection** *at the end of John Chapter 5*

ABOUT FRANCOIS AND LYDIA

Lydia and Francois met on the 25th of August 1974, while he was working with Youth For Christ. She was sixteen and he, nineteen. The following year he studied Greek and Hebrew at the University of Pretoria for three years while Lydia completed her nursing training. In 1978 Francois also spent a year with YWAM. They married in January 1979 and are blessed with four amazing children, Renaldo, Tehilla, Christo and Stefan; also, three darling grandchildren Nicola and Christiaan. And 3 month old Lydie-Anne, daughter of our youngest son, Stefan and Yaël. With Christo and Keryn's Sadie arriving in July 2021.

They pioneered and worked in full-time mission for fourteen years, during which time they also pastored a church and led a training facility for more than 700 students over a five-year period. During this time he translated several of the Pauline Epistles [The Ruach Translation], which were never published; although printed along with other booklets he wrote and distributed amongst their students.

They then left the ministry and for ten years did business mainly in the tourism industry.

They built and managed a Safari Lodge in the Sabi Sand Game Reserve and eventually relocated to Hermanus where they started Southern Right Charters boat-based whale watching.

In December 2000 Francois began to write the book, "God believes in You" which led to him being invited to speak at various Christian camps and churches. Since February 2004, they travelled regularly abroad and into Africa as well as South Africa.

Francois has written several books in both English and Afrikaans, including God Believes in You, Divine Embrace, The Logic of His Love; these are also available on Kindle. Also, The Mystery Revealed and Done, which are no longer in print - although still available in Afrikaans.

In order to focus their time on writing and translation, they relocated from Hermanus in 2015, to a remote farm in the Swartberg Mountains. They have since, also stopped most of their travelling.

Lydia has written 6 amazing children's stories of which Stella's Secret, The Little Bear And The Mirror, Kaa of the Great Kalahari as well as The Eagle Story, are already published in print and on Kindle. Her most recent story "King Solitaire's Banquet" was released in December '20.

Francois passionately continues his translation of the Mirror Bible, which will eventually include the entire NT as well as select portions of the Old. The 1st 250 page, A5 edition, was published in 2012. The 10th edition Mirror Study Bible is a 7 x 10 inch book, of 1144 pages, released in April 2021.

Lydia's books are already available in English Afrikaans, German and Spanish.

The Mirror Bible is currently available in Spanish, Shona, Xhosa and large portions in German.

More than 50000 people subscribe to their daily posts on Social Media; Lydia has her own fb page and Francois has 4 English pages and an Afrikaans, Spanish, Hungarian, French and Dutch page on Facebook.

Their email address is info@mirrorword.net

You can get more detail about them on www.mirrorword.net

The Mirror Bible is also on Kindle as well as an App, app.mirrorword.net

There are many of Francois' teachings on YouTube but they recently started their own

Mirror Word YOUTUBE channel, *https://m.youtube.com/channel/UC63YHkpabON9nHgQq-WeIPkA/videos*

Mirror Word PODCAST https://open.spotify.com/show/3qsgRsf2SNDx1bubxngw0W?fbclid=IwAR0zLo_wkVymqouQA3CvYxZ3lINrK-zUyXf4PuCql7bG-OGns4BTcgAgRLQ

REFERENCES & RESOURCES

Referred to by the author's name or by some abridgement of the title.

Adam Clarke (1762–1832 A British Methodist theologian)

Ackerman *[Christian Element in Plato]*

Bruce Metzger *(Textual Commentary on the Greek NT)*

Barnes Notes (Notes on the Bible, by Albert Barnes, [1834], at sacred-texts.com)

BBE (1949, Bible in Basic English)

Doddrich (Philip Doddridge 1702-1751 www.ccel.org/d/doddridge)

Dr. Robinson (Greek Lexicon by Edward Robinson1851)

E-Sword by Rick Meyers (www.e-sword.net)

Greek English Lexicon by C.Grimm Wilke - translated from Latin by J.H. Thayer DD - Edinburgh - T&T CLARK - Fourth Edition 1901)

J.B. Phillips Translation (Geoffrey Bles London 1960)

Jeff Benner http://www.ancient-hebrew.org/

KJV (King James Version - In 1604, King James I of England authorized that a new translation of the Bible into English. It was finished in 1611)

Knox Translation (Translated from the Vulgate Latin by Ronald Knox Published in London by Burns Oates and Washbourne Ltd. 1945)

Marvin R. Vincent (1834-1922) Word Studies.

NEB (New English Bible New Testament - Oxford & Cambridge University Press 1961)

Robert Charles *R. H. (Robert Henry), 1855-1931*

RSV (The Revised Standard Version is an authorized revision of the American Standard Version, published in 1901, which was a revision of the King James Version, published in 1611.)

Strongs (James Strong - Dictionary of the Bible)

The Message (Eugene H. Peterson Nav Press Publishing Group)

Walter Bauer (Greek English Lexicon - a translation of Walter Bauer's Griechisch-Deutches Worterbuch by Arndt and Gingrich 1958)

Wesley J. Perschbacher (The New Analytical Greek Lexicon Copyright 1990 by Hendrickson Publishers, Inc)

Westcott and Hort *The New Testament in the Original Greek 1881*

Weymouth New Testament *(M.A., D.Lit. 1822-1902)*

Zodhiates Complete Word Study Lexicon Mantis Bible Study for Apple

www.ingramcontent.com/pod-product-compliance
Lightning Source LLC
Chambersburg PA
CBHW082058230426
43670CB00017B/2888